Justices of the United States Supreme Court

MACMILLAN
PROFILES

Justices of the United States Supreme Court

Macmillan Reference USA

an imprint of the Gale Group

New York • Detroit • San Francisco • London • Boston • Woodbridge, CT

Copyright © 2001 by Macmillan Reference USA, an imprint of the Gale Group.

Macmillan Reference USA   Gale Group
1633 Broadway   27500 Drake Road
New York, NY 10019   Farmington Hills, MI 48331-3535

Printed in Canada
10 9 8 7 6 5 4 3 2 1

Cover design by Mike Logusz

Library of Congress Cataloging-in-Publication Data

Justices of the United States Supreme Court.
    p.cm.--(Macmillan profiles)
  Includes bibliographical references and index.
  ISBN 0-02-865634-2 (hardcover)
  1. United States Supreme Court--Biography. 2. Judges--United States--Biography. I.
Macmillan Reference USA. II. Series.

KF8744 .J875 2001
347.73\'922634--dc21
[B]   2001030282

Front cover, clockwise from top: Oliver Wendell Holmes, Jr., William H. Rehnquist, Sandra Day O'Connor, Thurgood Marshall. Photos of Holmes and O'Connor courtesy of the Library of Congress; photo of Rehnquist courtesy of Archive Photos: photo of Marshall courtesy of Fisk University Library.

Contents

Macmillan Profiles: *Justices of the United States Supreme Court* is a unique reference featuring biographies of every man and woman who has served on the United States Supreme Court since its establishment with the Judiciary Act of 1789. Macmillan Library Reference recognizes the need for accurate and accessible biographies of notable figures from American history. The Macmillan Profile series can help meet that need by providing new collections of biographies that were carefully selected to appeal to young readers and to complement the middle and high school curriculum.

From John Jay, America's first Chief Justice, to William Rehnquist and the eight justices who serve on the Supreme Court today, this volume offers an exciting introduction to America's judicial history. The shifting role of the Supreme Court in American government, the relative powers of the federal and state courts, and the impact of Supreme Court decisions on our day-to-day lives are issues of growing importance to students, teachers, parents, and voters. The goal of *Justices of the United States Supreme Court* is to bring these issues to life through engaging discussions of the lives and careers, as well as the judicial opinions and philosophies, of the men and women who have served on the country's highest court. Expanded attention is given to the 16 men who have served as Chief Justice, and to the pioneering women and African Americans who have served as associate justices.

FEATURES

To add visual appeal and enhance the usefulness of the volume, the page format was designed to include the following helpful features:

- ■ Timelines: Found throughout the text in the margins, timelines provide a quick reference source for dates and important events in the life and times of these men and women.

- ■ Notable Quotations: Found throughout the text in the margins, these thought-provoking quotations are drawn from interviews, speeches, and writings of the person covered in the article. Such quotations give readers a special insight into the distinctive personalities of these great men and women.

- ■ Definitions and Glossary: Brief definitions of important terms in the main text can be found in the margin. A glossary at the end of the book provides students with an even broader list of definitions.

- ■ Sidebars: Appearing in shaded boxes throughout the volume, these provocative asides relate to and amplify topics.

- Pull Quotes: Found throughout the text in the margin, pull quotes highlight essential facts.
- Suggested Reading: An extensive list of books and articles about the justices covered in the volume will help students who want to do further research.
- Index: A thorough index provides thousands of additional points of entry into the work.

This work would not have been possible without the hard work and creativity of our staff. We offer our sincere thanks to all who helped create this work.

Macmillan Reference USA

Baldwin, Henry

JANUARY 14, 1780–APRIL 21, 1844 ● ASSOCIATE JUSTICE

Henry Baldwin was born in New Haven, Connecticut, on January 14, 1780. His parents were Michael and Theodora Wolcot Baldwin. His family was prominent and had been in the New England area since the 17th century. A half-brother, Abraham Baldwin, later became a United States senator from Georgia, while his brother, Michael Baldwin, was a notable figure in Ohio politics.

Baldwin grew up on a farm and attended Hopkins Grammar School. After completing school, he returned to New Haven to study at Yale University. He was an excellent student and graduated at age 17. As was the custom at the time, aspiring attorneys learned the law as **apprentices** in law offices, and Baldwin found a good position working as a law clerk for a noted Philadelphia lawyer, Alexander J. Dallas. Soon, Baldwin was admitted to the bar in Pennsylvania, after which he headed west to seek his fortune, ending up in Pittsburgh, Pennsylvania. Because Pittsburgh was a growing community that didn't yet have a group of established community leaders, Baldwin was able to make a name for himself.

Henry Baldwin

apprentice: a young individual who learns a craft or skill under the supervision of a professional in that person's place of business or trade.

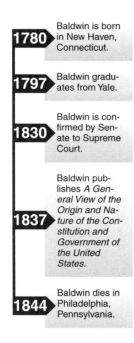

1780 Baldwin is born in New Haven, Connecticut.

1797 Baldwin graduates from Yale.

1830 Baldwin is confirmed by Senate to Supreme Court.

1837 Baldwin publishes *A General View of the Origin and Nature of the Constitution and Government of the United States.*

1844 Baldwin dies in Philadelphia, Pennsylvania.

Baldwin became so well liked that he was given the nicknames "Idol of Pennsylvania" and "Pride of Pennsylvania."

burgeoning: growing in prosperity and opportunity.
patronage: a system in politics wherein an elected official dispenses available jobs and posts to supporters and friends.

Baldwin took advantage of the opportunities that the **burgeoning** city offered. He formed a law firm with Tarleton Bates and Walter Forward that became known as the "Great Triumvirate of Early Pittsburg." The three men became highly active in the community, and together purchasing a newspaper, *The Tree of Liberty,* to further their Whig views. Baldwin became deeply involved in the affairs of the town, serving on various civic boards and working for the Whig party. Baldwin was also a businessman, purchasing several mills in Pennsylvania and Ohio.

Baldwin was well respected as an attorney. He was known for his extensive collection of legal books and for his courtroom arguments that relied on solid legal reasoning rather than the blustering speeches that were common at the time. When he was still only in his 20s, Baldwin became so well liked that he was given the nicknames "Idol of Pennsylvania" and "Pride of Pennsylvania."

After establishing himself professionally, Baldwin next set to work on his personal life. In 1802, he married a distant cousin, Marianna Norton. The year after their marriage she gave birth to Baldwin's only son, Henry, but she died only a month after Henry's birth. In 1805, Baldwin married Sally Ellicott, the daughter of a prominent local engineer.

Baldwin's work in politics soon paid off for him. In 1816, he was elected to the United States House of Representatives. In the House, he served as the chairman of the Committee on Domestic Manufacturers. He was re-elected twice more but had to resign his seat in 1822 for health reasons.

After spending two years recuperating from illness, Baldwin became actively involved in local and national politics again. In a move that ensured his political future, he urged Andrew Jackson to run for president in 1824, even though Jackson was not a Whig. When Jackson won the presidency in 1828, it was expected that the new president, who is recognized as the first to institute a system of political **patronage,** would give Baldwin a position in his administration. Baldwin did not get an appointment to the Treasury Department, as he had expected, but landed in the judiciary instead. After Justice Bushrod Washington died in 1829, Jackson nominated Baldwin to take the judge's place on the U.S. Supreme Court. Baldwin was confirmed by the Senate.

While he served on the Court, Baldwin generally voted in a consistent manner. He supported the preservation of states' rights, he considered slaves to be personal property, and he supported unobstructed interstate commerce. He considered himself to be a moderate on the question of whether the states or the federal government should have the most power, reasoning that there could be a middle ground where the two could share power.

But Baldwin became known for his personal style more than his specific viewpoints. Baldwin distinguished himself on the bench by being more than willing to go against the opinions of the rest of the justices. During the 1831 term alone, he dissented seven times. This was unusual because, at the time, there was an informal tradition that the Court would present unanimous decisions. Baldwin became so dissatisfied with the decisions the Court was handing down, that he seriously considered resigning that year. It took a personal appeal from President Jackson to keep Baldwin from leaving.

Baldwin stayed, but he refused to stop writing dissenting opinions. In 1837, Baldwin disagreed with the majority decisions in four different cases. He published his opinions on those cases in a special pamphlet called *A General View of the Origin and Nature of the Constitution and Government of the United States . . . Together with Opinions in the Cases Decided at January Term, 1837.*

Throughout his career, Baldwin suffered from mental health problems. As early as 1832, he was forced to miss one term on the Court because he suffered a mental breakdown and had to be hospitalized. As he aged, his behavior deteriorated further. In his later years, this one-time popular "Idol of Pennsylvania" started behaving more unusually. His peers disliked him because of his behavior on the bench, including his "nonconformity in writing opinions and his peculiar mannerisms during his last years on the court." Some accounts speculate that he might have had obsessive-compulsive disorder.

In his later years, Baldwin did not have the kind of life that would have been predicted from his early, promising years. Besides his mental problems, he also suffered from poor physical health and financial problems. Still, he served on the Court until his death from paralysis on April 21, 1844. At the time of his death, Baldwin was so poor that his friends had to take up a collection to pay for his funeral expenses. ◆

Throughout his career, Baldwin suffered from mental health problems.

Barbour, Philip Pendleton

MAY 25, 1783–FEBRUARY 25, 1841 ● ASSOCIATE JUSTICE

Philip Barbour was born in Orange County, Virginia, on May 25, 1783, to a prominent family that had lived in Virginia for many years. His mother, Mary Pendleton Thomas, was a fixture in local society circles, while his father, Thomas Barbour, was a wealthy planter who was active in politics and a member of the House of Burgesses. Although his family was considered to be upper class, by the time Barbour was born the family had suffered some financial setbacks. Thus, instead of attending the elite institutions that would have been expected from a young man of his status, Barbour attended local schools.

Barbour did well in school and showed a particular talent for languages and classical literature. At one point, he studied with the Reverend Charles O'Neil, an Episcopalian clergyman who was known for his liberal use of **flogging.** When Barbour was 17, he read law, then moved to Kentucky in 1800. Barbour started a law practice but quit after only a year to go back to school. Due to his financial situation, he had to borrow the money for tuition. He went to William and Mary College in Virginia for one semester, then resumed his law practice.

Two years later, Barbour's career was a success. Besides his social connections, he was known for his intelligence and his talent for public speaking. He quickly earned enough money to marry Frances Johnson, the daughter of a prosperous Orange County planter, in 1804. The couple would go on to have seven children. Although perhaps he did not intend to do so, he was in some ways following in the footsteps of his older brother, James Barbour, who was married to Frances' older sister. Barbour also followed his brother's lead

flogging: The beating of a criminal with a stick or rod.

Philip Barbour

in taking an interest in politics. James Barbour had an illustrious political career and was the governor of Virginia, a United States senator, and President John Quincy Adams' Secretary of War.

In 1812, at age 29, Barbour won his first political office when he was elected to be the Orange County representative to the Virginia **House of Burgesses.** Two years later, Barbour moved to the national level when he was elected to the United States Congress.

At first Barbour and his older brother agreed on political issues. Both were part of a group of states' rights advocates, meaning that they thought that the states—and not the federal government—should have the most power when it came to legal issues. Later the two brothers drifted apart ideologically when James Barbour changed his stance and began advocating increased powers for the national government.

Barbour served as the **Speaker of the House of Representatives** from 1821 until 1823, when he lost to Henry Clay. During his time as speaker, he worked hard to preserve states' rights. When Missouri joined the Union and a debate arose over whether or not slavery should be allowed to continue there, Barbour argued that it should, that it was a state-level decision. His position was that the issue was not the ethics of slavery, but rather the power of a state to control its own destiny.

After losing to Clay, Barbour was appointed to the General Court of Virginia. There, he continued to preserve states' rights. He argued against the **tariff,** a wider jurisdiction by the federal Supreme Court and internal improvements.

In 1827, Barbour returned to Congress to run again for speaker, but he lost to Andrew Stevenson. Barbour eventually served eight terms in Congress, ending his stay in 1830. During that time, he endeared himself to President Andrew Jackson by working to take power away from the Bank of the United States. This helped him in 1830, when President Jackson appointed Barbour to a federal district judge vacancy in Virginia. Barbour and Jackson were so closely aligned that when Jackson ran for president in 1832, Barbour was a serious contender for vice president. But party regulars dissuaded Barbour from running, thinking that he might split the ticket, causing the race to be decided in Congress, where there was a strong anti-Jackson sentiment.

Barbour was rewarded for backing down from the vice presidency in 1835 when Jackson nominated him for the U.S.

"Barbour, I really think is honest and conscientious; and he is certainly intelligent; but his fear or hatred, of the powers of this government is so great, his devotion to State rights so absolute, that perhaps [a case] could hardly arise, in which he would be willing to exercise the power of declaring a state law void."
Daniel Webster, *The Papers of Daniel Webster,* (C.M. Wiltse, ed., 1980)

House of Burgesses: a legislative body giving representation to residents of certain colonies in the years prior to the American Revolution.

Speaker of the House of Representatives: an individual elected by the majority of members of the House of Representatives to serve as the leader of the entire House; third in line of succession to the presidency.

tariff: a duty or tax added by a government to imported or exported goods.

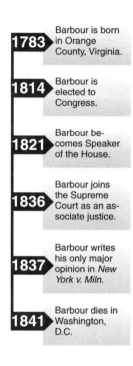

1783 Barbour is born in Orange County, Virginia.

1814 Barbour is elected to Congress.

1821 Barbour becomes Speaker of the House.

1836 Barbour joins the Supreme Court as an associate justice.

1837 Barbour writes his only major opinion in *New York v. Miln.*

1841 Barbour dies in Washington, D.C.

perspicacious: (Barbour) of sharply keen mental vision.

Supreme Court. Because he was such a staunch supporter of states' rights, Barbour was a controversial choice, but his nomination was overshadowed by the nomination of similarly controversial Roger Taney as chief justice at the same time. Of course, Barbour's fellow states' rights advocates were pleased with the choice. A reporter for the *Richmond Enquirer* said of Barbour's appointment, "the pride of the Democracy of Virginia, is now seated upon the bench of the Supreme Court, which he is so eminently fitted to adorn with his talents and enlighten with his inflexible and uncompromising states' rights principles."

Barbour did not sit on the bench long enough to compile a list of notable opinions. In cases such as *Charles River Bridge v. Warren Bridge* in 1837 or *Briscoe v. Bank of Kentucky*, also in 1837, Barbour predictably held up state sovereignty and supported the strengthening of state powers. His only major opinion was in *City of New York v. Miln* in 1837. This case concerned the states' jurisdiction over commercial activities and states' police power. Barbour wrote that a state has the same "undeniable and unlimited jurisdiction over all persons and things" as any foreign nation. According to his colleague, Justice Joseph Story, Barbour's "talents were of a high order; but he was distinguished less for brilliancy of effort, than for **perspicacious,** close, and vigorous reading. He sought less to be eloquent than to be accurate."

But Barbour did not live long enough to have much influence on the Court. In February of 1841, he became sick. He later seemed to have recovered and was working again by the end of the month. The night before he died, he attended a late meeting and seemed fine. The next morning, on February 25, 1841, he was found dead of a heart attack. He was 57 years old. ◆

Black, Hugo

FEBRUARY 27, 1886–SEPTEMBER 25, 1971 ● ASSOCIATE JUSTICE

Hugo Lafayette Black was born in Clay County, Alabama, in 1886. His father, William Lafayette, owned a small country store, while his mother, Martha, served as postmistress to the rural area. When Black was a young child, his parents moved to the nearby town of Ashland so that he and his seven siblings could receive a better education. As a child, Black would stop by the county courthouse with his parents, and he was always fascinated by the lawyers that he saw there. It surprised no one when Black decided to enroll in law school when he was older.

Black, who was an excellent student, attended a mix of private and public schools. After graduating from high school, he stayed in Ashland and attended Ashland College for a short time. He soon transferred to the University of Alabama, however, first attending the university's medical school and then, in 1904, switching to law school, from which he graduated in 1906.

Upon graduating, Black briefly opened his own law office back in Ashland, but he soon moved to the larger city of Birmingham, Alabama,

Hugo L. Black

a tough city known as a leading industrial center. In Birmingham, Black opened a law office that specialized in labor law and personal injury cases. In 1910, he took on additional responsibilities when he agreed to serve as a police court judge, hearing minor criminal cases.

Black's legal practice thrived and he became an active member of Birmingham society. In order to become better known in the community, Black joined as many local groups as he could, including the Freemasons, the Loyal Order of the Moose, and others. His efforts paid off, as he was named the county prosecuting attorney in 1917. His appointment coincided with the start of World War I, and Black quickly enlisted in the U.S. Army. After serving for two years, he returned to Birmingham in 1919 and re-opened his law office, where he gained a well-earned reputation as an outstanding lawyer who could win big cases. In 1921, he married local socialite Josephine Foster, with whom he would have three children. The couple was married until Foster passed away in 1951. Six years after her death, Black remarried, wedding Elizabeth Seay DeMeritte.

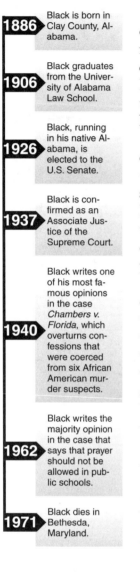

1886 Black is born in Clay County, Alabama.

1906 Black graduates from the University of Alabama Law School.

1926 Black, running in his native Alabama, is elected to the U.S. Senate.

1937 Black is confirmed as an Associate Justice of the Supreme Court.

1940 Black writes one of his most famous opinions in the case *Chambers v. Florida*, which overturns confessions that were coerced from six African American murder suspects.

1962 Black writes the majority opinion in the case that says that prayer should not be allowed in public schools.

1971 Black dies in Bethesda, Maryland.

By 1926, Black's local popularity and influence had grown enough that he decided to run for a seat in the U.S. Senate, running as a Democrat to replace retiring Senator Oscar Underwood. A surprise win in the Democratic primary earned Black the seat, as all of Alabama at that time was firmly in control of the Democratic party. Black's work in the Senate earned him re-election in 1932.

Black quickly became known as one of the leading supporters of President Franklin Roosevelt's New Deal government (the New Deal refers to Roosevelt's package of economic and social reforms). In fact, during Roosevelt's first term in office, Black voted for every one of the 24 pieces of New Deal legislation that the president introduced. His support for the president ensured that Black would move up quickly in the Democratic party.

Black sponsored several important pieces of legislation, including the Fair Labor Standards (Minimum Wage) Act, and the bill that oversaw the creation of the Tennessee Valley Authority. By supporting the president when Roosevelt attempted to expand the size of the Supreme Court so he could "pack" it with judges who supported the New Deal, Black gained Roosevelt's lasting appreciation. The president rewarded Black's loyalty by naming him to the Supreme Court in 1937, where he replaced Associate Justice Willis Van Devanter.

Soon after Black was confirmed for the Court by the U.S. Senate, one element of his past came under fire. As a young lawyer in rural Alabama, Black had served for four years as a member of the racial supremacy group, the Ku Klux Klan. When confronted about that membership, Black never apologized for joining the group. He claimed that he tried to serve as a moderate influence in the group and that he joined for financial reasons—all the other attorneys in the area were members and he had to keep up—and not for racial ones. He also felt compelled to join because he believed that the all-white juries of the time would be more sympathetic to his clients if he was a member of the Klan.

Black addressed the controversy head on and was able to counter most of the criticism by pointing out the numerous cases in which he had aided African American defendants. His court record during the years he was in the Klan seem to back up his claim that he did not endorse the Klan's racial views; when he later became a prosecuting attorney, he was far more lenient to and supportive of African American defendants than

Engel v. Vitale (1962)

In the early 1960s, there was a great deal of public controversy about prayer in the public schools. Because the United States Constitution prohibits Congress from the establishment of a state religion, and from prohibiting the free expression of religion, but many people felt that a school–sponsored prayer period was unconstitutional. In an effort to defuse the issue, the New York State Board of Regents authorized that the public schools open each school day with a short, voluntary, nondenominational prayer; the board hoped that the prayer's generalized wording would make it acceptable to people of all religious persuasions.

The parents of ten students filed a lawsuit against the state, claiming that the new, voluntary prayer violated the Constitution's provisions. Arguing on behalf of the parents as the case reached the U.S. Supreme Court, attorney William J. Butler stated that the prayer could not truly be considered voluntary, for any student refusing to participate would be exposed to peer pressure and possible ridicule.

The majority opinion, delivered by Justice Hugo Black and supported by Justices Clark, Brennan, Harlan, Douglas, and Chief Justice Earl Warren, sided with the parents. Justice Potter Stewart dissented, and Justices Felix Frankfurter and Byron R. White did not participate.

In the view of the Court, the central problem was that the Board of Regents, which is a government entity, had composed the wording of the prayer to be used. Even though the prayer was nondenominational, it was nevertheless dictated by the state. Noting that one of the primary reasons that the American colonies were established was to escape state–mandated religious practice in Europe, the majority ruled that the tradition of freedom of religious practice could not be compromised by state actions such as those taken in New York.

other prosecutors were. In the end, because it was clear that Black was not a racist and because he had quit the Klan as soon as he announced his run for the Senate back in 1925, Black suffered no lasting harm from the damaging revelation.

Black's appointment to the Supreme Court changed its dynamic for decades. In his early years on the Court, he was often in the minority—he wrote a dissenting opinion to the majority 13 times in his first eight months on the court—but his then-radical opinions usually came to become accepted principles of law as the years passed. Black served on the Court for 34 years, overseeing some of the most tumultuous and important years in American history.

For the duration of his time on the bench, Black earned a reputation as a strong defender of the U.S. Constitution who believed that the document should be interpreted literally. As he said in his opinion in the 1940 case *Chambers v. Florida* (which threw out confessions that were coerced from six

> Black's appointment to the Supreme Court changed its dynamic for decades.

Black continued his pattern of defending the Constitution and supporting the common man, often at the expense of big business.

African-American suspects): "No higher duty, no more solemn responsibility rests upon this court than that of translating into living law and maintaining this constitutional shield deliberately planned and inscribed for the benefit of every human being subject to our Constitution—of whatever race, creed, or persuasion."

Black was perhaps most vocal in his support of the First Amendment ensuring freedom of speech ("make no laws means make no law," he once said of that amendment, "not make some laws"). However, he is also known for extending the due process of law ideal that is part of the Fourteenth Amendment (the amendment that provides "equal protection of the laws" to all citizens). One of his most well-known minority opinions was in the 1948 case *Adamson v. California,* in which he argued that the amendment was designed to make all of the Bill of Rights (the first ten amendments to the U.S. Constitution) applicable to every state—in other words, no state could pass a law that bypassed the Bill of Rights in the name of "states' rights." While he might have been part of the minority in that case, in the years that followed, the rest of the Court gradually came to agree with his opinion and ruled in case after case that the entire Bill of Rights did in fact apply to all states.

An important example of that came in the 1963 case *Gideon v. Wainwright.* In that case, Black served as the spokesperson for the Court after it unanimously ruled that a person accused of a crime had a fundamental right to counsel (which is outlined in the Sixth Amendment) and that such a right was mandatory in every state because of the Fourteenth Amendment. Without such an application of the law, Black said, a fair trial could not be held. Black's opinion in this case showed his commitment to two principles—the right to a fair trial under due process of law, and the right to equal protection under the law for all defendants, regardless of their financial situation.

Throughout the 1950s and 1960s, Black continued his pattern of defending the Constitution and supporting the common man, often at the expense of big business. He never let his personal beliefs override his support of the Constitution. For example, although he personally hated pornography, he remained true to his First Amendment beliefs and repeatedly voted against attempts by the government to limit what could and could not be published.

Some of Black's most famous majority opinions included *Everson v. Board of Education* (1947), in which he ruled that states could use public funds to pay for transporting students to private, religious schools but that no other money could be given to such schools; *Marsh v. Alabama* (1946), which made it legal for Jehovah's Witnesses to distribute their religious materials; and *Wesberry v. Sanders* (1964), which led to apportioning (dividing) congressional districts to ensure that "one man's vote . . . is to be worth as much as another's."

Black's final opinion for the Court was written in 1970, and it was also one of his most important and most well-known. The case *New York Times v. United States* involved the infamous Pentagon Papers, which contained controversial information about the Vietnam War that the government did not want released. The papers had been written by a Pentagon consultant, who stole the information. In his opinion, Black staunchly defended the right of a free press and upheld the *Times's* First Amendment right to free speech.

Black's legacy as a Supreme Court justice is that of a liberal judge who was a passionate champion of equal rights and due process for all U.S. citizens. He believed in the Constitution so strongly that he carried a copy of it around in his back pocket at all times, and it was not uncommon for him to pull the tattered copy out of his pocket to give spur of the moment readings to groups of students or visitors. On September 17, 1971, Black resigned from the Supreme Court after he suffered a severe stroke; just eight days later, he passed away at Bethesda Naval Hospital in Maryland. Even after his death, Black caused a minor controversy when he ordered in his will that his bench papers and notes be destroyed after his death. While those papers would have been valuable to legal scholars, his son carried out Black's wishes. ◆

Blackmun, Harry

NOVEMBER 12, 1908–MARCH 4, 1999 ● ASSOCIATE JUSTICE

Harry Andrew Blackmun, who wrote some of the most important and controversial decisions handed down by the U.S. Supreme Court in the 20th century, was born in the small town of Nashville, Illinois, in 1908. Blackmun's parents—Corwin Manning Blackmun and Theo (Reuter) Blackmun—were fairly prosperous, but the family experienced

Harry Blackmun

the poverty that was so common during the Great Depression. His mother's family owned a flour mill in the town of Nashville, while his father was a successful businessman. The family moved to the St. Paul-Minneapolis area of Minnesota when Blackmun was a young child, and there the elder Blackmun owned a grocery store and a hardware store. From the time he was able, Harry worked at odd jobs to contribute money to the family.

In kindergarten in the Dayton Bluffs suburb of Minneapolis, Blackmun made a friend who would stay with him for life. Warren Burger, who later served as Chief Justice of the Supreme Court at the same time Blackmun served on the Court, became fast friends with young Blackmun, and the two remained friends throughout their lives. They were even called the "Minnesota Twins" in their early years together on the Court (not always fondly, either). Even though their relationship became strained in later years when Blackmun started siding with the more liberal side of the Court, they maintained their remarkable friendship for life.

After attending high school in the Minneapolis area, Blackmun attended Harvard University on a scholarship from the Harvard Club of Minnesota. At the prestigious university, Blackmun majored in mathematics, earning high honors in the subject. As an undergraduate, Blackmun earned Phi Beta Kappa academic honors and graduated summa cum laude; his accomplishments are even more impressive because he had to work as a janitor to make ends meet. Blackmun went on to attend the Harvard Law School, completing his degree in 1932. He then returned to Minneapolis to begin his legal career.

In Minneapolis, Blackmun's first job in the law was clerking for Eighth Circuit Court of Appeals Judge John B. Sanborn. Blackmun also taught classes at several colleges in the St. Paul area before going into private practice. The first firm he worked for was Dorsey, Colman, Barker, Scott & Barber. Blackmun stayed with that firm for more than 15 years, earning general partner status in 1949. In 1941, with his legal career in full swing, Blackmun married Dorothy Clark, with whom he had three daughters.

One of Blackmun's main clients at Dorsey, Colman, et. al., was the famous Mayo Clinic medical center in Minneapolis, and in 1950, he went to work as the hospital's general counsel. Nine years later, in 1959, his career came full circle when President Dwight D. Eisenhower named Blackmun as the judge in the Eighth Circuit Court of Appeals—the same court where he had clerked for Judge Sanborn in 1932. For Blackmun, the appointment marked his move onto the national judicial and political scene.

Blackmun served as head of the court of appeals for 11 years, writing more than 200 opinions during his time on the bench. As a result, he became nationally known as a politically conservative justice. When Associate Justice Abe Fortas retired from the Supreme Court in 1970, Blackmun was nominated to the high court by President Richard Nixon. Blackmun was Nixon's third choice ("[That] always kept me a little on the humble side," Blackmun said) behind Clement Haynsworth and G. Harrold Carswell, but he was a popular choice and was unanimously approved by the U.S. Senate.

Nixon called Blackmun a "strict constructionist" as a judge, meaning that Blackmun relied on building on existing case law instead of routinely creating new laws when new situations arose. Nixon was also convinced that he had appointed a justice who would remain true to Nixon's conservative viewpoints. For a time, it appeared that he was right. In his early years on the Supreme Court, Blackmun consistently voted with the conservative majority on the Court. He repeatedly sided with longtime friend Warren Burger, which eventually earned him the derisive nickname "Hip-Pocket Harry," implying that Blackmun would do whatever Burger did and whatever conservatives wanted him to do.

Within just a few years, however, Blackmun began to surprise people by siding with, and even authoring, more liberal court opinions. Nixon's hopes of maintaining a conservative Supreme Court began to fade, and in 1973, those hopes were completely destroyed when Blackmun wrote the liberal, majority opinion in one of the most famous cases in Court history.

That year, Blackmun shed his conservative reputation forever when a case came before the Court called *Roe v. Wade*. The case challenged the right of a woman to legally have an abortion as recognized by federal law. The incredibly controversial

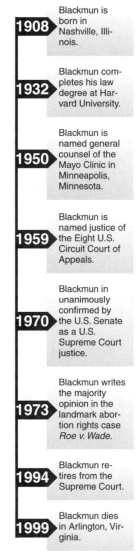

1908 Blackmun is born in Nashville, Illinois.

1932 Blackmun completes his law degree at Harvard University.

1950 Blackmun is named general counsel of the Mayo Clinic in Minneapolis, Minnesota.

1959 Blackmun is named justice of the Eight U.S. Circuit Court of Appeals.

1970 Blackmun in unanimously confirmed by the U.S. Senate as a U.S. Supreme Court justice.

1973 Blackmun writes the majority opinion in the landmark abortion rights case *Roe v. Wade*.

1994 Blackmun retires from the Supreme Court.

1999 Blackmun dies in Arlington, Virginia.

Roe v. Wade (1973)

Jane Roe is the pseudonym of a Texas woman named Norma McCorvey in whose name a lawsuit was filed in the early 1970s against Dallas County district attorney Henry Wade, challenging the right of a state to ban her from getting an abortion. At the time, Texas treated all abortions as criminal acts except when, in a medical doctor's opinion, the mother's life would be threatened by carrying the pregnancy to full term. After the case worked its way through the Texas courts, Attorney Sarah Weddington brought the issue before the Supreme Court.

What would ultimately become the watershed case for abortion rights in the United States got off to a rocky start at the first hearing in December 1971 because Weddington failed to make a clear connection between her case and the kind of constitutional issues required for Supreme Court involvement. Her opponent, attorney Jay Floyd, was no better prepared, however, so the case was scheduled for rearguments in October 1972.

This time, Weddington was much better able to make her case. She argued that Texas law infringed upon her client's Fourteenth Amendment rights to privacy by unreasonably interfering in her relationship with her doctor and constraining her choices regarding her body and physical well–being. The new attorney for the opposing side, Robert C. Flowers, however, attempted to raise the question of when life begins in a fetus. In its 7–2 decision (Justices White and Rehnquist dissenting), the Supreme Court rejected the invitation to speculate on metaphysical issues of when life begins, and held that a woman has total autonomy over the choice to continue a pregnancy during the first trimester, while granting some rights to the state to regulate later–term abortions.

The decision was the first to legalize abortion throughout the United States, and forced individual states to reasess their own statutes on the subject. It was, and remains, extremely controversial however, and continues to be challenged by pro-life legislators, organizations, and individuals, while being vehemently supported by pro-choice organizations and interest groups.

issue, then as now, sharply divided the American public. The *Roe* case centered on the question of a woman's constitutionally guaranteed right to privacy and was intended to determine if that right to privacy extended to her right to choose to end her pregnancy legally and without government interference. Writing the majority opinion in the 7–2 vote, Blackmun said that the right to privacy clause in the Constitution is "broad enough to encompass a woman's decision whether or not to terminate a pregnancy. The detriment that the state would impose upon pregnant women by denying this choice is apparent."

Roe v. Wade did set some limits on a woman's right to abortion. It established the trimester system, in which a woman could freely have an abortion in the first three months of pregnancy, could be denied one in the second three months only for health reasons, and could only have an abortion in the final three months if the mother's life was in imminent danger. The Court's decision also legalized the act of abortion for the first time by declaring unconstitutional any state laws against it.

Blackmun knew he was writing an important opinion. "It was a step that had to be taken . . . toward the full emancipation of women," he said looking back on the case when he retired from the Court in 1994.

Blackmun's majority opinion was hailed as a major victory by women's rights supporters. "Justice Harry Blackmun saved more women's lives than any other person in our nation's history," said Voters for Choice leader Gloria Steinem, in reference to Blackmun's famous opinion. "In supporting women's right to decide when and whether to have a child, the decision he authored confirmed women's fundamental right to their own bodies and freedom."

A great many other people opposed Blackmun's decision, however, and those opponents felt that Blackmun had done a great deal of harm to the rights of unborn children. The abortion issue is one of the most divisive topics in America, so it is not surprising that Blackmun received more than 60,000 pieces of mail attacking his *Roe v. Wade* decision. Blackmun claimed to have read every letter he received—even the ones that called him a Nazi and a murderer—because he felt it was important to know what the people were thinking.

The *Roe* case was just one of many to come in which Blackmun would take the liberal viewpoint in cases that matched an individual's rights against the power of government authority. In fact, by the time he retired in 1994, Blackmun was one of the most liberal justices in the history of the court. He was known as a champion of the separation of church and state, and at the end of his career he even changed his long-held support of the death penalty, opposing it in all cases and calling it a "failed experiment."

Other examples of his shift to a liberal viewpoint include his support in 1993 of Haitians who were trying to gain entrance into the United States after being expelled from their homeland. He was the lone dissenter in a case that ruled that the U.S. did not have to hold hearings before returning the so-called "boat people." He also dissented from the majority in a 1986 case involving the right to privacy and a person's sexual orientation. Blackmun essentially said that conduct between adults was none of the government's business, and that people had the fundamental "right to be left alone." In a 1977 ruling,

> *"Justice Blackmun was truly a profile in courage. His eloquence, his passion, and his commitment guarantee him an important place in the history of the Court and of the nation and to civil liberties."*
> Steven R. Shapiro, ACLU National Legal Director, in a March 4, 1999 press release on Justice Blackmun's death

he wrote that the right to free speech should be used to uphold the right of lawyers to advertise on television.

Throughout the 1980s and early 1990s, Blackmun felt it was his duty to remain on the Court as long as he could to contest the growth of conservatism in the United States. He feared that if he left, *Roe v. Wade* would be overturned—in fact, he had witnessed two challenges to that case (one in 1989 and one in 1992) that had nearly overturned all of the gains of *Roe*. In both cases, Blackmun sided with the narrow 5–4 majority that upheld the right to abortion while cutting back on some of the circumstances in which it would be allowed. After the second case, he knew abortion opponents were coming closer to overturning *Roe*, and he said, "I fear for the future. . . . The signs are evident and a chill wind blows." He later added regretfully: "I cannot stay on this Court forever."

However, after President Bill Clinton was elected in 1992 and new, liberal-leaning justices were appointed to the Court, Blackmun felt it was safe to retire. In 1994, after a distinguished 24-year career on the bench, Blackmun retired. He enjoyed his retirement with his three children and his five grandchildren until late February 1999, when he fell at his home in Virginia and broke one of his hips. The badly damaged hip was replaced a day later, but complications set in, and Blackmun never recovered. He died nine days after the surgery on March 4, 1999, in Arlington Hospital in Arlington, Virginia. ◆

Blair, John, Jr.

1732–AUGUST 31, 1800 ● ASSOCIATE JUSTICE

John Blair was born in 1732 in Williamsburg, Virginia. His parents, John and Mary Munro Blair, came from a privileged family that had owned land and had considerable wealth. His father was a colonial official for the state of Virginia and had served as acting Royal governor. Blair's uncle, James Blair, founded and was the first president of the prestigious College of William and Mary. Blair came from a large family and he was one of 10 children. He attended William and Mary, where he was a good student and graduated with honors in 1754. After college, Blair headed to London, England, to study law at Middle Temple.

When he returned home, Blair was ready to begin his professional career. In 1756, he began what would become a successful law practice in Virginia. He also married Jean Balfour, though little is known about her and it is unclear what year they married. The Blair family advocated having an active political life and Blair soon became involved in public service. He served as the representative from William and Mary in the Virginia House of Burgesses from 1766 until 1770, before resigning to become clerk of the Governor's Council.

During his tenure in the House of Burgesses, Blair was one of the members who opposed Patrick Henry's Stamp Act resolutions that challenged Great Britain's power in America, feeling that they were too extreme. Later, though, Blair changed his views. When the British Parliament passed the Townshend

John Blair

Revenue Acts in 1770, which led to higher taxes in the colonies for goods such as tea, paper, and glass, Blair signed the Virginia Association, which was an agreement to boycott British goods until the taxes were removed. Again in 1774, after Parliament passed the Intolerable Acts, Blair showed his support for his native land by joining the growing movement that was calling for a Continental Congress.

Blair was a clerk for the Governor's Council until 1775, but this did not stifle his revolutionary leanings. After the American Revolution began, Blair turned his focus to issues of the state. He was very involved with shaping the look of Virginia's new government and was one of the people who helped write Virginia's first constitution in 1776, as well as the state's Declaration of Rights, at the Virginia Convention. America's victory in war with Britain meant that government institutions were being totally reconfigured and, in some cases, were being invented by local leaders as they discovered the need for them. This meant that Blair was often one of the first members of a

1732 ▸ Blair is born.

1754 ▸ Blair graduates with honors from the College of William and Mary.

1787 ▸ Blair attends the Constitutional Convention.

1789 ▸ Blair is nominated to the Supreme Court by George Washington.

1793 ▸ Blair rules against Georgia in *Chisholm v. Georgia.*

1800 ▸ Blair dies in Williamsburg, Virginia.

On the bench, Blair was known for his strict adherence to the Constitution.

court or government body during its first year. In 1777, he was elected to the state of Virginia's General Court, which had not existed before. Two years later, he was voted chief justice.

In 1780, Blair became chancellor of the High Court of Chancery, which in turn helped him to be named a judge in the newly formed first Virginia Court of Appeals. There, Blair made one of his most important judicial decisions in the case *The Commonwealth of Virginia v. Caton et al.* In that case, Blair and another judge found that the court could nullify a legislative act if the court decided the act was unconstitutional. This affected the balance of powers between the legislature and the judicial system and would continue to have ramifications throughout American history.

Blair represented Virginia at the Constitutional Convention in 1787. The Virginia team of delegates was rather impressive, with Blair's peers at the time including George Washington and James Madison. Blair reportedly did not make any speeches at the convention, but he was a respected figure, and his counsel was valuable. During the meetings, the men worked on deciding whether the new federal government should have one president or two. Blair voted for two, which obviously, did not come to pass. There was also a vote on whether the people or the federal government should elect the president. Blair voted that the Congress should choose, though he later changed his vote.

Blair's work on the bench and his deep involvement during the Revolution did not escape the notice of his longtime friend, George Washington. When Washington was looking for judges for the newly formed United States Supreme Court, he called on Blair. Blair was nominated on September 24, 1789. When Blair was confirmed by the Senate two days later, he became one of the original members of the Court, along with John Jay, John Rutledge, William Cushing, and James Wilson. The Supreme Court first met in 1790 in New York. Only three judges arrived in time and the meeting had to be adjourned. But by the next day, Blair and Attorney General Edmund Randolph arrived and the court held its first real session.

On the bench, Blair was known for his strict adherence to the Constitution, his belief in the principles of the separation of powers, and his advocacy for a strong national government. Blair's most important ruling while a member of the Supreme Court was in the case *Chisholm v. Georgia* (1793), which concerned the right of an individual to sue a state in the federal court. Blair found nothing in the Constitution to disallow this and voted with four other judges that a person could indeed sue a state. The decision was not well received and ended up helping to spark a movement that eventually led to the creation of the Eleventh Amendment to the Constitution. The amendment overturned *Chisholm* and made it impossible for citizens to sue a state. Blair's most important circuit court case was *Hayburn's Case*. In that case, Blair decided that a federal statute violated the separation of powers doctrine. This marked the first time federal judges found an act of Congress to be unconstitutional.

Because the Court was so new, there was not yet a full schedule for the judges. When the Supreme Court was not in session, the justices spent their time "riding circuit." Riding circuit meant that the judges, in addition to their Supreme Court duties, were also in charge of presiding over a circuit court. At the time, riding circuit was a requirement for the Supreme Court justices.

During his early years on the court, Blair was often absent from its sessions. This was because the court met so infrequently and also because Blair's wife had become ill. In 1792, when his wife died, Blair became distraught and began to suffer from chronic headaches. Four years later, Blair resigned from the Court. He returned to Williamsburg and lived there until his death in 1800. ◆

During his early years on the court, Blair was often absent from its sessions.

Blatchford, Samuel

MARCH 9, 1820–JULY 7, 1893 ● ASSOCIATE JUSTICE

Samuel Blatchford was born on March 9, 1820, in New York City into a very prominent family. His father, Richard M. Blatchford, was a well-known Whig legislator and the attorney for the Bank of England and the Bank of the United States. His mother was Julia Ann Mumford, a socialite and the daughter of renowned publicist John P. Mumford. Blatchford's paternal grandfather, a member of the clergy who had fathered 17 children, arrived in Lansingburg, New York, from Devonshire, England, in the late 1700s.

Blatchford attended William Forrest School in Pittsfield, Massachusetts, as well as the grammar school associated with

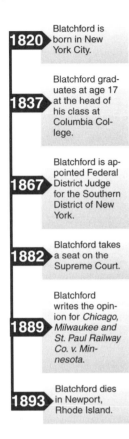

1820 Blatchford is born in New York City.

1837 Blatchford graduates at age 17 at the head of his class at Columbia College.

1867 Blatchford is appointed Federal District Judge for the Southern District of New York.

1882 Blatchford takes a seat on the Supreme Court.

1889 Blatchford writes the opinion for *Chicago, Milwaukee and St. Paul Railway Co. v. Minnesota.*

1893 Blatchford dies in Newport, Rhode Island.

bar examination: an examination given to individuals seeking to become certified by the state in which they wish to practice law.

maritime: relating to issues of navigation or commerce on the seas.

Columbia College. Blatchford was an excellent student and began attending Columbia College when he was only 13 years old. When he graduated in 1837, Blatchford was ranked at the top of his class.

Although Blatchford was certainly intelligent and resourceful enough to succeed on his own, he was not above taking advantage of the opportunities that his family's social status afforded him. His first job in the legal profession was working for New York governor William H. Seward, who was a close friend of his father's. Blatchford served as Seward's personal secretary and worked on getting the practical legal training he needed to pass the **bar examination.** In 1842, he passed the exam and was admitted to the bar. Again, he was able to use his family ties and got a job at his father's prominent law firm in Manhattan. During this time, in 1844, he married Caroline Appleton. The two never had children.

After three years of working with his father, Blatchford left the firm and began practicing at Seward's firm with Christopher Morgan in Auburn, New York. Blatchford spent nine years at the firm before leaving in 1854 to start a new firm, Blatchford, Seward, and Griswold, which he opened with Seward's nephew, William. In 1855, Blatchford was offered a post on the New York Supreme Court, but he turned it down to pursue his own interests.

During his legal career, Blatchford served in several legal posts, but before joining the Supreme Court, he was most well-known for painstakingly compiling years of decisions of the Circuit Court of the United States for the Second Circuit. He was particularly interested in cases involving admiralty, which had been previously uncollected. Blatchford published the results and went on to publish 24 volumes of the Circuit Court decisions in *Blatchford's Circuit Court Reports*, *Blatchford's and Howland's Reports* (concerning admiralty decisions), and *Blatchford's Prize Cases*, a compilation of local New York cases.

Blatchford's work attracted considerable attention in legal circles, and in 1867 he was appointed federal district judge for the Southern District of New York. In 1872, he was appointed to the Second Circuit Court. His decisions there on matters of patent law, copyright, and **maritime** torts made him well-respected by his peers.

That respect paid off when Blatchford was nominated by President Chester A. Arthur for a seat on the Supreme Court in 1882. Although this obviously placed Blatchford among the elite judges in the nation, he was not Arthur's top choice for the job. Blatchford got the position because the president's first choices—Roscoe Conkling of New York and Senator George F. Edmunds of Vermont—both refused the appointment. Still honored to be nominated, Blatchford was appointed and confirmed by the Senate, taking his seat on the Supreme Court on April 13, 1882. He replaced Justice Ward Hunt, who had recently resigned.

Once he was on the Court, Blatchford proved himself to be, if not a showy judge, a diligent and hard-working one. During his 10 years on the Supreme Court, he wrote 435 of the 3,237 signed opinions of the court. Through most of his decisions, he proved himself to be a centrist. His most noteworthy cases were on patent law, such as *Dobson v. Hartford Carpet Co.* in 1884 and *Dobson v. Dorman* in 1886. These cases weakened the standard that governed what types of designs could be patented. In *Counselman v. Hitchcock* (1892), Blatchford increased the scope of the circumstances under which the Fifth Amendment— which protects citizens against self-incrimination—could apply.

Despite all of his hard work, Blatchford's place in history remains small. One account of his life sums it up by saying, "Blatchford attracted slight public notice; he was most noteworthy for his businesslike approach, and his orderly, prosperous and placid career." Another account gives Blatchford small praise, describing him as a "quiet" man who was "widely appreciated in Washington for his modesty and courtesy."

Blatchford, however, did manage to stir up one bit of controversy during his final two years on the Court. In the case *Chicago, Milwaukee and St. Paul Railway Co. v. Minnesota* in 1890, he wrote the majority opinion, which struck down a law allowing an independent commission to determine whether railroad rates were "equal and reasonable." This decision essentially overturned a long-standing case, *Munn v. Illinois* (1877), which caused a bit of controversy. Further controversy erupted when another similar case, *Budd v. New York* (1892), came before the Court. In *Budd*, Blatchford decided that the state had the power to regulate businesses when the legislature had set the rates. In effect, his decision upheld *Munn v. Illinois*. The distinction that Blatchford found between the first and second cases was thought by most to be legal hairsplitting and some thought that Blatchford, by making these decisions that virtually canceled each other out, was trying to regain the safe, middle position that he was used to holding.

> **Once he was on the Court, Blatchford proved himself to be, if not a showy judge, a diligent and hard-working one.**

These decisions late in his career somewhat tainted his stellar, if rather dull, reputation. After Blatchford's death, Seymour D. Thompson, a progressive and the editor of the *American Law Review* said of him, "It was no great disparagement of him to say that he was probably a better reporter than judge." Blatchford died in Newport, Rhode Island, after a brief illness in 1893. He was 73. ◆

Bradley, Joseph P.

MARCH 14, 1813–JANUARY 22, 1892 ● ASSOCIATE JUSTICE

Joseph P. Bradley was born in Berne, New York, in 1813. He came from very modest circumstances. He was the oldest of 11 children and lived on a farm with his siblings, his father, Philo Bradley, and his mother Mercy Gardner. Bradley's great-grandfather, who moved to Berne after the Revolutionary War, was a farmer, as was Bradley's grandfather and father. The family did not have a lot of money and, as a boy, Bradley worked hard on the farm, working in the fields and selling homemade charcoal in town. Bradley went to a country school, but only for a few months each year. He also studied quite a bit on his own and was largely self-educated.

Joseph P. Bradley

When Bradley was 16, he met a clergyman who tutored him in Greek and Latin and got him a teaching job at the local school. Eventually the clergyman arranged for Bradley to attend Rutgers College. When Bradley set off to school, he was wearing clothes spun from wool from his family's sheep. Bradley entered Rutgers at age 20 and graduated a mere three years later in 1836. Even though he came from a less privileged background than his fellow students, he was a leader in his class and graduated with honors.

Bradley's first law job was with Archer Gifford, who was the collector of the port of Newark, New Jersey. In 1839, he was admitted to the bar at age 26, which at that time was considered somewhat old to be starting out. But the late start did not hinder him professionally or personally. In 1844, he married Mary Hornblower, the daughter of the chief justice of the New Jersey Supreme Court. He found a job working as an attorney for the New Jersey Railroad and Transportation Company and eventually became the attorney for the Camden and Amboy Line. The Camden and Amboy railroad was known for its corrupt business practices, such as bribing government officials. Even though Bradley was associated with the company for a long time, he was never accused of any wrongdoing himself. Besides railroad law, he also specialized in patent and commercial law. Bradley also worked on **actuarial tables** for the Mutual Benefit Life Insurance Company of Newark.

Politically, Bradley started out as a Whig, but became a Republican and a Union supporter after the Civil War began. In 1862, he ran for a seat in Congress, but lost. Bradley allied himself politically with Ulysses S. Grant, and in 1870, Grant nominated Bradley for a seat on the U.S. Supreme Court. There was controversy over Bradley's nomination because some thought that Grant chose Bradley—and William Strong, who was nominated the same day—hoping that the two would create a majority on the court that would uphold the Legal Tender Act. The two men did just that, but for the rest of his life, Bradley insisted that Grant did not know Bradley's opinion on the issue before nominating him.

Bradley was involved in more controversy after the 1876 presidential election. That year, there was a dispute over the voting in several states, so Congress chose a committee to determine who the winner was. There were seven Democrats and seven Republicans on the committee, plus Supreme Court justice David Davis, an independent. When Davis resigned from the committee after being elected to the United States Senate, Bradley was chosen to take his place since he was considered to be the most independent of the remaining justices. After careful consideration of the issues, Bradley sided with the Republicans and Rutherford B. Hayes was elected president. There was angry speculation that Bradley was unduly influenced by partisan politics, but in the end, it was generally agreed that Bradley had decided the case on purely legal grounds.

Bradley was known for his intellect, strong work ethic, and willingness to take a hard line on issues in which he believed. In *Hans v. Louisiana* (1890), a suit involving state-issued bonds,

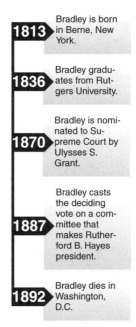

1813 ▶ Bradley is born in Berne, New York.

1836 ▶ Bradley graduates from Rutgers University.

1870 ▶ Bradley is nominated to Supreme Court by Ulysses S. Grant.

1887 ▶ Bradley casts the deciding vote on a committee that makes Rutherford B. Hayes president.

1892 ▶ Bradley dies in Washington, D.C.

actuarial tables: statistical calculations based on life expectancy yielding insurance annuities and premiums.

Bradley found that states could not be sued in federal court by their citizens. In *Burgess v. Seligson* (1883), he helped give the federal courts more power. He wrote that federal courts are an "independent jurisdiction" that was "not subordinate to that of the state courts."

The dark spot on Bradley's record is that he held the prejudices of his times. Many of his decisions on civil rights issues are now seen as unfair, racist, and sexist. He helped to break down many protections of civil rights for African Americans. In 1883, he was part of the majority ruling that declared that two sections of the Civil Rights Act of 1875 were unconstitutional. The act forbade discrimination on the basis of color in inns, public conveyances, and places of amusement. Bradley wrote that "to deprive white people of the right of choosing their own company would be to introduce another kind of slavery." *Bradwell v. Illinois* (1873) was another case where Bradley let his personal prejudices get in the way of making a fair decision. He rejected the arguments of Myra Bradwell, a woman who had studied law and wanted to be admitted to the bar. Bradley wrote, "The paramount destiny and mission of women are to fulfill the noble and benign offices of wife and mother."

The energy that helped Bradley become a self-made man stayed with him throughout his life. While serving on the court, Bradley kept up a wide variety of interests besides law. He was constantly reading books, especially those on philosophy, astronomy, math, and science. He once designed a perpetual calendar so that a person could tell on what day of the week any day of any year would fall. He had a huge personal library that had over 16,000 books. He wrote numerous essays on his personal philosophy and once wrote a history of the English translation of the Bible. He wrote an extensive history of his family, which was published after his death.

After serving on the court for 22 years, Bradley died at his home on January 22, 1892. He was 78. ◆

Brandeis, Louis

NOVEMBER 13, 1856–OCTOBER 5, 1941 ● ASSOCIATE JUSTICE

Louis D. Brandeis was born in Louisville, Kentucky, on November 13, 1856. His Bohemian Jewish parents, Adolph Brandeis and Frederika Dembitz Brandeis, had come to the United States in 1849 from the city of Prague in what is now Czechoslovakia. Adolph began a prosperous wholesale grain and produce business in 1851 in Louisville. Louis, his brother, and their two sisters enjoyed a home of privilege and culture. In his teens, Louis changed his middle name from David to Dembitz in honor of his mother's brother, Lewis Naphtali Dembitz, a leading lawyer and abolitionist.

After achieving honors at public schools in Louisville, Brandeis studied at the Annen Realschule in Dresden, Germany, after his father had sold the grain business and taken the family to Europe for three years. At age 18, Brandeis entered Harvard Law School and graduated at the head of his class in 1877.

After a year of graduate work at Harvard, Brandeis practiced law in St. Louis, Missouri, for less than a year. He returned to Boston to start what became a thriving practice with a former law school classmate. The pair earned plenty of business through personal contacts, but it was Brandeis's brilliance that raised the firm to a higher level.

Louis Brandeis

On March 23, 1891, Brandeis married a distant cousin, Alice Goldmark, and the couple took up residence in Boston. The couple had two daughters: Susan, born in 1893, who became an attorney, and Elizabeth, born in 1893, who became an economist. The Brandeis family lived simply, choosing to use its money for worthy causes. It did, though, acquire a vacation cottage on Cape Cod, and Brandeis would typically spend each August there.

Brandeis became known as the "people's attorney" because he often worked for causes in the public interest, taking on powerful business and financial institutions. His expertise led Brandeis to being called on to settle labor disputes as well as help in major public concerns. From 1893 to 1902, Brandeis fought against the Boston Elevated Railway's attempt to gain a railroad monopoly in Boston. He became nationally famous for his

1856 Brandeis is born in Louisville, Kentucky.

1916 Brandeis is appointed to the Supreme Court of the United States by President Woodrow Wilson.

1927 Brandeis delivers a concurring opinion in *Whitney v. California*, saying that penalties on speech should be applied only if the speech presents a "clear and present danger."

1939 Brandeis retires from the Supreme Court and devotes the rest of his life to the Zionist movement.

1941 Brandeis dies in Washington, D.C.

pro bono: Latin term meaning "public good"; the execution of legal services in exchange for no financial compensation.

involvement in the New Haven Railroad merger controversy. Famous financier J. P. Morgan tried to gain control over New England rail lines through a merger of his New York, New Haven and Hartford Railroad company with the Boston & Maine Railroad. Brandeis suspected a monopoly, and from 1905 to 1914 he waged a legal battle to oppose Morgan.

Brandeis often performed such legal work **"pro bono"** (for the public good), which means without pay. This practice has become a tradition among lawyers. In one of his efforts to make life better for workers, Brandeis created a new kind of life insurance that the average worker could afford. Brandeis argued that insurance companies were inefficient, and he proposed that savings banks could offer similar services without taking such great advantage of working people. Brandeis considered this one of his greatest achievements.

Brandeis fought for a shorter workday and a minimum wage for working women in Oregon and other states. From 1907 to 1914, he defended several state laws stating that women could not work too many hours and that they should have a minimum wage. In his defense of the state of Oregon in front of the U.S. Supreme Court in *Muller v. Oregon* (1908), Brandeis presented economic and sociological information to support his case instead of only outlining the legal details involved in the case. This was a new approach and has become known as a "Brandeis Brief." In such presentations, lawyers analyze the long-term social and economic effects that might result from a decision.

President Woodrow Wilson often consulted Brandeis on problems of business and labor law. Brandeis supported Wilson's theory of enforced competition among businesses. On January 28, 1916, Wilson appointed Brandeis an associate justice of the Supreme Court. Brandeis would be the first person of Jewish faith on the nation's high court, which led to some political opposition. However, stronger opposition came from the business community, who disliked Brandeis's views on labor and business issues. In spite of the conflict, the U.S. Senate confirmed the nomination, and Brandeis began his first Court term on June 5, 1916.

In his role as Supreme Court Justice, Brandeis continued his emphasis on individual rights and protection of individuals from the powerful forces of government and business. On most important issues, Brandeis joined with Justice Oliver Wendell Holmes, and the two often formed a minority. They criticized the conservatism of their colleagues and the Court's leader,

Opinion of the Court

When a case is decided by the Supreme Court, the Justices issue what is known as an *opinion of the court*, which is the formal expression of the legal reasons and principles upon which the decision has been based. The opinion is a detailed statement of the particular questions raised by the case and the ways in which the court has addressed those questions, citing precedents set by similar cases in the past.

After hearing a case and voting on its outcome, one of the Justices who voted with the majority is assigned by the Chief Justice to write the opinion of the Court, expressing the reasoning of all the Justices who agree with the decision. Sometimes one or more of the Justices feel so strongly about a decision that they are moved to explain their own position, especially if they feel that the official opinion does not adequately stress some of the issues that they consider important. This is released as a "concurring opinion." A third type of opinion is issued in cases where the Justices could not come to unanimous agreement. When the Court is split this way, one of the Justices in the minority writes a "dissenting opinion," explaining why they disagree with the majority ruling.

In some cases, the opinion of the Court is not actually written by the Justice to whom it has been assigned. Quite often, one of the assigned Justice's legal clerks is given the facts of the case and the reasons behind the decision and is charged with researching precedents and doing the actual writing. Once this is done, the assigned Justice reviews the document and signs it. In cases that are considered to be especially important, however, or when a Justice is particularly interested in a case it is not uncommon for the Justice to write the opinion personally.

Chief Justice William Howard Taft, a former U.S. President. The many cases in which Brandeis defended individual rights to privacy have been admired and referred to by other justices through the years.

Brandeis believed that state legislatures needed to be able to make laws that matched the changing needs of their people. However, he also saw fit to restrict states when they interfered with an individual's freedom of expression. In the case of *Whitney v. California* (1927), in which a communist woman had been convicted under a state law, Brandeis delivered an opinion stating that speech can be prohibited only if it meets the "clear and present danger" test formulated earlier by Justice Oliver Wendell Holmes.

During the 1930s, the court became more liberal, and Brandeis's opinions were less often in dissent. Following the Great Depression, President Franklin D. Roosevelt and the Congress passed many new laws to put the economy back on track. Sixteen major New Deal laws came before the Supreme Court, and Brandeis approved of all but six of them.

> *"The next generation must witness a continuing and ever increasing contest between those who have and those who have not. The industrial world is in a state of ferment. . . . The people are beginning to doubt . . . whether there is a justification for the great inequalities in the distribution of wealth."*
>
> Louis Brandeis, *Business—A Profession* (1914)

Zionist: an individual who is part of an international movement advocating the establishment of a Jewish state in Palestine.

Brandeis retired from the Supreme Court on February 13, 1939, at age 83.

Although he did not closely observe his Jewish faith, Brandeis became an internationally recognized leader of the **Zionist** movement that worked to found a Jewish homeland. At the end of World War I, Brandeis helped send several delegates to the Paris Peace Conferences to urge the creation of a Jewish homeland in Palestine. During the summer of 1919, Brandeis traveled to Paris and the Middle East. After leaving the Court, Brandeis devoted the remainder of his life to working for the Zionist movement. These efforts helped lead to the formation of Israel in 1948.

Brandeis wrote a volume of essays, *Other People's Money, and How the Bankers Use It* (1914), about how investment bankers control American industry. In his book, *Business—A Profession* (1914), Brandeis supported trade union rights, arguing that manufacturers should ensure that wages, hours of work, and sanitary conditions were fair for workers. Brandeis's writings are collected in *The Social and Economic Views of Mr. Justice Brandeis* (1930) and *The Brandeis Guide to the Modern World* (1941).

Brandeis died of a heart attack on October 5, 1941, in Washington, D.C., two years after retirement. In 1948, Brandeis University opened in Waltham, Massachusetts. ◆

Brennan, William J., Jr.

APRIL 25, 1906–JULY 24, 1997 ● ASSOCIATE JUSTICE

William Brennan was born on April 25, 1906, in Newark, New Jersey, to William and Agnes Brennan. The second of eight children, Brennan's opinions on social issues were shaped at an early age by his father, William Sr., who worked at a local brewery before becoming active in the growing union movement and in local Democratic politics. The elder Brennan served as the Commissioner for Public Safety in Newark for 16 years, and his dedicated public service had a lasting influence on his son.

After graduating from high school, Brennan went on to attend the University of Pennsylvania's Wharton School, where he graduated with a bachelor's degree in 1928. In 1927, while still in school, he married Marjorie Leonard, with whom he would have three children. After Penn, he attended Harvard Law School, earning his degree in 1931. He passed the bar exam in New Jersey that same year and went into private practice working for one of the top law firms in the state. When World War II broke out, Brennan served in the Army, working on the staff of the undersecretary of war to settle labor disputes.

When the war was over, Brennan returned to private practice, but that did not last long—he felt that his job intruded too much on his family life. In 1949, he was appointed as a New Jersey Superior Court judge and was promoted to the appellate division just a year later; in 1952, he was named to the state's Supreme Court. Brennan was one of the most prominent judges in the United States, and in 1956, he concluded his rise through the judicial ranks by being named to the U.S. Supreme Court by President Dwight D. Eisenhower. Brennan just missed a unanimous confirmation by the U.S. Senate—the lone "no" vote came from Senator Joseph McCarthy, who gained notoriety for his famous Communist witch hunts in the Senate.

William J. Brennan, Jr.

Justice Brennan, who served with eight presidents and held his seat for more than 30 years, is largely considered to be one of the greatest and most dedicated justices in American history. "His impact on the law was simply monumental," said Harvard law professor Laurence Tribe. As a libertarian justice, Brennan was a champion of individual rights and one of the Court's leaders in defending the freedoms guaranteed to all Americans by the First Amendment of the Constitution—especially the freedom of the press and the right to free speech. Because of his liberal leanings, and because his opinions were so well written, Brennan often wrote the opinion on important cases involving First Amendment issues.

1906 Brennan is born in Newark, New Jersey.

1931 Brennan graduates from Harvard University Law School.

1952 Brennan is named to the Supreme Court of New Jersey.

1956 Brennan is named to the U.S. Supreme Court by President Dwight D. Eisenhower.

1964 Brennan writes a famous opinion clarifying libel law and an individual's right to free speech in *The New York Times v. Sullivan*.

1990 Brennan retires from the Court after writing more than 1,300 opinions during his career.

1997 Brennan dies in Arlington, Virginia.

Among the most important of his career was the 1964 case, *The New York Times v. Sullivan*, in which the newspaper was accused of libel. The Court ruled that the newspaper had not committed libel (written words that damage a person's character) even if statements it had printed about a public official were false—as long as it could be shown that the paper had not shown "actual malice" when it printed the false statements. The press must be free to create a "robust . . . and wide-open" debate about public issues Brennan said, and the First Amendment protected that freedom. The inclusion of malice is still a necessary part of proving that libel was committed in the United States.

Besides his broad support of First Amendment rights, Brennan was a liberal in almost every possible way. He supported abortion rights and opposed the death penalty, calling it cruel and unusual punishment. He supported women's rights and gay rights. He was an expert on the line between pornography and art, and in such cases as *Roth v. United States* (1957), he routinely defended the rights of publishers while also recognizing that local communities should have some control over what could be sold there. And, although he was devoutly religious himself, he was absolutely insistent on the complete separation of church and state; at the same time, he was a champion of religious freedom. In a pair of 1963 cases, *Abington School District v. Schempp* and *Murray v. Curlett*, Brennan sided with the majority and wrote a stirring opinion in which he explained why reading the Bible and reciting the "Lord's Prayer" were unconstitutional when they were sanctioned by the state.

Brennan's time on the court can be divided into two time periods. The first 13 years of his tenure, he served along with Chief Justice Earl Warren, with whom Brennan shared most views on social issues and the Constitution. Together, the two men were the leaders on a Court that leaned toward a more liberal viewpoint. However, under the next two chief justices—Warren Burger and William Rehnquist—Brennan found himself either in the minority or as the deciding vote in numerous 5–4 decisions as the Court became more and more conservative. While his critics grew more vocal as the court leaned toward the right, Brennan held true to his beliefs throughout his career, which earned him the respect of most who followed the court.

For much of his time on the bench, Brennan, along with Thurgood Marshall, was one of the Court's champions of racial

Texas v. Johnson (1989)

During the Republican National Convention of 1984, Gregory Lee Johnson burned an American flag in front of the Dallas City Hall in protest of the policies of the Reagan administration. Under a Texas law banning the "desecration of a venerated object," Johnson was fined $2,000 and sentenced to a year in jail. The judgement was reversed by a Texas court of appeals, and the state took the case to the United States Supreme Court on March 21, 1989.

William Kunstler, arguing for the defendant, argued that Johnson's action, burning the flag, was "expressive conduct" and thus was a form of speech protected by the First Amendment. The Supreme Court, in a 5–4 decision, agreed. Justices Thurgood Marshall, Antonin Scalia, Anthony Kennedy, Harry A. Blackmun, and William J. Brennan (who delivered the opinion), stated that "the government may not prohibit the expression of an idea simply because society finds the idea itself offensive or disagreeable."

The majority opinion agreed that the state does have the right to prohibit free expression, but only in restricted situations where the public interest is directly threatened, such as by incitements to violence. It rejected the state's contention that it was "protecting a national symbol" because the protection was not consistently applied. The dissenting justices, John Paul Stevens, Sandra Day O'Connor, and Byron R. White, along with Chief Justice William Rehnquist, strongly disagreed with the majority opinion of the Court. They pointed out that the protection of national symbols, and particularly of the flag, has precedent in federal law. They noted that federal law has long governed the use, display, and disposal of the American flag, and cited Congressional anti flag–mutilation legislation, enacted in 1967.

rights and equality. He supported such controversial items as forced busing of students to desegregate public schools, affirmative action, and even using racial quotas in attempting to combat discrimination. Perhaps his most famous ruling on affirmative action was the 1979 case *Steelworkers v. Webber*, in which Brennan patched together the five votes needed to rule that racial quotas in hiring were sometimes necessary to uphold the "spirit" of Title VII of the Civil Rights Act of 1964. It was not a popular decision to many Americans, who thought that racial quotas themselves amounted to discrimination.

That 1979 ruling was a logical extension of rulings that Brennan had made earlier in his career. In the 1962 case *Baker v. Carr*, Brennan was part of a 6–2 majority that forever changed the face of U.S. politics on the national, state, and local level. The majority ruled that an individual could turn to the courts if he or she felt they had been discriminated against by the unfair apportionment of legislative districts (for example, the boundaries set up to determine the election of state and U.S. congressman, or other elected officials). The decision touched off a realignment of voting districts across the United States that caused dramatic changes in many elections by creating a system of representation based on population. The more people a given region had, the more state or U.S. senators and representatives that region had. It was a radical change.

One of Brennan's last rulings was one of his most controversial, but it was not surprising in light of his constant support of free speech. In the late 1980s, radicals who were unhappy with the U.S. government's foreign policy had made it a common practice to burn the U.S. flag at protest marches. This outraged the majority of the U.S. population and led to numerous lawsuits. Many local communities and even states passed laws making flag burning illegal, and there was even an attempt to pass a new constitutional amendment outlawing the practice. When the issue came before the Supreme Court, however, Brennan joined the majority in the case *Texas v. Johnson* (1989) in ruling that state laws making it illegal to desecrate religious objects violated freedom of speech when the object in question was the American flag. In other rulings since that decision, the Court has routinely upheld that burning the flag, as distasteful as it may be to most people, is protected by the First Amendment and is not unconstitutional.

Brennan's first wife, Marjorie, died in 1982, and he married his secretary, Mary Fowler, the following year. In the late 1980s, his health began to fail, and, after more than three decades of distinguished service, Brennan was forced to retire from the court on July 20, 1990. At age 84, after writing more than 1,300 opinions, Brennan was hailed by the *Washington Post* for "a vision that found the essential meaning of the Constitution not in the past but in contemporary life." In 1997, at age 91, Brennan died in an Arlington, Virginia, nursing home. ◆

Brewer, David

JUNE 20, 1837–MARCH 28, 1910 ● ASSOCIATE JUSTICE

David Josiah Brewer was born on June 20, 1837, in Smyrna, Asia Minor, in what is now Izmir, Turkey. His father, Reverend Josiah Brewer, and his mother, Emilia Field Brewer, were American missionaries of the Congregational church who had gone to Asia Minor to work at a school for women. When Josiah Brewer was assigned as chaplain of the St. Francis Prison, in Wethersfield, Connecticut, the family returned to the United States in 1840, and Brewer grew up in Connecticut. Brewer's mother was the daughter of a distinguished New England minister, and she had several high-achieving brothers. The Field brothers included prominent lawyers, a writer, and Cyrus W. Field, who helped create the first trans-Atlantic telegraph cable.

Brewer attended Yale University, his father's **alma mater,** and graduated with high honors in 1856. He then joined his uncle David Field's law office and was admitted to the New York bar in 1858. Following his uncle Stephen Field, Brewer explored the West, ending up in the frontier town of Leavenworth, Kansas, in 1859. Brewer met Louise R. Landon, from Burlington, Vermont, and married her in 1861. In that same year, at age 24, Brewer began serving as a judge in the U.S. Circuit Court for the District of Kansas. After serving in several elected judgeships, Brewer was elected to the Kansas Supreme Court in 1870, at age 33. In 14 years in this role, Brewer made several progressive decisions favoring women. In *Wright v. Noell* (1876), Brewer created a landmark decision on the rights of women when he allowed a woman to hold public office even though women did not yet have the vote. Brewer resigned the Kansas Supreme Court in 1984 to serve on the federal circuit court for five years.

In 1889, when Stanley Matthews of the U.S. Supreme Court died, the two senators of Kansas urged President Benjamin Harrison to appoint Brewer. After a vote of 53 to 11, the Senate confirmed Brewer on December 18, 1889.

In his 21 years on the bench, Brewer usually agreed with the conservatives in opposing a trend toward increased power and responsibility of the federal government. However, in an era that saw strong opposition to unions, Brewer supported the government's right to step into labor disputes. Union leaders were often found guilty of interfering with commerce by calling strikes, and judges issued court orders called **injunctions** forbidding strikes.

Brewer spoke for the Supreme Court majority in the principal injunction case of the period, *In re Debs* (1895), upholding the government's use of the injunction against unlawful strikes. In 1894, the Pullman Palace Car Company had reduced the wages of its workers. When the company refused arbitration, the American Railway Union called a strike. It began in Chicago

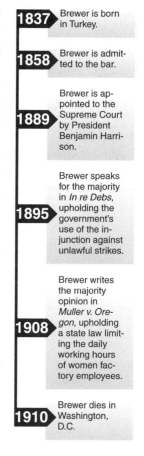

1837 Brewer is born in Turkey.

1858 Brewer is admitted to the bar.

1889 Brewer is appointed to the Supreme Court by President Benjamin Harrison.

1895 Brewer speaks for the majority in *In re Debs*, upholding the government's use of the injunction against unlawful strikes.

1908 Brewer writes the majority opinion in *Muller v. Oregon*, upholding a state law limiting the daily working hours of women factory employees.

1910 Brewer dies in Washington, D.C.

alma mater: a school, college, or university from which one has graduated.

injunction: a court order prohibiting an individual or entity from performing a specific action.

and spread to 27 states. The U.S. attorney general, Richard Ol-ney, sought an injunction under the Sherman Antitrust Act. This act had passed in 1890 after the public became angry over the misuse of trusts by large companies to accumulate wealth and power. The act prohibits restraint of trade and prohibits any person or business from monopolizing any market.

As a result of Olney's action, Eugene Debs, president of the American Railway Union, was arrested and imprisoned, in spite of the efforts of his famous lawyer, Clarence Darrow. When the case came before the Supreme Court, Brewer spoke for the Court, explaining why he refused the American Railway Union's appeal. This decision was a great blow against the trade union movement.

Brewer was particularly hostile to the emerging socialist movement. In his day, the American Socialist Party was close to its greatest strength, which it reached in 1912 with more than 118,000 dues-paying members. Brewer criticized all plans to redistribute wealth, and he made many speeches explaining the reasons for inequality. He expressed the belief that it was the natural law for some men to accumulate wealth, because they were capable of doing so while others were not.

Ironically, the case that Brewer is most noted for was a lib-eral decision that contrasted with his conservative decisions. In *Muller v. Oregon* (1908), Brewer wrote the majority opinion up-holding a state law that limited the daily working hours of women factory employees to 10. The case was also famous for the man who defended the state of Oregon in front of Brewer and the Supreme Court—Louis Brandeis, who later joined the Supreme Court. Brandeis presented economic and sociological information to support his case instead of only legal points. This was a new approach and has become known as a "Brandeis Brief." Brewer was sympathetic to Brandeis's arguments of the needs of women, and wrote that women needed special care be-cause of their "performance of maternal functions."

In 1895, Brewer began a two-year service as president of a commission appointed by the U.S. Congress to investigate a boundary dispute between Venezuela and British Guiana in South America. The commission prevented a war by settling the dispute with all the parties, which included Great Britain. This experience led Brewer to help found the American Soci-ety of International Law to help settle international disputes.

Brewer voiced his support of many political causes during his career on the nation's highest court. He supported charities, the right of women to vote, education, and rights of Chinese aliens to become U.S. residents. He also wrote many books, pamphlets, and articles. Colleagues considered Brewer a profound thinker as well as a warm, large, vigorous man. Three years after Brewer's wife Louise died in 1898, he married Emma Miner Mott of Washington, D.C.

Brewer remained a Supreme Court justice until he died in Washington, D.C., on March 28, 1910. ◆

Breyer, Stephen

AUGUST 15, 1938– ● ASSOCIATE JUSTICE

Stephen Breyer was born on August 15, 1938, in San Francisco, California. His father, Irving, worked as an attorney for the San Francisco Board of Education, while his mother, Anne, worked as a volunteer for the local Democratic Party and the League of Women Voters. Breyer's parents were only the second generation of the family to live in the United States—Irving Breyer's father had immigrated to the U.S. and made a hard-earned living as a cobbler, living in near poverty while ensuring his son would have the opportunity to do better. Irving made the most of that opportunity, and Stephen Breyer grew up in a comfortable, middle-class environment.

Education was a key principle in the Breyer household, so Breyer and his younger brother attended some of the best schools in San Francisco. In elementary and middle school, Breyer attended a religious school, although his family did not actively observe its Jewish heritage. When he reached high school, he attended the prestigious Lowell Academy,

Stephen Breyer

1938 Breyer is born in San Francisco, California.

1964 Breyer earns his law degree from Harvard University.

1973 Breyer works for the office of the special prosecutor investigating the Watergate break–in during Richard Nixon's administration.

1981 Breyer begins serving as a justice for the U.S. Court of Appeals, 1st District, in Boston, Massachusetts.

1985 Breyer begins four years of service on the U.S. Sentencing Commission, which establishes sentencing guidelines for criminal cases.

1995 Breyer is confirmed as an associate justice on the U.S. Supreme Court.

one of the best schools in the San Francisco public school system. While Breyer was easily one of the most intelligent students in his class, his mother wanted to ensure that he was well rounded, so she insisted that he play sports also, even though he was not very good at them.

After being voted "Most Likely to Succeed" as a senior and earning numerous academic awards, Breyer had his choice of either Stanford University or Harvard; to keep his parents happy, he chose to stay close to home and attend Stanford. His academic success continued there, and he graduated in 1959 with honors as a member of Phi Beta Kappa. Upon graduation, he earned a Marshall Scholarship to attend Oxford University in England. He completed his education by earning his law degree at Harvard University, where he was editor of the Law Review. He graduated from Harvard in 1964 and began his legal career.

Breyer's first position after law school was one of the top jobs in the country for a young, aspiring lawyer. He was selected as a clerk to U.S. Supreme Court justice Arthur Goldberg for the Court's 1964–1965 session. The prestigious job allowed him to work directly with the justice, helping him to research and write opinions on Supreme Court cases. One of the most important cases that Breyer worked on was the landmark *Griswold v. Connecticut* case, which involved right-to-privacy issues.

After the clerkship ended, Breyer moved through a series of jobs that took him higher and higher up the legal ladder. He also made his first foray into politics, paving the way for his later appointment. His first job after leaving Goldberg's office was with the U.S. Department of Justice, where he worked in the antitrust division until 1967. The same year he left the Justice Department, he married Joanna Hare of Great Britain, an aristocrat who was the daughter of Lord John Blakenham.

With his financial status secured after the wedding, Breyer decided to return to the academic world, taking a teaching position at Harvard. He was an assistant professor of law until 1970, at which time he earned full professor status. He remained active at Harvard until 1980, but while there he took a number of high profile jobs on the side that actually decided the path his career would take. In 1973, working for his former Harvard law professor Archibald Cox, Breyer served as part of the special prosecutor's office investigating the Watergate break-in and then-President Richard Nixon, who was forced to resign over the scandal.

Influential Senator Edward M. Kennedy of Massachusetts noticed Breyer's work for the prosecutor's office and appointed Breyer to the Senate Judiciary Committee staff in 1974, where he worked as legal counsel. In 1979, he was promoted to chief counsel of the Judiciary Committee. While serving that body, Breyer was known for two things—the fair and even-handed manner in which he ran his office, and his role in deregulating the airline industry, which created more competition among airlines.

Because of his hard work and competence, Breyer was rewarded by outgoing President Jimmy Carter by being named to the U.S Court of Appeals, First Circuit, in Boston. Breyer's nomination actually came after Carter had already lost the 1980 election but before Ronald Reagan took office, and Reagan could have vetoed the appointment. However, Breyer's reputation was as strong with Republicans as it was with Democrats, so his appointment was allowed to go through.

Breyer worked on the Court of Appeals from 1981 until 1994, serving as chief justice for the last four years of his stay. During his tenure, he developed the style that would earn him a seat on the Supreme Court. He firmly believed that the law was a fluid entity that should never be interpreted strictly. In many of his rulings, he looked at the "legislative intent" behind a law before he decided which way to vote. He considered the time period in which a law was passed, and tried to anticipate what future implications his decision would have.

Among the notable opinions he wrote while serving on the Court of Appeals was a dissenting opinion in what was known as the Bellotti case. In that opinion, he supported a law calling for parental consent in teen abortion cases. While Breyer has largely supported abortion rights, he knew that the Supreme Court had already voted overwhelmingly to uphold parental consent laws in two previous cases and that, even if the circuit court *did* rule against parental consent, there was no possible way the ruling would be upheld. In his mind, the law of the land had already been established, and there was no practical benefit in voting for striking down parental consent in one circuit court.

While some thought his 13 years of service on the Court of Appeals lacked "passion," many observers felt that Breyer was one of the best legal minds in the country. When President Clinton was presented with his first chance to name a Supreme Court justice in 1993, Breyer was one of the finalists for the position, which eventually went to Ruth Bader Ginsburg. When

"Law requires both a heart and a head. If you don't have a heart, it becomes a sterile set of rules removed from human problems, and it won't help. If you don't have a head, there's a risk that in trying to decide a particular person's problem in a case that may look fine for that person, you cause trouble for a lot of other people, making their lives yet worse. . . . It's a question of balance."

Stephen Breyer, quoted in the *New York Times*

Breyer is seen as an especially strong defender of the First Amendment.

another opening occurred in 1994, Clinton at first turned away from Breyer because the two had not hit it off during an interview for the first opening in 1993. However, Clinton soon realized that, because of Breyer's strong background with both Republicans and Democrats, he had the best chance of being confirmed by the U.S. Senate. This proved to be true, as his nomination was quickly approved by the Senate Judiciary Committee (the same body he had served on in the 1970s) and the full Senate. In August of 1994, Breyer became an associate justice of the Supreme Court.

Since his appointment, Breyer has adjusted to life on the Court during his first few terms. It is generally thought that he has not served long enough to determine what long-term effect he might have, or to guess what his place in history might be. On the court, Breyer is seen as a centrist, a coalition builder who brings both sides together on many issues. He often sides with the liberals on issues involving personal freedoms and big government, while he routinely votes with the conservatives on issues involving crime. Instead of letting one overriding principle guide his every decision, Breyer instead considers each case on a case-by-case basis, a style that has earned both criticism for its perceived lack of principles and praise for its flexibility.

Breyer is seen as an especially strong defender of the First Amendment, which dates back to his days on the circuit court. There, most notably, he ruled that the "gag order" imposed by President George Bush's administration preventing federally funded family planning clinics from telling patients about the option of abortion was unconstitutional. Other areas of strength are economic issues, the environment, and scientific issues.

As a moderate, Breyer most often sides with the other moderate members of the court—David Souter, Sandra Day O'Conner, and Anthony Kennedy—while he least often agrees with the most conservative member of the Court, Clarence Thomas. Breyer's fluid interpretation of the law is the exact opposite of Justice Antonin Scalia, who feels that written laws should be strictly interpreted as written.

Breyer is, however, conservative on criminal cases. His Supreme Court opinion upholding improper police testimony in a drug case because there was so much other evidence against the drug dealer met with a great deal of controversy. Critics thought that Breyer had abandoned his liberal background and gone too far in applying police powers in criminal cases.

Breyer's conservative work on criminal matters on the Supreme Court should come as no surprise to observers who have followed his career. Beginning in 1985, while serving the Court of Appeals, he also served on the U.S. Sentencing Commission, which was responsible for creating sentencing guidelines for criminal cases. These guidelines establish minimum and maximum penalties that judges must apply in criminal cases—a very controversial practice. Supporters say that the guidelines prevent criminals from receiving sentences that are too light or inappropriate, while critics argue that mandatory sentences handcuff judges by not letting them take special circumstances into consideration when they hand down sentences. Breyer received praise for his hard work on the commission and for his role in getting the group's members to finally put the standards into writing, but was also criticized for being too rigid and for supporting the government without also looking out for the people.

In the coming years, Breyer's role on the court will be watched closely. If he moves away from his centrist position towards either the liberal or conservative side, it could have a profound effect on the court. If he remains in the center, he could continue to be an effective coalition builder.

When not working, Breyer enjoys bike riding, cooking, and bird watching. He and his wife have three children. ◆

Brown, Henry Billings

MARCH 2, 1836–SEPTEMBER 4, 1913 ● ASSOCIATE JUSTICE

Henry Billings Brown was born March 2, 1836, in the little village of South Lee, Massachusetts. He came from a lineage traceable back 250 years to early New England Puritans. His father, Billings Brown, operated flour and saw mills in South Lee, and his mother, Mary Tyler Brown, taught Henry about religion and literature. She was also a talented artist. When the family moved to Ellington, Connecticut, Brown attended a private academy where he learned Latin and excelled in reading. After two years at an academy in Monson, Massachusetts, Brown entered Yale University at the age of 16, though he did not excel. One of his classmates was David Brewer, who would later serve with Brown on the United States

Henry Billings Brown

Supreme Court. Brown's father decided he would study law, and so he did, at Yale and then Harvard. After only six months at Harvard, though, Brown decided to head West to begin his career.

In 1859, Brown moved to Detroit, Michigan, where he was admitted to the bar the following year. In 1861, Brown was appointed deputy U.S. marshal for Detroit, at the time a city of not much more than 45,000 people. Because Detroit was a busy shipping port, Brown dealt with many shipping law cases, greatly affecting his career. In 1863, Brown earned a promotion to assistant U.S. attorney for the eastern district of Michigan. In 1864, Brown married Caroline Pitts, of a wealthy Detroit family. When her father died four years later, the family fortune made Brown and his wife independently wealthy. Forming a law partnership with two men, Brown specialized in shipping cases. He became the leading authority on maritime (sea) law in the Great Lakes region, and published an important volume of case reports from the Great Lakes district. Brown participated in local politics, but he did not win an office. In 1875, President Ulysses S. Grant appointed Brown as judge of the eastern district, where he spent 14 years as a federal judge.

In 1890, President Benjamin Harrison appointed Brown to the U.S. Supreme Court, where he replaced outgoing justice Samuel Miller after being confirmed by the Senate. Public reception ran favorably towards Brown, because it appeared he had achieved the position on his own merit. Brown was 54 years old and eagerly moved to Washington. He earned a reputation as a hard working, fair-minded judge who worked to find compromise. His hard work helped to reduce the Court's four-year backlog of cases. This jam occurred right before the circuit court of appeals was created, and the high court was overloaded. In 1891, Congress created the Courts of Appeals to relieve the Supreme Court of its great burden of work and to help citizens receive speedier justice. These courts decide on appeals from lower federal courts. Cases that are not resolved at that level, may be reviewed in the U.S. Supreme Court. The United States is now divided into 12 circuits, each of which has a court of appeals.

Brown's most important decision regarded *Plessy v. Ferguson* (1896), for which he wrote the majority opinion. It became a landmark court decision concerning racial segregation (separation). The case began in 1892, when a black man, Homer Plessy, sat in an area of a train reserved for white travelers. He was arrested for breaking a Louisiana law that required separate facilities for blacks and whites in railroad cars. Plessy and his lawyers argued that the Louisiana law violated a clause of the Fourteenth Amendment to the U.S. Constitution that guaranteed citizens equal protection of the law.

Brown and the Supreme Court ruled that the Fourteenth Amendment did not guarantee the social equality of all races, thus upholding the Louisiana law. In doing so, they established the legality of segregation as long as facilities were kept "separate but equal." In Brown's day, the ruling did not attract public opposition, and segregation of the races in the South continued. In spite of the fact that facilities for blacks were nearly always inferior to those for whites, the separate but equal standard dominated civil rights cases until 1954. That year, the standard was overruled by the Supreme Court in *Brown v. Board of Education of Topeka,* which declared racial segregation in public schools to be unconstitutional. That ruling attacked the "separate but equal" rule by arguing that segregation harms minority students by making them feel inferior and thus interfering with their ability to learn. The court declared that separate educational facilities could never be equal. Therefore, segregated schools violated the Fourteenth Amendment, which requires that all citizens be treated equally.

Another important case for Brown was *Pollock v. Farmers Loan & Trust Company,* usually called the "Income Tax Case." In this case, the Court declared the income tax act of 1894 as unconstitutional, and Brown dissented.

Brown served on the court during a group of cases called the "Insular Cases," which involved distant territories that the United States gained in the late 1800s. People of the new territories often had no experience of democratic self-government, so the U.S. Congress was unwilling to extend to these people full Constitutional protection. In the Insular Cases of 1901, the Supreme Court distinguished between incorporated and unincorporated territories. It held that all rights guaranteed by the

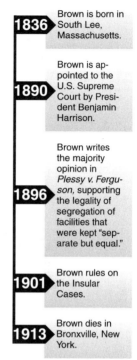

1836 Brown is born in South Lee, Massachusetts.

1890 Brown is appointed to the U.S. Supreme Court by President Benjamin Harrison.

1896 Brown writes the majority opinion in *Plessy v. Ferguson,* supporting the legality of segregation of facilities that were kept "separate but equal."

1901 Brown rules on the Insular Cases.

1913 Brown dies in Bronxville, New York.

"Laws permitting, and even requiring, their separation in places where they are liable to be brought into contact do not necessarily imply the inferiority of either race to the other, and have been generally, if not universally, recognized as within the competency of the state legislatures in the exercise of their police power."

Plessy v. Ferguson (1896) From opinion written by Brown

Constitution applied only in incorporated territories. Incorporated territories may become states, but unincorporated territories may not. In a controversial opinion concurring in *Downes v. Bidwell*, one of the Insular Cases, Brown said that people of **annexed** territories were not entitled to constitutionally guaranteed rights and privileges.

annexed: a piece of land which is incorporated through a treaty or agreement to a sovereign nation.

When his wife died in 1904, Brown married his cousin's widow, Josephine E. Tyler. As he aged, one eye became blind and the other nearly blind. On his 70th birthday, Brown submitted his resignation in 1906. He traveled abroad and then settled in Bronxville, New York, where he died in September 4, 1913. ◆

Burger, Warren

SEPTEMBER 17, 1907–JUNE 25, 1995 ● CHIEF JUSTICE

"We take on a burden when we put a man behind walls and that burden is to give him a chance to change. If we deny him that, we deny him his status as a human being, and to deny him that is to diminish our humanity and plant the seeds of future anguish for ourselves."

Chief Justice Warren Burger, addressing the New York State Bar Association, 1970

Warren Burger was born on September 17, 1907, in St. Paul, Minnesota, the fourth of seven children. His father, Charles, worked as a traveling salesman and a railroad cargo inspector, while his mother, Katharine, oversaw the children. The Burger family was not poor, but they had to work hard to maintain a middle-class standard of living. As soon as he was old enough, at age nine, Burger went to work delivering papers to help earn money for the family.

Throughout his youth, Burger was an excellent student. Although he received a scholarship to Princeton University, he could not afford to attend, and decided to remain in Minnesota for his higher education. He enrolled in the University of Minnesota and completed his classes in just three years, graduating in 1927. To obtain his law degree, he attended evening classes at the St. Paul College of Law; during the day, he worked as an insurance salesman to earn money for tuition.

Upon earning his law degree in 1931, Burger spent four years in private practice at a small firm before becoming a partner at the firm of Faricy, Burger, Moore & Costello, where he remained until 1953. There he handled both civil and criminal cases, and he also found time to teach classes at St. Paul College of Law for more than 12 years.

During his years at Faricy, Burger became well known on the local legal scene, and he made his name in political circles

Warren Burger

as well. He first became active with the Republican Party in 1934, where he met the charismatic Harold Stassen. Burger helped Stassen become governor of Minnesota in 1938, then served as the floor manager for Stassen's failed presidential election bids at the national conventions of 1948 and 1952.

While at the Republican National Convention in 1952, Burger was noticed by national Republican leaders when he switched allegiance to Dwight D. Eisenhower, helping the former general win the Republican nomination for president. Eisenhower returned the favor by bringing Burger to Washington with

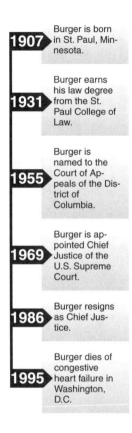

1907 Burger is born in St. Paul, Minnesota.

1931 Burger earns his law degree from the St. Paul College of Law.

1955 Burger is named to the Court of Appeals of the District of Columbia.

1969 Burger is appointed Chief Justice of the U.S. Supreme Court.

1986 Burger resigns as Chief Justice.

1995 Burger dies of congestive heart failure in Washington, D.C.

him. There he named Burger the head of the civil division of the Justice Department. It was a huge step up from his duties at Faricy back in Minnesota—as an assistant attorney general, Burger had more than 175 attorneys working for him. In just two years with the Justice Department, Burger established himself as one of the leaders of the conservative wing of the legal community in Washington, D.C.

That leadership became evident in 1955, just two years after his arrival in Washington, when Burger was appointed (by Eisenhower) to the U.S. Court of Appeals for the District of Columbia, considered by many to be the second most important court in the United States. Burger served on the court for 13 years and earned a reputation as a strong conservative who was especially active when it came to cases involving the police and the rights of criminals. In case after case, Burger sided with the police and made it easier to admit evidence that might have been gathered improperly and to use confessions or other information even when suspects were not properly arraigned. Burger believed that the court should do its part to support the police and the prosecutor's office, and his decisions during his time on the Court of Appeals reflected that belief.

Burger's conservative credentials had been noticed by the right people. When Richard Nixon became president in 1969, he nominated Burger to fill the seat of Chief Justice of the U.S. Supreme Court, a position that was previously held by Earl Warren. Warren had led one of the most active Courts in history as an extremely liberal and pro-active Chief Justice. Under his leadership, the court greatly expanded the rights of people accused of crimes and made numerous other decisions that leaned towards the left. President Nixon felt it was time to stop the liberal rulings, so he selected Burger based on his consistently conservative record. The appointment came as a shock to Burger because, in his words, he "hardly knew Nixon."

In appointing Burger, Nixon intended to create a "conservative counterrevolution" on the Court, but in the end, things did not happen the way that Nixon had hoped. In the final analysis, the Burger Court did not go nearly as far as Nixon had desired in revising or overturning the decisions made by the Warren Court. In fact, the Burger Court ended up making ruling after ruling that was interpreted as being too liberal for Nixon (Burger was often in the minority in those decisions). There was certainly no "constitutional counterrevolution," as Nixon had desired. Under Burger, the Court did make it easier

United States v. Nixon (1974)

During his presidency, Richard M. Nixon routinely recorded conversations that occurred in the Oval Office. These tapes became important evidence during the grand jury investigation of events associated with the Watergate break–in; many believed that the tapes contained records of the president and his associates while they were planning the break–in and other illegal acts. When a grand jury indicted seven of the Watergate conspirators, the special prosecutor issued a subpoena for these tapes, but President Nixon refused to hand them over. The president claimed executive privilege, asserting that the tapes contained confidential communications and were therefore exempt from the subpoena.

At the heart of the president's refusal to turn over the tapes was the idea of "separation of powers," which means that the executive branch of government (the presidency) could not be subjected to the demands of other branches of the government, such as the legislative branch (Congress) or the judiciary (the courts). The Supreme Court, however, did not agree.

Eight members of the Supreme Court held that the separation of powers and the need for confidentiality was not enough to keep the tapes out of evidence. Justice Rehnquist, a Nixon appointee, abstained. The Court said that while executive privilege and confidentiality were often valid claims in military or diplomatic affairs, they were not unlimited rights. Due process of law required that, in cases of criminal activities such as the Watergate break–in, there were limits on the right of the president to claim privilege, and the Court required that the tapes be made available as evidence. As a result of this decision, the president's direct involvement in the Watergate scandal was exposed, and Nixon ultimately resigned rather than face impeachment and a trial in the Senate.

for police departments to interrogate suspects, gain warrants, and gather evidence, but it did not completely overturn the exclusionary rule, which Burger had wanted to do when he took office.

On other important social issues, the Burger Court did lean towards the conservative side. The Court ruled that the use of busing to achieve desegregation in public schools was constitutional, but it repeatedly imposed additional restrictions on how the busing could be achieved. In addition, the court made it easier for employees to prove that they were racially discriminated against on the job.

There were seemingly dozens of other important cases decided during Burger's years, cases that had an important effect on the American system. The Burger Court upheld decisions increasing the freedom of the press, including the famous ruling that allowed the Pentagon Papers—a collection of documents on the Vietnam War—to be published. It also ruled that obscenity

The fact that Burger was never the "yes man" that Nixon might have hoped was made clear in 1974 at the end of the Watergate break-in scandal.

standards should be determined at the local level, and it increased the separation of church and state. Other notable rulings including one that allowed court cases to be televised even if the person on trial objected to the coverage, and one that struck down the congressional power known as the "legislative veto," which could be used to stop some actions taken by the office of the president.

Then, of course, there was the *Roe v. Wade* decision in 1973. In a decision that upset conservatives within the Nixon administration and mobilized public opinion on both sides of the issue, the Court ruled that all women had the right to obtain an abortion to end a pregnancy. Burger initially opposed the ruling, but in order to control who got to write the majority opinion, he voted with the majority on the case. Nearly three decades after the ruling, the abortion debate is still one of the most heated in the American political scene.

The fact that Burger was never the "yes man" that Nixon might have hoped was made clear in 1974 at the end of the Watergate break-in scandal. At that time, when there were still questions about who knew what in the growing scandal, Chief Justice Burger wrote the unanimous opinion that forced Nixon to turn over tape recordings made in his office to a special prosecutor. The tapes proved inconclusively that Nixon had known about the burglary of the Democratic Party offices and had participated in the cover-up of that illegal activity. Nixon was left with no choice but to resign the office of president just two weeks after the Court's decision. Burger called the ruling "one of the easiest decisions I ever made."

After Burger retired from the Court, he spent much of his time speaking around the country. Among his most common topics were two issues about which he felt passionately—prison reform and gun control. Burger had tried to bring about changes to the nation's prison system while he was a member of the Court, and he continued after he retired. He strongly opposed simply "warehousing" prisoners and felt that U.S. prisons were failing to educate or train prisoners, which led to more crime when they were released. He traveled extensively, studying other prison systems around the world, including the ones used by the Russians, who emphasized education for youthful offenders. "I would see that every prisoner who came in first has basic education so that he is literate," Burger once said. He also supported the Chinese principle of building "factories with fences" so that prisoners could learn job skills that they could use upon release.

On the matter of gun control, Burger was one of the leading—and rare—conservative voices that spoke out in support of limiting access to firearms. He strongly believed in former Chief Justice John Marshall's concept of a "living constitution," and felt that the conditions that were present when the Second Amendment (which protects the right to bear arms) was written were no longer relevant in the United States at the end of the 20th century. An avid hunter and sportsman, Burger felt that guns should be registered and that access to certain guns, such as automatic machine guns, should be strictly limited. For this strong stance, Burger was attacked by conservative gun supporters everywhere, but he remained unfazed by their attacks: "Nothing outrages me more than the conduct of the National Rifle Association [a firearms rights interest group]. . . . The fact is, they have trained themselves and their people to lie about this problem [of guns], and I can't use any word less than lie," he said.

In 1986, after 17 years on the Court, Burger surprised observers by resigning and taking over as head of the Bicentennial Commission of the U.S. Constitution. Appointed to the office of Chief Justice to create a conservative counterpoint to the court of Chief Justice Earl Warren, Burger had instead balanced liberal and conservative rulings and served as a transition between the Warren Court and the much more conservative court of William Rehnquist, his successor.

On June 25, 1995, Burger died of congestive heart failure in Washington, D.C.. He was 87 years old. ◆

Burton, Harold

JUNE 22, 1888–OCTOBER 28, 1964 ● ASSOCIATE JUSTICE

Harold Hitz Burton was born in Jamaica Plain (now part of Boston), on June 22, 1888. His father, Alfred Burton, served 20 years as dean of faculty for the Massachusetts Institute of Technology, one of the world's leading research universities, in Cambridge. Harold's mother, Gertrude Hitz Burton, was of Swiss descent. Burton spent his early childhood with his sick mother in Switzerland, where he learned

Harold Burton

"We conclude that in the field of public education the doctrine of 'separate but equal' has no place. Separate educational facilities are inherently unequal."

Brown v. Board of Education of Topeka (1954) Burton opinion supporting Court decision

French. Sadly, his mother died when he was seven, and Burton returned to his father's home. Burton received his education at Bowdoin, a coeducational liberal arts college in Brunswick, Maine. Famous Bowdoin graduates include the American writers Henry Wadsworth Longfellow and Nathaniel Hawthorne, as well as many of Maine's leading political figures. Burton was active in track and football, and won academic honors. He went on to Harvard Law School, graduating in 1912. That year he also married Selma Florence Smith. The couple had two children in a long and happy marriage.

As many had before him, Burton went West to seek greater opportunities. He practiced law in Cleveland, Ohio, also becoming an instructor in corporation law at Western Reserve University. He served in the army in World War I, earning a Purple Heart medal. A lifelong Republican, Burton became involved in politics, and between 1929 and 1932, he served as an elected member of the Ohio state legislature. He also served as director of law for the city of Cleveland. Burton then ran for election as mayor of Cleveland, and began the first of three terms in 1935.

In 1940, Burton won election as a U.S. Senator from Ohio, and began his term in 1941. In his stint on Capitol Hill, Burton worked with Harry S. Truman on the Senate Committee on the Conduct of the War which investigated defense contracts during World War II. After Truman became president, he appointed Burton to the U.S. Supreme Court in 1945. Even though Truman was a Democrat, he chose his long-time friend Burton, a liberal Republican, and Burton became the first Republican associate justice appointed by a Democratic president.

On the bench for 13 years, Burton voted conservatively. Burton was a **strict constructionist,** meaning that he relied mainly on a strict interpretation of the Constitution and of prior laws to support his decisions. In cases in which the government sought to discourage communism, Burton sided with the anticommunist laws. However, Burton generally voted with the liberal majority on questions of civil rights in the 1950s, supporting the desegregation of public schools and transportation.

Burton supported his colleagues in overturning the "separate but equal" doctrine in the famous case of *Brown v. Board of Education of Topeka* in 1954. In this landmark case about racially separate schools in various states, the court held that public school segregation violated the equal protection clause of the Fourteenth Amendment to the Constitution.

In the tragic case of Willie Francis, a black man of Louisiana, Burton passionately disagreed with the rest of the court. Francis had been convicted of murder in a state court and sentenced to be electrocuted. On May 9, 1947, he was prepared for electrocution, placed in the electric chair, and then the executioner threw the switch, giving Francis a shock intended to cause his death. However, because of a mechanical problem, Francis survived. He was removed from the chair and returned to prison, but the Governor of Louisiana issued another warrant for his execution at a later date.

When the case came to the Supreme Court, the Court ruled that Louisiana could go ahead and electrocute Francis again. They decided the execution would not violate the double jeopardy clause of the Fifth Amendment, it would not violate the cruel and unusual punishment clause of the Eighth Amendment, and it would not violate the equal protection clause of the Fourteenth Amendment. On May 3, 1946, Francis was executed.

Burton sometimes opposed the President on economic and commerce issues, and he upset Truman in 1952 when the Court ruled that the president did not have the authority to seize steel mills in the face of a labor strike. The administration had worked to prevent a strike that would close the country's steel mills, nevertheless, a strike date was set for early April 9, 1952. On nationwide radio, just hours before the scheduled strike, Truman ordered Secretary of Commerce Charles Sawyer to seize the mills. Truman wanted to ensure steel production would continue to support efforts for the Korean War. On June 2, 1952, the Supreme Court voted 6–3 in *Youngstown Sheet and Tube Co. v. Sawyer* that the seizure was unconstitutional. The Court said that Truman could have used the Taft-Hartley Act to delay the strike, but Truman disliked the law too much to use it because it addressed labor-management relations. The case did not end Burton's friendship with Truman, however, and Burton also became an ally of Truman's successor, Dwight D. Eisenhower.

1888 Burton is born in Jamaica Plain (now part of Boston), Massachusetts.

1940 Burton is elected to the United States Senate representing Ohio.

1945 Burton is appointed to the U.S. Supreme Court by President Harry S. Truman.

1952 Burton opposes Truman in *Youngstown Sheet and Tube Co. v. Sawyer*, declaring that presidential seizure of steel mills is unconstitutional.

1954 Burton supports overturning the "separate but equal" doctrine in *Brown v. Board of Education of Topeka*.

1964 Burton dies in Washington, D.C.

Burton earned a reputation on the court for his great respect for the law and the court and his diligent research. Other justices did not consider Burton witty or exceptionally intellectual compared with others, but all admired his hard work. His private life included the many parties his wife enjoyed, but he preferred bird watching and history reading. Burton retired from the Court in October 1958 due to failing health brought on by Parkinson's disease. He died in Washington, D.C., on October 28, 1964. ◆

Butler, Pierce

MARCH 17, 1866–NOVEMBER 16, 1939 ● ASSOCIATE JUSTICE

Pierce Butler was born in a log cabin in 1866 near Northfield, Minnesota, on March 17, St. Patrick's Day. His father, Patrick Butler, an Irish Roman Catholic, had earned a civil engineering degree from Trinity College in Dublin. He also traveled in Europe, even teaching English in Germany. Patrick Butler and his wife, Mary Gaffney Butler, moved to the United States from County Wicklow, Ireland, along with many Irish fleeing their nation's famine of 1848. The Butlers settled outside of St. Paul, Minnesota, to make a living at farming. Pierce and his seven siblings worked hard on the farm but also learned academic subjects from their father and at their local school.

Butler studied at a prep school at Carleton College in Northfield, then attended the college, paying his tuition by working in a local dairy. Butler graduated in 1887 and moved to St. Paul, where he was admitted to the Minnesota bar in 1888 at age 22. He also met Annie Cronin, who he married in 1891. The couple had eight children.

Butler served as assistant county attorney and then county attorney in St. Paul. In 1893, he formed a law firm with two partners. As the railroad became a large part of life in the American West, Butler's firm gained expertise in cases that dealt with such issues as property rights and railways. From 1899 to 1905, Butler was on **retainer** to a large railway company, earning the reputation as one of the leading railroad lawyers of the Midwest. He became known for his mastery of facts and figures, but also for being so tough on witnesses that he was accused of "bullying" them.

> *"The Constitution grants to the United States no power to pay unemployed persons or to require the states to enact laws . . . for that purpose."*
>
> Pierce Butler, dissenting in *Helvering v. Davis* (1937)

retainer: a fee paid by a client to an attorney for services in the present and future.

In addition to his private practice, Butler sometimes prosecuted antitrust cases for George Wickersham, attorney general under President William Howard Taft. When Wickersham called on Butler to take the federal government's side in cases, he found Butler very impressive.

In 1913, Butler argued the *Minnesota Rate Cases* before the U.S. Supreme Court. In this case, Butler helped determine the railroad methods for charging fares. Butler also worked on Canadian cases, saving large sums for the Canadian government in proceedings against the Western railroads. During one of these cases, Butler met and worked with former president Taft, and the two men became friends.

Taft went on to become Chief Justice of the Supreme Court, and on his recommendation, in 1922, President Warren G. Harding appointed Butler to the U.S. Supreme Court. A powerful group of liberal senators led by George W. Norris and Robert M. La Follette fought the appointment because, they said, Butler had strong loyalties to the powerful railroad industry. Butler also took criticism for his role in a firing of professors at the University of Minnesota when Butler was on the school's **Board of Regents.** The professors had expressed views promoting public ownership of streetcars, and Butler's opposition to their opinions showed his uncompromising spirit. In spite of the political forces opposing Butler's nomination, the President and the Congress made some political maneuvers, and Butler won the appointment.

In his 17 years on the bench, Butler behaved as a strict constitutional constructionist, meaning that he relied mainly on strict interpretation of the Constitution and of prior laws to support his decisions. He was a conservative justice and consistently opposed progressive taxation, social welfare programs, and government attempts to control the freedom of America's large corporations. He voted against giving a minimum wage to working women in *Morehead v. New York ex. rel. Tipaldo* (1936). He also dissented when the Court approved the Social Security tax in *Helvering v. Davis* (1937).

Butler voted conservatively together with three other Republican justices—Willis Van Devanter, James C. McReynolds, and George Sutherland—and the men became known as the Four Horsemen. They often turned over legislation that was part of President Franklin D. Roosevelt's New Deal.

Roosevelt, the Democratic Party candidate, had come into office the year after Butler joined the Court. Roosevelt tried to

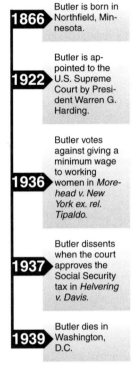

1866 Butler is born in Northfield, Minnesota.

1922 Butler is appointed to the U.S. Supreme Court by President Warren G. Harding.

1936 Butler votes against giving a minimum wage to working women in *Morehead v. New York ex. rel. Tipaldo.*

1937 Butler dissents when the court approves the Social Security tax in *Helvering v. Davis.*

1939 Butler dies in Washington, D.C.

board of regents: a group of elected members governing a public university or college.

put the economy back on track following the Great Depression, working with Congress to pass many laws to put social programs into place. Butler and the other conservative justices ruled against Roosevelt's National Recovery Administration (NRA), the Agricultural Adjustment Act (AAA), and ten other New Deal laws.

On February 2, 1937, Roosevelt made a speech attacking the Supreme Court for its actions over New Deal legislation. He pointed out that seven of the nine judges had been appointed by Republican presidents. Since Roosevelt had just won re-election by a massive number, he thought that the justices were vetoing legislation that the public supported. Roosevelt announced that he was going to ask Congress to pass a bill allowing him to expand the Supreme Court by adding new judges.

Chief Justice Charles Hughes realized that Roosevelt's Court Reorganization Bill would result in the Supreme Court coming under the control of the Democratic Party. He worked behind the scenes—convincing his colleagues to tone down their opposition to Roosevelt's laws—to make sure that the bill would be defeated in Congress. In July 1937, the Senate defeated Roosevelt's Court Reorganization Bill by 70–20. However, Roosevelt had the satisfaction of knowing he had a Supreme Court that was now less likely to block his legislation.

Butler was known as aggressive, stubborn, and domineering while working. At play, he was witty and loved golf and other outdoor activities. He visited his Irish ancestral home and served on the board of trustees of the Catholic University of America. In his later years, he enjoyed his farm in Maryland.

At age 73, while still on the Court, Butler died of a bladder problem on November 16, 1939, in Washington, D.C. ◆

Byrnes, James

MAY 2, 1882–APRIL 9, 1972 ● ASSOCIATE JUSTICE

Although James Francis "Jimmy" Byrnes served as an associate justice of the U.S. Supreme Court, he is best known as one of the nation's most important political figures in the 1930s and 1940s. He was born in 1882 in Charleston, South Carolina, although some sources list the date of his birth as 1879. As a young man Byrnes lied about his age to get a job, and he used the false date throughout his life. He was named after his father, a city clerk, who died before Byrnes was born. His mother, Elizabeth McSweeney, supported the family as a dressmaker.

At age 14, Byrnes went to work as a messenger in a law office for two dollars a week to help support his family. At the same time he took shorthand lessons to qualify as a court reporter, a job he held for eight years. In his spare time, he studied law under two local judges and, after passing the state bar examination in 1903, began practicing law in Aiken, South Carolina. He was born a Roman Catholic, but he converted to the Episcopal Church when he married Maude Busch in 1906.

Byrnes entered the political arena in 1908, when he was elected county prosecutor. Then in 1910 he won a seat in the U.S. House of Representative by a scant 57-vote margin. From 1911 to 1924 he gained a reputation in the House for his ability to forge compromises. As a member of the House Appropriations Committee, he became friends with Navy Secretary Franklin D. Roosevelt, who later as president would help shape Byrnes's career.

James F. Byrnes

Throughout his distinguished political career, Byrnes lost only one election. In 1924 he ran for a U.S. Senate seat against Coleman L. Blease. Blease was a ruthless campaigner who exploited Byrnes's Irish-Catholic heritage to turn South Carolina's overwhelmingly Protestant voters against him. Although Byrnes was a **segregationist,** he abhorred the violence of the Ku Klux Klan, who joined with Blease to defeat Byrnes. After the election, Byrnes settled in Spartanburg, South Carolina, and joined a prominent law firm.

Six years later, Byrnes won his coveted Senate seat, defeating Blease with the help of an endorsement from his Episcopal minister and the financial backing of Bernard M. Baruch. Byrnes

segregationist: supporter of the policy of legal separation of the races in public accommodations such as schools, restaurants, hotels, and other places.

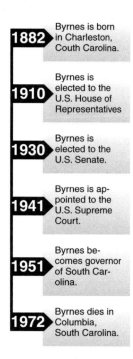

1882 Byrnes is born in Charleston, Couth Carolina.

1910 Byrnes is elected to the U.S. House of Representatives

1930 Byrnes is elected to the U.S. Senate.

1941 Byrnes is appointed to the U.S. Supreme Court.

1951 Byrnes becomes governor of South Carolina.

1972 Byrnes dies in Columbia, South Carolina.

Byrnes served only one term, 1941–1942, as a Supreme Court justice.

repeal: to invalidate a law or legislative act previously passed by a legislative body.

extended his power base by funneling some of Baruch's vast resources to other Senate Democrats, including the young Harry S. Truman.

Throughout his 10-year career in the Senate, Byrnes continued to function as an insider who knew how to get things done. An economic conservative, he opposed some of President Roosevelt's New Deal legislation, yet he remained one of the president's most valuable allies in Congress. As World War II approached, he was instrumental in helping the president in his efforts to **repeal** the Neutrality Act and pass the Lend-Lease Act to aid Great Britain in its war effort. For his support, Roosevelt nominated him to the Supreme Court in 1941. The Senate confirmed him unanimously without even holding hearings.

Byrnes served only one term, 1941–1942, as a Supreme Court justice. During his 16 months on the Court, he wrote no opinions. In fact, he chafed under the restrictions of the Court and wanted to take a more active role in the nation's war effort.

When Byrnes resigned from the Court in 1942, Roosevelt appointed him head of the Office of Economic Stabilization. In 1943 Roosevelt issued an executive order creating the Office of War Mobilization, later renamed the Office of War Mobilization and Reconversion. In doing so, the president relieved himself of the responsibility of directing the war effort on the home front so that he could concentrate on events overseas. As director of the new agency, Byrnes was in effect an "assistant president" with more power than Vice President Henry Wallace. From 1943 until the end of the war, Byrnes exercised wide-ranging authority over such matters as food rationing, sports schedules, the closing time for bars, and the procurement and distribution of war materials.

As the 1944 presidential election approached, Byrnes had high expectations that Roosevelt would select him as the vice presidential candidate. Given the president's failing health, Byrnes also reasonably expected that he might in time become president. Roosevelt disappointed him, however, by selecting Harry Truman for vice president. Byrnes then set his sights on becoming secretary of state, but Roosevelt again disappointed him when he named Edward R. Stettinius, Jr., to the post. Roosevelt did, however, invite Byrnes to attend the Yalta conference with him in February 1945. Byrnes again showed his talent as a troubleshooter in being able to reassure conservatives in the Senate that the president had made the best possible deal for postwar Europe with Soviet Premier Joseph Stalin.

After Roosevelt's death in April 1945, the new president, Harry Truman, finally appointed Byrnes secretary of state. Byrnes took his seat in the **cabinet** in July of that year. In the meantime, he was an important member of the Interim Committee, the group of policy advisers responsible for deciding whether to use the atomic bomb to end the war. Byrnes strongly supported use of the bomb, and it is likely that his access to Truman helped sway the new president's decision to unleash it on Japan.

cabinet: group of advisers of the head of the executive branch appointed by the executive and confirmed by the legislative branch of the federal government.

After the war, Byrnes conducted crucial negotiations with the Soviet Union. Although the evidence suggests that Byrnes took a hard line with the Soviets, many members of Congress accused him of "babying" America's postwar adversary. When Truman failed to defend Byrnes, the secretary resigned in 1947.

In the years that followed, Byrnes became increasingly disenchanted with the Democratic Party. He broke with Truman, and on a platform advocating resistance to federal intrusion into local and individual matters, he was elected governor of South Carolina, a position he held from 1951 to 1955. He remained a segregationist, and after the 1954 Supreme Court decision outlawing "separate but equal" schooling for blacks, he called for massive resistance to integration. In 1952, he supported Eisenhower for president, and in future elections he threw his support to Republican candidates Richard Nixon and Barry Goldwater.

James Byrnes died of a heart attack in Columbia, South Carolina, in 1972. ◆

Campbell, John Archibald

JUNE 24, 1811–MARCH 12, 1889 ● ASSOCIATE JUSTICE

John Campbell's life was one of remarkable achievement from an early age. Born in Washington, Georgia, he was the son of Duncan Green Campbell, a lawyer and state legislator, and Mary Williamson. At age 11 he entered Franklin College at the University of Georgia, and after he graduated with high honors at age 14, Secretary of War John C. Calhoun, his father's friend, nominated him for a cadetship at the U.S.

John Archibald
Campbell

Military Academy at West Point. But when his father died in 1828 (on the verge of being elected governor of Georgia), Campbell left West Point so that he could work to pay off his father's debts. He studied law under an uncle and the governor of Georgia and was admitted to the Georgia bar in 1829 when he was just 18 years old. In 1830 he moved to Montgomery, Alabama and began to practice law. There he met and married Anna Esther Goldthwaite, with whom he had five children.

Campbell rapidly earned a reputation as one of the leading attorneys of his time. He had a thorough knowledge of the law, and, in time, an extensive personal law library where he secluded himself to prepare

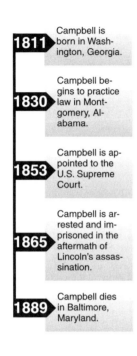

1811 Campbell is born in Washington, Georgia.

1830 Campbell begins to practice law in Montgomery, Alabama.

1853 Campbell is appointed to the U.S. Supreme Court.

1865 Campbell is arrested and imprisoned in the aftermath of Lincoln's assassination.

1889 Campbell dies in Baltimore, Maryland.

his cases. Twice he was nominated to the Alabama Supreme Court—the first time when he was just 24 years old—but he declined the position both times. In 1836 he was elected to the Alabama state legislature, where he served two terms, but he continued to argue important cases before the state supreme court, federal courts, and the U.S. Supreme Court. Perhaps his most famous case during these years was *Gaines v. Relf,* a decades-old inheritance case that found its way to the U.S. Supreme Court seven times. When the case was finally decided, the Court used the same line of reasoning that Campbell had used in arguing the case before the U.S. Court of Appeals.

In 1852, U.S. Supreme Court Justice John McKinley died. When the U.S. Senate refused to confirm President Millard Fillmore's nominee to fill the seat, two of the Court's justices wrote a letter to Fillmore's successor, Franklin Pierce, urging him to nominate Campbell. Pierce complied, and Campbell was confirmed as an associate justice in 1853. Throughout his judicial career, Campbell was a "strict constructionist," meaning that he strove to interpret the U.S. Constitution very narrowly by looking at what it actually says rather than by inferring a broader meaning.

As a Supreme Court justice in the 1850s, Campbell was deeply involved with events that led to the Civil War. Earlier, in 1850, he had been a delegate to the Convention of the Southern States in Nashville, Tennessee, where he wrote many of the convention's resolutions. He supported the view, prevalent throughout the Deep South, that the rights of the states should take precedence over those of the federal government. Thus, in the famous civil rights case *Dred Scott v. Sandford* (1857), he voted with the majority in overturning the Missouri Compromise. The result of this decision was that slaves were not regarded as citizens of the United States but rather were legally protected property.

Campbell, however, was by no means in favor of slavery. In circuit court cases he often upheld statutes prohibiting the buying and selling of slaves. He believed that slavery was already receding in the South and that in time it would disappear. He believed, however, that it was a state issue, not a federal one, and throughout the late 1850s and during the years of the Civil War, he advocated compromise positions that would avert the crisis facing the nation. Because he was moderate in his views, many political leaders saw him as a possible compromise candidate in the 1860 presidential election won by Abraham Lincoln.

When Alabama **seceded** from the Union in January 1861, Campbell worked feverishly to avoid war. He was a member of a commission that met with President Lincoln to serve as an intermediary between the **provisional government** in the South and the Union government. When the effort at compromise failed, Campbell felt that he was left with no choice. Although he did not support secession and war, he resigned from the U.S. Supreme Court and returned to Alabama, where in 1862 he took an administrative position in the office of the Confederate secretary of war.

The events surrounding the end of the Civil War were disastrous for Campbell. As the war was coming to a close, he met with Lincoln, in February 1865, to discuss peace. One of the proposals Campbell made to Lincoln was to allow the Virginia legislature to reconvene. The legislature's specific purpose would have been to discuss ways to cooperate with Lincoln's plans for reconstruction after the war. Lincoln agreed to the proposal, though he rescinded his agreement in April after the South surrendered. The next day, Lincoln was assassinated, and Campbell became a victim of the hysteria that followed. He was arrested because of the mistaken belief that he supported an independent "rebel" legislature. He spent four months in prison before Supreme Court Justices Benjamin Curtis and Samuel Nelson petitioned Present Andrew Johnson for his release.

After the war, Campbell set up a private law practice in New Orleans, Louisiana, for his home in Alabama had been destroyed during the war. Soon he was back at the Supreme Court, arguing cases before his former colleagues. One of the most famous of these cases was the *Slaughterhouse* case (1872). It involved the state of Louisiana, which had established a **monopoly** in the butchers' trade, forcing over 1,000 people out of work. Campbell argued that under the Fourteenth Amendment the states could not restrict economic liberty through this type of law. Although he lost the case, the Court adopted his reasoning later when it overturned similar state laws.

Campbell maintained his practice in New Orleans until his wife's death in 1884. He retired to Baltimore, Maryland, though he continued to accept clients and argue cases before the Supreme Court. He died at his home in Baltimore in 1889. ◆

The events surrounding the end of the Civil War were disastrous for Campbell.

secede: to remove oneself from a united group.

provisional government: government installed in conquered territory immediately after an armed conflict by the victor to restore law and order.

monopoly: ownership or control of an entity or product by one person or group, excluding all others.

Cardozo, Benjamin

MAY 24, 1870–JULY 9, 1938 ● ASSOCIATE JUSTICE

Benjamin Cardozo was born on May 24, 1870, to Albert and Rebecca Cardozo. Benjamin was the youngest of the couple's six children. Sephardic Jews who had lived in America since before the American Revolution, the Cardozo family was very well-respected in New York City. There, Albert had established a successful law career that saw him rise from lawyer to New York State Supreme Court justice. While he was generally held in high esteem, the elder Cardozo was forced to resign his position on the court because of connections to the infamous William M. "Boss" Tweed, a corrupt politician who ran the Democratic party in New York City out of Tammany Hall. When faced with charges that he took bribes, Cardozo retired in 1872 instead of dragging his family name though an embarrassing trial. Despite this negative incident, Benjamin decided to follow in his father's footsteps and become a lawyer.

Cardozo was a brilliant student and a child prodigy. He entered Columbia University (then called Columbia College) at the age of just 15 and took only two years to finish his bachelor's degree, graduating first in his class in 1889 and delivering the commencement address. It took him only one more year to earn his master's degree in political science. He then entered Columbia Law School, where he again excelled, although he did not complete his law degree. Instead he left school early to take a job at his father's law firm. He easily passed the bar exam in 1891 and began working as a lawyer.

Cardozo worked in private practice for more than 20 years and became one of the leading attorneys in the state of New York in the areas of commercial and appellate law. Often sought out by other attorneys for advice, Cardozo took on the tough-

Benjamin Cardozo

est cases and was not afraid to argue the most complex legal points. When approached in 1912 to run for office, Cardozo agreed, and in 1913, he defeated the same Tammany Hall politicians who had ruined his father's career and was elected to the State Supreme Court. In 1914, after just a year on the high court, he was appointed by the governor to the New York Court of Appeals, the highest court in the New York state system.

Cardozo served on the Court of Appeals until 1932, the last five years as the chief justice of that court. While on the Court of Appeals, he became better known than some of the judges serving on the U.S. Supreme Court, and he was more highly thought of in legal circles for his well-reasoned and important rulings. Usually taking a liberal stance, Cardozo believed that the law constantly changed with the times, shifting to meet changing social standards—a radical philosophy at the time. That attitude directly contradicted most of his contemporaries on the bench, who believed that the law was written in stone, static and unchanging.

Cardozo's opinions were always well-written, so it came as no surprise to his family and colleagues that he soon branched out and became a notable legal author. He wrote his first book, *Jurisdiction of the Court of Appeals of the State of New York,* in 1903, and in later works such as *The Nature of the Judicial Process* and *The Growth of the Law,* Cardozo greatly influenced a generation of American lawyers and judges.

One of Cardozo's most important decisions on the New York bench came in the case *MacPherson v. Buick Motor Company* (1916), which involved a consumer issue. In his ruling, Cardozo stated that a company issued an implied safety warranty on its product (in this case, a car) that remained intact even if that product was sold to a middleman, such as an automobile dealer, instead of directly to the consumer. The ruling held Buick directly liable for its products, instead of making the dealers liable. This concept that the manufacturer, not the retailer, is responsible for a warranty remains a cornerstone of U.S. consumer law.

In 1932, Cardozo was rewarded for his years of service to the law by being named to the U.S. Supreme Court. He was selected by President Herbert Hoover after Oliver Wendell Holmes retired. Upon selecting the New York justice, Hoover said that "the whole country demands the one man who could best carry on the great Holmes' tradition of philosophic approval to modern American jurisprudence." Cardozo accepted

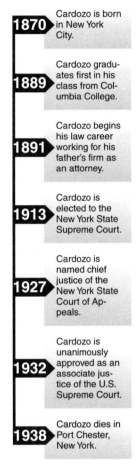

1870 Cardozo is born in New York City.

1889 Cardozo graduates first in his class from Columbia College.

1891 Cardozo begins his law career working for his father's firm as an attorney.

1913 Cardozo is elected to the New York State Supreme Court.

1927 Cardozo is named chief justice of the New York State Court of Appeals.

1932 Cardozo is unanimously approved as an associate justice of the U.S. Supreme Court.

1938 Cardozo dies in Port Chester, New York.

While Cardozo would only serve six years on the Supreme Court before suffering an untimely death, he left a lasting mark on the U.S. judicial process.

the appointment, was confirmed unanimously by the U.S. Senate, and took office on March 14, 1932.

While Cardozo would only serve six years on the Supreme Court before suffering an untimely death, he left a lasting mark on the U.S. judicial process. In his 1921 book *The Nature of the Judicial Process*, Cardozo cautioned against achieving a "good result" in a case if the outcome proved dishonest, and he strove to follow his own words in all of his decisions. During his six years on the court, Cardozo wrote more than 140 opinions, and thanks to his own brilliance and to the unusual turmoil of the time in which he served (which helped to create many important cases), many of those opinions carried judicial weight for decades.

Cardozo is perhaps best known for his opinions in two areas. One was a series of cases, including *Helvering v. Davis* (1937), in which the constitutionality of the newly founded Social Security administration was questioned. Many conservatives and business leaders felt that the program was illegal and that the federal government had no business handing out welfare to its citizens just because they reached a certain age. Cardozo sided with the majority in ruling that Social Security was, in fact, constitutional and wrote a distinguished opinion for the majority. In it, he explained how a government could intervene to help further the good of its people and that "Congress may spend money in aid of the 'general welfare,'" which of course is a basic tenet of the Constitution.

The second case for which Cardozo is best remembered is a case called *Palko v. Connecticut* (1937). The case involved a criminal named Palko who had been brought to trial on a charge of first degree murder. At his trial, the jury found him innocent of that charge but guilty of second degree murder, sentencing him to life in prison. However, even though Palko was found guilty, the state of Connecticut used a broad interpretation of the rules of appeal and asked that Palko's conviction be overturned so that it could retry him for first degree murder. The state Appeals Court agreed, and a new trial was ordered. At the second trial, Palko was again tried for first degree murder, but this time he was convicted, and his sentence was the death penalty. Palko appealed the verdict, saying that he was a victim of double jeopardy—that is, he had been tried and convicted for the same crime twice. (U.S. citizens are protected from double jeopardy by the Fifth Amendment to the Constitution.) The Connecticut Supreme Court upheld the second conviction, setting the stage for Palko's appeal to the U.S. Supreme Court.

Cardozo sided with the majority in a 8–1 ruling that held that Palko's constitutional rights had not been violated and that his conviction should be upheld. Cardozo's opinion made important statements about both the Fifth Amendment and the Fourteenth Amendment, which guaranteed a criminal's right to due process under the law. On the Fifth Amendment, the justice wrote that "This (privilege against self-incrimination) too might be lost and justice still done. Indeed, today as in the past, there are students of our penal system who look upon the immunity as a mischief rather than a benefit, and who would limit its scope, or destroy it altogether. . . . Justice, however, would not perish, if the accused were subject to a duty to respond to an ordinary inquiry."

What this quote implies, and Cardozo's opinion makes clear, is that individual states can make laws and legal decisions that conflict with the Bill of Rights of the Constitution (the first 10 amendments) and the Fourteenth Amendment if that conflict is not too serious in nature. The U.S. government, the Court ruled, could impose upon states only those provisions of the Bill of Rights that were "of the very essence of a scheme of ordered liberty." The Court's ruling left it up to state judges to determine, on a case by case basis, which laws fit that broad definition and which ones did not, and trusted that the states would make the right decisions. People could still challenge the states and bring their cases to the Supreme Court, but in *Palko*, the Court made it clear that it would let certain exceptions to the Constitution stand in order to benefit the greater good.

Cardozo's opinion was the standard by which the Supreme Court operated for more than 30 years, as the *Palko* decision was not reversed until 1969. Then, in the case *Benton v. Maryland*, the Court ruled that double jeopardy was so fundamentally wrong that a provision against it was a must if the due process of law was to be carried out.

During his tenure, Cardozo made a number of other rulings concerning President Franklin Roosevelt's New Deal social programs (which were designed to help get the country out of the Great Depression) that highlighted his intelligence and judicial skills. He became a fairly liberal justice, but not overly so, as some had feared he might. He never married and eventually the

> *It is when the colors do not match, when the references in the index fail, when there is no decisive precedent, that the serious business of the judge begins.*
> Benjamin Cardozo,
> *The Nature of the Judicial Process,*
> 1921

pressures of the job started to wear on him. In 1938, while visiting a friend, Cardozo became ill and never recovered, passing away in Port Chester, New York on July 9, 1938, as the result of a coronary thrombosis. ◆

Catron, John

1781–MAY 30, 1865 ● ASSOCIATE JUSTICE

ittle is known about the early life of John Catron, and nothing is known of his parents. By some accounts he was born in Pennsylvania, a descendant of German settlers, but according to others he was born in Virginia. Even the date of his birth is uncertain. He may have been born as early as 1778 or as late as 1787, although a niece reported that before he died he told her that he had been born in 1781. He spent much of his early life in Virginia, then moved to Kentucky and later Tennessee, where he married Matilda Childress in 1807. The two had no children.

John Catron

In 1812, Catron studied law, but he also served as an enlisted man under Andrew Jackson in the conflict with the Creek Indians and, by some accounts, in the War of 1812 at the Battle of New Orleans. After being admitted to the Tennessee bar in 1815, he worked as a local prosecutor, riding what were known then as the "mountain circuits." Then, in 1818, he opened a large—and lucrative—private law practice in Nashville, where he became an expert in land law, the source of much litigation in Tennessee at the time.

In 1824, the Tennessee legislature increased the number of judges on the state supreme court of errors and appeals and elected Catron to the new position. In this way the legislature was able to ensure a court majority in land dispute cases and thus put to rest some of the ongoing sources of dispute. In one of his most famous cases, in 1829, Catron ruled against an attorney who had been disbarred for killing a man in a duel. In his decision he said that dueling was a form of murder, and his opinion contributed greatly to the decline of **dueling,** still a prevalent way of settling disputes according to codes of honor in the South at the time. In his rulings, too, he supported the policies of President Andrew Jackson. Though he believed that the states, not the national government, should be the controlling authorities in Indian disputes, he made significant rulings in support of Jackson's Indian policies. He also sided with Jackson in his belief that a national bank was unconstitutional. Catron became the first chief justice of the state supreme court of errors and appeals when the title was created in 1831.

In 1834, the court of errors and appeals was abolished, so Catron returned to Nashville and private practice. In the meantime he had added to his personal fortune as a partner in the Buffalo Iron Works, a firm based near Nashville. He did, however, remain active in public affairs. In 1836 he directed Martin Van Buren's Tennessee campaign for the presidency. Then in March of the following year, Congress passed an act adding two justices to the U.S. Supreme Court. The following day, in one of his last acts as president, Jackson appointed Catron to one of the two seats. According to one tradition, Catron's wife went to the White House and personally asked Jackson for the appointment. According to another, Van Buren made the request. In either case, Jackson was happy to make the appointment, believing that Catron, though lacking formal education, showed sound common sense and a thorough knowledge of the law.

Inevitably, Catron played a role in the debate over slavery and the events leading to the Civil War. Although he himself was a slave owner, his views were more moderate than those of some of his **contemporaries.** For example, he denounced a proposal made in the Tennessee legislature that all free blacks should be enslaved. Privately, he believed that slavery could legally be abolished in the United States.

Nonetheless, Catron joined the Court majority in opinions enforcing the fugitive slave acts of 1793 and 1850 and in the famous *Dred Scott v. Sandford* case of 1857. In deciding that case, however, he wrote a separate opinion in which he disagreed with Chief Justice Roger Taney, who said that slaves could never be citizens. Catron argued that this was not a matter for the federal courts to decide. He did, however, support the

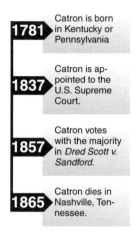

1781 Catron is born in Kentucky or Pennsylvania

1837 Catron is appointed to the U.S. Supreme Court.

1857 Catron votes with the majority in *Dred Scott v. Sandford.*

1865 Catron dies in Nashville, Tennessee.

Inevitably, Catron played a role in the debate over slavery and the events leading to the Civil War.

dueling: an armed conflict between two principles with witnesses with the primary purpose of settling a dispute.

contemporaries: individuals in the same relative age class and/or profession.

Court's majority opinion that the Treaty of 1803, by which the United States made the Louisiana Purchase, guaranteed the right of slavery to new states in that territory. He also cited the "privileges and immunities" clause in Article IV of the Constitution, which established the principle of equality of rights among the states. On this basis, he ruled that the Missouri Compromise of 1820, prohibiting slavery in new U.S. states above the 36th parallel, was unconstitutional. In connection with this case, Catron was guilty of a serious ethical lapse when, while the case was pending, he wrote to President James Buchanan asking him to pressure Justice Robert Grier to vote with the majority. He compounded this lapse when he informed Buchanan of the outcome of the case before it was announced to the public.

As civil war threatened, Catron remained loyal to the Union. He returned to Tennessee in an effort to persuade the state not to secede. In one statewide vote, Tennesseans had voted against secession, but in a second election, despite the efforts of Catron and many others, they voted to secede. Catron wanted to remain in Tennessee to do what he could to uphold the authority of the federal courts and persuade others to remain loyal to the Union. Soon, however, this proved impossible. A group of friends advised him that there were threats against his life and that he should leave the state. Later, Confederate authorities confiscated his property. Catron fled for a time, but eventually he returned to his judicial duties. In one of his last significant decisions, he ruled that the Federal Confiscation Act, which allowed the U.S. government to confiscate property owned by Confederate rebels, was constitutional.

John Catron died in Nashville, Tennessee, in 1865. ◆

Chase, Salmon P.

JANUARY 13, 1808–MAY 7, 1873 ● CHIEF JUSTICE

Salmon P. Chase, who led one of the most distinguished careers in the U.S. government that any person has ever had, was born on January 13, 1808, in Cornish, New Hampshire, the son of a tavern keeper who also was a local politician. One of 11 children born to Ithamar and Janette, Chase's family, which had been in America since Colonial times, was fairly well-off. While Salmon was still a child, the Chase family moved to Keene, New Hampshire, where Ithamar purchased his tavern and where the Chase children attended school; they also later received some tutoring from a private instructor in nearby Windsor, Vermont.

Salmon P. Chase

Chase's life took a drastic turn when his father died when Chase was nine years old. His mother was left with some property and money, but she thought it was best if her son went and lived with Ithamar's brother, Chase's uncle Philander Chase, in Ohio. Philander was a bishop of the Episcopal Church, first in Ohio and then in Illinois. In Ohio, Chase lived and worked on his uncle's farm and attended the bishop's school in Worthington, which is near Columbus. There, Chase studied Greek, religion, and other classical studies; his uncle hoped he would become a clergyman, but Chase did not wish to follow that path. After his uncle was named the president of Cincinnati College, Chase attended that school for a year, but when his uncle went to Great Britain on a fund-raising venture, Chase moved back to his native New Hampshire. There, he enrolled in Dartmouth College, from which he graduated in 1826,

Chase had decided that he wished to study the law, and to reach that goal, he moved to Washington, D.C. There, to make ends meet, he started a small private school for boys, teaching during the day and studying law at night. One of his students was the son of the U.S. Attorney General, William Wirt, who agreed to let Chase study and work under him. This was a great honor for Chase, since Wirt was one of the most distinguished lawyers in the United States. Chase was admitted to the bar in 1829, but he could not practice law in Washington because he did not meet the city's residency requirements. Instead, he moved back to Ohio, where he opened his first law office in Cincinnati. One of the first things he did there was to compile all of the state's written statutes into a three-volume work that

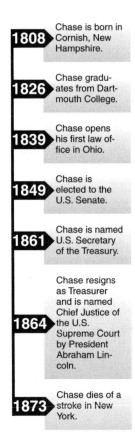

1808 Chase is born in Cornish, New Hampshire.

1826 Chase graduates from Dartmouth College.

1839 Chase opens his first law office in Ohio.

1849 Chase is elected to the U.S. Senate.

1861 Chase is named U.S. Secretary of the Treasury.

1864 Chase resigns as Treasurer and is named Chief Justice of the U.S. Supreme Court by President Abraham Lincoln.

1873 Chase dies of a stroke in New York.

became the standard reference in the state; he received great praise for this endeavor.

Chase married Katherine Jane Garniss on March 4, 1834. Unfortunately, she died just after childbirth in 1835, leaving Chase with a daughter named Catherine Jane, who also suffered an untimely death just four years later. These early deaths became a too common occurrence in Chase's life. He married twice more and had five more daughters, and three of those girls died at a very young age. The only daughters to reach adulthood were Katherine, born to his second wife, Eliza Ann Smith; and Janette, born to his third wife, Sarah Belle Dunlop Ludlow. In addition to the tragic deaths of his daughters, Chase endured the deaths of Smith, just six years after he married her in 1839, and Ludlow, who died five years after their 1846 marriage. Chase's touching, grief-stricken reactions to the horrific events in his life are carefully documented in his diaries, revealing a caring father and dedicated husband.

In Ohio, as he began his legal career, Chase also became actively involved in the anti-slavery movement. Ohio was a free state, but Cincinnati borders the state of Kentucky, which was pro-slavery. Because only the Ohio River separated the two states, Cincinnati was an important link in the Underground Railroad, which helped move former slaves to freedom in the northern United States. Chase became infamous for defending escaped slaves, earning the derisive nickname "the attorney general for runaway negroes," which he proudly bore. He became so well-known as a slave defender that he even argued one case before the U.S. Supreme Court; he lost, but he gained prominence in doing so. Chase was also actively involved in local politics, first as a member of the Whig party. He then formed the anti-slavery Freedom party, and later, also helped found the Free Soil party. In 1849, he was rewarded for his efforts when he was elected to the U.S. Senate as a Free Soil candidate.

Chase switched political allegiances to whichever party he thought was toughest on slavery, and eventually, that party was the Republican Party, which Chase joined. He returned to Ohio and continued his climb up the political ladder, winning election as the governor of Ohio in both 1855 and 1857. He was first mentioned as a presidential candidate in 1856, and in 1860, he ran for the top office (he had returned to the U.S. Senate by that time). He was one of the leading candidates, but at the Republican Convention, on the third ballot, he cast his support to Abraham Lincoln, helping Lincoln win the nomination. To thank Chase for his actions, Lincoln, after winning the presidential election, named Chase to the Secretary of the U.S. Treasury in 1861, an office that Chase would hold until 1864.

As Treasury secretary, Chase was in charge during one of the most difficult periods in U.S. history, helping the Union raise funds to fight the Civil War while maintaining the integrity of the U.S. dollar. He also oversaw the creation of the paper currency system that we have today (his face was on the $10,000 bill, which is no longer printed), and the creation of the national banking system (in 1863), which was one of his highest priority projects and one of his most lasting legacies. He received praise for his efforts, but he was so stridently anti-slavery that he no longer felt he could work with Lincoln, who was more moderate on the issue. In 1864, after trying to resign on two previous occasions, Chase succeeded in resigning as secretary. Lincoln hated to lose Chase, whom he respected, but felt he had to respect Chase's wishes.

Then, in an odd turn of events, Lincoln was presented with an opportunity to keep Chase in government service. When Roger Taney, Chief Justice of the Supreme Court, died on October 12, 1864, Lincoln named Chase to fill the vacancy. Many feel that Lincoln in part selected Chase so he would be less likely to run against Lincoln in the 1864 presidential election, as there was a growing movement to oust Lincoln and replace him with Chase. Despite his higher ambition, Chase accepted the appointment and was, in fact, the justice who swore in Andrew Johnson after President Lincoln was assassinated in 1865.

Just as his time at the Treasury had been one of great turmoil, so too was his time on the Supreme Court, due to the incredible uncertainty faced by the nation as it tried to heal the wounds of the Civil War. Most historians look back favorably on Chase's actions while he served as Chief Justice, citing his ability to do what was right while holding together fragile political factions. Northern politicians were trying to force reform on the defeated Southerners, while Southern politicians were still fighting the federal government at every turn when it came to issues involving slaves and the rights of African Americans. Two separate cases, *Mississippi v. Johnson* (1867) and *Georgia v. Stanton* (1868), allowed President Johnson and Secretary of War Edwin Stanton (or any member of the President's cabinet) to carry out provisions of the Reconstruction Act, which was intended to rebuild the South. Three other cases held important post-War ramifications. In *Texas v. White* (1869), Chase

"The very moment a slave passes beyond the jurisdiction of the state in which he is held as such, he ceases to be a slave; not because any law or regulation of the state which he enters confers freedom upon him, but because he continues to be a man, and leaves behind him the law of force which made him a slave."
Salmon Chase, arguing the case John Van Zandt, who was accused of harboring slaves, before the U.S. Supreme Court in 1842

While the impeachment trial was ongoing, Chase was fighting the last political fight of his life.

sided with the majority when it ruled that the Union was "indissoluble" and "perpetual;" in *Cummings v. Missouri* (1867), the Court ruled that the secession was null and void; and in *Ex parte Garland* (1867), the Court held that loyalty oaths that were meant to keep ex-Confederate soldiers from holding political office were unconstitutional.

Chase had to face many other difficult situations, such as determining when the federal courts should re-open in the Southern states. Chase only allowed the first of the courts to open (in Richmond, Virginia) after gaining promises that the military authorities who were in charge of the Reconstruction would not try to usurp the courts' powers. In 1868, Chase faced his two largest challenges. The first was overseeing the trial of Jefferson Davis, the Confederate president who was being tried for treason. Davis was turned over to civil authorities in late 1867 and brought to trial shortly after; in March of 1868, at the newly re-opened court in Richmond, Davis was convicted of treason and sentenced to death by Judge John Underwood. Chase disagreed with Underwood, who was extremely anti-South in all of his decisions, and felt that Davis should not face the death penalty; the case was about to be heard before the full Supreme Court when President Johnson issued full pardons for all those who had fought for the South during the war, thus ending the case.

The second challenge was overseeing the impeachment trial of President Johnson. The president was under attack by radicals who opposed the official government policy of Reconstruction, also known as the Stevens-Sumner-Wade policy. The anti-Johnson group made a mockery of the trial in the Senate, attempting to avoid the rules of evidence, slandering Chase and other political leaders, and arguing that a trial could not be held in the Senate. Chase put an end to all nonsense, refusing to let pro-Johnson senators be intimidated by the vocal opposition and refusing to be a figurehead at a hasty trial. He stood firm as the Chief Justice of the Supreme Court and insisted that his vote would be the deciding vote in all ties, as was his legal right. With Chase ensuring that the letter of the law was followed in all proceedings, President Johnson was acquitted of the impeachment charges.

While the impeachment trial was ongoing, Chase was fighting the last political fight of his life. He hoped to earn the presidential nomination of the Democratic party, which he had adopted as they became more anti-slavery—and as his own star faded in the Republican party. Most people thought he was still a Republican, so it came as a shock to many when Chase gave newspaper interviews in which he campaigned for the Democratic nomination. At the Democratic Convention, a team led by his daughter Kate actively tried to win the nomination for the "Chase platform," but he was soundly defeated by Horatio Seymour of New York.

By 1872, Chase's health was beginning to fail. The long and distinguished career of the deeply religious man of strong convictions was winding down, and on May 7, 1873, he died of a stroke in New York. ◆

Chase, Samuel

APRIL 17, 1741–JUNE 19, 1811 ● ASSOCIATE JUSTICE

Samuel Chase was one of the most colorful and controversial figures in the early years of the United States. Often described by his contemporaries as "boisterous" and "turbulent," he was tall and massive. His brownish-red complexion and large head earned him the nickname "Bacon Face" from his law colleagues. Although much of his personal life was a failure, he played a key role in the formation of the new nation, and as a Supreme Court justice he issued a number of important and far-reaching opinions.

Chase (not to be confused with Salmon Chase, the influential chief justice during the Reconstruction era in the 19th century) was born in 1741 in Somerset County, Maryland. His mother, Martha Walker, died when he was young, so he was raised by his father, Reverend Thomas Chase, an Episcopal minister who educated his son in the classics. When he was 18, Chase began to study law, and in 1761 he was admitted to the bar and began practice in the mayor's court in Annapolis,

Samuel Chase

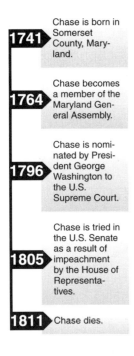

1741 Chase is born in Somerset County, Maryland.

1764 Chase becomes a member of the Maryland General Assembly.

1796 Chase is nominated by President George Washington to the U.S. Supreme Court.

1805 Chase is tried in the U.S. Senate as a result of impeachment by the House of Representatives.

1811 Chase dies.

Maryland. He lived in Annapolis until 1786, when he moved to Baltimore. He married twice, in 1762 to Anne Baldwin, and in 1784 to Hannah Giles.

Chase played a major role in the nation's quest for independence from England. In 1764 he became a member of the Maryland General Assembly, where he served until 1784. There he was a vigorous opponent of the British monarchy and of England's royal governor in the state. He was one of the leaders of the demonstrations by the Sons of Liberty that followed the Stamp Act of 1774. That year, too, he was a member of the Maryland Committee of Correspondence and a delegate to the First Continental Congress. The following year he was a delegate to the Second Continental Congress and served in the Maryland Convention and Council of Safety. In the Continental Congresses he played an important role in securing the Maryland delegation's support for the Declaration of Independence.

In the late 1770s and 1780s, though, Chase experienced some setbacks. In 1778, he used information he had obtained in Congress to conspire with others in an attempt to become rich by cornering the flour market. In response, the Maryland delegation to the Continental Congress dismissed him for two years. Throughout the 1780s he took part in a number of commercial ventures, including wartime supply businesses and coal and iron properties. None of these ventures succeeded, and in 1789 Chase declared bankruptcy.

Chase remained active in public affairs, though, and in 1788, following his move to Baltimore, he became chief judge of the criminal court. In 1791 he was also appointed chief judge of the General Court of Maryland, and he held both positions until 1796, despite efforts by the Maryland General Assembly to remove him from office. In the meantime, Chase opposed ratification of the new Constitution, arguing that the document was undemocratic.

In the 1770s, Chase had lent his support to George Washington against the general's congressional opponents. As president, Washington remembered Chase's loyalty and awarded him a federal appointment. His initial intention was to appoint Chase attorney general, but when Justice John Blair resigned from the Supreme Court in 1796, Washington selected Chase to replace him. Chase served as an associate justice on the Court until his death.

Chase's Supreme Court career had two distinct parts. During the first five years, he wrote a number of opinions that had far-reaching consequences, and he established precedents that still hold today. In *Hylton v. United States*, for example, he established a definition of "direct" taxation that remained in effect for nearly a century. In *Calder v. Bull* he defined **ex post facto** (retroactive) laws. His opinion in *Cooper v. Telfair* neatly summed up differing attitudes toward the developing concept of judicial review—the power of the Supreme Court to determine the constitutionality of the acts of other branches of government. His ruling in *United States v. Worrall* that the federal courts have no jurisdiction over **common-law** crimes was supported by later Supreme Court cases. During these years, he lived up to the praise of Washington's close friend Joseph McHenry, who told the president, "To his professional knowledge he subjoins a very valuable stock of political science."

The second part of Chase's career as a Supreme Court justice, the one for which he is perhaps best known, began in the early 1800s. Chase was infamous for his high-handed manner on the bench. He carried his contentiousness to new heights in his advocacy of the Alien and Sedition Acts, particularly in the 1800 trials of John Fries, who was tried twice for treason, and James T. Callender, who was tried for sedition. On another occasion, he sought to have Republican editors of newspapers opposed to his own Federalist Party indicted. Then, in May 1803, while making a jury charge, he delivered a **harangue** from the bench against the principles of Jeffersonian democracy, which he called "mobocracy." As a result of these and other incidents, he was impeached by the House of Representatives in March 1804. His trial in the Senate began in early 1805, and in spite of pressure from President Jefferson himself, the Senate failed to convict him.

Most senators agreed that Chase had acted improperly, but the Senate narrowly interpreted the "high crimes and misdemeanors" provision of Article III of the Constitution, and he retained his seat. Most historians believe that Chase's impeachment was politically motivated and that had he been convicted, his famous colleague, Chief Justice John Marshall, might have been impeached as well. Marshall, who enhanced the power of the Court, stood in strong opposition to Jefferson, who was wary of a strong Court. It is fair to say that the Senate's restraint changed the course of judicial history, for Marshall went on to

"The assault upon Judge Chase was unquestionably intended to pave the way for another prosecution, which would have swept the Supreme Judicial Bench clean at a stroke."

Letter from John Quincy Adams to his father, quoted in Charles Warren, *The Supreme Court in United States History*

Chase was infamous for his high-handed manner on the bench.

ex post facto: done or made after the fact; retroactive.

common law: body of law developed in England through judicial decisions of precedent and unwritten in code or statutes; basis of U.S. law in all states except Louisiana.

harangue: a loud, controversial speech in a public forum.

become one of the most influential Supreme Court justices in history.

Chase retained his seat on the bench, but he was already in ill health from **gout,** and during the last 10 years of his life he was often absent from his duties. Moreover, after Marshall was appointed, Chase rarely had an opportunity to speak for the Court. His turbulent career ended with his death on June 19, 1811. ◆

gout: a disease characterized by painful imflammation of joints and large amounts of uric acid in the blood.

Clark, Tom C.

SEPTEMBER 23, 1899–JUNE 13, 1977 ● ASSOCIATE JUSTICE

Although Thomas Campbell Clark—who preferred the less formal "Tom C."—was born in Dallas, Texas in 1899, his prominent family's roots were in Mississippi, where both of his grandfathers had been officers in the Confederate army. His father, William Clark, was an attorney and was active in Democratic Party politics. His mother was Virginia Falls. William Clark was an alcoholic, and as a result his lucrative legal practice began to collapse when Tom was a teenager, requiring Tom to work to help support the family.

Despite the demands on his time, Clark was active in speech and debate in high school, and he was one of the nation's first Eagle Scouts. After graduating from high school, he attended the Virginia Military Institute for one year, but the family's financial problems forced him to drop out. Returning to Texas, he joined the National Guard and served as a sergeant in an infantry division until the end of World War I. In 1919, he enrolled at the University of Texas, where he earned a bachelor's degree in 1921 and a law degree in 1922. In 1924, he married Mary Jane Ramsey, the daughter of a Texas Supreme Court justice.

Over the next several years, Clark practiced law alongside his brother Bill in their father's firm. In 1927, he was appointed district attorney in Dallas, but he returned to private practice in 1932. During these years he made a number of valuable contacts in the Texas oil industry. His career in public service began in earnest in 1937, when he was named a special assistant in the U.S. Justice Department. In the years that followed, he worked on antitrust cases and was the civilian coordinator of the **internment** of Japanese Americans on the West Coast during World War II. He also prosecuted fraudulent war claims, a duty

internment: movement of Japanese-Americans from their homes to camps during World War II by the United States government.

Tom Clark

that brought him into close contact with Harry S. Truman, who headed the Senate War Investigating Committee. In 1943, Clark was promoted to assistant U.S. attorney general.

Truman would have a major impact on Clark's career. Clark supported Truman's vice presidential bid at the Democratic National Convention in 1944. When Truman assumed the presidency on the death of Franklin D. Roosevelt in 1945, the new president remembered his supporter and appointed him U.S. attorney general. In his four years (1945–1949) as head of the Justice Department, Clark continued to pursue antitrust cases. He also fired some early rounds in the civil rights movement when he pressured the FBI to take action against lynchings of African Americans. Additionally, he was Truman's point man in the fight against communism. He prosecuted leaders of the American Communist Party, drew up a list of **subversive** organizations in the United States, and supported Truman in his hard line against the Soviet Union. During the 1948 presidential campaign, Truman relied on Clark's anticommunist zeal to help him fight the public perception that he was soft on communism.

subversive: description of acts contrary to the benefit of one's native nation; acting in behalf of a nation's enemies.

1899 Clark is born in Dallas, Texas.

1937 Clark is named special assistant in the Justice Department.

1945 Clark is named attorney general in Truman administration.

1949 Clark is named to the U.S. Supreme Court.

1967 Clark resigns from the Supreme Court.

1977 Clark Clark dies in New Yok City.

civil libertarians: individuals concerned with upholding the rights they see the Constitution providing to all citizens.

libertarian: political outlook advocating an extremely limited influence of government on the individual citizen.

In 1949, Truman nominated Clark for the seat on the Supreme Court vacated when Justice Frank Murphy died. Despite protests from liberals, who thought that he was too conservative, Clark won Senate confirmation by a vote of 73–8. During his 18 years on the bench, one of the most active periods in Supreme Court history, he issued far-reaching opinions in a large number of landmark cases.

Clark had always been loyal to Truman, but he showed his independence in an early case, *The Youngstown Sheet and Tube Co. v. Sawyer*. In this case, he ruled that the president had violated the Constitution when he invoked emergency executive power in seizing the nation's steel industry. The ruling placed limits on presidential power, and Truman never forgave Clark for joining the Court's majority in the ruling. In cases having to do with national security and anticommunism, he consistently unsettled **civil libertarians.** In *Uphaus v. Wyman*, for example, he ruled that the state's need to uncover subversive activities outweighed any claim of invasion of privacy.

In many of the social issues that confronted the Court during the 1950s and 1960s, Clark joined Chief Justice Earl Warren in taking a liberal path. He consistently upheld the civil rights of African Americans. In *Burton v. Wilmington Parking Authority*, for example, he wrote that a private restaurant had to comply with the equal protection clause of the Fourteenth Amendment. In similar cases he invoked the Constitution's commerce clause to uphold and enforce the Civil Rights Act of 1964. He also joined the Court in its historic unanimous ruling in *Brown v. Board of Education*, which outlawed school segregation.

Clark showed a **libertarian** bent in other social issues. In *Engel v. Vitale* he supported the Court in outlawing prayer in public schools, and in *Abington School District v. Schempp* he held that Bible reading in the public schools was unconstitutional. In *Burstyn v. Wilson* he struck down the state's right to censor films that were considered sacrilegious. In the area of criminal law, however, his record was mixed. He dissented from the Court's opinion in *Miranda v. Arizona*, in which the Court ruled that the police must inform suspects of their rights before questioning them. But in *Mapp v. Ohio* he ruled that state courts, like federal courts, had to exclude evidence seized in violation of the Fourth Amendment. Clark also supported the decriminalization of so-called victimless crimes, arguing that they clogged the court system.

One of Clark's abiding concerns was the fair and efficient administration of justice. Beginning in 1957 he chaired the Section of Judicial Administration of the American Bar Association, and in 1961 he helped establish the Joint Committee for the Effective Administration of Justice. Throughout the last decade of his Supreme Court career and beyond, he traveled around the country crusading for judicial reform.

In 1967, President Lyndon Johnson appointed Clark's son, William Ramsey Clark, attorney general, a position that would frequently require him to argue before the Supreme Court. Tom Clark wanted to avoid any appearance of conflict of interest, so he resigned. In his retirement, he continued to campaign for judicial reform, and he served as a judge in various federal courts of appeals. He died in his son's home in New York City on June 13, 1977. ◆

Clarke, John Hessin

SEPTEMBER 18, 1857–MARCH 22, 1945 ● ASSOCIATE JUSTICE

John Hessin Clarke, an important figure in progressive politics in the early 20th century, was born in 1857 in New Lisbon, Ohio, the son of John Clarke and Melissa Hessin. Clarke inherited his interest both in the law and in progressive politics from his father, who was a lawyer and judge and was active in the local Democratic Party. After attending Western Reserve College, where he graduated **Phi Beta Kappa** in 1877, Clarke returned to New Lisbon, where he studied law under his father. He passed the bar examination in 1878 and remained in New Lisbon to join his father's legal practice. He never married.

Two years later, Clarke moved to Youngstown, Ohio, where he practiced corporate law and was part owner of a Democratic weekly newspaper, the *Youngstown Vindicator*, a paper that advocated progressive reform. He was also active in local politics. In 1882, however, he sold his interest in the newspaper and suspended his political activity so that he could concentrate on his legal practice and hone his skills as a trial attorney. Corporate law might have seemed an odd choice for Clarke, for his progressive political views often ran counter to the views of his wealthy, conservative clients. Late in his life he commented, "Perhaps they preferred to have me with rather than against

Phi Beta Kappa: organization of individuals winning high scholastic distinction in undergraduate education in the United States.

John Hessin Clarke
gives a radio address.

imperialism: a practice
or policy of a nation to
extend its power and
domination by acquiring
territories or conquering
other nations for political
and economic superiority.

them in the court." He also contributed to Youngstown's cultural development. He lectured on Shakespeare and the poet James Russell Lowell and became an honorary trustee of the city's public library. In his will, he left $100,000 to the library.

In 1897, Clarke moved to Cleveland, Ohio, where he accepted a partnership at the firm of William and Cushing, specializing in railroad and corporate law. By this time he was well known for his progressive views—opposition to trusts, tariffs, colonialism, the free coinage of silver, and **imperialism;** support for women's suffrage, public disclosure of campaign spending, and the use of ballot initiatives and referendums. In 1904, he ran for the U.S. Senate, but in a state that voted heavily Republican, he lost to incumbent Mark Hanna, who characterized his opponent's politics as "populistic, socialistic and **anarchistic.**"

In 1914, after the Seventeenth Amendment to the Constitution called for direct popular election of senators, Clarke ran for the Senate again, but he withdrew his candidacy when he realized he was not likely to be popular with voters. His decision to withdraw was made easier when President Woodrow Wilson nominated him to a federal judgeship, one of a number of liberal, progressive judges Wilson appointed with an eye to grooming candidates for future seats on the Supreme Court. After just two years on the bench of the Federal District Court for the Northern District of Ohio, Clarke received a nomination from Wilson to fill the Supreme Court seat vacated by Charles Evans Hughes. Wilson's goal was to give a more liberal bent to a Supreme Court that for a number of years had been dominated by conservative Republican appointees. Unlike one of Wilson's other liberal nominees, Louis Brandeis, Clarke easily won confirmation in the Senate by a unanimous vote on July 24, 1916.

As an associate justice of the Supreme Court, Clarke acted on his progressive views, just as he had as a federal judge. In one of his most important cases, *United States v. Reading Co.* (1920), he ruled against the monopolistic activities of the Reading Railroad Company, setting an important precedent used years later to help enforce the Sherman Antitrust Act. In a dissent in another case, he invoked the Constitution's commerce clause to support Congress's efforts to enact child labor laws. Though a fierce advocate of free speech, in *Abrams v. United States* he ruled with the majority against a group of Russian-born aliens charged with violating the Espionage Act of 1918. The Russians had distributed leaflets condemning American policy toward the Russian Revolution. Clarke opposed his liberal colleagues, Oliver Wendell Holmes and Louis Brandeis, arguing that wartime considerations took precedence over the Russians' right to free speech.

Clarke found the duties of a Supreme Court justice tedious. He felt that rather than being able to speak out on the important issues of the day, he had to immerse himself in the details of unimportant cases—deciding "whether the digging of a ditch was constitutional or not." Additionally, both of his sisters died within a year's time, and his hearing began to fail. For these reasons he submitted his resignation to Wilson in 1922, to Wilson's immense

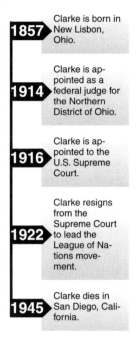

1857 Clarke is born in New Lisbon, Ohio.

1914 Clarke is appointed as a federal judge for the Northern District of Ohio.

1916 Clarke is appointed to the U.S. Supreme Court.

1922 Clarke resigns from the Supreme Court to lead the League of Nations movement.

1945 Clarke dies in San Diego, California.

Clarke found the duties of a Supreme Court justice tedious.

Anarchistic favoring total diarray within the political and social make-up of a nation or state.

disappointment. He did so shortly before becoming eligible for retirement benefits, believing he was not entitled to them because of his wealth. In his resignation letter Clarke told Wilson that he wanted to read and travel, but he also noted that he wanted to serve public causes. When an interviewer asked him about the causes he wanted to serve, he replied that he wanted to lend his support to America's entry into the League of Nations.

To that end, from 1922 to 1927 Clarke directed the League of Nations' Non-Partisan Association of the United States. He soon found himself in great demand as a speaker. His organization, though, faced obstacles from Wilson and his successors in the White House, and after a time it turned its attention to U.S. membership in the World Court. In the 1930s, Clarke continued to speak about world peace, and in 1937 he gave a nationwide radio address supporting President Franklin D. Roosevelt's effort to "pack" the Supreme Court with justices sympathetic to his New Deal economic policies.

Clarke would have been gratified by the results of the conference held in San Francisco in 1945 to create the United Nations. He died, however, at his home in San Diego, California, on March 22, shortly before that conference convened. ◆

Clifford, Nathan

AUGUST 18, 1803–JULY 25, 1881 ● ASSOCIATE JUSTICE

Nathan Clifford was born in 1803 in Rumney, New Hampshire, the oldest of seven children and the only boy. His father, Deacon Nathaniel Clifford, was a farmer whose family had lived in the state for many years; his mother was Lydia Simpson. As a child Clifford attended the village school in Rumney. At age 14, over the opposition of his parents, he attended Haverhill Academy, where he earned money teaching and giving singing lessons. In 1820 the death of his father put an end to his goal of attending Dartmouth College. Instead, he studied law with a local attorney, Josiah Quincy, and in 1827 was admitted to the state bar. He settled in Newfield, Maine, where he maintained a legal practice and with his wife, Hannah Ayer, eventually had six children.

For the next two decades, Clifford devoted his tremendous energy and capacity for hard work to politics as a member of the

fledgling Democratic Party. In 1830, he was elected to the lower house of the Maine legislature, where he served four one-year terms, including two (1833–1834) as Speaker. In 1834 he was appointed the state's attorney general. In 1837, his bid for a U.S. Senate seat in Maine was unsuccessful, but in 1838 he won a seat in the U.S. House of Representatives, where he served two terms. He lost his seat in 1843 when his own party redrew the congressional district lines in Maine, and he retired, grumbling, to Newfield.

Just three years later, though, Clifford returned to politics when Democratic president James Polk appointed him U.S. attorney general in 1846. Initially Clifford lacked confidence in his ability to serve in this position. He also worried about his family back in Maine, because he could not afford to move them to Washington, D.C. For these reasons he actually submitted his resignation to Polk shortly before the scheduled date of his first appearance in front of the Supreme Court. Polk talked him out of resigning, and a few days later he won his first case before the Court. Perhaps Clifford's chief accomplishment as the nation's attorney general was in acting as a liaison between Polk and his secretary of war, James Buchanan, who disagreed about how to conduct the war with Mexico. When that war ended, Polk sent Clifford to Mexico to negotiate a treaty and establish peaceful relations between the two countries.

Clifford's career in politics came to an end in 1848, when Polk, a Democrat, declined to run for reelection and Zachary Taylor, a **Whig,** was elected president. Clifford moved to Portland, Maine, where he practiced law for the next eight years, though again he ran unsuccessfully for U.S. Senate seats in 1850 and 1853. Then in 1858 Supreme Court Justice Benjamin Curtis suddenly resigned, and President James Buchanan, Clifford's old friend from the Polk administration, nominated him to the position.

Nathan Clifford

fledgling: a newly formed group or effort attempting to become estblished.

Whig: a political party which preceded and was replaced by the Republican Party in American politics.

Constitutionally, Clifford was distrustful of the authority of the federal government.

The nomination touched off a firestorm of controversy, for many Whigs and Republicans saw Clifford as what was then called a "doughface"—a Northerner who sympathized with the pro-slavery and states' rights views of the South. Despite the controversy, Clifford—a man who had never attended college—won confirmation to the Supreme Court by a Senate vote of 26 to 23. It was one of the closest confirmation votes in history.

In his 23-year career as a Supreme Court justice, Clifford won a reputation for what the *New York Tribune* called his "learning and integrity." He wrote the Court's majority opinion in nearly 400 cases, but he also wrote 49 dissenting opinions and dissented without writing an opinion in 42 other cases, suggesting his willingness to remain true to his principles. Although he had a strong political-party affiliation, constitutional scholars believe that his opinions were not marred by political bias—though they did tend to be long and difficult to read.

Constitutionally, Clifford was distrustful of the authority of the federal government, particularly when the exercise of that power seemed arbitrary and excessive. For this reason, in his opinions he drew a sharp line dividing the powers of the federal government from those of the states. He applied this principle in a number of important cases having to do with taxes, currency, and other economic matters. In *Collector v. Day* (1871), for example, he expressed his view that the federal government could not tax the salary of a state officer. The same principle led him to uphold the constitutionality of the Fugitive Slave Law in *Ableman v. Booth* (1859)—even though he personally opposed slavery. In *Ex parte Milligan* (1867) he sided with the Court in ruling that arbitrary arrests and martial law were invalid. In *Loan Association v. Topeka* (1875)—possibly his most important opinion—he wrote that state legislative powers were "practically absolute" unless the state's action is specifically prohibited by the U.S. Constitution.

In a number of opinions rendered during Reconstruction after the Civil War, Clifford continued to uphold the sovereignty of the states, often in opposition to other judges who wanted to expand the powers of the federal government. In *Test Oath Cases* (1867), for example, he voted with the majority to ban the use of loyalty oaths for public officials and voters. He also voted to restrict the federal government's authority to interfere with state authorities in protecting the rights of recently freed slaves.

In 1873 Chief Justice Salmon Chase died, and while the Court wrangled over who would replace him, Clifford, as the senior associate justice, presided over the Court for nearly a year. In 1877, he directed the Electoral Commission that settled the disputed Hayes-Tilden presidential election, in which Tilden won the popular vote but Hayes won the vote in the Electoral College. Clifford never accepted the legitimacy of Hayes's presidency because of the extreme partisanship of the Electoral Commission, which voted along strict party lines. For this reason, Clifford refused to resign in his declining years, even after a debilitating stroke in 1880. His goal was to wait for a Democrat to win the White House and be able to appoint his successor. He died in Cornish, Maine, in 1881. ◆

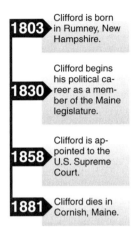

1803 Clifford is born in Rumney, New Hampshire.

1830 Clifford begins his political career as a member of the Maine legislature.

1858 Clifford is appointed to the U.S. Supreme Court.

1881 Clifford dies in Cornish, Maine.

Curtis, Benjamin

NOVEMBER 4, 1809–SEPTEMBER 15, 1874 ● ASSOCIATE JUSTICE

Remembered primarily for his dissent in the famous *Dred Scott* case of 1857, Benjamin Robbins Curtis was born in Watertown, Massachusetts, in 1809. His father was Benjamin Curtis III, an officer in the merchant marines whose ancestors had settled in Massachusetts in the early 17th century. The elder Curtis died when his son was five years old, but with the help of loans and an income from a dry-goods store, Benjamin's mother, Lois Robbins, managed to send him and his brother to Harvard College, where Benjamin completed a bachelor's degree in 1829.

Curtis started work on a law degree but left school to take over a small law practice in Northfield, Massachusetts. After returning to Harvard to complete his law degree in 1832, he married Eliza Maria Woodward and moved back to

Benjamin Curtis

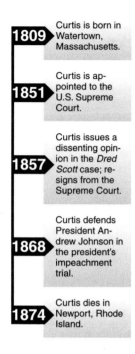

1809 — Curtis is born in Watertown, Massachusetts.

1851 — Curtis is appointed to the U.S. Supreme Court.

1857 — Curtis issues a dissenting opinion in the *Dred Scott* case; resigns from the Supreme Court.

1868 — Curtis defends President Andrew Johnson in the president's impeachment trial.

1874 — Curtis dies in Newport, Rhode Island.

admiralty law: laws and statutes which govern maritime questions and disputes.

Northfield to settle into the role of old-fashioned country lawyer. He and Woodward had five children. Later, in 1846, he married Anna Wroe Curtis and had three more children. In 1861 he married for a third time, and he and his wife, Maria Malleville Allen, had four children.

Curtis's career took a major turn in 1834, when he accepted a job offer in Boston from Charles Curtis, a distant relative and Anna Wroe's father, in a law firm that served the city's affluent merchant class. Over the next 17 years he became one of the city's leading attorneys and a prominent member of Boston society. As a member of the Whig establishment, he attracted the attention of such notable figures as Noah Webster. He also became increasingly active in politics, and he served in the Massachusetts legislature in the 1849 and 1851 terms. When Supreme Court Justice Levi Woodbury died in 1851, the Whig president, Millard Fillmore, wrote Webster, asking him his opinion about Curtis. Webster assured the president that Curtis would be a sound choice, and accordingly, Fillmore made the appointment.

Curtis served on the Supreme Court for six years. During that time he wrote the opinion of the Court in 51 cases and dissented in just 13, a surprisingly low number given that the Court at that time was dominated by southern Democrats. He wrote a number of important opinions in the areas of **admiralty law,** tax collection, and interstate commerce. Some of these opinions became the basis of later constitutional law.

Curtis is best known, however, for the part he played in the national debate over slavery. His involvement in the issue dated back to 1836, when, as a young associate in Charles Curtis's firm in Boston, he argued his first slave case, *Commonwealth v. Aves.* His opponent in the case was the Boston Female Anti-Slavery Society, which argued that by accompanying her mistress into a free state, a black child named Med was emancipated. Curtis, however, was concerned about militant abolitionists, whose activities, he believed, threatened to divide the Union. In court, he argued unsuccessfully that slave owners visiting the state could restrain their slaves for the purpose of returning them to their home states.

Curtis once again took the stage in the slavery issue in 1850, when Noah Webster advised the U.S. attorney to employ Curtis to defend the Fugitive Slave Act. Curtis took the position that while slaves had natural rights, helping them to escape might set off a civil war. The following year he defended the arrest warrant of Thomas Sims, a fugitive slave who had been captured in Boston.

In 1857, the Supreme Court, under Chief Justice Roger Taney, issued what was arguably its most famous ruling. The case was *Dred Scott v. Sandford*, and oddly enough, the attorney arguing for Dred Scott was Curtis's brother, George Ticknor Curtis. Benjamin Curtis joined Justice John McClean in dissenting from Taney's majority opinion. In his written opinion, Curtis supported the terms of the Missouri Compromise, arguing that Congress had the constitutional authority to regulate slavery in the nation's new territories. Thus, he concluded, by residing in the Illinois and Wisconsin Territories, Scott was a free man. Curtis also rejected the majority opinion that a black was not a citizen of the United States simply because he was black. He argued that black citizens of a state were automatically citizens of the United States, because under both the Articles of Confederation and the Constitution, U.S. citizenship was derived from state citizenship. Thus, as a citizen, Dred Scott was entitled to sue in federal court.

It should be noted, though, that Curtis was not taking a position against slavery. Rather, he was arguing that the rights of citizens should be determined by the individual states, not the federal government. He wrote: "To what citizens the elective franchise shall be confided is a question to be determined by each state in accordance with its own views of the necessities or expediencies of its condition. What civil rights shall be enjoyed by its citizens, and whether all shall enjoy the same, or how they may be gained or lost, are to be determined in the same way."

As a result of the *Dred Scott* case, Curtis became disenchanted with the Supreme Court and resigned on September 1, 1857. Though he claimed that he needed a larger income, in reality he left because he believed that his colleagues, including Chief Justice Taney, were influenced by politics in their decision in the *Dred Scott* case.

That year, Curtis returned to Boston, where he opened a law practice and continued to speak out on the issues of the day. He cautioned that any forcible interference with slavery on the part of the federal government could lead to war. Although he remained loyal to the Union during the Civil War, he was critical of President Lincoln's Emancipation Proclamation. He was in the public eye again in 1868, when he was one of the attorneys defending President Andrew Johnson in his impeachment trial. He continued to argue cases before the Supreme Court

> *"He is a slave-catching Judge, appointed to office as a reward for his professional support given to the Fugitive Slave bill."*
> New York Tribune, April 9, 1855

As a result of the *Dred Scott* case, Curtis became disenchanted with the Supreme Court and resigned.

and taught for two years at the Harvard Law School. He fell ill at his villa in Newport, Rhode Island, in the summer of 1874 and died there on September 15. ◆

Cushing, William

MARCH 1, 1732–SEPTEMBER 13, 1810 ● CHIEF JUSTICE

probate judge: a judge who determines the validity of a deceased person's estate.

squatters: individuals who settle on property without title or payment of rent.

That William Cushing became the first associate justice of the Supreme Court is not surprising, given his family background. He was born in Scituate, Massachusetts, to John Cushing and Mary Cotton. His maternal grandfather had been a county judge and a member of the Massachusetts legislature, and both his father and paternal grandfather were members of the superior court, the highest court in the province.

After receiving a bachelor's degree from Harvard College in 1751, Cushing taught at the Roxbury Grammar School for a year. He began his legal career in 1752, when he apprenticed in Boston with the famous lawyer Jeremiah Gridley. He was admitted to the bar in 1755 and took up practice in Scituate, working primarily in the Plymouth Court of Common Pleas. In 1759, though, a new county was created in Maine, and Cushing moved there to accept the post of **probate judge,** a position he held until 1764. At the same time he continued to practice law, specializing in the litigation of land disputes between real estate companies and **squatters.** He remained in Maine until 1771 and was the only lawyer in the backwoods community surrounding Pownalborough, the county seat.

That year, John Cushing retired after 23 years as a superior court judge, and in early 1772, his son William returned to Massachusetts when Lieutenant Governor Thomas Hutchinson agreed to appoint him to the post. Over the next two years, Cushing and his colleagues on the

William Cushing

bench became embroiled in a controversy that had a bearing on the colonies' quest for independence from Great Britain. The British crown, in an effort to make the judiciary independent of the colony, insisted on paying judges' salaries; the Massachusetts legislature, asserting its independence from the crown, voted to pay judges' salaries itself and asked judges to refuse money from the crown. Chief Justice Peter Oliver accepted the crown salary and was impeached. Cushing joined three other judges in accepting the legislature's salary, raising his profile as a leader in the movement for American independence.

After the colonies broke with Great Britain, Massachusetts reorganized its court system. Cushing became the only superior court judge from before the revolution to be retained. As senior associate, he presided over the court in the frequent absence of Chief Justice John Adams, and when Adams resigned in 1777, Cushing took the post in name as well as in fact. During his 12 years as chief justice of the supreme judicial court in Massachusetts, he issued rulings in a number of important cases, particularly *Commonwealth v. Jennison* (1783). The case was a criminal action against Jennison, who committed assault while trying to capture an escaped slave. In his instructions to the jury, Cushing reminded them that the Massachusetts constitution—which Cushing had helped draft in 1779—said that "all men are born free and equal." For some historians, this case marked the beginning of the end of slavery in Massachusetts.

Cushing played a part in at least two important historical events in the 1780s. In 1786, unrest and even violence erupted in rural New England areas over harsh debt-collection practices. This unrest culminated in Shays' Rebellion. Among other actions, the malcontents attempted to disrupt court proceedings in Springfield, Massachusetts, in September of that year. Cushing insisted that the law required the court to sit, and at some personal danger, he walked firmly through the crowd and opened court. The other historical event was the debate over the newly drafted U.S. Constitution. Cushing became vice president and presiding officer of the state convention that was called to ratify the Constitution.

By this time, Cushing was one of the most distinguished jurists of the day, so when the U.S. Supreme Court was organized, President George Washington nominated him for one of the seats. Cushing was confirmed in the Senate on September 27, 1789, and thus became the first associate justice of the United States Supreme Court.

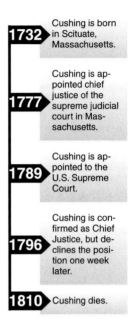

1732 Cushing is born in Scituate, Massachusetts.

1777 Cushing is appointed chief justice of the supreme judicial court in Massachusetts.

1789 Cushing is appointed to the U.S. Supreme Court.

1796 Cushing is confirmed as Chief Justice, but declines the position one week later.

1810 Cushing dies.

*"I very well re-
member the strong
impression [Cush-
ing's] appearance
made upon my
mind when I first
saw him. . . . He
was a man whose
deportment sur-
passed all the
ideas of personal
dignity I had ever
formed. His wig
added much to the
imposing effect."*

J. D. Hopkins,
*Address to the
Cumberland Bar,*
1833

jurisdiction: the area of
law over which a particu-
lar court has the authority
upon which to issue a
resolution to a dispute.

Cushing served on the Court until his death 21 years later. During his tenure, he wrote just 19 opinions, most of them relatively brief, and it is fair to say that he did not have a significant impact on the development of case law in the United States. He ruled with the majority in three cases of note. One was *Chisholm v. Georgia* (1793), in which the Court ruled that the state of Georgia could be sued in federal court for a debt owed to a man in South Carolina. The basis of Cushing's opinion was that the Court retained **jurisdiction** over the states, despite the states' "sovereign immunity." The ruling was controversial, and when Cushing ran against Samuel Adams for governor of Massachusetts in 1794 (though he never campaigned), it may have contributed to his defeat. The second case of note was *Ware v. Hylton* (1796), in which the Court ruled that the state of Virginia had to honor the 1783 peace treaty with Great Britain and pay its prewar debts to British merchants. The third was *Calder v. Bull* (1798), in which the Court ruled that the *ex post facto* (retroactive) clause of the Constitution applied to criminal rather than civil criminal cases. Taken together, these cases were important because they asserted the power of the federal courts to strike down state laws.

In 1796, John Jay resigned as Chief Justice of the Supreme Court and President Washington nominated John Rutledge for the position. The Senate, though, rejected the nomination, so Washington turned to Cushing. The Senate confirmed him in January, but just one week later, Cushing declined the position, citing ill health. Financially, though, he could not afford to retire, so he retained his position as an associate justice. And, as all Supreme Court justices did at that time, he presided over federal circuit courts—often attracting attention as he traveled in state throughout the New England circuit with his wife, Hannah Phillips, who read aloud to him in their neatly equipped carriage. Cushing was the last American judge to wear a British wig in court, a practice he finally abandoned when the wig attracted undue attention on the streets.

Cushing's health continued to decline, limiting his activities on the Court. He died in Scituate on September 13, 1810. ◆

Daniel, Peter

APRIL 24, 1784–MAY 31, 1860 ● ASSOCIATE JUSTICE

Peter Vivian Daniel was born in 1784 in Stafford County, Virginia, to Travers Daniel and Frances Moncure. The Daniel family roots as Southern planters and members of the local **aristocracy** in Virginia extended back to the early 17th century. Following a family tradition of public service, Daniel's grandfather had been a justice of the peace. Peter Daniel was privately tutored on his family's extensive estate, Crows Nest, before enrolling at the College of New Jersey (which later became Princeton University). He left college after just a year and returned to Virginia, where he studied law in Richmond with Edmund Randolph, formerly the governor of the state and U.S. attorney general in the Washington administration.

aristocracy: governing body made up of wealthy individuals of inherited nobility.

Peter Daniel

In 1808, the year he was admitted to the Virginia bar, Daniel was elected to the Virginia House of Delegates, despite having fought a duel earlier in the year and killing his antagonist. The following year he married Randolph's daughter, Lucy, and the two divided their time between Richmond and Spring Farm, a nearby plantation Daniel had bought from his father-in-law.

1784 Daniel is born in Stafford County, Virginia.

1808 Daniel is elected to the Virginia House of Delegates.

1836 Daniel is appointed judge of the U.S. District Court for eastern Virginia.

1841 Daniel is appointed to the U.S. Supreme Court.

1860 Daniel dies in Richmond, Virginia.

Daniel's elevation to the U.S. Supreme Court came suddenly.

de facto: in reality; exercising power as if legally entrusted to do so.

In the years that followed, Daniel continued to practice law, but he spent most of his energy on politics. He left the House of Delegates in 1812 to serve on the Privy Council, an advisory body formed to limit the power of the state governor. Among his immediate duties was organizing the state defenses during the War of 1812. Additionally, the Privy Council functioned in some matters as an appellate court in the state, and Daniel, who examined the cases before the Council in constitutional terms, vigorously defended the rights of criminal defendants and urged the state to moderate the severity of its criminal code. In 1818 he was named presiding officer of the Council and, in that capacity, he was the **de facto** lieutenant governor of the state. He remained in that position until 1835, when a Whig majority in the legislature swept him out of office.

In the 1830s, Daniel was active in Democratic Party politics. He was a member of the "Richmond Junto," a group of influential citizens who advocated the principles of Jacksonian democracy in Virginia. He also figured prominently in the presidential election campaigns of Andrew Jackson and Martin Van Buren. Jackson, in an effort to reward Daniel for his support, offered him the post of U.S. attorney general, but Daniel declined, citing the post's low salary. He did, however, accept Jackson's offer of a judgeship for the U.S. District Court for eastern Virginia.

Daniel's elevation to the U.S. Supreme Court came suddenly. Fellow Virginian Philip Barbour had been appointed to the Court in 1836, but he died suddenly in 1841. By now, Van Buren was in the White House, and the president, eager to appoint Daniel as Barbour's replacement, placed his name in nomination just two days after Barbour's death. Whigs in the Senate tried to block the nomination, but their efforts failed, and Daniel was confirmed in March, just one day before Van Buren left office. The annoyed response of the incoming party to Daniel's last-minute appointment was to rearrange the circuits on which the Supreme Court justices sat and assign to Daniel Arkansas and Mississippi, the two hardest states to reach on bumpy stagecoaches.

Consistent with his background as a member of Virginia's rural gentry, Daniel was an unrepentant conservative—in fact, a kind of throwback who stubbornly resisted the changes taking place in America and who therefore often wrote dissenting opinions. A good example was a case involving navigation on inland waterways. At the time the Constitution was framed, water navigation took place largely on tidal waters such as the Atlantic Ocean and its adjacent rivers, bays, and sounds. As the nation expanded westward, though, more and more navigation took place on inland waters rather than tidewaters. Led by Chief Justice Roger Taney, the Court took this change in the nation's geography into account and extended federal admiralty law to inland waterways. Daniel, though, wrote a stinging dissent, refusing to accept any enlargement of federal authority, though he later conceded that his opinion was "antiquated, unsuited to the day in which we live." Daniel even refused to endorse federal attempts to apportion money for improvements—roads, for example—in the states.

In his early years on the Court, Daniel's opinions tended to focus on land disputes and procedural issues. In time, however, he wrote about broader issues, and he consistently fought expansion of federal authority and growing economic concentration. Throughout his life he was a staunch Jeffersonian, believing in agrarianism, strict construction of the Constitution, states' rights, and limited government. Following Jackson, he was an opponent of central banks and powerful corporations. He tried to restrict the access of corporations to the federal courts, arguing that corporations were not really "citizens" as the Constitution used the word. In several cases, he insisted that the states, not the federal government, should regulate business.

Daniel was also a Southern partisan who defended the institution of slavery. In an 1842 case, *Prigg v. Pennsylvania*, he argued, consistent with his states' rights position, that the Missouri Compromise was unconstitutional and that Congress had no authority to regulate slavery in new U.S. territories. As time went on, he grew increasingly bitter against the northern states, largely because of their opposition to slavery. Thus, in the famous *Dred Scott* case of 1857, he joined the majority but went farther than the other justices did in contending that, because they had once been property, "subjects of commerce or traffic," freed slaves were not citizens.

The final years of Daniel's life were marked by considerable sadness. His wife died in 1847, and Daniel took solace in his daughter and in his friendship with Taney. In 1853, he married Elizabeth Harris, and the two had two children. Although Elizabeth was much younger, she died in 1857. Broken in spirit and in poor health, he retired from the bench in 1859. He died a year later in Richmond, Virginia, on the eve of the Civil War. ◆

"Neither Congress nor the Federal Government in the exercise of all or any of its powers or attributes possesses the power to construct roads, nor any other description of what have been called internal improvements, within the limits of the States."
Peter Daniel,
Searight v. Stokes,
1845

Davis, David

MARCH 9, 1815–JUNE 26, 1886 ● ASSOCIATE JUSTICE

malaria: a disease in humans caused by the bite of certain mosquitoes and characterized by periodic attacks of chills and fever.

David Davis

D avid Davis—remembered today primarily for his close association with Abraham Lincoln—was born in Cecil County, Maryland, in 1815. He was named for his father, a physician of Welsh descent who died before Davis was born; his mother was Ann Mercer. When he was just 17 he completed a course of study at Kenyon College in Ohio, then moved to Lenox, Massachusetts, where he studied law under Judge Henry W. Bishop. After a year at the Yale University law school, he moved in 1835 to Pekin, Illinois, at that time a frontier river town, where he started a legal practice and met for the first time a young attorney named Abraham Lincoln. After just a year, however, a bout of **malaria** forced him to move to the more healthful climate of Bloomington, Illinois, where he purchased a legal practice. In 1838, he married Sarah Woodruff, the daughter of Judge William Walker, whom he had met while he was studying law in Massachusetts. The couple had two children who survived to adulthood.

Politics dominated much of Davis's attention during the 1840s and, in fact, throughout his career. In 1840 he ran unsuccessfully as a Whig for a seat in the Illinois legislature. Five years later he ran again, and this time he was elected. He quickly came to be regarded as an influential member of the legislature and in 1847 was named to the state's Constitutional Convention. As a member of the convention, he focused on legal issues and strongly advocated popular election of state court judges. He benefited from his own proposal in 1848, when he was elected judge of the Eighth Judicial Circuit of Illinois.

Davis served in this position for three terms until 1862 and showed such practical common sense that his decisions were rarely appealed or reversed by higher courts. One of the attorneys who frequently argued before Davis was Lincoln, and during these years he formed an intimate friendship with the future president; after Lincoln's assassination, he served as administrator of the fallen president's estate. When the Whig Party broke up over the slavery issue in 1856, both men joined the Republican Party. Davis supported Lincoln's unsuccessful bid for a seat in the U.S. Senate in 1858.

Two years later, Davis was instrumental in helping Lincoln secure his party's nomination for president, and he was active in the campaign that followed. When Lincoln won the presidency, Davis followed him to Washington, where observers believed that it was inevitable that Lincoln would appoint him to the U.S. Supreme Court. Lincoln did, but only after he had filled two other open seats on the Court. In December 1862 Davis took his seat on the Court, where he served as an associate justice for 14 years.

As a Supreme Court justice, Davis is perhaps best remembered for delivering the Court's opinion in *Ex parte Milligan* in 1866. This famous case involved Lambdin Milligan, a leader of the Sons of Liberty, a group of "Copperheads" from Indiana who opposed the Civil War. In 1862, Lincoln had issued a wartime proclamation suspending the *writ of* **habeas corpus** (a provision of the Constitution ensuring that arrests are legal). By doing so, he allowed the arrest of civilians in the North who were guilty of disloyal acts such as resisting the draft or interfering with army volunteers. The proclamation also allowed such people to be tried before military courts or commissions. Davis joined the Court majority in overturning Milligan's conviction by a military commission. He maintained that the president had acted unconstitutionally in suspending the writ of habeas corpus and had no authority to authorize the use of military courts. Fellow Republicans harshly criticized Davis, but he insisted that the decision was necessary to protect civil liberties.

Otherwise, Davis tended to support the Court's Republican majority, ruling during Reconstruction, for example, that the citizens of the South could be treated as wartime **belligerents,** that the government's plan for Reconstruction in Georgia could proceed, and that loyalty oaths could be used to determine whether to grant political rights to Southerners.

Davis remained an imposing figure in politics—perhaps as much because of his immense girth as his talent for politics. (One observer noted that Davis had to be "surveyed" for a new pair of trousers.) In 1864, he supported Lincoln's bid for reelection, though he vigorously opposed the president's Emancipation

1815 Davis is born in Cecil County, Maryland.

1848 Davis is elected judge of the Eighth Judicial Circuit of Illinois.

1862 Davis is appointed to the U.S. Supreme Court.

1877 Davis resigns from the Supreme Court to become a U.S. senator

1886 Davis dies in Bloomington, Illinois.

One observer noted that Davis had to be "surveyed" for a new pair of trousers.

habeas corpus: a legal writ requiring a law enforcement body bringing a party who is being charged with a crime or offense to the court in person.

belligerents: individuals involved in waging war or conflict..

Proclamation. After the war, he became increasingly disen-chanted with the Republican Party. He thought that Presidents Andrew Johnson and Ulysses S. Grant were inept and that the radical Republicans in the North were treating the South vindic-tively.

In 1872, Davis flirted with running for president and in fact won the nomination of the Labor Reform Convention, a stepping-stone that could have led to nomination by either of the two major political parties, but in time his support waned and his candidacy did not go anywhere. By this time, Davis's sympathies wavered between the Democrats and the Republicans.

Davis left the Supreme Court under peculiar circumstances. The year 1876 was noteworthy for the contested presidential election between Rutherford B. Hayes, who won the vote in the Electoral College and went on to become president, and Samuel Tilden, who won the popular vote. To settle the dis-pute, Congress appointed a special Election Commission that consisted of 10 members of Congress and five Court justices. Democrats in Congress agreed to the formation of the commis-sion only because they believed that Davis would be the fifth justice and support Tilden. Oddly, however, while the bill to create the commission was being considered, Democrats in Illi-nois unwittingly thwarted this plan by electing Davis to a seat in the U.S. Senate. (At that time, senators were not elected by popular vote.) In 1877, Davis resigned from the Supreme Court to accept the position. The fifth justice appointed to the com-mission was a Republican, and Hayes won the election.

Davis served one term as a senator, where he frequently tipped the balance of power, sometimes voting with Democrats, sometimes with Republicans, in a Senate that was evenly di-vided between the two parties. In 1879 his wife, Sarah, died. In 1883 he married Adeline Burr, and the two lived in Blooming-ton, Illinois, until Davis's death on June 26, 1886. ◆

Day, William

APRIL 17, 1849–JULY 9, 1923 ● ASSOCIATE JUSTICE

Seemingly destined at birth for a career as a jurist, William Rufus Day was born on April 17, 1849, in Ravenna, Ohio, to Luther Day and Emily Spalding. His maternal great-grandfather had been chief justice of the supreme court in Connecticut, and his maternal grandfather had been an associate justice on the Ohio Supreme Court, where his father had served as chief justice. Day graduated as a literature major from the University of Michigan in 1870, but he decided to follow in his family's footsteps and returned to Ravenna to read law. Back at the University of Michigan Law School he studied for a year before being admitted to the Ohio bar in 1872. That year he settled in nearby Canton, Ohio, where he practiced law and, in 1875, married Mary Elizabeth Schaefer, a Southern woman whose ancestors had fought in the Revolutionary War.

William Day

Canton was a growing industrial town, and Day practiced both criminal and corporate law there for 25 years as a partner in the prosperous firm of Lynch and Day. He was also active in local Republican Party politics and became friends with future president William McKinley, who got his start in politics by beating Day's partner, William Lynch, in an election for county prosecutor in Canton. Winning the respect of the members of the legal community, Day was elected judge of the common pleas in 1886, but he resigned six months later for financial reasons. In 1889, President Benjamin Harrison offered him the chance to become a federal judge for the northern district of Ohio, but he resigned from the post before taking office, citing ill health—a problem that plagued him throughout much of his life. While he occasionally golfed and fished, he preferred watching baseball games and leading a quiet domestic life with his wife and four sons.

Day continued to act as a political adviser to McKinley while the latter served in Congress and as governor of Ohio. When McKinley became president, he offered Day the post of attorney general, but Day turned him down. In 1897, McKinley finally persuaded Day to join his administration when Secretary of State John Sherman's physical and mental condition began to deteriorate, and the president needed someone competent to

1849 Day is born in Ravenna, Ohio.

1899 Day is appointed to the U.S. Court of Appeals for the Sixth Circuit.

1903 Day is appointed to the U.S. Supreme Court.

1922 Day resigns from the U.S. Supreme Court.

1923 Day dies on Mackinac Island, Michigan.

Day served as an associate justice of the Supreme Court for nearly 20 years.

mediate: to attempt to bring agreement or accord between two opposing parties.

antitrust cases: cases involving legislation intended to break up and eliminate unlawful restraints of trade by large monopolies.

serve as first assistant in the State Department. Day had no experience in diplomacy, but equipped with a gentle, scholarly manner, innate tact, and sound judgment, he served well as the de facto secretary of state for 20 months during the Spanish American War. (The fact that the State Department's second secretary was completely deaf led some in the diplomatic community to quip, "The head of the Department knows nothing; the First Assistant [Day] says nothing; the Second Assistant hears nothing.") During this time Day often met with the French ambassador, who tried to **mediate** the dispute between the United States and Spain. Following the war he went to Paris, where he led the U.S. peace commission that signed the treaty ending the war and, for $20 million, gave the United States access to one of Spain's former holdings, the Philippine Islands.

When his work in Paris was done, Day hoped to return to private life, but McKinley called on him again, this time to serve as a judge on the U.S. Court of Appeals for the Sixth Circuit. Day was devastated when his old friend McKinley was assassinated in 1901. In 1902 the new president, Theodore Roosevelt, twice offered a seat on the Supreme Court to William Howard Taft, but Taft, then governor of the Philippines, refused each time. In 1903, Roosevelt turned to Day, who once again put his personal preferences aside to serve his country.

Day served as an associate justice of the Supreme Court for nearly 20 years. During that time he wrote 439 opinions, only 18 of which were dissents. A single thread linked many of those decisions: Day's immense distrust of concentrations of power, both business and governmental. Day distrusted large corporations, and from that distrust he consistently ruled against them in **antitrust cases,** including *Northern Securities Co. v. U.S.* in *1904;* the *Standard Oil, American Tobacco,* and *Union Pacific* cases in 1911 and 1912; and the *Southern Pacific* case in 1922.

Day also wanted to keep the federal government out of what he considered the business of the states, relying frequently on the Tenth Amendment of the Constitution to limit the police power of the federal government. At the same time, he granted broad authority to the states to regulate such affairs. Thus, for example, in *Coppage v. Kansas* (1915) he wrote a dissent in which he upheld the constitutionality of a state law in Kansas outlawing yellow-dog contracts—labor contracts that require workers not to join a union as a condition for the job. In

1921, in *Minnesota ex rel. Whipple v. Martinson,* he upheld the right of a state to regulate drug use.

Sometimes Day's views brought him into sharp disagreement with others. In perhaps his most famous opinion, in *Hammer v. Dagenhart* (1917), he swam against the tide in opposing both President Woodrow Wilson and Chief Justice Oliver Wendell Holmes, who saw the case as an opportunity to curb child-labor abuses. The case hinged on how much power the Constitution gives the federal government to regulate interstate commerce. In delivering the Court's ruling, Day distinguished between "production" and "commerce," arguing that the federal government had power only over interstate commerce, or the buying and selling of goods across state lines, but not production. Day's ruling thus invalidated the Child Labor Act of 1916, which sought to prohibit the interstate transportation of goods made by overworked minors.

In late 1922, Day resigned from the Supreme Court to serve on the Mixed Claims Commission, a body formed to rule on the claims of American citizens against Germany stemming from World War I. His health failed in 1923, though, and he resigned this position. In June of that year he went to his summer home on Mackinac Island, Michigan, but an earlier bout of pneumonia had left him in a weakened condition, and he died there a few weeks later on July 9. ◆

> *"The head of the Department knows nothing; the First Assistant says nothing; the Second Assistant hears nothing."*
> Quoted by Margaret Leech, *In the Days of McKinley,* 1959, referring to the State Department during Day's tenure.

Douglas, William O.

OCTOBER 16, 1898–JANUARY 19, 1980 ● ASSOCIATE JUSTICE

William O. Douglas, whose name is synonymous with judicial activism in the mid-20th century, was born in the town of Maine, Minnesota, in 1898. His childhood was a difficult one, and his determination to overcome the effects of poverty and illness undoubtedly shaped his later career. At age four he was stricken with polio, but in time he regained his strength by hiking and mountain climbing, and throughout his life he was an ardent nature lover, hiker, and preservationist.

When Douglas was six, his father, an **itinerant** preacher for whom William was named, died, and his mother, Julia Bickford Fisk, moved the impoverished family in with relatives

itinerant: an individual who travels to complete the duties of his occupation.

William O. Douglas

in Yakima, Washington. Douglas worked at odd jobs to help support the family but still managed to graduate as **valedictorian** of the Yakima High School class of 1916. After graduating Phi Beta Kappa from Whitman College in Walla Walla, Washington, in 1920, he returned to Yakima, where he taught high school English and Latin for two years.

Douglas, though, wanted to be an attorney, so he packed his bags for New York and Columbia University Law School in 1922. Almost penniless, he worked his way through school and graduated second in his class. He went to work for a large Wall Street firm in 1925, where he practiced corporate law, but two years later he returned to Yakima and tried to set up his own private practice. When that endeavor failed, he returned to New York to accept a faculty position at Columbia Law School. He resigned that position just a year later to protest the actions of his dean, but a chance meeting with the dean of the law school at Yale led to an appointment there. Douglas remained at Yale for five years, and his growing reputation led Yale to appoint him Sterling Chair of Commercial and Corporate Law in 1932.

In the wake of the Great Depression of the 1930s, Douglas's strong background in corporate law opened doors for him in the New Deal administration of President Franklin D. Roosevelt. In 1934, the Securities and Exchange Commission (SEC), directed by Joseph P. Kennedy, enlisted him to help write regulations for the nation's banks, financial markets, and the securities industry. Douglas's efforts led to his appointment as a member of the SEC in 1936. Just a year later, he was appointed commissioner. Largely through his efforts, the SEC wrote bold regulations to ensure that the nation's securities markets were fairer and more stable, especially for smaller, less sophisticated investors.

Douglas was witty and a good conversationalist. He quickly became part of Roosevelt's inner circle and a regular attendee at the president's poker parties. It came as little surprise, then, that in March 1939 Roosevelt appointed Douglas to the U.S. Supreme Court. Douglas was confirmed two weeks later and went on to serve on the Court for 37 years and seven months, the longest tenure of any Supreme Court justice. During those years he wrote more than 1,200 opinions. Twice—in 1944 and 1948—he was a leading contender for nomination as the vice presidential candidate. As if his judicial activities were not enough, he was a prolific author, writing speeches, articles, two autobiographies, and books on foreign policy, civil liberties, and wilderness preservation.

His private life kept him busy, too—but not out of trouble. In 1923, he had married Mildred Riddle, an English teacher he met in Yakima. She divorced him in 1953. In 1954, he married Washington socialite Mercedes Hester Davison. She divorced him in 1963. Just a few months later he married Joan Martin, a 24-year-old college student. That marriage lasted until 1966, when Douglas married 23-year-old Cathleen Ann Heffernan, also a college student. These divorces and remarriages, particularly to women young enough to be his granddaughters, added to Douglas's controversial reputation.

Douglas, though, had been a controversial figure on the Supreme Court almost from the start. Following in the footsteps of his idol, Justice Louis Brandeis, Douglas was a liberal, activist justice. He did not believe in "judicial neutrality," nor did he believe that the Supreme Court was bound by precedent or by a strict, literal interpretation of the text of the Constitution. In his later years, on the Court led by Earl Warren, he was at home with a liberal majority. But during the early Cold War years under Chief Justice Fred Vinson, Douglas was often a dissenting voice on a more conservative Court. In the eyes of many Americans, Douglas took positions that were un-American, and on at least two occasions there were loud calls for his impeachment.

Douglas stirred ire in part because of his belief in the absolute right of free speech and his staunch defense of the Bill of Rights. In 1951, for example, he dissented sharply when the Court upheld the conviction of members of the American Communist Party. In 1953, he attempted to stay the execution of Julius and Ethel Rosenberg, who were convicted for espionage after passing information about the atomic bomb to the Soviets.

On the Warren Court, Douglas joined a majority in far-reaching decisions on a number of pressing issues. On school

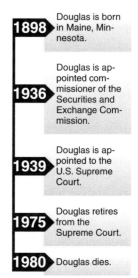

1898 Douglas is born in Maine, Minnesota.

1936 Douglas is appointed commissioner of the Securities and Exchange Commission.

1939 Douglas is appointed to the U.S. Supreme Court.

1975 Douglas retires from the Supreme Court.

1980 Douglas dies.

Douglas, though, had been a controversial figure on the Supreme Court almost from the start.

> "The Constitution was designed to keep government off the backs of the people."
>
> William O. Douglas, in *Laird v. Tatum*, 1972

penumbra a surrounding or adjoining region wherein something exists in a smaller degree.

emanation: the action of an object or thing coming out of another source.

desegregation, he voted to strike down "separate-but-equal" education in *Brown v. Board of Education*. In the area of criminal justice, he dissented in *Johnson v. Louisiana*, arguing that states should not be allowed to convict criminals with non-unanimous jury verdicts. In obscenity cases, he defended the absolute right of freedom of speech, leading to charges that he defended "smut." In cases having to do with religion in the schools, he insisted on an absolute separation of church and state.

Douglas also coined the famous expression "**penumbras, formed from emanations,**" in arguing that the Constitution implicitly grants individuals the right to privacy, even though it does not specify that right. Thus, in a famous case, *Griswold v. Connecticut* (1965), he upheld the right to marital privacy in striking down a state law banning the sale of contraceptives. These, however, are just a few of the areas in which Douglas helped to reshape the American social landscape.

On the last day of 1974, a stroke partially paralyzed Douglas, and in November 1975 he retired from the bench. He continued to work on his autobiography until his death at the Walter Reed Army Medical Center on January 19, 1980. ◆

Duvall, Gabriel

DECEMBER 6, 1752–MARCH 6, 1844 ● ASSOCIATE JUSTICE

> "It will be universally admitted that the right to freedom is more important than the right of property."
>
> Gabriel Duvall in *Mima Queen and Child v. Hepburn*, 1813

Gabriel Duvall was born on his family's plantation near Buena Vista in Prince Georges County, Maryland, on December 6, 1752. The 3,000-acre plantation was just part of the family's extensive estates, which dated back to his great-grandfather, Marin Du Val (sometimes written Mareen Duvall), a French Huguenot merchant who had fled religious persecution and settled in the area in the mid-17th century. His parents were Benjamin Duvall and Susanna Tyler, and Gabriel was their second son and the sixth of 10 children. It should be noted that various members of his family spelled their name DuVal or Duval, but Duvall is the way he signed his name.

As a child, Duvall was tutored in the classics, mathematics, and grammar at home on the family's estate. The family considered sending him to London for a legal education, but growing tension between the colonies and Great Britain forced him to study law in Annapolis, Maryland, and he was admitted to the bar in 1778. In the meantime he became a clerk for the Maryland Convention, the legislative assembly that took control of the colony in 1775 as war with Britain threatened, and he also served as a clerk for that body's executive arm, the Council of Safety. In 1777, he began a ten-year term as a clerk for the Maryland House of Delegates, the state's first elected legislature. He also took part in the war effort, serving as the **mustermaster** and commissary of stores for the state militia and, later, as a private in the militia.

In the years following the war, Duvall practiced law in Annapolis and became one of the state's most distinguished attorneys. He was also active in politics. In 1782, he was elected to the Maryland State Council, and in 1787 he rose from clerk to membership in the House of Delegates. That year, too, he was chosen as a member of the Maryland delegation to the Constitutional Convention, but he declined the post because he had just married Mary Brice. His political career received a further boost in 1794 when he was elected to complete the unexpired term of John Francis Mercer in the U.S. House of Representatives.

Duvall served in the House for just two years. In 1796, he resigned to become a judge of the General Court of Maryland, and for the next six years he served happily on the bench. One of the lawyers who appeared before him to argue his first case was Roger B. Taney, who went on to become a distinguished Chief Justice of the U.S. Supreme Court. During these years Duvall became involved in national politics, serving as an elector in the 1796 and 1800 presidential elections.

Duvall emerged on the national scene in 1802 when President Thomas Jefferson appointed him comptroller of the Treasury under Albert Gallatin, the secretary of the Treasury. By all accounts he was an efficient and knowledgeable comptroller, and Gallatin, Jefferson, and Congress often relied on him to provide accurate and unvarnished information. After James Madison became president in 1809, Duvall remained in this position

Gabriel Duvall

mustermaster: a military position in which an individual is charged with assembling his or her particular regiment for inspection.

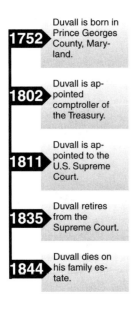

1752 Duvall is born in Prince Georges County, Maryland.

1802 Duvall is appointed comptroller of the Treasury.

1811 Duvall is appointed to the U.S. Supreme Court.

1835 Duvall retires from the Supreme Court.

1844 Duvall dies on his family estate.

hearsay evidence: evidence based on the knowledge of a witness on a matter told to him or her by someone else.

until Madison appointed him to the Supreme Court in 1811—but not before encountering some difficulties in filling the seat on the bench left open by the death of Justice William Cushing in 1810. Madison's first choice to replace Cushing declined, his second was rejected by the Senate, and while his third, John Quincy Adams, was confirmed in the Senate, he also declined. Madison, though, did not know of Adams's decision until several months later because Adams was in Russia at the time serving as a diplomat, and the mail routes were slow. In the meantime, Justice Samuel Chase died, so Madison faced the need to fill two seats. Finally, in 1811 he nominated Joseph Story and Duvall, who by now was almost 60 years old, and both were confirmed by the Senate three days later.

Duvall served on the Supreme Court until early 1835. During his entire 23-year tenure, the Court was dominated by Chief Justice John Marshall, known for asserting federal power over that of the states. Duvall consistently voted with Marshall—with one noteworthy exception, *Dartmouth College v. Woodward* (1819). Unfortunately, Duvall wrote few opinions and none in this case, so his reason for opposing Marshall is unknown. He is perhaps best remembered for his opinion in two cases having to do with slavery, and although his family owned slaves, his opinions were advanced for the times. In *Mima Queen and Child v. Hepburn* (1813), the issue was whether **hearsay evidence** could be used to support a slave's contention that she was free because her mother had been freed. The Court majority disallowed the evidence, but Duvall dissented: "It will be universally admitted that the right to freedom is more important than the right of property. And people of color from their helpless condition under the uncontrolled authority of a master, are entitled to all reasonable protection." In an 1829 case, *LeGrand v. Darnall*, Duvall wrote the opinion for the unanimous Court in ruling that a master in effect freed a slave by leaving property to the slave.

During his final years on the Court, Duvall's hearing began to fail, and he was increasingly absent. For years there was speculation that he would resign, but he refused to do so, afraid that "too much of a politician" would be appointed to replace him. When President Andrew Jackson indicated that he wanted to appoint Roger Taney to the bench, Duvall finally agreed to step down in 1835. Duvall, widowed in 1790, had remarried in 1795, but the death of his second wife in 1834 likely contributed to his decision to retire. Ironically, the Senate rejected Taney, and

Duvall's replacement turned out to be Philip Barbour, a states' rights Virginian whose views were in sharp contrast to those of Duvall.

Duvall lived for nine years after his retirement, and although he was almost completely deaf, he took an active part in the management of the family estates. He died peacefully at age 92 on March 6, 1844. ◆

Ellsworth, Oliver

APRIL 29, 1745–NOVEMBER 26, 1807 ● CHIEF JUSTICE

Oliver Ellsworth was born on April 29, 1745, in Windsor, Connecticut. His father, David, was a military officer, while his mother, Jemima, tended to the family home. The Ellsworth family had been in America since the mid-1600s, when Oliver's great-grandfather, Josiah, moved there from his home in Yorkshire, England. The Ellsworth family was well off,

Oliver Ellsworth

and, although David was disappointed when his son did not become a clergyman as David had hoped he would, he still provided Ellsworth with every educational advantage that was available at that time.

As a young boy, Ellsworth was tutored by the Reverend Joseph Bella, which prepared him for classes at Yale University, where Ellsworth enrolled in 1762. He later switched to Princeton, where he completed his bachelor's degree around 1766. While no clear records are available, it appears that Ellsworth did not leave Yale of his own accord, although he still liked the university well enough to later send his sons there. He first studied theology after leaving Yale, but that

1745 Ellsworth is born in Windsor, Connecticut.

1771 Ellsworth enters the bar and begins working as an attorney.

1777 Ellsworth is appointed to the first of six consecutive terms on the Continental Congress.

1787 Ellsworth represents Connecticut at the Constitutional Convention and is credited as one of the main framers of the Bill of Rights and the Connecticut Compromise.

1789 Ellsworth is named one of Connecticut's first two senators, where he is largely responsible for establishing the federal court system.

1796 Elsworth is appointed the third Chief Justice of the U.S. Supreme Court.

1807 Ellsworth dies in Windsor, Connecticut.

did not last long, as he was drawn to the law. After four years of study, he entered the bar in 1771 and began working as a lawyer. In 1772, he married Abigail Wolcott.

It was a time of prosperous growth and rapid change in America. While Ellsworth's law practice struggled in its early years—records show he averaged only three pounds of the Connecticut state currency per year for his first three years—but he was successful in other areas. While he was a talented and knowledgeable lawyer, he proved to be an even better politician. In 1777, he was selected to represent his state in the Continental Congress in Philadelphia. He also strongly supported the U.S. war effort against the British, serving on a committee that oversaw Connecticut's war expenses and later serving on the Council of Safety, which oversaw all of Connecticut's military operations. By the time he served on those bodies, his law practice had begun to prosper, and by 1779, he had one of the busiest law offices in the country. A young clerk named Noah Webster—who would go on to found the famous dictionary that bears his name—worked for Ellsworth and reported that, at any given time, Ellsworth always had more than 1,000 clients in the books. In no time, Ellsworth was extremely wealthy and he became a prominent land owner. In 1777, he was appointed to be the state's attorney for Hartford County, which made his practice grow even further.

Ellsworth served on six consecutive sessions of the Continental Congress (1777–1783) while remaining active in state politics at the same time. From 1780 to 1784, he served on a special council that advised the Connecticut governor, and for the next five years after that, he resumed his law career by serving on the State Superior Court.

While serving on the Continental Congress, Ellsworth served on a number of committees, including the Committee of Appeals. That body, which was charged with overseeing marine disputes, represented the first instance of a federal court in the United States. The committee had the power to issue legal judgements in cases that came before it, although it could not always enforce those laws. In a complex case involving ownership of a captured British ship, the committee's ruling that the ship be awarded to a group of Connecticut men was completely ignored by the state of Pennsylvania, where the ship had reached land. As a result, the case actually remained in litigation for more than 30 years before it was finally completely resolved.

At the national level, Ellsworth earned a reputation as an excellent writer an a strong statesman. He again represented his state at the Constitutional Convention in 1787, and he is credited with being one of the Committee of Five, which is the group that wrote the first draft of the U.S. Constitution. He was also widely praised for his part in authoring the Connecticut Compromise (also known as the Great Compromise) at the convention, which provided a framework for how the states would be represented in the two houses of the newly formed Congress. In addition, history credits him with popularizing the term "United States" in reference to the 13 states. He reportedly changed the wording in a document from "national government" to "the government of the United States," and from that point forward, the term United States was commonly used in reference to the states in official government documents.

In 1789, Ellsworth was again asked to serve his state in Washington, D.C., when he was named one of Connecticut's first senators. Because the federal government was in its infancy after starting from scratch just a few years before, Ellsworth was given the opportunity to serve on numerous committees that were responsible for creating the U.S. government. For example, he helped create the national army and the U.S. Post Office; helped bring North Carolina and Rhode Island into the union; and served on the committee that created a national bank of the United States and determined how to fund the national debt. However, the action for which Ellsworth is best remembered is chairing the committee that created the Judiciary Act of 1789. The act created the framework for a federal judiciary and court system, and Ellsworth received most of the credit for its final draft. "That the Judiciary Bill which came from this Committee was to a large extent, drafted by Ellsworth is now well established," wrote Charles Warren in a Harvard Law Review article in 1923.

Ellsworth served nearly his full, seven-year term as senator, but in 1796, he resigned after he was elevated to a higher position—Chief Justice of the U.S. Supreme Court. He was actually President George Washington's third choice to replace John Jay; first, the Senate refused to approve the appointment of John Rutledge, after which associate justice William Cushing refused the promotion to chief justice. Ellsworth accepted the position and was sworn in on March 4, 1796.

Ellsworth would serve as chief justice for only three-and-a-half years. While he was widely recognized as an excellent

"Let there be vigilance, constant diligence, and fidelity for the execution of the laws—of law made by all and having for their object the good of all. So let us rear an empire sacred to the rights of man and commend a government of reason to the nations of the earth."

Oliver Ellsworth, addressing a grand jury at the federal circuit court in Savannah, Georgia, April, 1796

Justices may still write their own opinions, but the use of *per curiam* opinions became commonplace after Ellsworth's court.

lawyer, and his work as a politician was unrivaled, he proved to be an only adequate judge. Part of the reason for that might lie in the fact that, at that time, the chief justice was responsible for doing what was known as "riding circuit"—traveling around the 13 states to visit each of the federal circuit courts to hear cases there. Given the state of the roads and the forms of transportation available at the time, this was a difficult task that made the job of chief justice much more difficult.

During Ellsworth's tenure, few decisions were handed down by the Court, and few had any real lasting historical significance. Perhaps the one well-known case is *United States v. Isaac*, in which the U.S. Circuit Court for Connecticut (one of the circuits he presided over) ruled that a U.S. citizen could not expatriate himself unless he was granted consent to do so by the U.S. government.

The one notable accomplishment that Ellsworth achieved while chief justice was his reworking of the manner in which case opinions were issued. Prior to his service, each justice on the Supreme Court would issue his own opinion on each case (known as seriotimopinions), a tradition that followed English common law. However, Ellsworth switched the Court to the use of *per curiam* opinions, in which one person (who usually remains anonymous) writes an opinion that represents the view of the court as a whole. Justices may still write their own opinions, but the use of *per curiam* opinions became commonplace after Ellsworth's court.

In 1799, while still the chief justice, Ellsworth was appointed a special U.S. commissioner to France, a position he held until 1800. After a difficult, stormy four-month trip to France, in which his health failed due to a kidney ailment, Ellsworth negotiated a treaty with French leader Napoleon that ended an undeclared naval war that had been ongoing between the two nations. While war was avoided, no one in the U.S. government was particularly happy with the terms that Ellsworth had settled for, and it was widely recognized that his health may have impaired his ability to do his job. When his health continued to decline, he was forced to remain in France and England until early 1801, when he was finally able to return to his home in Windsor, Connecticut. There he lived out the final few years of his life, finally retired from the civil service that he had served so well throughout his life. He died in his home on November 26, 1807. ◆

Field, Stephen J.

NOVEMBER 4, 1816–APRIL 9, 1899 ● ASSOCIATE JUSTICE

Members of the nation's highest court are often remembered primarily for their impact on the evolution of law and for their insight into the application of the Constitution to contemporary conditions. While Stephen J. Field was a dominating voice on the Supreme Court in the latter half of the 19th century, he is probably best remembered for his eventful, sometimes boisterous, personal and professional life.

Stephen J. Field

Field was born in Haddam, Connecticut, on November 4, 1816. His father, David Dudley Field, was a hellfire-and-brimstone Congregationalist preacher in the tradition of Jonathan Edwards. His mother bore the unusual name Submit Dickinson. When he was just 13, Field began the far-flung travels that would mark much of his life when he joined an elder sister and her husband in Turkey for two and a half years. There he learned a number of foreign languages, and some thought that he might grow up to become a language professor.

Instead, Field turned to the law. After graduating at the head of his class from Williams College in 1837,

1816 Field is born in Haddam, Connecticut.

1857 Field elected to the California Supreme Court.

1863 Field appointed to the U.S. Supreme Court.

1897 Field resigns from the Supreme Court.

1899 Field dies.

alcalde the chief judicial officer in a Spanish town.

he studied law with his older brother, then in the office of the New York state attorney in Albany. He gained admission to the bar in 1841, then practiced with his brother for seven years. After a year touring Europe, he returned to the United States, only to be bitten by the California "gold rush" bug. In late 1849, after an arduous journey, he reached the West Coast with only $10 in his pocket. His initial goal was to set up a law practice in San Francisco, but after just a month he took a boat inland to Marysville, a backwoods settlement of about 600 people, who leaped to the conclusion that he was a wealthy capitalist. After convincing them of the need for a local government, he was elected the town's alcalde, a judicial office that was a remnant of Mexican rule in the area.

In 1850, California ratified a new state constitution, eliminating the position of **alcalde.** The new local official was William Turner, a state district court judge. Relations between Field and Turner were openly hostile, and after a heated exchange, Turner fined Field, jailed him, and had him expelled from the California bar. Field persuaded the state supreme court to overturn the decision, but relations between the two men remained strained, almost leading to a shoot-out in the California Assembly after Field was elected to the lower house in 1850.

Field was a valuable addition to the lower house. In the states' early years, he was responsible for blending U.S. precedent, Spanish law, and the rough-and-ready practices of the frontier into a coherent legal code. With his practical good sense and a firm decisiveness rooted in his upbringing, he was the ideal man for that job at that time and in that place.

In 1851, Field ran for a state Senate seat, but he lost the primary election when some of his "supporters" traded away their votes for political favors. Field returned to private practice but entered politics again in 1857 when he ran unsuccessfully for a U.S. Senate seat. The attention he attracted during the campaign helped him to gain election to the California Supreme Court.

In 1859, Field married Sue Virginia Swearington, who managed over the next 40 years to keep her blunt, bullish husband in check—but not before he became embroiled in a bitter feud with California Chief Justice David Terry, who killed Field's friend, U.S. Senator David Broderick, in a duel. (Field never forgot an enemy, and the feud erupted nearly 30 years later, in 1888. Field, as circuit judge in California, issued a ruling unfavorable to Terry and his wife, and Terry threatened Field's life. When Terry and Field bumped into one another at a restaurant, Terry slapped Field. Field's bodyguard shot Terry and was charged with murder—and Field was charged as an accomplice. Eventually, the case reached the Supreme Court and was resolved in Field's and the bodyguard's favor.)

Congress created an additional seat on the U.S. Supreme Court in 1863. President Abraham Lincoln had at least three criteria for selecting the new judge. First, since the judge would ride the California/Oregon circuit, he wanted someone familiar with laws pertaining to land use, mineral rights, and the like. Second, he wanted an outspoken supporter of the Union who would uphold the legality of his actions in prosecuting the Civil War. Finally, he wanted someone who would support reconstruction following the Civil War. Although Field was a Democrat, he fit the Republican president's bill and was appointed to the Supreme Court in March 1863.

In the years that followed, Field often regaled Washington society with tall tales from the California frontier. And he never lost his abiding interest in politics. He served on the Electoral Commission that decided the disputed Hayes-Tilden presidential election of 1876, voting with the Democrats. In 1880 and again in 1884 he sought the Democratic presidential nomination.

As a jurist, Field wrote clear, unequivocal opinions—and many of them—some 640, including 220 dissents. During the late 1800s the nation's economy was changing and growing, and Field consistently sided with private business in opposing regulation by the federal government. His opinions helped shape contemporary interpretations of the Constitution's commerce clause, due process clause, and the equal protection clause of the Fourteenth Amendment in protecting capital and private property, particularly from what he called "communistic" invasions. He consistently voted against efforts to impose an income tax, arguing that they were an "assault on capital" and that a progressive tax would lead to a "war between the poor and the rich."

By the mid-1890s, Field—who coincidentally sat on the Court with his nephew, Justice David Brewer—was growing increasingly infirm and irritable. He was in constant pain from a knee injury that would not heal. He resisted colleagues who urged him to resign until November 30, 1897, when he passed John Marshall's record for the longest tenure on the Court.

Field died on April 9, 1899. The relatively modest size of his estate finally cleared him of charges, which plagued him throughout his judicial career, that he was bribed by the businesses and corporations whose interests he so staunchly defended. ◆

"If the provisions of the Constitution can be set aside by an act of Congress, where is the course of usurpation to end? The present assault on capital is but the beginning."
Stephen J. Field in *Pollock v. Farmers' Loan and Trust Co.*, 1895

As a jurist, Field wrote clear, unequivocal opinions.

Fortas, Abe

JUNE 19, 1910–APRIL 5, 1982 ● ASSOCIATE JUSTICE

A be Fortas, who resigned from the Supreme Court after just four years amid charges of improprieties, was born in Memphis, Tennessee, on June 19, 1910. He was the youngest of five children of William Fortas, a cabinetmaker, and Ray Berson. As a child he showed considerable talent on the violin, which he continued to play in a semiprofessional string quartet even as a sitting Supreme Court justice. A scholarship enabled him to attend Southwestern College in Memphis, where he graduated first in his class in 1930. As a student he showed skill as a debater, so he decided on a career in law. The law schools at both Yale and Harvard offered him scholarships, but Yale's was $50 a month more, so he packed his bags for New Haven, where he came under the influence of a young professor, future Supreme Court Justice William O. Douglas.

Fortas graduated second in his class in 1933, and Yale offered him a position on the faculty. For the next six years he divided his time between the university and Washington, D.C., where he worked in President Franklin D. Roosevelt's New Deal administration to help curb some of the effects of the Depression. His first position was with the Agricultural Adjustment Administration, but in 1935—the year he married Carolyn Eugenia Agger—he was lured to the Securities and Exchange Commission by Douglas. In 1939, Fortas was appointed general counsel of the Public Works Administration. Then in 1941, he joined the Department of the Interior, where in 1942 he was promoted to undersecretary under the colorful Harold Ickes.

Fortas left government service in 1946 to go into private practice as a lawyer. He teamed up with Thurman Arnold to form Arnold and Fortas, which became one of the top

Abe Fortas

law firms in Washington, D.C., over the next two decades. While Fortas usually represented some of the nation's corporate giants, he also volunteered to represent individual clients, including the indigent. During the McCarthy years of the early 1950s he successfully defended a low-level policy expert against charges of disloyalty. In 1954 he represented a client in a precedent-setting case that extended the boundaries of insanity defenses. In 1963, he argued before the Supreme Court in defense of Earl Gideon in *Gideon v. Wainwright*, a landmark case that established the right of suspects to be represented by a lawyer.

At the same time other paths were leading Fortas to the Supreme Court. In the 1930s he had met a young congressman from Texas, Lyndon B. Johnson. Fortas was slim, soft-spoken, and refined—in other words, not at all like Johnson. Despite the sharp contrast between the two men, they became fast friends. In 1948, Fortas defended Johnson against charges of ballot-box stuffing in the Texas senatorial primary, which Johnson had won by fewer than 100 votes. In the years that followed, Fortas often served as an informal adviser to Johnson during Johnson's tenure as a senator, vice president, and then president. As president, Johnson offered Fortas a cabinet appointment as attorney general, but Fortas declined.

Fortas was appointed to the U.S. Supreme Court in 1965. Johnson had persuaded Justice Arthur Goldberg to take the post of ambassador to the United Nations. Wanting to continue the tradition of the "Jewish seat" on the Court, he informally offered the seat to Fortas, who was an Orthodox Jew. Fortas declined, not wanting to leave his lucrative law practice and his role as adviser to the president. A determined Johnson placed his name in nomination anyway, and the Senate confirmed the appointment. Oddly, Fortas never did formally accept the position, but he joined the Court in October of that year.

In his four years on the Court, Fortas staked out a clear position as a civil libertarian. His was the fifth vote that provided the majority in *Miranda v. Arizona*, the 1966 case that required the police to inform criminal suspects of their legal rights. In *In re Gault* in 1967, he wrote for the majority in ruling that juveniles as well as adults have the right not to incriminate themselves: "Under our Constitution, the condition of being a boy does not justify a **kangaroo court**."

Fortas also wrote the majority opinion in the landmark case *Tinker v. Des Moines Independent Community School District*

> *"They can't even fix traffic tickets. They don't have time to take anybody to lunch; and if they did, they'd have to get the other fellow to pick up the check."*
>
> Abe Fortas, commenting on the change from affluent lawyer to Supreme Court justice, quoted in Fred Graham, *The Justices of the United States Supreme Court 1789–1969*

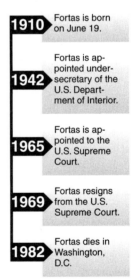

1910 Fortas is born on June 19.

1942 Fortas is appointed undersecretary of the U.S. Department of Interior.

1965 Fortas is appointed to the U.S. Supreme Court.

1969 Fortas resigns from the U.S. Supreme Court.

1982 Fortas dies in Washington, D.C.

kangaroo court: a court making decisions without regard to proper authority or procedures.

Salary and terms of service for justices to the Supreme Court

Supreme Court Justices are appointed and serve for life, until they resign, or until they choose to retire from the bench. There is no mandatory retirement age, but a Justice must have served at least 10 years to qualify for a pension. There is also no process by which a sitting Justice can be removed from the bench for political or ideological reasons, but they can be impeached for serious misconduct. The salary for Justices of the Supreme Court is set by Congressional statute and has been adjusted periodically to reflect changes in the cost of living. As of 1998, the salary for the Chief Justice was set at $175,000 per year, while Associate Justices receive $167,900 annually.

Both the salary level and terms of service are intended to insulate the Supreme Court Justices from outside pressures when they are judging the cases that come before them. Because they are appointed, they need not court popular opinion the way elected officials do every few years. Even so, without a lifetime tenure in office they would still be subject to political pressure if they had to worry about being re-appointed. This means that they need not worry about the consequences of taking an unpopular stand.

The salaries of Supreme Court Justices are also insulated from manipulation by the executive and legislative branches. Although Congress sets the actual salary level, it is not empowered to cut the pay of a sitting Justice. However, Supreme Court salaries have not always been particularly generous, especially in the early years of the court. Several Justices retired citing inadequacy of pay during the 1800s. Today, however, salaries are set fairly high, in general accord with the pay scales of other high government officials in Congress. The system seems to work: even during periods when the populace has had a low opinion of the honesty of elected officials, the Supreme Court has enjoyed an enviable reputation for honesty and even-handedness.

(1969). The case arose as the nation was divided over the war in Vietnam. Two high school students, Mary Beth and John Tinker, wore black armbands to school to protest the war. For their efforts, they were suspended. The Supreme Court ruled, however, that the First Amendment to the Constitution gives students the right to engage in peaceful, non-disruptive protest. Finding that the wearing of an armband was symbolic speech, Fortas and the Court ruled that the school district had violated the students' right to free speech.

The events that led to Fortas's resignation from the Court began in 1968. That year, burdened with an unpopular war, Johnson decided not to seek reelection. Further, Chief Justice Earl Warren indicated that he wanted to retire. Johnson placed Fortas's name in nomination for chief justice, but Johnson's growing unpopularity led to charges that he was trying to "pack" the Supreme Court while he still could. Republicans and conservative Democrats cried "cronyism" in light of Fortas's personal relationship with the president. They also charged Fortas with impropriety in accepting payment from a local law school while serving on the Court. Fortas asked Johnson to withdraw his nomination, but he remained on the Court as an associate justice.

Then in 1969 *Life* magazine published an article accusing Fortas of taking $20,000 from the family foundation of a convicted stock swindler. Amid talk of impeachment, Fortas denied the charge but resigned from the Court in May 1969—the first Supreme Court justice to resign under the pressure of public opinion.

Fortas returned to private practice in the capital. He also continued to play the violin and served as a board member for the Kennedy Center for the Performing Arts. He died at his Georgetown home on April 5, 1982. ◆

Frankfurter, Felix

NOVEMBER 15, 1882–FEBRUARY 22, 1965 ● ASSOCIATE JUSTICE

Felix Frankfurter, the last of just six Supreme Court justices born outside the United States, was born in Vienna, Austria, on November 15, 1882. He immigrated with his Jewish parents to the United States when he was 12, and the family settled on the Lower East Side of New York City. As a child, Frankfurter quickly learned English, and he developed a habit of reading several newspapers each day—perhaps contributing to his belief that the judiciary cannot function without integrating the law into the social and economic currents of everyday contemporary life.

Frankfurter graduated from the City College of New York in 1902. He worked briefly for the city's Tenement Department, then enrolled at the Harvard Law School. After graduating at the top of his class in 1906, he was one of the first Jews ever to be offered a position at a leading New York City law firm. His private law career was short-lived, however, for that same year he accepted a position under Henry L. Stimson at the U.S. Attorney's office in New York, beginning a career in public service that would span nearly six decades. Later Frankfurter worked as a campaign aide for Stimson when Stimson ran for governor of New York, and he joined Stimson in Washington, D.C. when Stimson was appointed secretary of war in President William

"The core of the difficulty is that there is hardly a question of any real difficulty before the Court that does not entail more than one so-called principle. Anybody can decide a question if only a single principle is in controversy."

Felix Frankfurter,
Of Law and Men,
1956

Felix Frankfurter

Taft's cabinet in 1911. In the nation's capital Frankfurter was part of an energetic group of budding young statesmen, and he became personal friends with Justice Oliver Wendell Holmes and future justice Louis Brandeis. Frankfurter's ability to forge strong personal relationships with influential people was a hallmark of his career.

In 1914, Frankfurter was offered a position on the Harvard Law School faculty. It was Brandeis who urged Frankfurter to accept the position, and in the years that followed, he successfully combined academics with public service. As a teacher, he was highly esteemed by his students, who remembered the way that he probed and dissected cases and taught students to think like lawyers. It was to Frankfurter, in large part, that future generations of law students owed a teaching approach that emphasized not legal principles but the examination of cases. As a jurist, he earned a reputation as perhaps one of the most scholarly members of the bench.

Washington, though, continued to beckon. During World War I Frankfurter was appointed secretary and general counsel to the President's Mediation Commission on labor relations. In 1918, he met future president Franklin D. Roosevelt while serving as chair of the War Labor Policies Board. In 1919, he married Marion A. Denman in a ceremony performed by his predecessor on the Supreme Court, Judge Benjamin Cardozo, at that time of the New York Court of Appeals.

By this time, Frankfurter had a reputation as a liberal, sometimes a controversial one. Prior to World War I, he had worked on behalf of a minimum wage and maximum hours provision for the National Consumers League in Boston. In the 1920s, he defended alleged communists charged by the U.S. attorney general during that period's "red scares." In a celebrated case, he demonstrated that Nicola Sacco and Bartolomeo Vanzetti, anarchists convicted of a robbery and shooting, had been denied due process because they were Italian-born immigrants. He also

Writ of Certiorari

When a judgement has been reached in a lower court (local, district, or state level), the losing side has the right to appeal the decision to a higher court, even to the highest court in the land, the United States Supreme Court. The first step of this process is to file a petition requesting that the higher court consider the case, an action that is commonly called "filing for cert." This phrase comes from the Latin word, "certiorari" (pronounced ser-tee-oh-RAH-ree), which means "to be informed."

If the higher court is persuaded by the legal arguments for considering the case, it issues a *writ of certiorari*, the legal instrument by which the court signals its decision to hear both sides of the dispute present their sides of the case. By issuing a writ of certiorari, the court calls upon the lower court that originally heard the case, requiring that the lower court send all records, evidence, and documents pertaining to the case, which the higher court then reviews along with new arguments presented by both sides to the dispute.

The Supreme Court, as the highest judicial body in the nation, is the final court of appeal, and thus receives many requests for writs of certiorari to settle disputes. However, the Supreme Court only reviews cases that meet certain standards. Chief among these are cases that touch upon constitutional issues, such as free speech, discrimination, and states' rights. A petition to the Supreme Court for a writ of certiorari, therefore, must include an explanation of how the original decision somehow conflicts with or violates an article or amendment to the U.S. Constitution.

gave his help to the National Association for the Advancement of Colored People (NAACP) and was a founding member of the American Civil Liberties Union.

Frankfurter also attracted controversy for openly tendering advice to high public officials, even making recommendations to President Roosevelt about cabinet posts. While in England teaching at Oxford University in 1933–34, he met physicist Niels Bohr, and thus became one of the first Americans to learn about the early development of the atomic bomb. Some Americans believed that there was little about the inner workings of the United States that Felix Frankfurter did not know.

When Justice Cardozo retired from the Supreme Court, President Roosevelt sought to appoint a successor who would uphold his New Deal legislation. In January 1939, he turned to Frankfurter, who was unanimously confirmed by the Senate and went on to serve on the Court for over 23 years. Given his scholarly—as opposed to doctrinaire or political—approach to the law, it is difficult to classify him. Despite his early reputation as a liberal, he was perhaps best known for advocating judicial restraint. While he believed that the provisions of the Constitution were "adaptable to the changes of the time," he did not

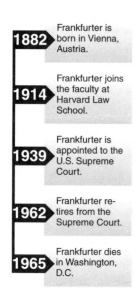

1882 Frankfurter is born in Vienna, Austria.

1914 Frankfurter joins the faculty at Harvard Law School.

1939 Frankfurter is appointed to the U.S. Supreme Court.

1962 Frankfurter retires from the Supreme Court.

1965 Frankfurter dies in Washington, D.C.

believe that any "vagueness" in the Constitution gave the judiciary the right to overturn the lawful actions of the legislative branch of government. He was, however, inclined to review the actions of the executive branch, particularly when those actions, in his opinion, violated the Bill of Rights, in particular the due process clause.

In social and economic cases, Frankfurter generally upheld Roosevelt's New Deal legislation. In criminal cases, he showed no hesitation in rigorously scrutinizing the actions of the police. In cases having to do with freedom of speech and religion, he refused to take an absolute position. While some jurists insisted that freedom of speech was absolute and a "preferred" freedom, Frankfurter balanced freedom of speech against other freedoms. Similarly, in freedom of religion cases, he believed that the First Amendment banned public financing of busing for parochial school children, religious classes after hours, and releasing students to attend religious services. At the same time, he ruled that a public school district could require Jehovah's Witnesses to salute the flag.

In sum, "liberal" and "conservative" are words that never applied to Frankfurter. Rather, Frankfurter weighed each case on its own merits, taking into consideration not only the social and economic conditions of the times but also any historical currents that had a bearing on the case.

In 1962 Frankfurter suffered a stroke, followed by a heart attack, forcing him to retire in August. He died in Washington, D.C., on February 22, 1965. ◆

Fuller, Melville Weston

FEBRUARY 11, 1833–JULY 4, 1910 ● CHIEF JUSTICE

Melville Weston Fuller was born on February 11, 1833, in Augusta, Maine. He was the youngest of two boys born to Frederick Augustus Fuller and Catherine Weston, who both came from prominent families. When Fuller was just two months old, his mother accused his father of adultery and the couple divorced. Catherine took her sons and moved in with her parents; her father was a judge on the Maine Supreme Court, which sparked Fuller's early interest in the law. That interest was nurtured by other family members, as well—in addition to his grandfather, Fuller's father and six of Fuller's uncles were lawyers or judges. Even after his mother remarried when he was 11, Fuller continued to live with his grandparents.

Fuller attended Bowdoin College, where he graduated Phi Beta Kappa in 1853 after being very active in campus politics. Like his father and his grandfather, Fuller decided to study law and become an attorney. At first he studied law on his own while living in Bangor, Maine, but he then enrolled in law school at Harvard University. After just six months at Harvard, he passed the bar exam in 1855 and opened a private practice in his hometown of Augusta. Besides the law, Fuller's other passion in college had been writing, and he decided to remain active in that area as well when, at the same time he was starting out as a lawyer, he became an editorial writer for *The Age*, a small, Democratic newspaper owned by an uncle on his father's side.

Melville Fuller

In 1856, Fuller grew restless and decided to join the thousands of people who were moving west, settling in the growing city of Chicago. There, Fuller again established his own law office, which proved to be successful. He and his partners handled all areas of the law but specialized in real estate and commercial law. He received a great deal of attention for defending Charles Edward Cheney against charges of canonical disobedience in front of an ecclesiastical tribunal (a case that led to the formation of the Reformed Protestant Episcopal Church). In more traditional civil law, he also made a name for himself in what was known as the Lake Front litigation, a case involving the city of Chicago and the rights it held to the Lake Michigan shoreline. Fuller also wed for the first time in Chicago, marrying Calista O. Reynolds, who died just six years later. Fuller remarried in 1866, to Mary Ellen Coolbaugh.

In Chicago, Fuller also renewed the love of politics he had first displayed at Bowdoin College, successfully running for a

1833 Fuller is born in Augusta, Maine.

1855 Fuller passes the bar exam.

1862 Fuller is elected to the House of Representatives in Illinois.

1888 Fuller is appointed Chief Justice of the U.S. Supreme Court.

1900 Fuller begins ten years of service on the Permanent Court of Arbitration at the Hague, Netherlands.

1910 Fuller dies in Sorrento, Maine.

spot as a Democratic representative to the Illinois State Constitutional Convention in 1861. A year later, he was elected to the new state's House of Representatives. A lifelong Democrat, Fuller served as a representative to that party's presidential nominating conventions in 1864, 1872, 1876, and 1880.

Fuller's appointment as chief justice came out of the blue to most political observers. In fact, he is widely considered to be the least experienced of all nominees for chief justice, before or since. While he was well-known in Illinois, Fuller was not prominent on the national scene. However, he had met President Grover Cleveland when the president was on a trip out west, and the two had hit it off. Alexander, who respected Fuller's opinions on economic and legal policies, offered Fuller two civil service positions in Washington, D.C., but both times Fuller turned him down. However, in 1888, Alexander approached Fuller one more time, and this time he offered him the position as Chief Justice of the Supreme Court, replacing Morrison R. Waite; Fuller accepted the nomination.

At the time of his appointment to the Court, there were a number of better-known and highly respected jurors who were considered to be front-runners for the position, including sitting justices Oliver Wendell Holmes, Samuel F. Miller, and John Marshall Harlan, as well as attorney Edward J. Phelps, who Alexander initially favored. Also, Fuller was viewed as being too strongly Democratic by Republican members of Congress. All of these factors combined to make Fuller's confirmation as justice a difficult process. Finally, after three months and a great deal of haggling, Fuller's nomination was approved by a vote of 41–20 in the Senate and he was became chief justice, a position he would hold for 22 years.

As chief justice, Fuller was known for his easy-going manner, his staunch impartiality, and his skill at managing meetings and conferences, always keeping them focused on the matter at hand. His friendliness and impartiality helped him arbitrate the disputes that regularly broke out on the Court, usually managing to avoid serious arguments. Fuller did not write many memorable opinions while he was on the Court, but he was prolific, writing more than 850 total. What he is most remembered for, however, is running one of the best-organized and efficient Courts in history. Justices Holmes and Miller, two highly respected justices who together served more than 70 years on Supreme Court, called him "the best presiding judge they had ever known." The years that Fuller served as chief justice were a time of turmoil that saw many important cases, and it is widely agreed that Fuller did a good job in steering the Court through challenging times.

Because he was a lifelong Democrat, Fuller was a strong believer in states' rights and the rights of the individual. As a result, he strived to ensure, in every decision, that government powers did not overly trample on the political and economic rights of U.S. citizens and that the federal government did not usurp too much of the states' powers. He routinely ruled that Congress had limited powers that had to be created by specific laws, that there was no "national sovereignty" that allowed Congress to act as it pleased.

In addition, Fuller favored a free business climate in which government rules and restrictions were kept to a minimum. "Fuller presided over and was supported by a Court that became a veritable bastion of economic *laissez-faire*, espousing a policy of preserving *in extremis*, the notion of 'freedom of contract,'" said legal scholar Henry J. Abraham of the chief justice. In two famous rulings, Fuller demonstrated his support of business and his belief that the government should not have too much power. Both cases were in 1895—the first was *United States v, E. C. Knight Co.* In his ruling, Fuller issued such a tightly construed view of the Sherman Anti-Trust Act of 1890 that the legislation could really only be used against the transportation industry. This allowed other businesses to continue near-monopolistic practices without government interference. The other, *Pollock v. Farmers' Loan and Trust Co.*, ruled that the federal income tax act of 1894 was unconstitutional. It would be more than 20 years before the *Pollock* ruling was overturned and an income tax was ruled constitutional.

Fuller is also remembered for helping to pass a law that saved the U.S. court system from drowning in a sea of cases. By the late 1880s, the courts were incredibly overworked, with the Supreme Court alone receiving more than 550 case filings each year. When Congress approached the Court with an offer to pass a law to improve conditions, Fuller worked closely with fellow justice Horace Gray to provide important feedback on the law that became the Circuit Court of Appeals Act of 1891. The act created nine new Courts of Appeals that were given the power of final disposition over many types of cases, subject to Supreme Court review and appeal. As a result, the huge backlog of court cases clogging the U.S. system was largely gone by 1900.

The years that Fuller served as chief justice were years of upheaval and rapid growth for the United States and the world at

> *"I am fond of the work of the Chief Justiceship. It is arduous, but nothing is truer than the labor we delight in physical pain."*
> Melville Fuller, 1893, explaining to President Cleveland why he could not become the Secretary of State

Plessy v. Ferguson (1896)

In the late 1800s, Louisiana law required that all railways maintain separate cars for blacks and whites. One day in 1892, Homer Adolph Plessy, who was of mixed race (7/8ths white), was arrested on the train when he took a seat in a whites–only car. He took his case to the Supreme Court, where he raised the question: Is legally mandated segregation of the races unconstitutional?

Plessy's lawyer argued that mandatory segregation violated the Fourteenth Amendment of the Constitution, which grants everyone "equal protection" and equal rights and privileges. The majority of the Court, however, disagreed. Justice Henry B. Brown, arguing for the majority, stated that he agreed with the plaintiff (Plessy) that the Fourteenth Amendment was aimed at establishing absolute equality, but qualified this by saying "it could not have been intended to abolish distinctions based upon color, or to enforce social, as distinguished from political, equality, or a commingling of the two races [upon terms] unsatisfactory to either."

The Court's decision had an impact that reached far beyond the *Plessy v. Ferguson* case. It's ruling gave rise to what came to be called the separate–but–equal doctrine, which legitimized such practices as "whites only" drinking fountains, schools, hotels, beaches, and other public facilities. These practices remained unchallenged until the Supreme Court opinion in the *Brown v. Board of Education of Topeka* (1954) and the Civil Rights Movement of the late 1950s and 1960s.

large. The Industrial Revolution was in full swing in the United States, and businesses were growing at record rates. Internationally, the nation was adding colonies and expanding on several fronts, while at the same time, millions of immigrants wished to move to the States. The U.S. was taking an active leadership role on the international scene, and Fuller did his part to contribute to that role. While still serving as justice, Fuller also served for 10 years (1900–1910) on the Permanent Court of Arbitration at the Hague Court of International Arbitration in the Netherlands, and he also served as an arbitrator in a land dispute between Venezuela and Great Britain.

Fuller's legacy on the court is a long one, as the Fuller court is seen today as the first "modern" Supreme Court. With the rapid industrialization of the United States and the increasing concern with personal liberties, the Court was required to rule on many cases that were unprecedented in U.S. history, and Fuller was able to successfully navigate the difficult waters that those cases presented. He remained active on the court for his entire tenure. On July 4, 1910, he unexpectedly died of heart failure at age 77 while vacationing at his summer home in Sorrento, Maine. ◆

Ginsburg, Ruth Bader

MARCH 15, 1933– ● ASSOCIATE JUSTICE

Ruth Bader Ginsburg

uth Bader Ginsburg was born Joan Ruth Bader on March 15, 1933, in the Bronx borough of New York City. She was the second child born to Nathan and Cecilia Bader, but she was left an only child when her sister died at a young age. The Bader family was a typical, hardworking middle class family, and Ginsburg was raised in a multicultural blue collar neighborhood.

Ginsburg attended public school in New York and succeeded at every level. A popular student who was known for her hard work, through most of her high school years Ginsburg had to contend with the fact that her mother had terminal cancer, a fact she kept hidden from all but her closest friends. Celia Bader died in the spring of 1951, just one day before her daughter graduated sixth in her high school class.

Ginsburg's hard work in school paid off, as she received a full academic scholarship to attend Cornell University in upstate New York. There, she graduated first in her class and decided to attend Harvard

1933 Ginsburg is born in the Bronx, New York City.

1959 Ginsburg graduates first in her class from Columbia University Law School.

1972 Ginsburg becomes the first tenured female professor at the Columbia Law School.

1973 Ginsburg serves as counsel in the first of six cases she will argue in front of the Supreme Court in the next three years for the American Civil Liberties Union.

1981 Ginsburg is appointed judge on the U.S. Circuit Court of Appeals in Washington, D.C.

1993 Ginsburg is appointed an associate justice of the U.S. Supreme Court.

University's law school. However, there was a two-year gap between finishing her undergraduate degree and enrolling at Harvard when Ginsburg moved to Oklahoma to be with her husband Martin, whom she had met at Cornell. Martin, who also attended Harvard Law School, was in his first year there when he was drafted by the U.S. Army and stationed at Fort Sill in Oklahoma. The couple married before they made the move west.

Ginsburg's life was again touched by cancer when Martin came down with testicular cancer while both of them were attending Harvard. He eventually was declared cancer-free after months of difficult treatment. For Ginsburg, the cancer created an almost impossible schedule, as she had to care for her husband as well as the couple's new daughter, attend her own classes, and also attend her husband's classes to take notes for him. Still, she succeeded, earning a spot on the law review at Harvard. After successfully helping Martin graduate from Harvard, Ginsburg transferred to Columbia University Law School when Martin received a high-paying job offer in New York City.

At Columbia, Ginsburg also made the law review, becoming the first woman in the history of Columbia to earn that distinction; she added to her honors by finishing first in her law class in 1959. Upon graduating, Ginsburg ironically had her first brush with the court on which she would later serve. Because of her amazing academic record, Ginsburg should have had her choice of top internships and jobs. Because she was a woman, though, that was not the case. No less than Supreme Court Justice Felix Frankfurter, in fact, passed her over for a clerk position, openly admitting that he simply was not ready to hire a woman. It was that rejection that led Ginsburg to fight so adamantly for feminist issues.

Immediately after graduating, she worked for two years as a law clerk for Judge Edmund Palmieri in the Southern District Court of New York. However, based on her successes in school, it is no surprise that Ginsburg decided to return to the academic environment after she completed her clerkship. She spent a number of years working as a research assistant and teaching, first at Columbia and then at Rutgers University Law School, where she moved in 1963. She was only the second female to teach at Rutgers Law School, and it is estimated that she was one of the first 20 women in the country to teach law at the university level.

During her nine years at Rutgers, during which time she rose to full professor, Ginsburg also became politically and socially active, participating in various feminist projects and actively working with the American Civil Liberties Union. In fact, her support of feminism and free speech came together when she was named to head the national Women's Rights Project for the ACLU. In 1972, she again scored a significant first at Columbia when she became the first female tenured faculty member at the law school.

At Columbia, Ginsburg began to participate in more activities that would propel her to the national stage. More actively involved than ever on women's rights issues, Ginsburg participated on several national commissions around the country and used her great legal mind to provide assistance to those commissions. In her role as general counsel for the ACLU and leader of its Women's Rights Project, she even argued six cases before the Supreme Court between 1973 and 1976; all were groundbreaking cases involving gender discrimination, and she won five of the six. For example, in 1973, she successfully argued against a provision in the Social Security Act that gave male soldiers better housing and medical benefits than it did female soldiers.

One of Ginsburg's main weapons in the legal arena was to attack all laws that favored one sex over another, even if they favored women. One example of this was an Oklahoma law that allowed women to legally drink at age 18, but men not until they turned 21. By successfully fighting to have that law, and others like it, overturned, Ginsburg strengthened her cause by showing that she opposed bias in all its forms, not just those that hindered women.

After a short stay in Stanford, California, where she worked for a research group, Ginsburg was appointed to be a judge on the U.S. Court of Appeals in Washington, D.C., by President Jimmy Carter. Her appointment was supported by the Democratic and Republican parties, both of which thought that her politics favored their side. The Democrats held this belief because of Ginsburg's long history of support for free speech and nondiscrimination, while the Republicans liked her because she followed their belief that judges should simply interpret the law and let Congress and the President create new policies through legislation.

On the Court of Appeals, where Ginsburg served from 1981 until 1993, it was the Republicans who appeared to have

"I pray that I may be all that she would have been had she lived in an age when women could aspire and achieve and daughters are cherished as much as sons."
Ruth Bader Ginsburg, speaking about her mother, *The New York Times*, August 1993

During her tenure on the Court, Ginsburg has been active, rather than passive.

guessed right about Ginsburg. A study completed after Ginsburg was nominated for the Supreme Court showed that Ginsburg could almost have been considered ultra-conservative, as 85 percent of the time she sided with fellow judge Robert Bork, one of the country's leading conservative justices whose own nomination for the Supreme Court had been turned down because he was thought to be too conservative. Only 38 percent of the time did she side with the most liberal judge on the appeals court. Despite that record, even the Democrats admitted that Ginsburg was an excellent judge who was good at building consensus and at drafting well-reasoned opinions.

Her bipartisan support paid off in the biggest way possible in 1993 when President Bill Clinton selected her as his first nominee to the Supreme Court, replacing retiring justice Byron White. Conservatives were overjoyed that Clinton had not nominated an ultra-liberal candidate, while liberals were convinced that she was strong enough to counter the Court's staunchest conservatives, Antonin Scalia and Clarence Thomas. Her confirmation hearings in front of the Senate Judiciary committee went very smoothly and met with a minimal amount of resistance, and she was officially named an associate justice of the Supreme Court. In addition to becoming just the second woman to serve on the court, Ginsburg was also the first Jewish justice since 1969.

During her tenure on the Court, Ginsburg has been active, rather than passive. In her first year, the Tribune News Service reported that "in her rookie year, [she] proved to be anything but a novice. . . ." Some of the cases she asserted herself on during that first term were those involving gender equality, the separation of church and state, workers' rights, and property rights. Just as both sides thought, she was enough of a centrist that neither side seemed to gain an inordinate amount of power based on her rulings, although liberals were a bit disappointed that she did not lean a little further to the left in her decisions.

In 1997, Ginsburg was implicated in a small scandal involving her husband. Journalists revealed that, in 21 separate cases, Ginsburg did not recuse (disqualify) herself from hearing a case even though it involved a company that Martin Ginsburg had a financial stake in through his retirement investment plan. Under a federal statute, judges must formally recuse themselves in such instances; the Ginsburgs answered the charges by saying that they did not realize that Martin's plans even had holdings involving those companies. They then sold off all of the stocks in his retirement plan, choosing to invest in mutual funds and bonds only. Despite the violation, Ginsburg faced no disciplinary action because the statute prohibiting such behavior failed to provide a penalty for Supreme Court justices. Many feel that it may have ended any chance she had to become chief justice in the future, however.

As a justice, Ginsburg has favored moderation, caution, and restraint. By the year 2000, she had been involved in very few cases of historical importance, but that changed drastically by the end of that year. In November, the entire nation was transfixed by the drama that ensued when George W. Bush and Al Gore became tangled in an election controversy in the state of Florida after the presidential election. With the outcome of the presidential race at stake, the Supreme Court was asked to make several rulings regarding the legality of vote recounts in Florida. Ultimately, the Court ruled that additional recounts ordered by the Florida supreme court were above and beyond what the law required, and that Governor George W. Bush won the state of Florida, which put him over the top in the race for the necessary electoral votes for the presidency. ◆

Goldberg, Arthur J.

AUGUST 8, 1908–JANUARY 19, 1990 ● ASSOCIATE JUSTICE

Arthur J. Goldberg, known primarily for his advocacy of individual rights and the rights of workers, was born on August 8, 1908, in Chicago, Illinois. He was the youngest of eight surviving children of Joseph and Rebecca Goldberg, Russian Jews who had immigrated to the United States. Goldberg's early life was one of poverty. His father sold produce to hotels from a cart drawn by a blind horse, and the family moved frequently to escape a month's rent. As a youngster Arthur worked as a delivery boy, a shoe salesman, a fish wrapper, and other jobs to help support the family.

Goldberg's life, though, became a classic "rags-to-riches" story. He completed high school at age 15, then simultaneously attended Crane Junior College and De Paul University in Chicago. He transferred to Northwestern University, where he graduated first in his class with a bachelor's degree in 1929, then a law degree in 1930. After working briefly for a firm that

Arthur J. Goldberg

handled mortgage foreclosures—a job he hated in the early, dark days of the Great Depression—he clerked for a Chicago law firm, then opened his own law practice. One of his first major clients was the American Newspaper Guild, a labor group mired in a strike against the Chicago newspaper owned by publishing magnate William Randolph Hearst. In 1931 Goldberg married Dorothy Kurgans, a painter who later became a well-known name in the women's movement.

In 1936, Goldberg got his first taste of politics, when he worked for the reelection campaign of President Franklin D. Roosevelt. When World War II broke out, he served as a special assistant in the U.S. Office of Strategic Services, the nation's intelligence-gathering agency. Following the war he continued to represent labor clients, including the United Steelworkers of America and the Congress of Industrial Organizations. In 1955 he played a major role in the merger of the CIO and the American Federation of Labor, and he wrote the new organization's constitution.

Goldberg became intimate with the Kennedy family after he cooperated with Robert Kennedy in his 1957 investigation of corrupt labor practices. He was a prominent supporter of labor reform legislation proposed by Senator John F. Kennedy, and he won the support of organized labor for John Kennedy in his 1960 presidential campaign. After winning the presidency, Kennedy naturally turned to Goldberg to fill the post of secretary of labor. In this role Goldberg mediated a number of disputes, including one between Kennedy and the U.S. Steel Corporation over wages and prices. He also developed procedures to deal with labor strikes at missile construction sites, balancing the concerns of labor with those of national security. He worked for an increase in the minimum wage, and he oversaw the reorganization of the Office of Manpower Administration, the agency that supervised employment and job-training programs.

His tenure as labor secretary lasted only 15 months. In August 1962, Supreme Court Justice Felix Frankfurter retired, and Kennedy, wanting to preserve the tradition of the "Jewish seat"—filled by Frankfurter and, before him, Benjamin Cardozo—nominated Goldberg the next day. In September, the Senate unanimously confirmed him by voice vote.

Although Goldberg served only three terms on the Court—rom 1962 to June 1965—he wrote a number of important majority opinions and often provided the important fifth vote for the liberal wing of the Court under the leadership of Chief Justice Earl Warren. He was particularly concerned about individual rights. In an important 1963 case, *Kennedy v. Mendoza-Martinez*, he struck down a section of the immigration law that allowed the government to revoke the citizenship of anyone who left the country to avoid service in the military. In desegregation cases such as *Watson v. City of Memphis* (1965), he made it clear that the Court would brook no delay in the pace of desegregation by communities.

His most notable opinion was in the famous 1964 case, *Escobedo v. Illinois*. Danny Escobedo had been charged with murder. During an **interrogation** in which he made incriminating statements, the police denied his repeated requests to talk to a lawyer, and eventually he was convicted. After the case reached the Supreme Court, a 5–4 majority overturned his conviction on the grounds that Escobedo had been denied his constitutional right to remain silent. Goldberg wrote: "If the exercise of constitutional rights will thwart the effectiveness of a system of law enforcement, then there is something very wrong with that system." The *Escobedo* case became an important precedent in later criminal procedure cases.

In 1965, President Lyndon B. Johnson asked Goldberg to resign from the Court to become the U.S. ambassador to the United Nations. Some observers speculated that Johnson was motivated by his desire to appoint his friend Abe Fortas to the bench. Goldberg accepted the appointment, though with great reluctance, for he found his experience on the Supreme Court richly satisfying—though he once joked that he felt "demoted" from Cabinet secretary to Supreme Court justice because in the latter capacity he had to park his own car.

Goldberg served as U.N. ambassador for three years. In 1967, he helped negotiate a resolution of the Arab-Israeli conflict, and he showed his skill as a negotiator in winning the support of the Soviet ambassador for the peace plan. One of

1908 Goldberg is born in Chicago, Illinois.

1961 Goldberg is appointed secretary of labor in the Kennedy administration.

1962 Goldberg is appointed to the U.S. Supreme Court.

1965 Goldberg resigns from the Supreme Court to become U.S. ambassador.

1990 Goldberg dies.

interrogation: a formal period of questioning under systematic rules.

Goldberg's chief duties was to find a way to resolve the widening war in Vietnam, but this goal remained elusive, and Johnson became increasingly irritated with Goldberg's calls for de-escalation of the war.

After three frustrating years, Goldberg resigned from the U.N. post in 1968 and returned to private law practice in New York City. In 1970, he ran unsuccessfully for governor of New York as a Democrat against Republican Nelson A. Rockefeller. In 1971, he returned to Washington, D.C., to practice law and lecture at local universities. During the 1970s, he was often called on to arbitrate international disputes, and in 1977–78 he was President Jimmy Carter's ambassador-at-large. In 1978 Carter awarded him the Presidential Medal of Freedom.

Goldberg continued to practice law until his death on January 19, 1990. ◆

Gray, Horace

MARCH 24, 1828–SEPTEMBER 15, 1902 ● ASSOCIATE JUSTICE

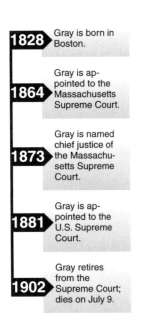

1828 Gray is born in Boston.

1864 Gray is appointed to the Massachusetts Supreme Court.

1873 Gray is named chief justice of the Massachusetts Supreme Court.

1881 Gray is appointed to the U.S. Supreme Court.

1902 Gray retires from the Supreme Court; dies on July 9.

One of New England's foremost intellectuals in the second half of the 19th century, Horace Gray was born on March 24, 1828, to a prominent merchant and shipbuilding family in Boston, Massachusetts. His grandfather had risen from poverty to affluence by developing trade with Russia, China, and India, and he served as the lieutenant governor of Massachusetts for two terms. His father, who built and sustained the family fortune, was Horace Gray, Sr.; his mother, Harriet Upham, the daughter of a U.S. congressman, died when the younger Horace was just six years old.

As a child Gray attended private schools in the Boston area. Because he was so tall—six feet, five inches at age 13—his father insisted that he pursue outdoor activities for his health, and throughout his life Gray enjoyed long walks, hunting, and fishing. Gray graduated from Harvard University in 1845 with an undistinguished record, though he showed some facility for modern languages and, under the influence of naturalist Louis Agassiz, developed an interest in insects and birds. But like many young men of his class, he gave little thought to a profession—until his father's business collapsed and the family lost its entire fortune. Needing a career that would pay him well, Gray returned to Harvard and the law school there, where he threw himself into his studies. After graduating in 1849 he continued to read law and clerked for a law firm until he was admitted to the bar in 1851.

Gray established a private law practice, but it was during this period that he discovered his niche in life—an interest in legal history and historical records. He did some work for Luther S. Cushing, the reporter of decisions for the Massachusetts Supreme Court, and when Cushing became ill, Gray took on more and more of the work until he was officially appointed reporter, a prestigious position at the time. He also continued his legal practice, and between 1854 and 1864 he argued 31 cases before the Massachusetts Supreme Court, winning 24 of them.

Horace Gray

It was Gray's reporting and independent scholarship that began to win him a reputation, however. An opponent of slavery, he wrote a book entitled *Slavery in Massachusetts* that examined the history of slavery in the state. In a lengthy article in the *Monthly Law Review*, he examined in detail the famous *Dred Scott v. Sandford* case that had reached the U.S. Supreme Court in 1857. In these and other works he discovered obscure legal precedents and historical references that bolstered his positions.

In 1864, on the strength of his growing reputation, Gray was appointed to the Massachusetts Supreme Court. In 1873, he was elevated to the position of chief justice, where he remained until 1881. Gray disliked divided courts, which he believed weakened the judiciary and public trust in its decisions, so he worked tirelessly to find common ground with the rest of the court and in 17 years wrote only one dissent among almost 1,400 opinions. In manner he was stiff and formal; on more than one occasion he sent witnesses away with instructions to dress more formally. He brought the same **punctiliousness** to his examination of cases, and not one of his appellate decisions was ever overturned by a higher court. And he continued to rely on precedent. In his first case on the court, he issued a five-page ruling that cited a textbook; eight English cases, some going

punctilious: careful and precise in matters of conventional style or wisdom.

augmented: made greater.

back to the reign of Henry VIII; 26 state cases; one federal case; and 21 statutes, some going back to 1641. The case was a suit to recover a lost cow.

Gray was appointed to the U.S. Supreme Court on December 19, 1881, by President Chester A. Arthur and confirmed the following day in the Senate. His appointment was widely applauded, largely because he had endeavored to avoid political partisanship throughout his life and was not seen as a "crony" of the president. Despite the fact that he wrote more than 450 opinions during his 20 years on the Court, constitutional scholars find it difficult to pinpoint any overriding judicial philosophy that animated his opinions, although he tended to support a strong federal government and protect private property rights. Instead, he continued to function as the Court's scholar and historian, consistently governed by history and precedent.

A good example is provided by *Budd v. New York,* an 1892 case that had to do with the rates companies could charge for grain storage. In his dissent Gray cited a colonial Virginia statute and an act of the British Parliament that were still in effect at the time the constitutions of New York and the United States were written. In another case, the last of three so-called *Legal Tender* cases, he cited cases from the English Court of Chancery and a precedent from the Austro-Hungarian empire to write that the issuance of paper currency was not a judicial question but one that was under the exclusive constitutional authority of the legislative branch.

Gray has been the object of some speculation in connection with *Pollock v. Farmers' Loan & Trust Company,* an 1895 case that would have imposed a 2 percent income tax. Ultimately, the Court ruled the tax unconstitutional, but not before one of the justices changed his vote when the case had to be reheard. For many years it was believed that Justice George Shiras changed his vote, but many scholars make a case that it was Gray.

In his personal life, Gray was widely respected for his intellect **augmented** by an extensive library. He met many of the foremost minds of his time, and was even invited to join the famous Saturday Club, a group of Boston intellectuals and writers that included James Russell Lowell, Henry Wadsworth Longfellow, Ralph Waldo Emerson, Oliver Wendell Holmes, Sr, Nathaniel Hawthorne, and others. Gray remained a bachelor for over 60 years, but in 1889 he met and married Jane Matthews, the young daughter of fellow Supreme Court Justice Stanley Matthews.

Illness forced Gray to miss a good deal of the 1894 Court term. In 1896 his share of the Court's work load began to drop off, but he persisted doggedly until February 3, 1902, when he suffered a stroke. In July of that year he submitted his resignation to President Teddy Roosevelt. He died on September 15 in Nahant, Massachusetts. He was succeeded by Oliver Wendell Holmes, Jr., who coincidentally had succeeded him on the Massachusetts Supreme Court. ◆

Grier, Robert

MARCH 5, 1794–SEPTEMBER 25, 1870 ● ASSOCIATE JUSTICE

Robert Cooper Grier's family was firmly rooted in eastern Pennsylvania. He was born on March 5, 1794, in Cumberland County, near Harrisburg. His father, Isaac Grier, was a Presbyterian minister who supplemented his income with farming and by conducting a grammar school. His mother was Elizabeth Cooper. Shortly after Grier's birth the family moved to Lycoming County; then when he was 12 to Northumberland, where Isaac Grier accepted a post as head of a private school and pastor of three nearby churches.

Grier was educated at home in the classics, and even as an adult he read the Bible in Greek. He was an apt student and was admitted to Dickinson College in 1811 as a junior. After graduating a year later, he remained at Dickinson to teach for a year, then returned home to help his father with the school, Northumberland Academy, where he taught Latin, Greek, mathematics, chemistry, and astronomy. His father died in 1815, and Grier—just 20 years old—was appointed principal.

Grier also began to study law with Charles Hall in nearby Sudbury, and he was admitted to the bar

Robert Grier

1794 Grier is born in Cumberland County, Pennsylvania.

1833 Grier is appointed judge of the District Court of Allegheny County.

1846 Grier is appointed to the U.S. Supreme Court.

1870 Grier resigns from the Court in February; dies later that year.

carpetbagger: derogatory political term applied to individuals who are seen as running for office in an area with which they have little or no association.

treason: the overt act or attempt to overthrow the government of a state to which an individual owes allegiance.

in 1817. He then practiced for a year in Bloomsbury, Pennsylvania, before moving to Danbury, where he practiced for 15 years, and his income enabled him to support his mother and 10 brothers and sisters. His 1829 marriage to Isabella Rose improved Grier's financial position, and eventually he inherited his father-in-law's extensive estate, which he returned to throughout his life to indulge in his favorite pastime, fly fishing.

In 1833, Grier entered public service. The Pennsylvania governor was entangled in a political struggle that led him to offer Grier the judgeship of the District Court of Allegheny County, near Pittsburgh. The governor was fully expecting Grier to decline the position and was both surprised and disappointed when Grier accepted. Grier, a "**carpetbagger**" in the western part of the state, received a cool reception from the governor's supporters when he assumed the post, but in time his competence and disposition won him acceptance from his colleagues. Grier remained a district court judge for 13 years.

In 1844, the "Pennsylvania judge" on the U.S. Supreme Court, Justice Harry Baldwin, died, and for two years President John Tyler's nominees were rejected by the Senate. Tyler's successor in office, James Polk, ran into similar obstacles until he finally offered the seat to Grier in 1846. The Senate confirmed him the next day, largely with the help of supporters from Maryland and Pennsylvania who applauded his position on the issue of slavery.

Defining that position is difficult. On the one hand, Grier was not in favor of slavery. But on the other hand he believed, first, that the Supreme Court was obliged to uphold the laws that then existed with regard to slavery, and, second, that many abolitionists (as well as pro-slavery forces) were too extreme in their views. Thus, when Congress strengthened the fugitive slave laws in 1850, Grier felt obligated to uphold those laws against violent abolitionists who called for massive resistance. In a case that he heard in his capacity as judge on the Pennsylvania circuit in 1851, his instructions to the jury led to an acquittal of blacks and Quakers who had taken up arms against Marylanders who crossed the border into Pennsylvania searching for escaped slaves. The defendants had been charged with **treason**, and although Grier deplored their actions, he told the jury that those actions did not rise to the level of treason. Based on the outcome of this sensational and widely publicized case, prosecutors dropped charges against other defendants.

In the famous *Dred Scott v. Sandford* case of 1857, Grier did not want to confront the constitutional questions the case raised. He was fearful that the Court would divide along sectional lines, and he worried about what he saw as the extreme views of some of the Southern justices. At the urging of President James Buchanan, Grier ruled on the constitutional issues, and he was the only justice from a Northern state who ruled that Scott was not a citizen and therefore could not sue in federal court. He also ruled that the Missouri Compromise, which gave Congress the power to prohibit slavery in new western states, was unconstitutional. His decision drew sharp criticism from abolitionists.

In spite of this decision, Grier vigorously opposed the secession of the Southern states and supported the Union in the Civil War. In 1861, he ruled that rebels were traitors and could not plead that they were citizens acting under the orders of the Confederate States of America. He issued perhaps his most significant ruling in the 1863 *Prize Cases*, which would have a significant bearing on any future president's war-making power. In April 1861, three months before Congress formally declared war on the South, President Abraham Lincoln ordered a blockade of Southern ports. At issue was whether the president had acted illegally, usurping Congress's authority in war-related matters. Grier wrote the opinion for the 5–4 majority, ruling that the president did not need Congress's authority or even a formal declaration of war.

The decision did much to enhance the president's war powers and to limit judicial scrutiny over the president's decisions in wartime. Grier wrote: "A civil war is never solemnly declared; it becomes such by accident. . . . The President was bound to meet it in the shape it presented itself, without waiting for Congress to baptize it with a name; and no name given to it by him could change the fact."

In 1864, rumors began to circulate that Grier was not in good health. Though he quit riding circuit in Pennsylvania, he continued his perfect attendance record at sessions of the Supreme Court until he became partially paralyzed in 1867. Colleagues urged him to step down, but Grier was waiting for a new law to take effect that would provide him with retirement benefits. Finally, Chief Justice Salmon Chase and Associate Justice Samuel Nelson visited him at his daughter's home, where he lived while the Court was in session, urging him to retire. He reluctantly agreed and submitted his resignation in late 1869, to take effect in February 1870. He died in his daughter's home on September 25 of that year. ◆

Grier vigorously opposed the secession of the Southern states and supported the Union in the Civil War.

Harlan, John Marshall

JUNE 1, 1833–OCTOBER 14, 1911 ● ASSOCIATE JUSTICE

J ohn Marshall Harlan's political and judicial views reflected the **schisms** of his native Kentucky, a neutral state in the Civil War. He was a slave owner who fought for the Union, a Republican who opposed Abraham Lincoln, and a foe of the antislavery Thirteenth Amendment who later championed the rights of African Americans during his 34 years on the U.S. Supreme Court.

schisms: divisions between people, groups, or two points of land.

John Marshall Harlan

Harlan's forebears settled in Pennsylvania in the 17th century and later emigrated to Kentucky. His father, James, was a prominent lawyer and Whig politician who served as a U.S. congressman, attorney general of Kentucky, and local U.S. attorney. John was born in Boyle County, Kentucky, on June 1, 1833. He atended Centre College in Danville, Kentucky. After graduating in 1850, he enrolled in the law program at Transylvania University at Lexington, Kentucky. He then continued his legal studies in his father's office in Frankfort and was admitted to the bar in 1853.

In 1858, Harlan was elected to a one-year term as judge of the county

1833   Harlan is born in Boyle County Kentucky.

1853   Harlan is admitted to the Kentucky bar.

1876   Harlan leads the Kentucky delegation at the Republican National Convention.

1877   Harlan becomes associate justice of the United States Supreme Court.

1897   Harlan writes a vigorous dissent in *Plessy v. Ferguson*.

1911   Harlan dies.

exigencies: situations which demand urgent action or a sudden change of previous plans.

court of Franklin County, his last judicial post until his appointment to the U.S. Supreme Court nearly 20 years later. A member of the Know-Nothing Party during the 1850s, Harlan shifted to the Democrats and ran for Congress in 1859 in the Ashland District. After his narrow defeat in that race, he returned to private practice but remained passionately involved in the bitter controversies tearing at Kentucky as the Union lurched toward breakup and civil war. A temperamentally conservative slaveholder, he was opposed to secession but demurred from following other pro-Unionists in supporting Lincoln in the 1860 presidential election.

With the onset of the Civil War, Harlan helped to organize the 10th Kentucky Volunteer Infantry, which he directed in battle as a colonel until 1863, when personal and professional **exigencies** obliged him to resign his commission. He then mounted a successful campaign to become attorney general of Kentucky. Still not reconciled to Lincoln, Harlan supported the presidential bid of General George B. McClellan in 1864 and threw his weight against the proposed federal abolition of slavery as embodied in the Thirteenth Amendment to the Constitution, arguing that it was "a flagrant invasion of the rights of self-government."

After serving out his term in 1867, Harlan resumed his private law practice in Louisville. By 1868 he had made his peace with the Republican Party after grudgingly accepting the "war amendments" as an unavoidable prerequisite for restoring the Union. The conservative Republicans deserted to the Democrats, leaving Harlan in an alliance with the more radical Kentucky Republicans, with whose support he secured the party's 1871 nomination for governor. Although soundly defeated, his campaign helped reconstitute the Republicans as a viable political force. After another unsuccessful gubernatorial campaign in 1875, Harlan led the Republican delegation to the 1876 National Convention, where he ended up supporting Rutherford Hayes, who won the presidency in a bitterly contested election.

In gratitude Hayes offered Harlan an ambassadorship that he declined for professional reasons. He did accept an assignment to serve on a special federal commission to help Louisiana settle a stalemated dispute over the overall structure of the state government. That mission successfully completed, Hayes nominated Harlan to the U.S. Supreme Court. Despite opposition from both Southern conservatives—who doubted his support for states' rights—and Northern Republicans—who recalled his opposition to Lincoln—the nomination was confirmed on November 29, 1877, and he took his seat on December 11, 1877.

In a Court career that spanned more than three decades, Harlan became known as a champion of the rights of blacks and a supporter of federal regulation of big business. He was the sole dissenter from the Court's underminding of the Sherman Antitrust Act in the case of *U.S. v. E.C. Knight* (1894), and he also objected to the majority ruling against the income tax in *Pollack v Farmer's Loan and Trust Co.* (1895). In that case he contended that the Court should apply judicial review sparingly and base its rulings on the Constitution rather than abstract notions of natural law. In *Standard Oil Company of New Jersey, et al., v. United States*, and *United States v. American Tobacco Company* (both 1911), he vigorously decried the Court's **interpolation** of the notion "unreasonable" into the Sherman Antitrust Act's prohibition of restraint of trade, thus inhibiting antitrust enforcement.

Harlan's mistrust of untrammeled free enterprise is evident in his remarks from 1905: "We must have corporations, but we must see that they do not corrupt our government. . . . We have reached that point in the management of politics when educated men . . . [are] willing to receive from officers of corporations money for political purposes. . . ." Yet Harlan tempered his regulatory zeal with frequent opinions defending the rights of private property.

Harlan's most famous dissent, however, concerned not the rights of property but of people. He bitterly denounced the Court's tolerance of racial segregation in its "separate but equal" ruling in *Plessy v. Ferguson*, writing: "Our Constution is color-blind and neither knows nor tolerates classes among citizens."

John Harlan died on October 14, 1911, at the age of 78. ◆

Harlan became known as a champion of the rights of blacks and a supporter of federal regulation of big business.

interpolation: insertion of a word or words into a text which did not previously exist in that text.

Harlan, John Marshall

MAY 20, 1899–DECEMBER 29, 1971 ● ASSOCIATE JUSTICE

When John Marshall Harlan took his seat on the Supreme Court on March 28, 1955, he followed in the footsteps of his grandfather, also an associate justice of the Court, in more than just job description. Both were progressive Republicans who endured difficult confirmations

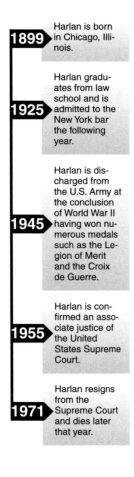

1899 Harlan is born in Chicago, Illinois.

1925 Harlan graduates from law school and is admitted to the New York bar the following year.

1945 Harlan is discharged from the U.S. Army at the conclusion of World War II having won numerous medals such as the Legion of Merit and the Croix de Guerre.

1955 Harlan is confirmed an associate justice of the United States Supreme Court.

1971 Harlan resigns from the Supreme Court and dies later that year.

because of the reservations of both Southern conservatives and Northern liberals. Each confounded expectations, but in the opposite way: the elder Harlan proved more progressive than anticipated, the younger more conservative.

The son of a prominent Chicago attorney and city alderman, John Marshall Harlan was born in Chicago on May 20, 1899. He attended various private schools growing up, first the Appleby School in Oakville, Ontario, Canada, and then the Lake Placid School in New York. He enrolled in Princeton University in 1916, where he achieved good but not outstanding grades while editing the school newspaper and winning election as class president three times. In 1917 and 1918, during World War I, he trained with the Students' Army Training Corps and served as a seaman, second class, with the Great Lakes Naval Training Station.

After graduating from Princeton in 1920, Harlan traveled to Oxford to study as a Rhodes Scholar at Bailliol College, from which he received an M.A. in jurisprudence. He then returned to the United States and enrolled at the New York Law School, from which he received his LL.B. degree in 1924. By the time he was admitted to the bar in 1925, he had already spent two years as an apprentice at the law firm of Root, Clark, Howland, Buckner & Ballantine, where he remained for some three decades, becoming a partner in 1932.

When the firm's leading partner, Emory R. Buckner, became United States Attorney for the Southern District of New York in 1925, he hired Harlan as an assistant, making him chief of the Prohibition unit in 1926. Harlan gained considerable press attention for his prosecution of Earl Carroll, a theatrical producer who had violated the ban on alcohol by throwing a party that featured a naked woman in a champagne-filled bathtub from which guests filled their glasses. He also helped to prosecute a former attorney general, Harry Daugherty, for official improprieties. In 1927, after returning briefly to his law firm, Harlan and Buckner took another two-year leave to become special prosecutors in a corruption probe in the borough of Queens.

After working as a legal consultant in the U.S. War Department in 1942, Harlan joined the army and became chief of operations of the analysis section for the U.S. Army Air Forces Eighth Bomber Command in England, for which he earned the Legion of Merit, the French **Croix de Guerre,** and the Belgian Croix de Guerre. After his discharge from the army in 1945, Harlan spent six years in private practice before returning to

Croix de Guerre: a French military medal for distinguished and gallant action in war.

Miranda v. Arizona (1966)

"You have the right to remain silent. . . ." These words are familiar to any fan of police shows on television. However, prior to the Supreme Court's *Miranda* decision of 1966, people arrested or even merely brought in for questioning by the police were not routinely advised of their rights.

The *Miranda* case was actually only one of several that the Supreme Court heard simultaneously (also heard were *Vignera v. New York*, *Westover v. United States*, and *California v. Stuart*). All the cases involved individuals who had been interrogated by the police (or, in one case, the FBI) and made to sign statements or confessions without being told that they could not be legally required to incriminate themselves, as guaranteed by the Fifth Amendment of the U.S. Constitution. Defending the standard interrogation procedures in use at the time, lawyers argued that the state's need to interrogate witnesses and criminals was paramount, and that since modern interrogation methods did not involve violence, they were not coercive.

Chief Justice Earl Warren, along with Justices Abe Fortas, William O. Douglas, Potter Stewart, William Brennan, and Hugo Black, delivered an opinion that not only challenged standard interrogation procedures, but also set out very specific steps that law enforcement officials must follow when questioning a witness or suspect, including the now familiar "Miranda Warning." They stated that since the possibility of abuse was so great, and the remedy was so simple, there was no excuse for failing to tell suspects or witnesses what their rights were prior to questioning. The Court was split on this issue however. Justices John Harlen, Byron White, and Tom Clark dissented, expressing a grave concern that, by placing restraints on how interrogations could be conducted, the ability of law enforcement to solve crimes or prosecute criminals would be seriously hampered.

public service as the chief counsel of the five-member New York State Crime Commission, investigating gambling and waterfront **racketeering** for two years.

Harlan's success in that assignment brought him to the attention of President Eisenhower, who appointed him to the U.S. Court of Appeals of the Second Circuit, which covers New York, Vermont, and Connecticut. After he took the oath of office in March 1954, Harlan resigned from his law firm. Less than a year later, on November 9, 1954, Eisenhower asked Harlan to fill the Supreme Court vacancy created by the death of Robert Jackson.

Associating Harlan with the anti-segregationist views of his grandfather, Southern conservatives held up his confirmation, hoping thereby to forestall the Warren Court's zeal to overturn the South's segregation laws. Eisenhower had to wait for a new Congress to resubmit the nomination, which still faced protracted hearings in the Senate Judiciary Committee before the full Senate approved it on March 16, 1955.

racketeering: participating in a fraudulent operation the primary purpose of which is to obtain money, usually by intimidation and threat.

It was fitting that among the first arguments Harlan heard on the Court concerned enforcement measures for its historic May 1954 decision to end school desegregation by striking down the "separate but equal" doctrine of *Plessy v. Ferguson*, from which Harlan's grandfather had bitterly dissented. During his quarter century on the Court, Harlan proved himself to be an able, industrious justice who injected a conservative note of caution to the social activism and aggressive federalism typical of the Warren Court. Of the 613 opinions he wrote in his Court career, nearly half—296—were dissents; he wrote only 168 majority opinions.

Some key rulings in which Harlan diverged from the sweeping reforms of the Warren Court were the reapportionment of state legislatures according to the "one man, one vote" rule, striking down the poll tax, requiring police to issue to suspects the now-famous "Miranda" reading of rights to counsel and silence, and the requirement that poor defendants be provided with free legal counsel in appellate actions. He was at one with the Court, however, in its vigorous defense of free speech. In 1971 he wrote the majority opinion upholding a defendant's right to enter a courtroom wearing a jacket bearing an obscenity.

Poor health forced Harlan to resign from the Court on September 23, 1971. He died on December 29 of that year, at the age of 72. ◆

Holmes, Oliver Wendell, Jr.

MARCH 8, 1841–MARCH 6, 1935 ● ASSOCIATE JUSTICE

Oliver Wendell Holmes, Jr., became one of the best-known American associate justices of the United States Supreme Court of the 20th century. In his 30 years on the court, he stood out for his great legal learning, wisdom, wit, and eloquence.

Oliver Wendell Holmes, Jr., was born in Boston, Massachusetts, on March 8, 1841, into a long-distinguished New England family. Descended from the **Puritan** poet Anne Bradstreet, Holmes's father, also named Oliver Wendell Holmes, was a renowned physician and professor at Harvard Medical School. The senior Holmes also became popular as a public speaker and a famous writer. In 1857, he helped launch a new

Puritan: a member of a group of Protestants in England and New England during the sixteenth and seventeenth centuries opposed to the dominance of the Church of England.

magazine, *Atlantic Monthly*, and joined the staff as a columnist. His wise, witty column made both him and the magazine famous. He also wrote poetry and books.

The junior Holmes's mother, Amelia Lee Jackson, was the daughter of a renowned Boston attorney and associate justice of the Supreme Judicial Court of the State of Massachusetts. Holmes had one brother and one sister. During the late 1840s, John Quincy Adams, U.S. President from 1825 to 1829, frequently visited the Holmes house and became a mentor to young Holmes.

Holmes attended a private preparatory school and then followed the family tradition of going to Harvard College. He graduated in 1861, after being elected class poet just as his father had been years earlier. Following his abolitionist beliefs, Holmes served for three years in the Union Army in the American Civil War (1861–1865).

Oliver Wendell Holmes, Jr.

During his Civil War service, Holmes received three serious wounds. He was shot in the chest at the battle of Ball's Bluff, shot in the neck at Antietam, and caught a piece of shrapnel at Fredericksburg that almost destroyed his leg. He attained the rank of lieutenant colonel but resigned as a captain in 1864. In a Memorial Day speech years later, Holmes described the passion of his military experience by saying, "In our youth our hearts were touched with fire." Throughout his life, he remained proud of his contribution to the war.

Homes returned to Boston and entered Harvard Law School in 1864. William James, who became one of the greatest philosophers of the 20th century, was one of Holmes' closest friends, and Holmes considered becoming a philosopher himself. After finishing college in 1866, Holmes toured Europe, meeting a variety of distinguished people. In 1867, Holmes was admitted to the Massachusetts bar and began to practice law in Boston with his brother. Three years later, Holmes became coeditor of the *American Law Review*, also writing articles for the journal.

Although considered a bit of a ladies' man, on June 17, 1872, Holmes married longtime friend, Fanny Bowditch

During his Civil War service, Holmes received three serious wounds.

Schenck v. United States (1919)

During World War I, a man named Schenck, who was the general secretary of the Socialist Party, protested the imposition of the military draft in the United States, calling it a tool of oppression used by the capitalist system. He was arrested for sending out a mass mailing of circulars to men of draft age, encouraging them to refuse induction into military service and suggesting that citizens take peaceful action to protest the draft, such as organizing petitions for the repeal of the Conscription Act. He was convicted of conspiracy to violate the Espionage Act and for obstructing recruitment.

The case was taken up by the Supreme Court, where attorney Henry John Nelson, speaking for Schenck, portrayed the case as a free–speech issue. The government position, however, was that Schenck was guilty of the espionage charge, and that he was also guilty of conspiracy to commit an offense against the United States. It further charged that, by mailing the petitions across state lines, Schenck was guilty of the unlawful use of the mails.

The Supreme Court rejected the free speech defense raised by Schenck's attorney and upheld the lower–court convictions. In justifying its position, the Court specifically stated that times of war allowed greater powers of control over the conduct of its citizenry, and could even infringe upon constitutionally guaranteed rights, stating that "during wartime, utterances tolerable in peacetime can be punished."

Dixwell, daughter of his childhood schoolmaster. Their happy marriage lasted 57 years and produced no children. After his wedding, Holmes set up a lucrative law partnership with two other Boston lawyers.

In the 1880–1881 academic year, Holmes lectured on common law at the prestigious Lowell Institute in Boston. He published his lectures in a collection called *The Common Law* (1881), which became an international classic on the subject. Holmes asserted in his work that the law is always changing and evolving with society's changing needs. His fame led Harvard to give him a position as professor of law in 1882. Holmes resigned his professorship that same year to accept an appointment as associate justice of the Supreme Judicial Court of Massachusetts. He served in that position until 1899 and as chief justice from 1899 until 1902—a total of 20 years of service to that court.

President Theodore Roosevelt appointed Holmes, age 61, an associate justice of the Supreme Court of the United States in 1902. He was to serve as a member of the Supreme Court of the United States for nearly 30 years, until his retirement in 1932. During that period, he made great contributions to the changing concepts of law. His sharp intellect, humor, and ability to express himself influenced American thought. His written opinions showed brilliant legal reasoning.

Roosevelt selected Holmes in hopes that his Republican views would match his own. But Holmes surprised Roosevelt by making many independent decisions. Holmes became known as "the Great Dissenter," as he often disagreed with the rest of the Court. But that nickname also referred to the brilliance of his writings and opinions. Holmes became famous for his liberal interpretations of the U.S. Constitution, taking each case on its own merit, judging each case on facts, and not seeking a specific outcome. Associate Justice Louis D. Brandeis often joined him in his dissents.

One of his most famous dissents occurred in *Lochner v. New York* (1905), in which the Supreme Court upheld the right of employers and employees to create contracts for working hours without government interference. This decision reflected the view that business and industry should be allowed to operate with as little government control as possible. The case involved a New York law limiting bakers to a 60-hour workweek. The U.S. Supreme Court declared the law unconstitutional because it interfered with the "liberty of contract," a vague idea derived from the Fourteenth Amendment to the Constitution. The court said that the law restricted the right of an individual to contract for employment. The court ruling in *Lochner v. New York* was a major setback for the American labor movement. After this ruling, employers were able to use the liberty of contract principle to defeat local minimum-wage laws.

Scholars, though, consider Holmes's opinion in the case the most famous dissent ever given. Holmes wrote in the dissenting opinion: "General propositions do not decide concrete cases." He also said that the ruling was based on "an economic theory which a large part of the country does not entertain." In later years, the *Lochner* ruling was discredited and Holmes' views were embraced.

Holmes became a master of his craft, and in later years, as new judges replaced some of conservatives on the Court, his views became more accepted. By insisting that the Court look at facts in a changing society, instead of hanging on to old formulas, Holmes exercised a deep influence on the law. He influenced judges to keep from allowing their personal opinions to affect their decisions. This doctrine, known as judicial restraint, has since come to dominate American judicial thinking. Holmes' sharp phrases as well as his philosophy caught the public imagination. People understood him because he was "down to earth," and he is equally famous as a philosopher and as a judge.

In the case of *Schenck v. United States* (1919), Holmes agreed with a unanimous Court. During World War I, Charles

1841 Holmes is born in Boston, Massachusetts.

1866 Holmes graduates from Harvard Law School.

1872 Holmes marries Fanny Bowditch Dixwell.

1882 Holmes becomes associate justice of the Supreme Judicial Court of Massachusetts.

1902 Holmes becomes associate justice of the Supreme Court of the United States.

1920 Holmes publishes *Collected Legal Papers*.

1935 Holmes dies.

"The life of the law has not been logic; it has been experience."
Oliver Wendell Holmes, Jr., *The Common Law* (1881)

T. Schenck had produced a pamphlet saying the military draft was illegal. He was convicted under the Espionage Act of attempting to cause insubordination in the military and of obstructing recruiting. In his opinion for the Supreme Court, Holmes rejected the argument that the pamphlet was protected by the First Amendment to the U.S. Constitution. He argued that speech may be suppressed if it creates a "clear and present danger" that it will produce a "substantive evil" that can be prevented. In later Court decisions, the clear and present danger test would be limited to violent actions, and not just promoting ideas. Holmes himself later agreed that the 1919 decision had been abused by the federal government in prosecuting political dissidents.

Holmes' *Collected Legal Papers* was published in 1920 and *The Dissenting Opinions of Mr. Justice Holmes* in 1929.

Holmes almost never missed a session of the Court, and he walked two miles to work every day from his house. He sat on the Supreme Court to an older age than any other person, retiring on January 12, 1932, just before his 91st birthday. In 1933, President-elect Franklin Roosevelt paid retired Holmes a courtesy call and found Holmes reading Plato in Greek. When Roosevelt asked him why, Holmes, then 92 years old, answered, "Why, to improve my mind."

invalidism: a chronic state of suffering from disability or disease.

When his beloved wife Fanny, after many years of **invalidism,** died on April 30, 1929, Holmes wrote to a friend, "For 60 years she made life poetry for me. . . . I shall keep at work and interested while it lasts—though not caring very much for how long." He died two days before his 94th birthday on March 6, 1935, and was buried next to his wife in Arlington National Cemetery. ◆

Hughes, Charles Evans

APRIL 11, 1862–AUGUST 27, 1948 ● CHIEF JUSTICE

Charles Evans Hughes, the 11th chief justice of the United States Supreme Court, was thought by many to have been the greatest chief justice of the United States since John Marshall.

Charles Hughes was born in Glens Falls, New York, on April 11, 1862. Hughes's father, David Charles Hughes, was a Protestant minister from Wales who married Hughes' mother,

Mary Catherine Connelly, a schoolteacher, in 1858. Hughes remained the couple's only child, and they raised him with a strong religious training and hoped he would become a minister.

The young Hughes amazed his teachers and parents at age six, when he convinced his parents that his public school was too boring and that he could do better studying at home. His parents agreed and taught him at home. By age eight, he was studying Greek. When the family moved to New York City, Hughes earned a high school diploma at age 13, ranking second in his class. At Brown University, Hughes began to have some fun, learning to smoke and play cards. However, he still engaged in numerous school activities. Informing his parents that he no longer wished to join the ministry, he went on to Columbia University Law School in New York City. After graduating with highest honors in 1884, Hughes passed the New York bar examination with a score of 99.5. He practiced law in New York City for most of the following 22 years. In 1888, he married Antoinette Carter, daughter of one of his law firm partners. The couple had three daughters and a son who later became solicitor general of the United States.

Charles Evans Hughes

As a member of a major New York City law firm, Hughes gained national attention in 1905, acting as **counsel** for New York legislative committees that investigated the gas industry and the insurance business. His work resulted in a reorganization of the state laws concerning life insurance companies and established his reputation for fearlessness and integrity. His arguments became models for future similar inquiries.

counsel: an attorney engaged in a trial; an attorney hired for the purposes of legal advice to a corporate or public entity.

Hughes's fairness and skill in exposing major scandals led to his election as governor of New York in 1906. With the help of President Theodore Roosevelt, he defeated his Democratic opponent, newspaper publisher William Randolph Hearst. Hughes won a second term in 1908. During his terms in office, he put many political reforms into place, including welfare and

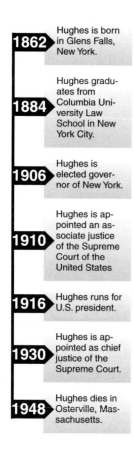

1862 Hughes is born in Glens Falls, New York.

1884 Hughes graduates from Columbia University Law School in New York City.

1906 Hughes is elected governor of New York.

1910 Hughes is appointed an associate justice of the Supreme Court of the United States

1916 Hughes runs for U.S. president.

1930 Hughes is appointed as chief justice of the Supreme Court.

1948 Hughes dies in Osterville, Massachusetts.

labor legislation, and he eliminated a great deal of political corruption.

President William Howard Taft appointed Hughes an associate justice of the Supreme Court of the United States in 1910. He filled the place left by the death of David Brewer. Hughes worked hard for the four years he served, but he resigned in 1916 to run for the presidency as a Republican against President Woodrow Wilson. In one of the nation's closest elections, Hughes lost by 594,188 popular votes and the narrow margin of 23 electoral votes to Wilson. Hughes returned to private practice, and five months later the United States entered World War I.

In 1921, President Warren G. Harding appointed Hughes to be his secretary of state. In the early postwar years, Hughes negotiated a peace treaty with Germany after the Senate had failed to confirm the Treaty of Versailles. He supported U.S. entry into the League of Nations. He planned and then served as chairman of the Washington Disarmament Conference of 1921–22. In 1924, he initiated the Dawes Plan, a program designed to help Germany pay its World War I debts. Charles G. Dawes, a banker who later became vice president of the United States, led the committee that formed the plan.

Hughes remained secretary of state into the administration of President Calvin Coolidge, which began in 1923 and ended in 1929. Hughes then returned to his private practice. In 1928, he was appointed a judge of the International Court of Justice, often called the World Court, the highest judicial agency of the United Nations.

President Herbert Hoover appointed Hughes to the Supreme Court in 1930, this time as chief justice. Hughes was confirmed despite opposition by liberals in the Senate.

History has credited Hughes for guiding the Supreme Court during one of its most turbulent periods, making him one of the country's great chief justices. In many cases involving problems raised by the Great Depression of the 1930s, Hughes favored the exercise of federal power. On February 18, 1935, he delivered three opinions upholding the right of the government to forbid payment of public and private debts in gold. In *Schechter Poultry Corporation v. United States* (1935), however, he spoke for the Court in invalidating the National Industrial Recovery Act, one of the principal New Deal statutes.

During Hughes's early years as chief justice, the Supreme Court held many of President Franklin D. Roosevelt's New Deal laws to be unconstitutional. Following the Great Depression, Roosevelt and the Congress had passed many new laws to put the economy back on track. Sixteen major New Deal laws came before the Supreme Court. The Court ruled that the laws violated the rights of states and of property owners.

In 1937, shortly after his second inauguration, Roosevelt proposed a reorganization of the Supreme Court. Congress approved six of the seven changes recommended by the President. In the seventh, Roosevelt proposed that when a Supreme Court justice reached the age of 70, a younger person should be appointed to sit with the justice on the Court. The total number of justices was not to exceed 15. The seventh proposal provoked many people, who charged that Roosevelt was trying to "pack" the Supreme Court with judges who would always favor the New Deal.

In a letter to the Senate Judiciary Committee, Hughes attacked the plan, and on April 12, 1937, he delivered the opinion in *National Labor Relations Board v. Jones & Laughlin Steel Corporation*, sustaining the right of collective bargaining under the National Labor Relations Act of 1935 (Wagner Act). A few weeks later, the Court upheld various provisions of the Social Security Act. While Congress debated the President's proposal, the Supreme Court approved some legislation considered essential to the New Deal program. For these reasons, the proposal did not pass.

Later, in response to pressure from the executive branch, Hughes led the court in overturning the earlier anti-New Deal rulings and in focusing more on the protection of civil rights and civil liberties. Hughes became well known for his opinions that upheld human liberties.

Hughes retired in 1941 at the age of 79. He died in Osterville, Massachusetts, on August 27, 1948. He wrote *Foreign Relations* (1924), *The Pathway of Peace* (1925), *The Supreme Court of the United States* (1928), and *Pan-American Peace Plans* (1929). ◆

> *"Extraordinary conditions may call for extraordinary remedies. But . . . extraordinary conditions do not create or enlarge constitutional power. The Constitution established a national government with powers deemed to be adequate, as they have proved to be both in war and peace, but these powers of the national government are limited by the constitutional grants."*
>
> from *Schechter Poultry Corporation v. United States*, (1935), opinion of the Court written by Charles Hughes

Hunt, Ward

JUNE 14, 1810–MARCH 24, 1886 ● ASSOCIATE JUSTICE

During his nine-year term on the United States Supreme Court (1873-1882) Ward Hunt was responsible for no landmark opinions or groundbreaking jurisprudence. A stroke prevented him from taking part in the Court's

Ward Hunt

proceedings for the last four years of his term, which he served out only because of financial exigency.

Hunt's North American pedigree extended back to 1650, when his forebear Thomas Hunt arrived in Stamford, Connecticut. The son of a banker, Ward Hunt grew up in secure surroundings in Utica, New York. He was educated at two private schools—Oxford Academy and Geneva Academy. Hunt spent his college years first at Hamilton College and then at Union College, where he obtained his degree in 1828. He then moved to Licthfield, Connecticut, to study law at a private academy run by James Gould. Upon graduating he took a position in the Utica law office of Judge Hiram Denio.

Shortly after his admittance to the bar in 1831, Hunt was obliged to spend several months in the South recuperating from an illness. When he returned to Denio's office, he established a thriving and influential law practice that brought him enough public notice to warrant a run for the New York Assembly in 1838 as a Jacksonian Democrat. He won the election but spent only one term in the state house, during which time he became a prominent opponent of the spread of slavery beyond the South.

Hunt was elected mayor of Utica in 1844, during which time the intensifying controversy over slavery led him to break with the Democratic Party. In 1848 he campaigned for the Free-Soil Party presidential candidate, Martin van Buren. Hunt waged two unsuccessful campaigns for the state supreme court—the second, in 1853, foundering because of lingering Democratic resentment over his defection to the Free Soil ticket five years earlier.

Exasperated by the Democrats' temporizing over slavery, Hunt helped to found the New York State Republican Party in 1856 and was briefly in contention for its nomination for the U.S. Senate the following year. His first successful bid for elective office came in 1865, when he was voted onto the state court of appeals, where he succeeded his former law partner, Judge Denio. After three years Hunt rose to that panel's chief judgeship, retaining the title commissioner of appeals after the state's court system was reorganized in 1869.

In the fall of 1872, when Samuel Nelson announced his intention to resign from the Supreme Court, Senator Roscoe Conkling suggested that Grant appoint Hunt, his friend from Utica, to replace him. The nomination breezed through the U. S. Senate, and Hunt was sworn in on January 9, 1873. Hunt served with competence if not distinction for the next five years, issuing 152 opinions and seven dissents.

Hunt's finest hour was his 1876 dissent from the Court's evisceration of the Enforcement Act of 1870, which protected the rights of black voters under the Fifteenth Amendment. Writing for the majority in *United States v. Reese*, Chief Justice Waite ruled the entire act unconstitutional due to an alleged lack of specificity in penalizing voting-rights violations. Hunt's lone dissent clearly demonstrated the falsity of this claim, which seemed governed less by legal scruple than by political pressure to conform to the spirit of the Compromise of 1877. Hunt argued that the Fifteenth Amendment clearly intended to guarantee citizens the franchise in all state and federal elections as an integral part of the "republican form of government."

Today law students most often encounter Hunt's name in connection with his dissent in *Pennoyer v. Neff* (1877), in which the Court overturned a judgment against an absentee landlord because the state statute governing the case was deemed unconstitutional. Other noteworthy rulings pertain to Hunt's inclination to support state governments' power to regulate their economies. For example, *Munn v. Illinois* allowed the state to limit charges on storage charges in grain silos; and the *Slaughter House Cases* (1873) ratified a monopoly approved by a state government. Hunt also joined the Court in supporting bondholders' rights against states that attempted to renege on obligations, as in *Commissioneres of Johnson City v. Thayer* (1877), *Randolph Cty. v. Post* (1877), and *Burlington Township v. Beasely* (1877).

After suffering a disabling stroke in January 1879, Hunt was no longer able to participate in the Court's work. Because of financial need, however, he retained his seat until 1882, when Congress passed a special act that extended to him the provisions of an 1869 law allowing federal judges to retire at the age

1810   Hunt is born in Utica, New York.

1828   Hunt earns a bachelor's degree from Union College

1831   Hunt is admitted to the New York bar.

1856   Hunt is instrumental in founding the New York Republican Party.

1865   Hunt is elected to the state court of appeals.

1873   Hunt is confirmed an associate justice of the Supreme Court.

1876   Hunt dissents in *United States v. Reese* and argues that all citizens of legal age are entitled to vote.

1882   Hunt resigns his seat on the Supreme Court.

1886   Hunt dies in Washington, D.C.

of 70 with full pay. Since the original law required ten years of service and Hunt had only been on active duty for six years, he incurred stinging criticism from some congressmen for clinging to his office so long while incapacitated.

Ward Hunt died in Washington, D.C., on March 24, 1886. ◆

I

Iredell, James

OCTOBER 5, 1751–OCTOBER 20, 1799 ● ASSOCIATE JUSTICE

James Iredell

A native of England who turned against the British crown, James Iredell emerged as one of the sharpest legal minds of the American movement for independence. He helped to draft the laws of the new state of North Carolina, was a persuasive proponent of the federal Constitution, and was appointed by George Washington to the Supreme Court, where he participated in several significant decisions and dissents over his nine-year term (1790–1799).

The son of a merchant from Bristol, England, James Iredell was born on October 5, 1751, in Lewes, Sussex, England. When he was a young child, his family migrated to Edenton, North Carolina, where James launched his career in public service at the age of 17, accepting the British government's appointment as comptroller of the local custom house. The position afforded him ample spare time for reading and study, and he took up legal studies with Samuel Johnson, the town's most prominent lawyer. A year after completing his legal studies in 1771,

1751 ▶ Iredell is born in Edenton, North Carolina.

1779 ▶ Iredell becomes state attorney general of North Carolina.

1790 ▶ Iredell is appointed to Supreme Court.

1799 ▶ Iredell dies on October 20.

Iredell also took a major role in the debates over the ratification of the proposed federal constitution.

eludicate: to give clarity to an issue or word.

Iredell began to write essays in local newspapers expressing sympathy for the colonists' grievances against the British monarchy. After serving as collector of the local port from 1774 to 1776, Iredell went into private law practice full time. Although he was active in the brewing colonial rebellion, he harbored hopes of a peaceful compromise until just before independence was declared on July 4, 1776.

As a member of a special committee after the outbreak of the Revolutionary War, Iredell helped to draft the legal system of the newly independent state of North Carolina, especially the provisions that re-established the court system. His public service during the war included a six-month stint as a superior court judge (1777–78) and a two-year term as state attorney general (1779–1781), after which he returned to private practice while maintaining a high profile in public affairs.

Iredell wrote the *Instructions to Chowan County Representatives* (1783), which called for adequate, stable salaries for judges, stating that "otherwise they cannot be truly independent, which is a point of the utmost moment in a Republic where the Law is superior to any or all the Individuals, and the Constitution superior even to the Legislature, and of which the Judges are the guardians and protectors."

After the establishment of the new North Carolina state constitution, Iredell became a leading voice among conservatives who sought to strengthen judicial power at the expense of the legislature, a principle he advanced in his arguments in *Bayard v. Singleton* (1787). Iredell won the case in which he had argued against a state statute that permitted confiscation of property without challenge by a jury trial.

Iredell also took a major role in the debates over the ratification of the proposed federal constitution. In 1788 he published, under the pseudonym "Marcus," a tract entitled "Answers to Mr. Mason's Objections to the New Constitution." Serving as the Federalist's floor leader at the convention of 1788, he patiently, paintstakingly **elucidated** and defended key provisions of the nation's new charter, winning over a number of wavering delegates. His publication of the transcripts of those debates is credited with helping to win ratification of the Constitution in 1789.

Iredell's energetic and persuasive arguments for the Constitution brought him to the attention of George Washington, who appointed him to the Supreme Court on February 10, 1790. Iredell proved to be an able and meticulous jurist whose opinions were, as one scholar put it, "lucid, logical, compact, comprehensive." On the Court he became an influential advocate for a strong judiciary. In 1792, for instance, he informed Washington in a letter that he viewed as unconstitutional the Invalid Pensions Act. This recently passed law required federal circuit judges to review the pension claims of Revolutionary War veterans yet subjected their verdicts to the review of the Secretary of War, thus making that office a kind of appellate court and breaching the separation of powers.

Iredell's views on judicial review emerged even more forcefully in *Calder v. Bull* (1798), in which he stated that if any state or federal statute contravened the federal constitution, it was "unquestionably void." He added that "as the authority to declare it void is of a delicate and awful nature, the Court will never resort to that authority, but in a clear and urgent case."

Iredell's most famous opinion was his dissent in *Chisolm v. Georgia* (1793), in which he argued that federal courts should not hear suits brought by citizens of one state against another state. He thus anticipated the key provisions of the Eleventh Amendment to the Constitution, known as the "states' rights" amendment.

In the early days of the Supreme Court, justices were subjected to the grueling demands of circuit riding, which Iredell compared to "the life of a post boy in a circuit of vast extent, under great difficulties of travel and the perils of life in the sickly season." Eventually the rigors of those rounds took their toll on his health, and after less than a decade on the court, Iredell took ill and died at his home in Edenton, North Carolina, on October 20, 1799. He was 48. ◆

Jackson, Howell Edmunds

APRIL 8, 1832–AUGUST 8, 1895 ● ASSOCIATE JUSTICE

Howell Edmunds Jackson's appointment to the Supreme Court in 1893 was the summit of his legal career, but, ironically, it proved to be the place where he had the least impact. Shortly after his confirmation, he contracted tuberculosis, and the resulting debility prevented him from taking part in most of the Court's work. He did manage to summon sufficient strength to cast a dissenting vote in one important case, *Pollock v. Farmer's Loan and Trust Co.* (1895), in which an income tax was held to be unconstitutional.

Jackson was born in Paris, Tennessee, on April 8, 1832, to a distinguished Tennessee family. His father, Dr. Alexander Jackson, a prominent physician, and his mother, Mary, a minister's daughter, were natives of Virginia who had moved to Tennessee in 1830. After taking his undergraduate degree from West Tennessee College in 1849, Jackson pursued further studies at the University of Virginia from 1851 to 1852. He took his law degree in 1856 from Cumberland College in Lebanon, Tennessee and practiced law briefly in Jackson before moving to Memphis in 1858, where he married Sophia Molloy in 1859.

With the Civil War looming, Jackson was true to his Whig lineage in opposing Tennessee's secession from the Union, but during the war he remained loyal to the Confederacy, working for the government as a receiver of stolen property that had been recovered by the state. After the war he returned to his law practice in Memphis but later resettled in Jackson, where, in 1874, he took his second wife, Mary Harding.

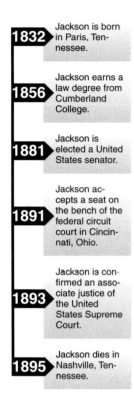

1832 Jackson is born in Paris, Tennessee.

1856 Jackson earns a law degree from Cumberland College.

1881 Jackson is elected a United States senator.

1891 Jackson accepts a seat on the bench of the federal circuit court in Cincinnati, Ohio.

1893 Jackson is confirmed an associate justice of the United States Supreme Court.

1895 Jackson dies in Nashville, Tennessee.

probity: adherence to high ideals and principles.

Although unimposing in stature and demeanor, Jackson won wide respect and important corporate clients with his diligence, wide learning, and unquestioned **probity.** In 1875 he assumed his first judicial post, a seat on the court of arbitration for western Tennessee, a temporary panel set up to address legal conflicts engendered by the Civil War. Jackson was also an activist in the Democratic Party, and his vocal opposition to state debt repudiation helped to lift him to a narrow victory in his first electoral campaign, a race for a seat in the Tennessee House of Representatives in 1880.

It wasn't long before Jackson's political fortunes took a major if unexpected leap forward. Amid harsh partisan bickering, the Tennessee House in 1881 assembled to elect a United States senator, but the vote remained deadlocked after several days. In a dramatic gesture, a Republican legislator rose to put Jackson's name in nomination, and he won the votes of enough lawmakers to break the deadlock.

Jackson's thorough, unassuming style served him well in the Senate, where he steered an independent path that occasionally diverged from the Democratic party line, especially in his speech endorsing the Blair bill on education. Jackson's renown as a legal expert led President Grover Cleveland to offer him a seat in the federal judiciary, sixth circuit, in 1886. Although reluctant to resign from the Senate, Jackson accepted the offer. After serving with distinction for five years, he was appointed the presiding judge of the newly created federal circuit court in Cincinnati, Ohio, in 1891. He established a reputation there as one of the country's ablest circuit jurists.

Nearing the end of his term in 1893, President Benjamin Harrison, a Republican, sought a candidate for a Supreme Court vacancy who would be acceptable to the Democratic-controlled Senate yet independent enough to win confidence in his own party. Howell Jackson seemed the perfect choice, and after his confirmation breezed through the Senate, Jackson took his seat on the high court on March 4, 1893.

In his first year on the bench, Jackson conformed to the Supreme Court's basically conservative bent in key economic and civil rights issues. In *Fong Tue Ting v. United States* (1893), he voted with the majority to deny redress to a Chinese plaintiff denied due process in a deportation proceeding under the Chinese Exclusion Act. The following year he joined David J. Brewer in dissenting from the majority's view that the Constitution permitted state regulation of grain elevators (*Brass v.*

North Dakota). When Tennessee attempted to overrule a prior tax exemption granted in a state charter, Jackson voted with the majority to overrule the measure in *Mobile & Ohio R.R. v. Tennessee* (1894).

The tuberculosis that afflicted him several months into his term limited Jackson's participation in most of the Court's cases in the second half of 1894. In March 1895 the Court was evenly divided on one of its most significant cases, *Pollock v. Farmers' Loan & Trust Company*, also known as The Income Tax Case. Determined to cast his potentially decisive vote, Jackson rallied his strength to hear the lawyers' arguments. In the meantime, one of the other justices had switched sides, and the Court voted 5–4 to invalidate the income tax. Jackson's opinion in the case, his most famous, was his last. A few months later, on August 8, 1895, he died in Nashville at the age of 63. ◆

Jackson, Robert Houghwout

FEBRUARY 13, 1892–OCTOBER 19, 1954 ● ASSOCIATE JUSTICE

A fourth-generation Democrat, Robert Jackson was a self-educated lawyer, the last Supreme Court justice to have learned the law as an apprentice, with no formal degrees from a college or law school. He solidified his reputation in the 1930s as a soldier for Franklin Roosevelt's New Deal, ascending the rungs of the legal establishment in Washington, D.C.—assistant United States attorney general, solicitor general, and attorney general—on his way to the Supreme Court. He was also the chief U.S. prosecutor at the International War Crimes Tribunal in Nuremberg, Germany, where prominent members of Germany's Third Reich were put on trial for the mass murder of European Jews.

Robert Houghwout Jackson's forebears originally settled in Warren County, Pennsylvania, in the 18th century. He was the son of William Eldred Jackson, a horse breeder, and Angelina Houghwout. Shortly after young Robert was born on February 13, 1892, on the Pennsylvania farm that had belonged to his great-grandfather, William Jackson moved his family to Jamestown, New York, to run a livery stable and inn. Robert attended elementary school in Spring Creek and high school in Jamestown. Thinking he might like to practice law in Jackson,

Robert Jackson

New York, he studied briefly—for about a year—at the nearby Albany Law School, after which he returned to Jamestown, where he pursued further private law study before passing his bar exam in 1913.

As he launched his private law practice in Jamestown, Jackson also sought a foothold in state politics, winning election as a Democratic state committeeman at the age of 21. Stung by controversy over his parceling out of patronage jobs, Jackson did not seek another term. He returned to private practice, temporarily swearing off politics, which he felt had "filled my office with people who came there asking political favors and waging political fights."

But it was not long before Jackson answered the siren song of public life again. In 1918 he became Jamestown's corporate counsel, while his array of influential clients helped him to become the vice-president and general counsel of two regional railways and the Jamestown Telephone Company.

Jackson's prominence in upstate legal and corporate circles led Governor Franklin D. Roosevelt (FDR) to appoint him to a government panel investigating the New York State court system. In 1934 FDR, now the president of the United States, again called on Jackson, this time to serve as general counsel for the Bureau of Internal Revenue (as the Internal Revenue Service was called then). Jackson made headlines with his successful tax-evasion prosecution of the Mellon oil and aluminum interests, which yielded the national treasury $750,000 (about $10 million in 1999 dollars) in back taxes and penalties.

Jackson's rise in the political establishment proceeded through the legal departments of the Treasury Department, the Securities and Exchange Commission, and the Department of Justice before Roosevelt appointed him solicitor general (the government's lawyer in cases before the Supreme Court) in 1938. He went on to win 38 of the 44 cases he argued before the

Court, including critical pieces of New Deal legislation involving public utilities, social security and agricultural legislation, and regulation of stock transactions. One reporter at the time called him "the legal **buttress** of the New Deal." He was also one of Roosevelt's closest advisers and confidants, having played an active role in his re-election efforts in 1936 and 1940.

Roosevelt appointed Jackson attorney general in 1940. His major achievements as attorney general included the investigation of subversive activities in the United States without compromising civil liberties and the devising of a legal strategy for aiding the British with 50 U.S. destroyers in exchange for British naval and air bases in the Western Hemisphere. He was also obliged to defend before Congress Roosevelt's unsuccessful scheme for packing the Supreme Court with justices sympathetic to the New Deal.

Although Roosevelt was not able to expand the number of justices on the Court, he did eventually get to put his imprint on it with seven appointments, one of which was Robert Jackson, who took his seat on October 6, 1941. On the high bench Jackson resisted easy ideological classification, tempering his New Deal liberalism with a canny pragmatism. His more liberal side was evident in *Edwards v. California* (1941), in which he joined the majority in overturning as unconstitutional a California law barring impoverished people from entering the state, holding that U.S. citizenship implied freedom of movement.

Jackson's firm belief in the separation of church and state guided what some consider his most famous opinion, which he wrote for the majority in *West Virginia State Board of Education v. Barnette* (1943). Overturning a 1941 Court ruling that permitted a public school to expel Jehovah's Witness students for refusing to salute the American flag, Jackson wrote that "those who begin coercive elimination of dissent soon find themselves exterminating dissenters," thereby achieving "the unanimity of the graveyard." He concluded: "The case is made difficult not because the principles of its decision are obscure but because the flag involved is our own. . . . But freedom to differ is not limited to things that do not matter much. That would be a mere shadow of freedom. The test of its substance is the right to differ as to things that touch the heart of the existing order. If there is any fixed star in our constitutional constellation, it is that no official, high or petty, can prescribe what shall be orthodox in politics, nationalism, religion, or other matters of opinion of force citizens to confess by word or act their faith therein."

1892 Jackson is born in Pennsylvania.

1913 Jackson is admitted to the bar in the state of New York.

1918 Jackson is named the chief counsel for the corporation of Jamestown, New York.

1934 Jackson is named counsel for the Internal Revenue Service by President Franklin Roosevelt.

1938 Jackson is appointed Solicitor General.

1941 Jackson is confirmed an associate justice of the United States Supreme Court.

1954 Jackson dies in Washington, D.C.

buttress: support.

Jackson was a cautious civil libertarian.

Jackson was a cautious civil libertarian. While on circuit he overturned as unconstitutional the revocation of bail pending appeal for a group of communists convicted of conspiracy to propagate and practice the violent overthrow of the U.S. government. He wrote that an infringement of their rights would "cast aside protection for the liberties of more worthy critics who may be in opposition to the Government of some future day." By contrast, in 1951 he joined the majority decision to uphold the convictions of 11 communists for violation of the Smith Act on the grounds that the Communist Party was a "criminal conspiracy that forfeits the constitutional guarantee of free speech."

In Jackson's final years on the Court, illness interfered with his effectiveness, but he made a point of joining his fellow justices at the May 17, 1954, announcement of the unanimous ruling outlawing school desegregation. He died of a heart attack six months later in Washington, D.C. ◆

Jay, John

DECEMBER 12, 1745– MAY 17, 1829 ● CHIEF JUSTICE

diplomat: an individual representing a nation and skilled in negotiation and mediation in foreign affairs on behalf of that nation.

John Jay became the first chief justice of the United States Supreme Court under the new U.S. Constitution. He also served the young nation as a valued **diplomat,** a canny negotiator, and a pioneering jurist.

Jay was born in New York City on December 12, 1745, of a Dutch descended mother, Mary Van Cortlandt Jay, and a French descended father, Peter Jay, a prosperous merchant. Jay grew up on a farm in Rye, New York, the youngest of ten children. At age 14 he entered King's College (now Columbia University), where he graduated with honors in 1764. He then clerked at a New York law office, gained admission to the bar in 1768, and went on to become one of New York's most successful lawyers. In 1774, Jay married Sarah Van Brugh Livingston, the cousin of a former law partner and daughter of a future governor of New Jersey. The couple had six children, two of whom pursued law careers.

When New York elected Jay as their delegate to the First Continental Congress in 1774, he gave up his private practice to serve the newly forming nation. The Continental Congress was a convention of delegates from the American Colonies that met in Philadelphia to unify the colonies. It also became the governing body of the newly forming nation. The first Congress sought fair treatment from Great Britain, but not independence, and set forth a Declaration of Rights, adopted on October 14, 1774. The Second Continental Congress began meeting in Philadelphia on May 10, 1775. The congress organized an army and appointed George Washington as **commander in chief.** With the outbreak of the Revolutionary War in 1775, the Second Continental Congress encouraged the colonies to adopt new republican governments. On July 4, 1776, the Congress approved the Declaration of Independence.

John Jay

commander in chief
(Jay) An individual who holds the supreme command and final authority in an armed force

Jay did not sign the Declaration of Independence, because he was helping to draft the first constitution of New York State. He was then appointed chief justice of the state in 1777.

He left that position to serve on the Second Continental Congress in 1778, and he was president of the Congress from December 1778 until September 1779.

The Second Continental Congress drafted the *Articles of Confederation*, the agreement under which the 13 original states established a federal government in 1781. The states called their confederation the United States of America, continuing the name used in the Declaration of Independence. The Articles of Confederation served as the new nation's charter of government until the first government under the Constitution of the United States was formed in 1789.

In 1779, Jay visited Spain as a U.S. ambassador, seeking that country's support in the War of Independence. He traveled to Paris in 1782 to serve as one of the commissioners who negotiated the Treaty of Paris with Great Britain. This treaty, which ended the Revolutionary War in America, was signed in 1783.

When Jay returned to the United States, he found that Congress had chosen him as secretary of foreign affairs, a position he held from 1784 to 1789. Jay's experiences as a diplomat in Europe

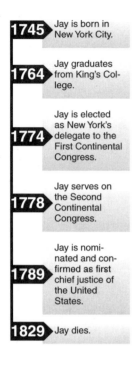

1745 — Jay is born in New York City.

1764 — Jay graduates from King's College.

1774 — Jay is elected as New York's delegate to the First Continental Congress.

1778 — Jay serves on the Second Continental Congress.

1789 — Jay is nominated and confirmed as first chief justice of the United States.

1829 — Jay dies.

convinced him that the Articles of Confederation were not adequate, and that the United States needed a stronger central government. The Articles of Confederation gave independence to the states but provided no way for states to work together.

Leading statesmen had gathered in Philadelphia in 1787 to revise the Articles of Confederation, but they wrote a new plan of government instead—the Constitution of the United States. With Alexander Hamilton and James Madison, Jay wrote a series of 85 letters that were sent to newspapers urging ratification (confirmation) of the U.S. Constitution. The collected essays have become known as "The Federalist Papers" and later appeared in book form as *The Federalist*. The authors pointed to weaknesses in the Articles of Confederation, the dangers of foreign powers, the need of a stronger central government, and the safeguards of the new Constitution.

The Constitution of the United States was ratified in June 1788.

On September 24, 1789, President George Washington nominated 43-year-old Jay as the first chief justice of the United States Supreme Court. Two days later, the Senate confirmed the appointment.

One important case for Jay and for the newly forming nation was *Chisholm v. Georgia* (1793), in which a man from South Carolina sued the state of Georgia over an inheritance. Georgia argued that it could not be sued in federal court, but the Supreme Court under Jay ruled that the state could be sued. The Congress later overturned this ruling with the 11th Amendment to the Constitution, which makes it impossible for a citizen of one state to sue another state in federal court.

An important ruling occurred with *Glass v. The Sloop Betsey* (1794), in which the Court ruled that foreign powers on U.S. soil had no jurisdiction over maritime (sea) law. Jay's opinion in this case set the tone for having other nations respect the sovereignty of the United States.

Jay set an important example for future Supreme Court justices when he declined to advise Secretary of State Thomas Jefferson and Washington on the constitutionality of certain issues. He and the other justices agreed that the high court should not give advisory opinions, but should handle actual legal cases that came before them. This has been the custom of the Court to this day.

In those days, each of the Supreme Court justices was required to travel to areas that needed their judicial services, since there were no circuit courts then. Jay found this twice-annual chore difficult, and he complained of the bad food, loneliness, and uncomfortable inns.

In 1794, the United States came close to war with Great Britain due to controversies over the Treaty of Paris. Although the treaty had ended the Revolutionary War in 1783, neither Britain nor the United States had lived up to the agreement. Washington sent Jay to London to negotiate a settlement of the differences while Jay was still chief justice.

Jay successfully concluded the Treaty of Amity, Commerce, and Navigation with Great Britain. It became known as the Jay Treaty. The negotiators signed the treaty on November 19, 1794, giving the United States control of all military posts on its side of the Great Lakes. It also provided that neutral commissions would decide possession of disputed areas on the Canada-U.S. border, the amount U.S. debtors owed the British, and the amounts Britain owed for losses in the blockade.

The Jay Treaty improved U.S. relations with Britain, and Jay and other members of the Federalist Party called it the best arrangement, considering Britain's superior strength. However, the opposing Democratic-Republican Party insisted that Jay could have won better terms by threatening to cut off trade with the British. The U.S. Senate narrowly passed the treaty, and Washington approved it in August 1795.

On his return to the United States, Jay discovered that during his absence he had been elected governor of New York. He resigned from the Court on June 29, 1795, and served as governor from 1795 to 1801. He spent the remaining 28 years of his life in retirement on his 800–acre estate in Westchester County. Sadly, his wife died in 1802.

Jay spent his later years involved in politics as an advisor. He was an active Episcopalian and helped form the American Bible Society. He died on May 17, 1829. ◆

> *"Nothing is more certain than the indispensable necessity of government, and it is equally undeniable, that whenever and however it is instituted, the people must cede to it some of their natural rights in order to vest it with requisite powers."*
> John Jay, *The Federalist,* 1787–1788

Johnson, Thomas

NOVEMBER 4, 1732–OCTOBER 26, 1819 ● ASSOCIATE JUSTICE

Although he never attained the heroic stature of the chief leaders of the American Revolution, Thomas Johnson played a significant role in the birth and infancy of the

Thomas Johnson

United States. He served as a member of the Continental Congress (1774–1777), as the man who nominated George Washington as commander in chief of the Continental army, as a three-term governor of Maryland (1777–1779), and as an associate justice of the United States Supreme Court (1791–93).

One of 12 children, Johnson was born in Calvert County, Maryland, on November 4, 1732. The descendant of a line of distinguished English Puritans on his mother's side, Johnson was educated at home as a child. While still a young man he moved to Annapolis, Maryland, where he worked as a clerk before studying law with Stephen Bordley. In 1762, after several years in private law practice, he became a delegate to the Provincial Assembly, representing Anne Arundel County.

Thereafter Johnson's political commitments multiplied. In response to the Stamp Act, he served on a committee that sought to advance the colonists' rights against the British Crown. He helped to oversee the building of the Maryland State House and was chosen by the Maryland convention to travel to Philadelphia to represent the state at that year's Continental Congress, where he helped to write a petition of colonial demands to the British government.

Mindful of sectional rivalries, John Adams sought out a Southern representative to nominate George Washington as commander-in-chief of the Continental Army, and the task fell to Johnson, who nominated Washington for the post on June 15, 1775. Johnson then returned to Annapolis to aid in the formation of a local revolutionary government, helping to draft its founding document, the Association of the Freemen of Maryland. He became an eloquent presence in the proceedings of the early Continental Congress, lauded by John Adams as the Maryland delegation's "most frequent speaker."

At first Johnson counseled moderation and conciliation with Britain, but when the Crown's intransigence forced the colonists to declare independence, Adams wrote that Johnson "and all his State came cordially into our system."

Although absent from Philadelphia on the day the Declaration of Independence was signed, Johnson participated, two days later, in the vote for the Declaration of the Delegates of Maryland, which severed the colony's ties to Great Britain. Later that year he was a leading force at Maryland's constitutional convention, helping to draft many of the state charter's key provisions. The following year, as the Maryland militia's brigadier-general, he commanded a march of some 2,000 troops to General Washington's New Jersey command post.

In 1777 the Maryland assembly elected Johnson to the first of three one-year terms as governor of the fledgling state. After his last term as governor, he was elected to the Maryland legislature, where he was an early advocate of the Articles of Confederation. In 1785 Johnson and George Washington became founding board members of the Patowmack Company, which oversaw traffic on the Potomac River. Returning to the Maryland house in 1786, he served two one-year terms before participating in the state convention that approved the U.S. Constitution in 1788.

After a year and a half as chief judge of General Court of Maryland (April 1790 to October 1791), Johnson was nominated to the United States Supreme Court on a temporary commission on August 5, 1791. He had to overcome an initial reluctance to serve because of the requirement that justices ride a circuit, conducting courts in outlying areas. His appointment was confirmed on November 7, 1791, and he ascended to the bench on August 6, 1792.

Although he served only one full term on the nation's high court, Johnson participated in two key decisions. One of these was *Hayburn's Case* (1792), in which he opined that the attorney general had the authority to proceed without the president's permission to move for a mandamus to require a federal circuit court to hear Hayburn's petition (since the Court was evenly divided, the motion was denied). In another case, *Georgia v. Brailsford* (1792), Johnson dissented from a ruling permitting the state of Georgia to sequester money owed to a British subject as a result of a circuit court judgment. Johnson wrote that Georgia's "right to the debt in question . . . may be enforced at common law." Georgia later lost this case when the high court instructed a jury in the case that the peace treaty with Britain

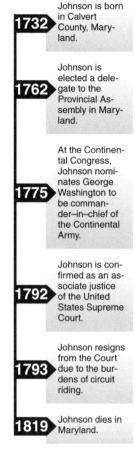

1732 Johnson is born in Calvert County, Maryland.

1762 Johnson is elected a delegate to the Provincial Assembly in Maryland.

1775 At the Continental Congress, Johnson nominates George Washington to be commander–in–chief of the Continental Army.

1792 Johnson is confirmed as an associate justice of the United States Supreme Court.

1793 Johnson resigns from the Court due to the burdens of circuit riding.

1819 Johnson dies in Maryland.

overrode the state's sequestration rights, but by this time, Johnson had left the Court.

Overtaxed by the circuit-riding duties of that era's justices, Johnson resigned from the Court on January 16, 1793. In 1795, burdened by illness, he spurned Washington's offer to become secretary of state. He died in Maryland on October 26, 1819. ◆

Johnson, William

DECEMBER 27, 1771–AUGUST 4, 1834 ● ASSOCIATE JUSTICE

Coming of age during the infancy of the American public, William Johnson exemplified his country's democratic ideal of boundless opportunity for the ambitious common man. The son of a blacksmith, Johnson swiftly climbed the rungs of political power to the House of Representatives and then the Supreme Court, where he became the bench's first great dissenter, a Jeffersonian thorn in the side of the Federalist Chief Justice John Marshall.

William Johnson was born on December 27, 1771, in Charleston, South Carolina. After his father's imprisonment during the Revolutionary War, the family moved to Philadelphia, Pennsylvania. Johnson attended the nearby College of New Jersey (now Princeton University). After graduating in 1790, he returned to South Carolina to study law with the distinguished lawyer and diplomat Charles Pinckney.

Shortly after his admission to the South Carolina bar in 1793, Johnson was elected to the South Carolina House of Representatives, where he remained for the next five years, serving as speaker for the last two. During these years he married into a wealthy family and became a rising star in rarefied social and political circles, cultivating a close relationship with his political mentor, Thomas Jefferson.

In 1799 Johnson was appointed to what was then South Carolina's highest court, the Court of Common Pleas. During his five years in that post he became a cofounder of a college in Columbia that later evolved into the University of South Carolina.

In 1804 Jefferson appointed Johnson to the Supreme Court, and his nomination breezed through the Senate in just two days. As the first Jeffersonian on the Court, Johnson often found himself at odds with the daunting paternalism of Chief Justice John Marshall, a Federalist whose conception of the national interest included pressing for unanimity and discouraging the publication of dissents where there was disagreement. Johnson, on the other hand, was steeped in the South Carolina high court's practice of publishing separate opinions, and he did not hesitate to introduce this custom into the nation's highest tribunal.

He nonetheless managed to stake out a middle ground of cooperation. As Johnson wrote in a letter in 1822, "I found that I must either submit to circumstances or become such a cypher . . . as to effect no good at all. I therefore bent to the current."

In balancing his Jeffersonian convictions with his judicial duties, Johnson often confounded Jefferson's expectations. In 1807, for example, he cited Marshall's opinion in *Marbury v. Madison* in dissenting from the Court's granting of a writ of mandamus (a command from a higher court to a lower one) in the treason proceedings against Aaron Burr. In 1808 Johnson, while touring the Southern circuit, ruled against the Republican-approved policy that allowed the detention of a sailing vessel (*Gilchrist v. Collector*), arguing that the federal executive was not empowered to restrain commerce and thus "individual liberty." This decision earned Johnson denunciation by Attorney General Caesar Rodney as a traitor to Jeffersonian principles.

But over the long term Johnson proved no more pliant to the Federalists' wishes than to the Jeffersonians' as evidenced by the hearty animosity between Johnson and Joseph Story, a staunch Marshallian. Fearing an unchecked federal power, Johnson consistently voted to assign authority over criminal law to the states, as in *United States v. Hudson and Goodwin* (1812). Equally suspicious of concentrated economic power, Johnson also opposed efforts by corporations to attain legal recognition as "persons," as in his 1808 ruling in *United States v. Deveaux* that corporate banks had no right to file suit in federal courts. Although he championed creative capitalism on the local and state level, he maintained a steadfast vigilance against the potential tyranny of centralized governmental or economic authority.

Johnson countenanced federal authority chiefly as a means of encouraging state and local power, free trade, and the building or roads and waterways to foster economic growth. Thus, Johnson supported Marshall's assertion, in *Gibbons v. Ogden* (1824), of the unconstitutionality of New York State's grant of

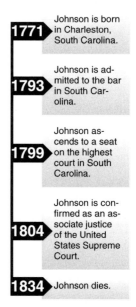

1771 Johnson is born in Charleston, South Carolina.

1793 Johnson is admitted to the bar in South Carolina.

1799 Johnson ascends to a seat on the highest court in South Carolina.

1804 Johnson is confirmed as an associate justice of the United States Supreme Court.

1834 Johnson dies.

In balancing his Jeffersonian convictions with his judicial duties, Johnson often confounded Jefferson's expectations.

a navigation monopoly on the Hudson River to the Fulton-Livingston company. Johnson wrote: "The power of a sovereign state over commerce . . . must be exclusive. . . . The grant of this power carries with it the whole subject, leaving nothing of the state to act upon."

A slaveholder who yet advocated the humane treatment of slaves, Johnson had a decidedly mixed record in ruling on the peculiar institution. In *Elkison v. Deliesseline*, Johnson overturned a South Carolina law banning black seamen from several ports, including Charleston. In 1832 he roused the wrath of many of his fellow South Carolinians by denying the constitutionality of state nullification of federal law in *Holmes v. United States*.

William Johnson served on the Supreme Court for three decades, until his death on August 4, 1834, at the age of 62. ◆

Kennedy, Anthony M.

JULY 23, 1936– ● ASSOCIATE JUSTICE

Anthony M. Kennedy

Anthony McLeod Kennedy was born July 23, 1936, in Sacramento, California, into an Irish Roman Catholic family of which he was the second of three children. Kennedy's father, Anthony J. Kennedy, had worked his way through law school as a dockworker. He became a successful lawyer with a well-established law practice. He also worked as a lobbyist for various businesses, developing a reputation for influence in the California legislature. Kennedy's mother, Gladys McLeod Kennedy, graduated from Stanford University, near San Francisco, in 1928. She taught school, then became a secretary in the California Senate, where she met her husband. After the couple married in 1932, she went on to become a leader in Sacramento civic activities.

While Kennedy attended a Sacramento high school, he met such high-level people as the future Supreme Court justice Earl Warren through working in his father's office and in senate offices. Kennedy graduated from Stanford in 1958, after earning a Phi Beta Kappa key

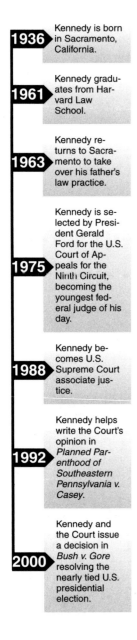

1936 Kennedy is born in Sacramento, California.

1961 Kennedy graduates from Harvard Law School.

1963 Kennedy returns to Sacramento to take over his father's law practice.

1975 Kennedy is selected by President Gerald Ford for the U.S. Court of Appeals for the Ninth Circuit, becoming the youngest federal judge of his day.

1988 Kennedy becomes U.S. Supreme Court associate justice.

1992 Kennedy helps write the Court's opinion in *Planned Parenthood of Southeastern Pennsylvania v. Casey.*

2000 Kennedy and the Court issue a decision in *Bush v. Gore* resolving the nearly tied U.S. presidential election.

cum laude: to graduate from a higher educational institution with distinction.

and spending his senior year at the London School of Economics. After Stanford, Kennedy enrolled in Harvard Law School, where he graduated **cum laude** in 1961.

Kennedy returned to California, began working as an associate for a law firm in San Francisco, and was called to the bar in 1962. When his father died suddenly in 1963, Kennedy returned to Sacramento to take over his father's practice. That same year, he married longtime acquaintance Mary Davis, who had earned a master's degree in education from Stanford. She worked as a teacher and librarian for many years. The couple would have three children, Justin Anthony, Gregory Davis, and Kristin Marie, each of whom attended Stanford.

Kennedy practiced law in Sacramento until 1975. For 22 years, he also taught constitutional law part time at the McGeorge School of Law, University of the Pacific. Although Kennedy lacked experience as a lawyer at first, many of his father's important clients stayed with him out of respect for his father. Kennedy's clients soon discovered their new lawyer to have just as much, if not more, legal skills than his father. Kennedy had a talent for socializing and soon made many friends among influential Californian politicians. He often entertained clients and guests at lavish parties and exclusive restaurants. Kennedy also donated large sums of money on behalf of himself and his clients to various political officials in the state.

Through his work as a lobbyist, Kennedy befriended Edwin P. Meese, III, who represented the California District Attorney Association at that time. The two became close friends. After Meese began working for California Governor Ronald Reagan in 1966, Kennedy kept in touch with him, and Kennedy helped Meese and Reagan in various ways.

In 1973, Meese recruited Kennedy to help Reagan draft a plan to cut taxes and government spending. They drafted Proposition 1, a ballot initiative to limit the state's spending. Kennedy campaigned throughout the state to push for passage of the proposal, and his efforts won him Reagan's favor. Despite the initiative's failure, Reagan rewarded Kennedy for his work by recommending him to President Gerald Ford for a vacancy on the U.S. Court of Appeals for the Ninth Circuit. In 1975, President Ford appointed Kennedy to the position. Close to 40, Kennedy was the youngest federal judge of his day.

As the Ninth Circuit Court filled with liberal judges, Kennedy soon headed up the Court's conservative minority.

Kennedy's careful case-by-case approach, though, won him the support of many colleagues, and even his opponents could admire his thoughtful opinions.

When U.S. Supreme Court Justice Lewis Powell, Jr., retired in 1987, President Reagan put his old associate Kennedy on a short list of candidates to replace Powell. Reagan nominated conservative Judge Robert H. Bork first, but the Senate fiercely opposed him because of his outspoken conservative views on constitutional law. Bork was not confirmed. Reagan then turned to Douglas Ginsburg, a judge from the U.S. Court of Appeals in the District of Columbia Circuit. Ginsburg, however, soon withdrew himself from consideration when news leaked of his possible past marijuana use. On the advice of Meese, Reagan turned to Kennedy to fill the Supreme Court vacancy.

Few people resisted Kennedy's nomination, as even liberals considered him fair-minded. The Senate unanimously confirmed Kennedy on February 3, 1988, and he took the oath of office a few days later.

Kennedy's experience as a federal judge allowed him to move quickly and easily into his Supreme Court role. In his first term, he proved to be markedly conservative, voting with hardline conservatives Chief Justice William H. Rehnquist and Antonin Scalia more than 90 percent of the time. He upheld the constitutionality of testing employees for drugs in *Skinner v. Railway Labor Executives Association* (1989) and in *National Treasury Employees Union v. Von Raab* (1989). In subsequent years, Kennedy continued to vote conservatively in cases seeking to abolish affirmative action, abortion rights, and other liberal policies. He also remained conservative on crime issues.

However, in his years as a lobbyist, Kennedy had learned to use his personality to win over allies and form unlikely coalitions. This skill helped Kennedy as he became key to building coalitions on the Court. Rehnquist often relied on Kennedy to build bridges between the Court's conservatives and liberals. Kennedy became an important axis on which close decisions turned, and he later moved into the Court's growing centrist bloc. In 1992, Kennedy joined Sandra Day O'Connor and David Souter to write the Court's opinion upholding abortion rights in *Planned Parenthood of Southeastern Pennsylvania v. Casey.* An opinion is the essay explaining the logic and principles underlying a ruling.

Kennedy and associate justice O'Connor became known as the "swing votes" on the Court. They were the moderates—not

"To protect the central right recognized by Roe [v. Wade] *while at the same time accommodating the State's profound interest in potential life . . . the undue burden standard should be employed. An undue burden exists, and therefore [such a] law is invalid, if its purpose or effect is to place substantial obstacles in the path of a woman seeking an abortion."*

Planned Parenthood
of Southeastern
Pennsylvania v.
Casey (1992)

Kennedy is generally considered an advocate of judicial restraint.

too conservative and not actually liberal—whose votes could swing a Court decision either way. Thus, many Court decisions hinged on one vote, with 5–4 rulings.

The U.S. presidential elections of November 2000 drew the Court into a case unlike any it had dealt with in the past. In the nearly tied contest between Vice President Al Gore and Texas Governor George W. Bush, the state of Florida became the final battleground, as numerous disputes arose over how votes were counted. In one case, the Florida Supreme Court ruled that Florida's Secretary of State had set an unreasonable deadline for counties to turn in their vote tallies. According to the decision, her deadline had prevented many votes from being recounted, allowing Bush to keep his slim lead.

On December 4 the Court issued an unusual unsigned decision that sent the matter back to the Florida Supreme Court "for further consideration." By doing this, the Court declined to decide the merits of the case, saying they found "considerable uncertainty" in the Florida court's decision. Court observers commented that the nation's highest court had managed to save its image as a nonpartisan body by not siding with either political candidate.

Kennedy is generally considered an advocate of judicial restraint. Judicial restraint is the doctrine advocating that judges should keep from allowing their personal opinions to affect their decisions. Kennedy did not advocate Court interference with legislative policy unless that policy was clearly unconstitutional.

The modest and friendly Kennedy won the respect and admiration of his colleagues over the years. Kennedy's consistency and competence earned him a reputation for reliability among his peers. Colleagues admired his hard work and loyalty. His staff found him easy to approach, and he took them to such events as Shakespeare plays. Kennedy was an avid reader, enjoying history and English literature especially. He also enjoyed sports such as tennis, golf, swimming, jogging, and bicycling. He remained a devoted Roman Catholic. ◆

Lamar, Joseph R.

OCTOBER 14, 1857–JANUARY 2, 1916 ● ASSOCIATE JUSTICE

A product of the political aristocracy of the South, Joseph Lamar progressed to the U.S. Supreme Court along ground broken by his distinguished forebears, who included Merabeau Lamar, president of the Republic of Texas, and Lucius Quintus Cincinnatus Lamar, a Supreme Court justice.

Lamar's father trained to enter the bar but became a minister instead. His mother, Mary Rucker, descended from one of Georgia's most influential planter families. Joseph spent his early childhood on the family plantation, but at seven years of age, after the death of his mother, he moved to Augusta, where his father led a congregation of the Disciples of Christ. He attended school at Joseph T. Derry's academy and at the Martin Institute in Jefferson, Georgia. He later enrolled at the University of Georgia, where he remained briefly before transferring to Bethany College in West Virginia.

After graduating from Bethany in 1877, Lamar attended the law school of Washington and Lee University, where he completed his two-year curriculum in only one year. He then apprenticed in the law office of Henry Clay Foster in Augusta, gaining admission to the Georgia bar in 1878. After a year back in Bethany, where he taught Latin and married Clarinda Huntington Pendleton, Lamar returned to Augusta, where he formed a partnership with Foster that became one of Georgia's most successful corporate law firms.

Lamar complemented his private practice with public service, serving two terms in the Georgia state legislature (1886–1887, 1888–1889) and applying himself to scholarly

1857 Lamar is born.

1878 Lamar graduates from law school and is admitted to the Georgia bar.

1896 Lamar is part of a commission that recodifies Georgia law.

1903 Lamar is named to the Georgia supreme court.

1911 Lamar is confirmed an associate justice of the United States Supreme Court.

1916 Lamar dies in Washington, D.C.

meticulous: careful and precise.

research and writing on the history of Georgian jurisprudence. His expertise led to his appointment, in 1893, to a three-man commission charged with the recodification of Georgia's civil code. Lamar's three-year effort yielded the two-volume *Code of the State of Georgia* (1896), which garnered wide praise and led to his appointment to the Supreme Court of Georgia in 1903.

After a two-year stint on Georgia's high bench, Lamar returned to private practice in Augusta, where he soon became involved in a landmark case that led him to argue before the United States Supreme Court. In *Central of Georgia Railway Company v. Wright, Comptroller-General of Georgia*, Lamar persuaded the nation's high court that Georgia's statutory scheme for assessing the taxable value of railroad property violated the Constitution's due process provisions. Legal scholars still commend his argument before the Court as a model of **meticulous** legal scholarship and cogent reasoning.

When William H. Moody retired from the Supreme Court in 1910, President William Howard Taft nominated Lamar to succeed him. He was confirmed without opposition by the Senate and took his seat on January 3, 1911. During his five years on the Court, Lamar wrote 113 majority opinions that are esteemed for their lucidity and concision.

Lamar's economic conservatism on the Court is evident in a number of key cases. In *Gompers v. Bucks Stove & Range* (1911), he upheld the constitutionality of an antitrust regulation that barred the American Federation of Labor from pursuing a secondary boycott by publishing lists of companies it deemed unfair or unworthy of patronage. *Smith v. Texas* (1914), overturned a state law requiring railroad conductors to have previous experience on the grounds that it violated freedom of contract. In *Kansas City Southern Railway v. Anderson* (1914), Lamar dissented from the Court's upholding of damages for a plaintiff whose cows were killed by a train. *German Alliance Insurance Co. v. Luis* (1914) also found Lamar dissenting from the Court's defense of state regulation of insurance rates.

Lamar seemed more receptive to federal than to state regulation of economic activity. In *United States v. Grimaud* (1911), he upheld Congress's ability to grant expanded oversight to regulatory agencies. He also joined the majority in putting more teeth into the Pure Food and Drug Act through the *Hipolite Egg Company Case* (1911) and the Interstate Commerce Commission through the *Minnesota Rate Cases* (1913).

Lamar was not consistent in his decisions on civil rights cases. In *McCabe v. Atchison, Topeka & Santa Fe Railway Co.* (1914), he upheld an Oklahoma law mandating separate cars for black passengers. By contrast, he joined the majority in overturning such civil rights violations as Alabama's peonage law in *Bailey v. Alabama* (1911), a discriminatory tax on Chinese laundries (*Ouong King v. Kirkendall*), and a withdrawal of tax-exempt status for Indian lands in Oklahoma in *Choate v. Trapp* (1912).

In 1914 President Wilson dispatched Lamar to Canada as a U.S. envoy to negotiations among several Latin American nations over the disputed presidency of Mexico. The following year Wilson named Lamar a delegate to the Pan American Conference in Chile, but illness prevented him from attending. Despite visits to various spas to treat his ailments, Lamar's health continued to deteriorate, and he died in Washington, D.C., on January 2, 1916, one day shy of his fifth anniversary on the Supreme Court. ◆

Lamar was not consistent in his decisions on civil rights cases.

Lamar, Lucius Q. C.

SEPTEMBER 17, 1825–JANUARY 23, 1893 ● ASSOCIATE JUSTICE

Ascion of the antebellum Southern aristocracy, Lucius Lamar loyally fought for the Confederacy but later proved a moderating, conciliatory influence as a postwar congressman and senator from Mississippi. His eloquent statesmanship at a time of national trauma won him high regard among his colleagues, including Grover Cleveland, who appointed him secretary of the interior and later an associate justice of the Supreme Court. As a member of the high court, he recorded important opinions on interstate commerce, the separation of powers, and states' rights.

Lucius Quintus Cincinnatus Lamar's ancestors were French Huguenots who had emigrated to Maryland in the 17th century and later settled in Georgia, where Lucius was educated in the finest schools of Baldwin and Newton Counties. He attended Emory College in Oxford, Georgia, and, after graduating in 1845, he studied law privately with a relative, Absalom Chappell, in Macon, Georgia, for two years. He was admitted to the

Lucius Q.C. Lamar

bar in 1847, the same year he married Virginia Longstreet, the daughter of the president of Emory. In 1849, Lamar and his wife moved to Oxford, Mississippi, where Virginia's father had just been made president of the state university. He launched a law practice there while teaching mathematics at the university and dabbling in politics.

In 1852 Lamar returned to Newton County, Georgia, where he became a member of the county legislature the following year. He then moved to Macon for a year before returning to Oxford, where he plunged in earnest into public life. In 1857 he won election to the United States Congress for the first of two terms. Faced with the growing secession crisis, he was torn between his loyalties to the Union and to his region. At the Charleston Democratic Convention in 1860, he voted against secession, but when the die was cast with Lincoln's election, he resigned from Congress and joined the Confederate cause.

During the Civil War Lamar led the 19th Mississippi Regiment as a lieutenant-colonel until ill health led forced him to resign from the army in October 1862. The next month he left for Europe, assigned to serve as the Confederate commissioner to Russia, but he got only as far as London and Paris, since the Russian government never accorded diplomatic recognition to the rebel regime. Arriving back in Virginia in 1864, he served as a judge-advocate there until the end of the war, when he returned to Oxford to teach metaphysics and law at the University of Mississippi.

In 1872 Lamar was again elected to Congress, where he won wide respect as a healer of sectional bitterness, especially after his moving eulogy for Charles Sumner in April 1874. He furthered the cause of national reconciliation by supporting the Hayes-Tilden compromise of 1876. Having emerged as Mississipi's leading national political figure, Lamar was elected to the U.S. Senate in 1876, where his statesmanship and eloquence soon made him a leading force, especially in resolving such contentious policy debates as the tariff question and the free coinage of silver.

When the Democrat Grover Cleveland became president in 1885, he appointed Lamar secretary of the interior, a post he accepted, as he put it in a letter at the time, to "impress the country with a desire of the South faithfully to serve the interests of a common country." Two years later, on December 6, 1887, President Cleveland nominated Lamar, then 62, to a seat on the Supreme Court after the death of Justice Woods. Lamar's age and former Confederate loyalties stirred some controversy in the Senate, but the appointment was confirmed 32–28 on January 16, 1888.

During Lamar's five years on the Court, he was scrupulous in his devotion to the separation of powers. In the case *In re Neagle* (1890), for example, his dissent opposed the Court's liberal interpretation of of executive power. His dissent from the majority's opinion in *Chicago, Milwaukee, and St. Paul Railway Company v. Minnesota* (1890), in which the Court deemed unconstitutional Minnesota's powerful state railroad commission, was typical of Lamar's support for states' rights. Chief Justice Fuller appraised Lamar's work on the Court this way: "He rendered few decisions, but was invaluable in consultation. His was the most suggestive mind that I ever knew, and not one of us but has drawn from its inexhaustible store."

Lamar died in Vineland, Georgia, on January 23, 1893. ◆

1825	Lamar is born.
1847	Lamar is admitted to the bar in Georgia.
1857	Lamar is elected as a member of the U.S. Congress from Georgia.
1860	Lamar resigns from Congress to serve in the Confederate army.
1872	Lamar is again elected to the U.S. Congress.
1888	Lamar is confirmed an associate justice of the U.S. Supreme Court.
1893	Lamar dies in Vineland, Georgia.

Livingston, Henry Brockholst

NOVEMBER 25, 1757–MARCH 18, 1823 ● ASSOCIATE JUSTICE

In a time when distinguished birth was a prerequisite to high political office in the United States, Henry Brockholst Livingston began life with an excellent résumé. His father, William Livingston, a governor of New Jersey, and his mother, Susannah French, both came from wealthy and powerful families. Young Henry was a 1774 graduate the College of New Jersey (the precursor of Princeton University), where he was a classmate of James Madison.

With the onset of the Revolutionary War, Livingston enlisted in the Continental Army, serving with distinction in a

Henry Livingston

succession of roles. He was an aide to General Philip Schuyler and then to General St. Clair, a soldier in the siege of Ticonderoga, and an assistant to Benedict Arnold, under whose command he fought in the Saratoga campaign and witnessed the surrender of General Burgoyne.

After a brief additional tour of duty with Schuyler, Livingston returned to civilian life to accompany his brother-in-law, John Jay, on a diplomatic mission to seek aid from Spain in 1779. While sailing back to American three years later, he was captured on the high seas by the British and then briefly held as a prisoner in New York City. He then moved to Albany to study law under Peter Yates and, after gaining admission to the bar in 1783, he moved to New York City to establish a private practice.

While prospering as a New York attorney, Livingston took a lively interest in politics, gaining a seat in the New York Assembly. Even though he had favored ratification of the Constitution and had admired Alexander Hamiltion, Livingston evolved into such an ardent anti-Federalist and pro-Jeffersonian that he took part in a demonstration against the Jay treaty at which an effigy of his eminent brother–in–law was set aflame.

In 1802, after a decade of political activism, Livingston was appointed to the Supreme Court of New York, where James Kent was one of his fellow jurists. Jefferson considered him for a Supreme Court appointment in 1804, but passed him over in favor of William Johnson. Two years later, however, another vacancy arose with the death of Justice William Patterson, and this time Jefferson rewarded Livingston's loyalty with an appointment to the nation's highest court.

Jefferson pinned great hopes on Livingston as a counterbalance to the Federalist leanings of the Court, but after taking his seat on February 2, 1807, Livingston seemed to bend to the

Court's prevailing winds, obliging John Marshall's discouragement of strong dissent from key rulings, which the chief justice usually wrote himself. It was a practice that makes it hard to discern distinctive views among individual justices of that era. Hence, during his 17 years on the bench, Livingston wrote only eight dissents and only 38 majority opinions, none of which were landmark cases. In 1817, for example, he voiced strong support for the retroactive applicability of state bankruptcy statutes but failed to dissent from a ruling in 1819 (*Dartmouth College v. Woodward*) that held such provisions to be a breach of the Constitution's contract provisions.

Most of the rulings penned by Livingston concerned the maritime and commercial law issues in which his background was strongest. In most such cases Livingston again conformed to Marshall's Federalist bent by siding with creditors. In *Lennox v. Prout* (1813), for instance, Livingston ruled that if someone defaulted on a promissory note, the endorser could not claim the protection of an equity court but was subject, along with the maker of the note, to legal action by the claimant. He took a similar view in *Dugan v. United States* (1818), in which he ruled that that the federal government had the right to seek damages for what it deemed to be failure to perform parts of a contract agreement. According to Livingston, "It would be strange to deny to them [the federal government] a right which is secured to every citizen of the United States."

Livingston's most important maritime case was *United States v. Smith* (1820). The case asked the Court to judge the extent of Congress's purview in a federal anti-piracy law it had passed specifically in relation to the criminal conviction of American citizens for raiding and plundering a Spanish ship in international waters. In a rare departure from the majority's opinion, Livingston argued that the vagueness of the law's definition of piracy demanded the overturning of the conviction.

Although Livingston's written record as an associate justice bespeaks no great distinction in style or substance, he was highly regarded by his fellow jurists. Justice Joseph Story characterized Livingston as "a very able and independent judge," whom he found to be "luminous, decisive, earnest, and impressive on the bench."

Henry Livingston died in Washington, D.C., on March 18, 1823, at the age of 65. ◆

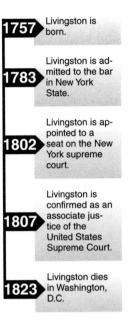

1757 Livingston is born.

1783 Livingston is admitted to the bar in New York State.

1802 Livingston is appointed to a seat on the New York supreme court.

1807 Livingston is confirmed as an associate justice of the United States Supreme Court.

1823 Livingston dies in Washington, D.C.

Lurton, Horace

FEBRUARY 26, 1844–JULY 12, 1914 ● ASSOCIATE JUSTICE

Horace Lurton's appointment to the Supreme Court in 1910 was distinctive in more than one respect: he was one of the last Civil War veterans to serve on the Court and, at 66 years old, the oldest appointee up to that time. As a Southern Democrat, his appointment to the bench by the Republican William Howard Taft surprised many observers when it was made. But it was a canny choice—both parties united behind his candidacy, and Lurton's deeply conservative outlook dovetailed with Taft's pro-business agenda.

Horace Lurton was the son of Sarah Ann Harmon and Lycurgus L. Lurton, a physician-turned-Episcopal minister. Several years after Horace's birth in Kentucky in 1844, the family moved to Clarksville, Tennessee, where Horace was educated mostly at home by private tutors. He entered the University of Chicago in 1859, but he returned home after only one year, upon the outbreak of the Civil War. In 1861 Horace enlisted in the Confederate army, in which he served as an infantryman in a Tennessee regiment. After a disability discharge in 1862, he re-enlisted, this time in a Kentucky regiment. Captured during Grant's siege of Fort Donelson, he escaped from Camp Chase in Ohio and participated in General John Hung Morgan's raids on Ohio, which led once again to his imprisonment in July 1863.

After Lurton contracted tuberculosis in prison, his mother traveled to Washington, D.C. to appeal directly to Lincoln, who paroled Lurton in 1865.

Upon recovering from his illness, Lurton enrolled at Cumberland University Law School in Lebanon, Tennessee, from which he graduated in 1867. Later that year

Horace Lurton

he married Mary Francis Own and moved back to Clarksville to set up a private law practice. He became one of the area's most successful and respected lawyers and found himself gravitating toward Democratic party activism under the influence of his law partner, James A. Bailey. In 1875 Lurton became the youngest chancellor in Tennessee history when the governor appointed him to head the state's sixth chancery division.

After serving out his term in 1878, Lurton returned to Clarksville, where his immensely successful private law partnership with Charles G. Smith brought him such local distinctions as the presidency of the Farmers' and Merchants' National Bank, a trusteeship of the University of the South, and a leading role in the Trinity Episcopal Chruch of Clarksville. His growing **eminence** led to his election to the Supreme Court of Tennessee in 1886, where he served for seven years before his appointment as chief justice in 1893. Several months thereafter, President Cleveland appointed Lurton to fill the spot on the U.S. Court of Appeals just vacated by Howell Jackson, whom Cleveland had named to the Supreme Court.

When the circuit court's presiding judge, William Howard Taft, resigned to become governor general of the Phillipines, Lurton succeeded him. While serving on the federal bench, Lurton also spent seven years as a professor of constitutional law at Vanderbilt University, where he served as dean from 1905–1909.

By 1909 William Howard Taft was president of the United States. Taft thought of his old friend Lurton when a spot opened on the Supreme Court. For the Republican Taft, this was a doubly risky move: not only was Lurton a Democrat, but, at 66, he was the oldest man ever nominated for the nation's highest court. But Taft was adamant—"There was nothing I had so much at heart in my whole administration," he later said—and the nomination breezed through the Senate.

Lurton took his seat on the Court on January 3, 1910. He proved an able if predictably conservative jurist, respected for the clarity and technical mastery of his opinions. His conservatism was evident in an essay he published in 1911 in which he endorsed Montesquieu's belief in a division of powers as the key to defending a government of laws against a "government of men."

Of Lurton's 97 opinions during his four-year term, none were legal watersheds. His pro-business **proclivities** were evident in cases such as *Henry v. A. B. Dick Co.* (1912), in which

1844 Lurton is born in Kentucky.

1861 Lurton enlists in the Confederate Army.

1867 Lurton earns a law degree from Cumberland University in Tennessee.

1886 Lurton is elected to the supreme court of Tennessee.

1910 Lurton is confirmed as an associate justice of the United States Supreme Court.

1914 Lurton dies in Atlantic City, New Jersey.

Eminence (Lurton) A high degree of importance

proclivities: tendencies or leanings.

Lurton was, however, amenable to some degree of government regulation.

Lurton judged that it was not a restraint of trade for a manufacturer of duplicating machines to require customers to purchase only its ink and related supplies. Lurton was, however, amenable to some degree of government regulation. He joined the Court majority in such cases as *Second Employer Liablity Case* (1912), which defended an employer liability insurance law; *Hipolite Egg Co.* (1912), which enhanced enforcement of the Pure Food and Drug Act; and the *Minnesota Rate Cases* (1913), which broadened the purview of the Interstate Commerce Commission.

Ill health forced Lurton to take a leave of absence in Florida early in 1914. He returned in April of that year to serve the remainder of that year's term. He then repaired to Atlantic City for the summer and died there of a heart attack on July 12, 1914. ◆

Marshall, John

SEPTEMBER 24, 1755– JULY 6, 1835 ● CHIEF JUSTICE

John Marshall, the fourth chief justice of the United States, earned a place in history for establishing the Supreme Court as the strong branch of the federal government that it is today.

Marshall was born in a log cabin near Germantown, Virginia, on September 24, 1755. His mother, Mary Randolph Keith Marshall, was the daughter of an Anglican minister and was related to Thomas Jefferson. His father, Thomas Marshall, served in the Virginia House of Burgesses and as a county sheriff. The eldest of 15 children, young Marshall spent much of his first 20 years helping to raise his younger brothers and sisters on the family farm in Fauquier County, Virginia. He received tutoring from several local ministers.

After the Revolutionary War began, Marshall joined the Continental Army in 1776 and served as a lieutenant. He spent the winter of 1777–1778 with General George Washington's forces at Valley Forge, and he was promoted to captain in 1778. After his service, Marshall received his only formal education in

John Marshall

185

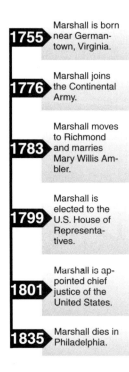

1755 Marshall is born near German-town, Virginia.

1776 Marshall joins the Continental Army.

1783 Marshall moves to Richmond and marries Mary Willis Ambler.

1799 Marshall is elected to the U.S. House of Representatives.

1801 Marshall is appointed chief justice of the United States.

1835 Marshall dies in Philadelphia.

1779, when he briefly studied law at the College of William and Mary. He was admitted to the Virginia bar in 1780.

In 1782, Marshall was elected to his first term in the Virginia legislature. That same year, he became a member of the Council of State, the executive branch of government in Virginia.

In 1783, Marshall moved to Richmond, Virginia, where he was to become a highly successful lawyer. In that same year, he married Mary Willis Ambler, daughter of the state treasurer. The couple had 10 children, six of whom survived to adulthood. Mary, nicknamed Polly, suffered from mental and physical illness most of her life.

In 1788, Marshall was elected to his state's convention that decided to ratify the proposed Constitution of the United States. After Marshall's final term in the Virginia legislature was completed in 1797, President John Adams sent him and two other ambassadors to Paris to negotiate with the French government over French interference with American trade. When Marshall returned in 1798, he had become famous for refusing to give in to French demands in what became known as the "XYZ Affair," named after three French agents who became known as X, Y, and Z. The XYZ Affair led to fighting at sea between the United States and France, though war was never declared.

Marshall was elected to the U.S. House of Representatives in 1799. He quickly became the leader of the moderate Federalists and championed the policies of Adams. This position made him a rival of his distant cousin and fellow Virginian, Thomas Jefferson, and the two men never agreed on many issues thereafter. In 1800, Marshall became secretary of state in the cabinet of Adams, handling foreign relations for the United States for nine months.

Near the end of his presidential term, Adams appointed Marshall chief justice of the United States Supreme Court in January 1801. The U.S. Senate confirmed the nomination by January 27, and Marshall took the position on February 4, 1801.

At the time that Marshall took his post, the Supreme Court did not command the respect and power that it does today. In Marshall's 34 years on the court, he raised the level of the Court to equality with the executive and legislative branches of the government. Marshall believed that the Constitution must be accepted as the supreme law of the land. He also helped define the young nation's division of power between the states and the federal government. Marshall was responsible for establishing fundamental judicial principles that have served as the foundation for many future court decisions.

Marshall believed in a strong judiciary and a strong central government. Most of the leaders in power during Marshall's years as chief justice—President Thomas Jefferson, in particular—believed in states' rights. Marshall, however, believed that the United States, still a young nation, greatly needed a strong central government. Marshall believed that was the way for the United States to grow strong.

One of Marshall's first and most famous cases came in 1803, when he wrote the opinion in the landmark case of *Marbury v. Madison.* This case marked the first time the Supreme Court declared a federal law unconstitutional, thus establishing the supremacy of the Constitution over laws passed by Congress. It also established the Supreme Court as the arbiter of whether or not legislation was constitutional.

In 1801, Adams had appointed William Marbury justice of the peace in the District of Columbia. But Adams' term ended before Marbury took office, and James Madison, the new secretary of state, withheld the appointment. Marbury asked the Supreme Court, under a section of the Congressional Judiciary Act of 1789, to force Madison to grant the appointment. But the Court refused to do so because the section gave the Supreme Court powers not provided by the Constitution. Therefore, the court declared, the section was unconstitutional. The Supreme Court thus struck down an act of Congress that conflicted with the Constitution, creating the power of judicial review.

After that ruling, judicial review became the most important power of U.S. courts. Any court in the United States can declare laws or the actions of public officials illegal if they conflict with the U.S. Constitution. The Supreme Court, then, is the final authority on all such matters.

In the case of *Fletcher v. Peck* (1810), Marshall established that the Constitution protects an individual's property rights against interference from the states. In this case, the Court declared a state law unconstitutional for the first time.

In what came to be called the Dartmouth College case, *Dartmouth College v. Woodward* (1819), the court upheld the rights of private property and protected the development of the free enterprise system. In 1769, King George III of Britain had granted Dartmouth College a charter as a private school. This charter was to last "forever." In 1816, New Hampshire tried to

"The very essence of civil liberty certainly consists in the right of every individual to claim the protection of the laws, whenever he receives an injury. One of the first duties of government is to afford that protection. [The] government of the United States has been emphatically termed a government of laws, and not of men."

Marbury v. Madison (1803)

Marbury v. Madison (1803)

William Marbury and several others were granted political appointments during the final days of the John Adams presidency; Marbury was appointed Justice of the Peace in the District of Columbia. Unfortunately for these new appointees, their positions were not yet confirmed when the new administration took office, and Congress overturned their appointments by a legislative act. Marbury was angry, and he applied to the Supreme Court for reinstatement.

The Supreme Court took the case, seeing three separate questions that needed to be resolved. First, the Justices considered whether or not it was appropriate for Marbury to use a lawsuit as the method of regaining his job. In the Court's opinion, the answer was yes, so the Justices moved on to ask if the Supreme Court was the proper venue for the lawsuit to take place. The issue here was whether or not the Supreme Court had the power to review, and perhaps overturn, Acts of Congress, which was how Marbury had lost his job in the first place. The answer here, too, was yes; but only in certain circumstances. Finally, having established its jurisdiction in Marbury's case, the Court decided that, indeed, Marbury did deserve to be reinstated to his appointed post.

The importance of this decision goes far beyond whether an individual appointed official got to keep his job. Chief Justice John Marshall, who wrote the Court opinion, introduced the concept of judicial review, a power not explicitly given to the Court, nor never before specifically claimed by the Supreme Court. *Marbury v. Madison* firmly established that the Supreme Court had the right to review Acts of Congress, stating flatly that "when the Constitution conflicts with an act of the legislature, the Constitution wins."

make Dartmouth College their state university by canceling the charter. Former trustees of the college claimed that the royal charter was still valid. The Court ruled that the trustees were right.

One of the most important cases in the Court's history was *McCulloch v. Maryland* (1819). The Court ruled that Congress possessed implied powers—that is, powers not specifically stated in the Constitution. In this case, Marshall upheld the power of Congress to create the United States Bank and ruled that the state of Maryland's attempt to tax the bank was unconstitutional. This decision was crucial to the growth of the United States, because it allowed for changes in the nation's needs over time. It also firmly established the superiority of federal power over state power in cases of conflict.

In *Gibbons v. Ogden* (1824), the Court rejected the authority of a New York law that hindered out-of-state commercial steamboats from doing business in its waters. Marshall's opinion defined national power over interstate commerce, opening the way for easy trade between the states and national economic growth. The case confirmed congressional control over foreign and interstate commerce.

Marshall became known as the "Great Chief Justice" because of his tremendous impact on the U.S. judicial system. He earned wide admiration for his personal integrity, humble attitude, wit, charm, and devotion to his nation. A precise and clear style, literary skill, and thorough, logical analysis characterized his legal opinions. These skills led him to write *Life of George Washington*.

In his later years, Marshall suffered from illness and loneliness. He barely survived surgery for bladder stones in 1831, only to have his wife die later that year. Suffering an intestinal blockage, he attended his last term of the Court in February 1835 before going to Philadelphia for medical care. He died there on July 6, 1835, at nearly 80 years of age. On the day of Marshall's funeral, July 8, the Liberty Bell cracked while ringing for him. ◆

Marshall, Thurgood

JULY 2, 1908– JANUARY 24, 1993 ● ASSOCIATE JUSTICE

Thurgood Marshall, the first African American justice of the Supreme Court of the United States, was born July 2, 1908, in Baltimore, Maryland. Marshall's mother, Norma Arica Marshall, was one of the first blacks to graduate from Columbia Teacher's College in New York City. She taught in a segregated elementary school. His father, William Canfield Marshall, worked as a railroad porter and as chief steward at a private white club. Marshall was named for his paternal grandfather, a freed slave who changed his name to Thoroughgood when he joined the United States Army during the Civil War.

Marshall grew up in Baltimore and graduated from an all-black high school at age 16. He attended Lincoln University in Chester County, Pennsylvania, the nation's oldest black college. In college, Marshall began his lifelong fight against segregation when he joined a protest at a local movie theater. The protesters sat in "whites-only" seats, forcing the theater to stop making blacks sit in a segregated balcony section.

Marshall soon met Vivien "Buster" Burey, a student at the University of Pennsylvania, and the couple married in 1929. Marshall graduated with high honors in 1930, then studied at

Thurgood Marshall

Howard University Law School in Washington, D.C., graduating first in his class in 1933. Marshall began practicing law that same year.

Marshall's law career soon found its direction as he became a great advocate for the rights of minorities and the poor. In 1936, he left his private practice in Baltimore to move to New York City. There he became a staff lawyer of the National Association for the Advancement of Colored People (NAACP). Founded in 1909, the NAACP is a civil rights organization in the United States that works to end discrimination against blacks and other minority groups.

From 1939 to 1961, Marshall worked as chief of the NAACP legal staff. In addition to cases before local, state, and federal courts, Marshall and his staff argued 32 cases before the United States Supreme Court, winning an amazing 29 of them. Marshall earned the nickname "Mr. Civil Rights."

These cases included *Chambers v. Florida* (1940), in which he persuaded the Supreme Court to overturn a criminal conviction based on a forced confession. In *Smith v. Allwright* (1944), the Court declared a Texas practice of excluding black voters from primary elections as unconstitutional. In *Shelley v. Kraemer* (1948) the Supreme Court agreed with Marshall that courts could not enforce "restrictive covenants," private agreements not to sell land to blacks. In *Sipuel v. University of Oklahoma* (1948) and *Sweatt v. Painter* (1950) Marshall won unanimous decisions forcing the universities of Oklahoma and Texas to give equal treatment to black students.

These cases became the basis for a long-term NAACP strategy, which Marshall helped develop, to fight racial segregation throughout the United States. Citizens in local communities across the country became part of the effort. The most important victory of this effort came in the famous *Brown v. Board of Education of Topeka* (1954) case. The NAACP and Marshall used the *Brown* case and its companion cases to challenge the "separate but equal" principle. (In *Plessy v. Ferguson* (1896), the Supreme Court had declared that "separate but equal" public facilities for blacks and whites was permissible. That decision had supported segregation in the South for over 50 years.)

In the *Brown* case itself, Oliver Brown, an African American railroad worker in Topeka, Kansas, sued the Topeka Board of Education for not allowing Linda Brown, his daughter, to attend Sumner Elementary School, an all-white school near her home. Marshall and his team added other cases involving similar suits from other parts of the country. Marshall attacked the "separate but equal" rule by arguing that segregation harms minority students by making them feel inferior and thus interfering with their ability to learn. He argued that the "equal protection clause" of the Fourteenth Amendment to the Constitution of the United States requires that states treat all citizens alike, regardless of race.

The Court unanimously declared segregation in public schools unconstitutional. This decision marked a major landmark in the civil rights movement of the 1950s and 1960s. Sadly, Marshall's joy over the *Brown* victory was cut short with the news of his wife's cancer. He spent many months caring for Buster before she died in February 1955. In December 1955, though, Marshall married a colleague, Cecilia "Cissy" Suyat. The couple had two sons, Thurgood, Jr., and John William.

Marshall tried to spread the philosophy of the *Brown* case into other areas in which blacks were excluded. He won six Supreme Court victories in the 1950s, leading to the desegregation of beaches, parks, swimming pools, bus systems, and recreational facilities.

Recognizing Marshall as one of the most successful lawyers in America, in 1961, President John F. Kennedy appointed him to the United States Second Circuit Court of Appeals, which had jurisdiction over New York, Connecticut, and Vermont. Southern senators strongly opposed the appointment, delaying Marshall's confirmation for 11 months. However, in four years as a Court of Appeals judge, Marshall wrote 98 majority opinions that were upheld by the Supreme Court.

In 1965, President Lyndon B. Johnson appointed Marshall Solicitor General of the United States. The solicitor general is responsible for arguing cases before the Supreme Court when the United States government itself is one of the parties in the case. He was confirmed quickly and became the first black to hold the position. He won 14 out of 19 cases.

1908 Marshall is born in Baltimore, Maryland.

1936 Marshall begins career in New York City with NAACP.

1954 Marshall argues and wins *Brown v. Board of Education of Topeka* before the United States Supreme Court.

1967 Marshall nominated to and confirmed as associate justice of the Supreme Court.

1993 Marshall dies in Bethesda, Maryland.

Marshall tried to spread the philosophy of the *Brown* case into other areas in which blacks were excluded.

Brown v. the Board of Education of Topeka (1954)

Since 1857, race relations in the United States were ruled by the doctrine of "separate but equal," which meant that states were free to permit segregation of the races as long as necessary facilities and services offered to whites were also made available, separately, to blacks. Thus there were "whites only" and "blacks only" drinking fountains, beaches, restaurants, and even schools.

In 1952, this policy was challenged in several states, including Kansas, South Carolina, Virginia, and Delaware. The Supreme Court bundled these challenges together under the title *Brown v. the Board of Education of Topeka*, which was argued in December, 1952, and reargued one year later. The petitioners charged that the separate-but-equal policy, at least as applied to education, did not work. Even though African–Americans might have school facilities of similar quality to those available to whites, discrimination still occurred, measured in "intangibles" such as perceptions of inferiority and opportunity.

The Supreme Court decided unanimously in favor of the petitioners. In delivering the Court's opinion, Chief Justice Earl Warren explicitly rejected the guiding constitutional principles of the *Plessy v. Ferguson* decision (1896) that had instituted the separate–but–equal doctrine. He said that the Constitution could not be taken literally in this case, for its framers lived in an entirely different set of circumstances. At the time that the Constitution was written, it was even illegal in many states for blacks to receive an education. This decision set the stage for the Civil Rights Movement that followed during the rest of the 1950s and 1960s.

Johnson nominated Marshall to the Supreme Court on June 13, 1967. Two months later, the United States Senate confirmed Marshall as associate justice of the Supreme Court. Marshall joined the Supreme Court's liberal majority, led by Chief Justice Earl Warren and later by Justice William Brennan. The Court leaned in favor of a broad-minded view of the Constitution and individual rights. Marshall defended the First Amendment rights when he wrote the majority opinion in *Stanley v. Georgia* (1969), overturning a Georgia law that prohibited private possession of obscene material. He spoke for the court in *Grayned v. City of Rockford* (1972), striking down an anti-picketing ordinance that had been used against civil rights demonstrators. In *Police Department of Chicago v. Mosely* (1972), the Court held that the police could not allow some people to picket while banning others.

As the Supreme Court became increasingly conservative in the 1970s and 1980s, Marshall was often a dissenting voice. He frequently spoke out against the Court's endorsement of **capital punishment.** Marshall believed the death penalty was "cruel and unusual punishment" in violation of the Eighth Amendment to the Constitution. In his years as a lawyer, Marshall had defended clients who faced the death penalty, and he believed it was applied to minorities more often than whites. The Court ruled in 1972 against the death penalty, but changed back four years later. After that, Marshall and Brennan dissented in each case involving the death penalty.

In *San Antonio Independent School District v. Rodriguez* (1973), Marshall dissented from a decision that refused to require San Antonio to give money to schools equally. Marshall pointed out that students from the city's poorest neighborhoods received a lower education, even though their parents paid a greater percentage of their income in school taxes than did parents in wealthy areas of the city.

Marshall continued to side with the poor and underprivileged, whose lives he understood in ways that other justices did not. When his colleagues supported a $50 fee for people filing bankruptcy—thinking it was not too large a sum—Marshall dissented, criticizing his colleagues' inability to understand how much that sum would mean to a poor person. In *Florida v. Bostick* (1991), Marshall protested when the Court found that it was acceptable for police to board inter-city buses and ask passengers to allow their bags to be searched. Marshall argued that people on a bus, many uneducated and poor, would not understand that they could legally refuse to agree to a search on constitutional grounds.

"Equal means getting the same thing, at the same time and in the same place."
Thurgood Marshall, responding to a justice in *Brown v The Board of Education*, 1954

capital punishment: policy of an individual state whereby a conviction for murder may result in the state executing a guilty party.

Citing poor health, Marshall retired from the Supreme Court on June 27, 1991, at age 82. By that time, he was one of the last remaining liberal members of a Supreme Court dominated by a conservative majority. Although his conservative colleagues did not always agree with him, they admired Marshall for his honesty, his commitment, and his accomplishments.

Marshall died of heart failure January 24, 1993, in Bethesda, Maryland. Thousands of people waited for hours in the cold to file past his body, which lay in state in the Supreme Court building. Many more came to a ceremony at Washington's National Cathedral. He was buried in Arlington National Cemetery. His second wife, Cissy, and their two sons survived him.

Like many Supreme Court justices, Marshall left his personal papers to the Library of Congress. However, unlike other justices, Marshall allowed his papers to be available immediately for research by scholars, journalists, and others. ◆

Matthews, Stanley

JULY 21, 1824–MARCH 22, 1889 ● ASSOCIATE JUSTICE

Called by one biographer "an unusual combination of liberal and conservative premises," Stanley Matthews zigged now right, now left, through a number of conspicuous public roles—prosecutor, judge, U.S. attorney, soldier, counselor to the Hayes-Tilden Electoral Commission, and U.S. Senator—before he joined the U.S. Supreme Court in 1881.

The first child of Thomas Johnson Matthews and Isabella Brown, Stanley Matthews was born Thomas Stanley in Cincinnati, Ohio, in 1824 (he dropped the Thomas as an adult). His father was a professor of mathematics and natural philosphy at Transylvania University in Lexington, Kentucky. He later moved back to Cincinnati to assume the presidency of Woodward College—later Woodward High School—where Stanley began his college studies before transferring to Kenyon College in his junior year. After graduating from Kenyon in 1840, he spent the next two years in Cincinnati studying law. In 1842 Matthews moved to Maury County, Tennessee, to work at the Union Seminary there. Later that year he was admitted to the Tennessee bar and moved to Columbia, where he launched both a private law practice and a pro-Polk weekly newspaper, the *Tennessee Democrat*.

In 1844 Matthews married the daughter of a wealthy farmer, Mary Ann Black, who eventually bore eight children. Later that year he moved his family and his law practice to Cincinnati, where his legal talents won him an appointment as assistant prosecuting attorney. His newspaper experience led to a year's stint as editor of the abolitionist *Cincinnati Morning Herald*. The public visibility afforded him through the newspaper led to his election as clerk of the Ohio House of Representatives for the 1848–1849 term.

Stanley Matthews

After the Ohio state constitution was ratified in 1851, Matthews ran successfully for one of three judgeships of the Court of Common Pleas in Hamilton County, but he didn't serve out his term because he preferred the more ample compensation of private practice. Still ambitious for public office, however, he won election to the Ohio Senate in 1855, and after three years in that post was named U.S. attorney for southern Ohio by President Buchanan. In that post the abolitionist Matthews was obliged to swallow hard and enforce the Fugitive Slave Act by prosecuting W. B. Connelly, a journalist who had aided in the attempted escape of two slaves. Matthews's role in the case became a political albatross he carried for the rest of his career, contributing to his defeat in an 1876 campaign for Congress and, many years later, threatening his confirmation by the Senate for the Supreme Court.

With the outbreak of the Civil War, Matthews served with the Ohio Infantry and the Ohio Volunteers until 1863, when he resigned from the army to accept election to the Cincinnati Superior Court. After two years of financial sacrifice on the bench, he again returned to private practice, representing major corporate and railroad interests and gaining renown as one of the country's ablest attorneys. He retained his lively interest in public affairs, however, serving as a Republican **presidential elector** in 1864 and 1868, and chairing the 1872 Liberal Republican

presidential elector: an individual elected to serve in the Electoral College, which selects the president and vice president of the United States

1824 Matthews is born in Cincinnati, Ohio.

1842 Matthews is admitted to the Tennessee bar.

1855 Matthews, who had moved back to Ohio, is elected to the Ohio senate.

1858 Matthews is named the U.S. attorney for southern Ohio.

1863 Matthews is elected to the Cincinnati Superior Court.

1881 Matthews is confirmed as an associate U.S. Supreme Court justice by one vote.

1889 Matthews dies in Washington, D.C.

convention. His quest for a congressional seat that year foundered on bitterness over his prewar prosecution of Connelly.

Matthews's national political prominence was boosted considerably by his retention as one of the lawyers who presided over the electoral commission that adjudicated the disputed Hayes-Tilden election of 1876. The commission ended up adopting Matthews's argument that the verdict of the Florida State authorities should govern the result.

In 1877, when Senator John Sherman of Ohio vacated his seat to accept appointment as secretary of the treasury, the Ohio legislature elected Matthews to replace him. His two-year term in the Senate was notable for the passage, in 1878, of the "Matthews Resolution," which allowed silver interest payments on U.S. bonds and declared silver to be a legally recognized form of currency.

When Supreme Court Justice Noah Swayne resigned in 1879, President Hayes's nomination of Matthews to fill the seat was rebuffed by the Senate, which deemed the appointment an unsavory political payback for Matthews's pro-Hayes advocacy in the disputed election of 1876. The move smacked of cronyism as well, since the two men had attended Kenyon College together and had both served in the Ohio Infantry during the Civil War.

The Court seat remained vacant until 1880, when the newly elected President Garfield again offered the vacancy to Matthews. But the confirmation still faced stiff opposition among the senators because of Matthews's longstanding association with corporate and railroad interests as a private attorney. After a heated debate, the Senate approved the nomination by one vote on May 12, 1881, and Matthews remained on the Court until his death eight years later.

Among Matthews's most important decisions were *Hurtado v. California* (1884), in which he ruled that the grand jury indictment clause of the Fifth Amendment did not apply to defendants in state criminal trials; *Yick Wo v. Hopkins* (1886), where he overturned a San Francisco law that required permits to operate laundries in wooden buildings but denied them to Chinese workers, arguing that it violated the Constitution's equal-protection provisions; and *Poindexter v. Greenhow* (1885), in which Matthews wrote the majority opinion that states could not disavow debts under the contract clause of the Constitution.

Matthews died in Washington, D.C., on March 22, 1889. ◆

McKenna, Joseph

AUGUST 10, 1843–NOVEMBER 21, 1926 ● ASSOCIATE JUSTICE

There are two equally compelling ways to spin the story of Joseph McKenna's rise to the Supreme Court. It can be seen as a classic parable of the American Dream, in which a man rises from humble immigrant roots to the nation's highest court, or as a cautionary tale about the political cronyism that pushed an unqualified man to an unmerited judicial eminence for purely political ends.

McKenna's parents, John and Mary (Johnson) McKenna, were Irish immigrants who landed first in Philadelphia, where Joseph was born on August 10, 1843. John McKenna waged a losing battle to sustain his bakery business in the face of a wave of anti-immigrant, anti-Catholic sentiment. Lured by the prospect of a fresh start out west, in the winter of 1854 the McKennas booked third-class passage on a Panamanian steamer for the grueling journey to California.

They settled in the small coastal town of Benicia, where John McKenna improved his lot until his untimely death in 1858, when Joseph was only 15 years old. Now the head of the family, Joseph forsook his training for the priesthood in favor of law courses, which he pursued while holding a series of odd jobs. He graduated from the law department of Benicia State College in 1865 and passed the bar exam later that year.

McKenna's ensuing private law practice proved to be merely a springboard for his true passion, politics. His activism in the state's burgeoning Republican Party led to his election as Solano County district attorney for two terms (1866–70) and then as a representative in the state legislature (1875–1877), where he vied unsuccessfully for the speakership. McKenna then suffered two defeats in races for the U.S. House of Representatives before finally winning a seat in 1885.

He was an able and effective legislator. During his four terms in Congress, he helped to pass several important laws, including an extension of land grants to the railroads and an upgrade of major ports. Less laudable was his support for restrictions on the rights of Chinese immigrants, especially in view of his own immigrant roots. While serving in the House, McKenna cultivated two key political allies who later proved critical in advancing his fortunes in Washington: Senator Leland Stanford of California

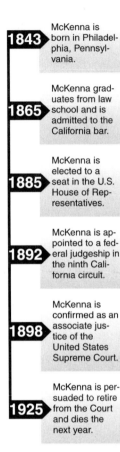

stacks: a compact storage space for books usually found in college libraries.

paucity: lacking.

surfeit: overabundance.

and Congressman William McKinley, the future president with whom he served on the Ways and Means Committee.

In 1892 Senator Stanford persuaded President Benjamin Harrison to appoint McKenna to the ninth circuit of California's federal court, where he served for five years until he resigned to become United States attorney general under President McKinley.

A few months into McKinley's term, Stephen Field retired from the Supreme Court, and the president nominated McKenna to succeed him. Because of McKenna's association with Leland and the railroads (his was one of the few Congressional votes cast against the creation of the Interstate Commerce Commission in 1887), the nomination stirred some controversy in the Senate, which nonetheless confirmed him.

Acknowledging the limitations of his legal training, McKenna traveled to New York to bury himself in the **stacks** of the Columbia law library, furiously straining to compress years' worth of legal training into a few months. The futility of this cram course was apparent in the months after he took his seat on the Court on January 26, 1898. A Court librarian noted in a letter that McKenna seemed unequal to the duties of his post. Some of his early opinions, such as *Magoun v. Illinois Trust,* sought to compensate for a **paucity** of verbal clarity and logic with a **surfeit** of case law, much of it of questionable relevancy.

In his ensuing 26 years on the bench, McKenna never seemed to develop a consistent or identifiable legal outlook. After his first decade on the Court, however, McKenna did seem to develop a more lucid and readable style of exposition. In his opinion in *United States v. United States Steel Corporation* (1920), he concisely enunciated the "rule of reason," which interpreted the Sherman Antitrust Act to apply only to unreasonable restraints of trade, not to every corporate combination. In other cases, however, he proved more sympathetic to the commercial regulatory power of the federal government, as in *Hipolite Egg Company v. United States* (1911), which reinforced the Pure Food and Drug Act, and *Hoke v. United States* (1913), which upheld the Mann Act.

In the 1920s, McKenna's mental capacities began to decline to the point that he no longer seemed able to grasp key issues in the cases brought before the Court. In 1924, the associate justices reached an informal agreement to try to avoid situations in which McKenna's vote would be decisive. He was finally persuaded to retire in 1925. He died in Washington, D.C., on November 21, 1926. ◆

McKinley, John

MAY 1, 1780–JULY 19, 1852 ● ASSOCIATE JUSTICE

On the way to becoming as associate justice of the United States Supreme Court, John McKinley served as a congressman and senator. A physician's son, he was born in Culpeper County, Virginia, on May 1, 1780. When John was a young child, his family moved to Kentucky. As a young man McKinley worked as a mechanic and then studied law privately. After gaining admission to the bar in 1800, McKinley practiced law in Kentucky for the next 18 years, first in Frankfort and later in Louisville.

In 1818 McKinley moved to Hunstville, Alabama, a thriving center of political and economic activity. Having cultivated influential friends and professional colleagues among the planters and local politicians, McKinley ran for circuit judge in 1819, Alabama's first year of statehood. Defeated in that race, he rebounded to win a seat in the state legislature the following year. When John Walker resigned from his U.S. senate seat in 1822, McKinley entered the race to succeed him but was defeated by one vote. When another senate seat went vacant in 1826 with the death of Henry Chambers, McKinley again entered the fray, this time against a wealthy planter, Clement Clay. McKinley, applying the political capital he had accumulated with his support of Andrew Jackson, carried the election by three votes.

After serving out his term, McKinley ran for re-election but lost to Gabriel Moore. He then won a contest for the state legislature, where he served for two years before successfully running for Congress. After a single term in the U.S. House, McKinley preferred to run once again for the Alabama state legislature, where he planned to bide his time for two years while

John McKinley

waiting to contest Moore's Senate seat, to which he was indeed elected in 1836. But before McKinley could begin his term, Martin Van Buren appointed him to the Supreme Court, where he remained for the rest of his life after assuming his seat on January 9, 1838.

In his early years on the bench, McKinley was assigned to the ninth circuit, which covered Arkansas and parts of Alabama, Mississippi, and Louisiana. The rigors of riding circuit—which entailed yearly travel of 10,000 miles and a crushing case load—took a fearful toll on his stamina and health, which resulted in frequent absences from Court sessions. Since his circuit rulings were not preserved in writing, the only published record of his 14-year tenure on the Court is the 18 majority opinions, two concurring rulings, and two dissents that he wrote during his sporadic sessions with the full Court in Washington, D.C.

As a Jacksonian Democrat, McKinley's opinions usually followed the party's line on states' rights and corporations. In *Bank of Augusta v. Earle* (1838), a circuit case, McKinley sided with an Alabamian defendant who refused to pay a bill of exchange on the grounds that the creditor institution, having been chartered in another state, was a "foreign bank" and thus forbidden by state law to operate in Alabama.

McKinley's decision sent a shudder through banking and financial circles. Joseph Story wrote that McKinley's extreme states' rights ruling had "frightened half the lawyers and all of the corporations out of their proprieties." When the case reached the U.S. Supreme Court in January 1839, Chief Justice Taney wrote the majority opinion overturning McKinley's decision on the grounds that the "law of comity" permitted out-of-state enterprises to operate across state lines in the absence of specific laws to the contrary. The Alabama constitution did not expressly disallow the negotiation of bills of exchange by such "foreign" entities.

McKinley's advocacy of states' rights was equally apparent in other cases. He dissented from the majority's overturning of the Mississippi constitution's ban against slaves from other states. McKinley disputed the majority view that such regulations required the passage of particular state laws. He likewise opposed the majority view in *Lane v. Dick* (1845), in which he held that the Supreme Court's countermanding of a ruling by the Mississippi Supreme Court gave too much power to the federal judiciary.

Among McKinley's major opinions, only his decision in the *Passenger Cases* (1849) contrasts with his overall Jacksonian proclivities. In this case, which so divided the Court that it issued eight separate opinions, McKinley upheld the Court's reversal of New York's and Massachusetts's laws governing the arrival of foreign ship passengers, although the rationale for his pro-federalist opinion was ambiguous.

Declining health limited McKinley's participation in the Court's work in his last few years on the bench. He died in Louisville, Kentucky, on July 19, 1852. ◆

McLean, John

MARCH 11, 1785–APRIL 4, 1861 ● ASSOCIATE JUSTICE

The son of Irish-Scottish immigrants, John McLean served as a congressman, postmaster-general, judge, and associate justice of the Supreme Court. Although most scholars do not find anything remarkable in his record as a jurist, he served ably and conscientiously during his three decades on the court, rendering a significant dissent in the *Dred Scott* decision that anticipated the principles of the Fourteenth Amendment to the Constitution.

John McLean

John McLean's parents—Fergus, a weaver, and Sophia—immigrated from Ireland and in 1775 settled in Morris County, New Jersey, where John was born in 1785. Fergus soon abandoned weaving to take up farming, and in 1779 he moved his growing family to Morgantown, Virginia, the first of several moves over the ensuing decade—to Jessamine, Kentucky; Maysville, Kentucky; and, finally, Warren County, Ohio, in 1799. There young John was able to settle into regular attendance at school. Determined to improve his

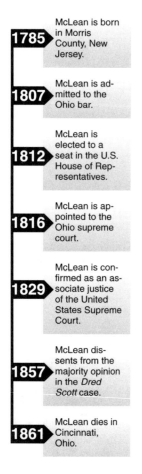

1785 McLean is born in Morris County, New Jersey.

1807 McLean is admitted to the Ohio bar.

1812 McLean is elected to a seat in the U.S. House of Representatives.

1816 McLean is appointed to the Ohio supreme court.

1829 McLean is confirmed as an associate justice of the United States Supreme Court.

1857 McLean dissents from the majority opinion in the *Dred Scott* case.

1861 McLean dies in Cincinnati, Ohio.

education, he earned enough at part-time jobs to hire private tutors, one of whom, Reverend Matthew G. Wallace, afforded him first-rate and inspiring instruction in Greek and Latin.

At the age of 18, McLean moved to Cincinnati, where he spent two years working as an apprentice to the clerk of the Hamilton County Court of Common Pleas while studying law in the evenings with Arthur St. Clair, an eminent lawyer in that area. After his admission to the bar in 1807, McLean married Rebecca Edwards and went into private law practice in Lebanon, Ohio, where he also opened a printing office and launched a weekly Jeffersonian newspaper, the *Western Star*. His brother took over the newspaper in 1810 so that John could devote himself full-time to his thriving law practice and his deepening engagement with politics.

McLean's political activism led to his election to the United States House of Representatives in 1812 as a War Democrat. He was re-elected in 1814, receiving every vote cast for congressman in his district. During his four years in the House, McLean was a staunch supporter of Madison's war policies and an opponent of the creation of the Second Bank of the United States.

After resigning from the House in 1816, McLean was elected by the state legislature to the Ohio Supreme Court, where he spent the next three years. In gratitude for McLean's effective campaigning on his behalf in 1816, President Monroe appointed him land commissioner in 1822 and then postmaster general in 1823. In his six years at the head of the post office, McLean proved himself an outstanding administrator and canny politician, working to undermine the 1828 re-election of campaign of his boss, President John Quincy Adams. A grateful president-elect Jackson took note of McLean's help, and two days into his term, he nominated McLean to the Supreme Court. The Senate confirmed his appointment on March 7, 1829.

McLean established himself as an able, thorough, if undistinguished associate justice, lauded for his unbending nonpartisanship, which was in evidence early on in his opposition to Jackson's federal patronage schemes. In opposition to the Jacksonian chief justice, Robert B. Taney, McLean tended to support the prerogatives of the federal government in dealing with the states and regulating economic activity. He was also in favor of a strong federal government. For example, in the *License Cases* (1847), he joined a majority opinion in upholding a challenge to the states' ability to regulate liquor sales. Likewise, in the *Passenger Cases* (1849), McLean wrote the majority 5–4 opinion, **abrogating** state laws that imposed a levy on ship captains for every immigrant they carried to the United States. The Court held such fees to be an unconstitutional "regulation of commerce" that "cannot be laid by a State, except under the sanction of Congress."

McLean further asserted the rights of federal power in *Pennsylvania v. Wheeling Bridge Co.* (1852), in which he ruled that the Wheeling Bridge must be raised to accommodate interstate commerce on the Ohio River.

McLean proved one of the most consistent opponents of slavery among his fellow justices. Most of his opinions on this subject challenged the legal underpinnings of the peculiar institution, beginning with his 1841 endorsement of Joseph Story's opinion that freed the captives who arrived on the *Amistad*. In 1848 the antislavery activist Samuel P. Chase said that McLean was "the most reliable man, on the slavery questions, now prominent in either party." McLean's most notable antislavery opinion was his dissent in the Dred Scott case, in which the majority held the Missouri Compromise to be unconstitutional and ruled that Congress could not outlaw slavery. McLean's dissent argued that slavery was "emphatically a state institution," supported only by local law, and that the federal government was entitled to regulate affairs in the territories and thus to outlaw slavery there.

Although Thaddeus Stevens and others supported him for the presidential nomination in 1860, the 75-year-old McLean never posed any real threat to Lincoln. McLean died the following year in Cincinnati. ◆

> **McLean proved one of the most consistent opponents of slavery among his fellow justices.**

abrogate: abolish.

McReynolds, James

FEBRUARY 3, 1862– AUGUST 24, 1946 ● ASSOCIATE JUSTICE

James McReynolds first made his name on the national scene as a reforming, trust-busting assistant attorney general, first under Theodore Roosevelt and later under Woodrow Wilson, for whom he also served as attorney general. Ironically, he is best known to posterity as an adamantly anti-reformist Supreme Court justice, one of the "nine old men"

James McReynolds

whom Franklin Roosevelt derided in the 1930s as an impediment to his New Deal measures.

McReynolds's Scottish forebears immigrated from Ireland in 1740 and landed in what is now Appomatox County, Virginia. James McReynolds was born on February 3, 1862, in Elkton, Kentucky, a strongly pro-Confederate community. He grew up under strict religious authority on the plantation owned by his parents, devoted followers of the Campbellite fundamentalists.

McReynolds attended college at Vanderbilt University in Nashville, Tennessee. After graduating in 1882, he enrolled at the law school of the University of Virginia at Charlottesville, where he took his law degree in 1884.

After law school McReynolds returned to Nashville, where he developed a thriving law practice that served some of the state's leading corporate clients. Although esteemed chiefly as a private attorney, McReynolds also served on the Vanderbilt Law School faculty and had a taste of public service during his brief stint as secretary to Senator Howell Edmunds Jackson (himself a future Supreme Court Justice). That experience spurred McReynolds to run for the U.S. Congress on the Gold Democratic ticket in 1896, but his haughty style put off enough voters to send him to defeat.

This setback notwithstanding, McReynolds's impressive private legal work among influential interests and his rising political profile led Philander C. Knox, the U.S. attorney general, to appoint him as assistant attorney general in 1903. For the next four years he supervised the prosecution of violators of the Sherman Antitrust Act, crossing swords in the courtroom with the powerful anthracite coal trust and the tobacco trust, which he once described as composed of "commercial wolves and highwaymen."

McReynolds returned to private practice in 1907, this time with the prestigious New York City firm of Cravath, Henerson, & Gersdorff. He did, however, continue to consult with the Justice Department on key antitrust cases. He campaigned for Woodrow Wilson in 1912, and Wilson in turn appointed him attorney general that year. McReynolds persisted in his vigorous pursuit of antitrust cases, but his arrogant personal manner often overshadowed his professional accomplishments.

Not wishing to lose the benefit of his legal expertise but recognizing the political limitations of his personal style, Wilson decided that McReynolds's talents would be put to better use on the Supreme Court, where **hauteur** could be more of an asset than a drawback. McReynolds was nominated on August 19, 1914, and confirmed by the Senate ten days later, by a 44–6 vote.

Because of his zealous antitrust prosecutions, some conservatives viewed McReynolds as a liberal or even as a radical. And some of his early rulings on the Court do indeed reflect an activist bent. In Meyers v. Nebraska he wrote a majority opinion overturning a state law banning the teaching of German in elementary schools. In 1929 he wrote for the court majority in upholding the five-cent transit fare in New York City. But over

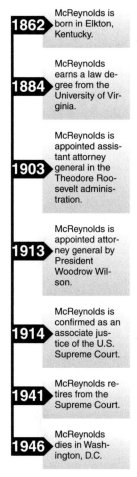

1862 McReynolds is born in Elkton, Kentucky.

1884 McReynolds earns a law degree from the University of Virginia.

1903 McReynolds is appointed assistant attorney general in the Theodore Roosevelt administration.

1913 McReynolds is appointed attorney general by President Woodrow Wilson.

1914 McReynolds is confirmed as an associate justice of the U.S. Supreme Court.

1941 McReynolds retires from the Supreme Court.

1946 McReynolds dies in Washington, D.C.

hauteur: arrogance.

McReynolds's aversion to the New Deal persisted with little abatement as he dissented from various key liberal rulings.

the long term McReynolds's rulings swerved in a consistently conservative direction, beginning with *St. Louis & O'Fallon Railroad v. United States*, which ruled against the Insterstate Commerce Commision.

It was in opposition to the advancing tide of social and political activism during FDR's New Deal that McReynolds's conservatism opened up full throttle. A long-time advocate of states' rights, McReynolds dissented from the Court's order of a new trial for the seven black men convicted in the Scottsboro case, arguing that the ruling transgressed the limits of federal authority. He also dissented, along with four other justices, from the majority ruling on the Minnesota mortgage moratorium.

McReynolds was in the same minority of four on other key New Deal cases. In *Norman v. the Baltimore & Ohio Railroad Company*, McReynolds voiced opposition to the majority view that gold payment of private bonds could not be enforced. An irate McReynolds wrote: "It seems to us impossible to overestimate the result of what has been done here," adding that he thought that it was not "too much to say that it [the Constitution] is gone." He added, "the impending legal and moral chaos is appalling."

Soon, however, the embattled minority was joined by other justices in becoming a majority bulwark against a whole raft of key New Deal measures. The Court overturned the Railroad Retirement Act, the National Recovery Act, and the Agricultural Adjustment Act. McReynolds was, however, the lone dissenter in opposing the creation of the Tennessee Valley Authority. By October of 1936, McReynolds had voted against all 13 New Deal laws brought before the Court. Over the ensuing six months, his views began to moderate slightly, as he opposed New Deal initiatives in only half of 14 cases that came before the Court.

In February 1938, exasperated with the Court's intransigent conservatism, Roosevelt proposed legislation to revamp the Court by expanding its membership to 15, thus allowing him to "pack" it with more cooperative justices—one for every member over 70 who refused to quit. By that year, however, the Court's opinions became less persistently hostile to Roosevelt's reforms, especially in its upholding of the Social Security Act.

But McReynolds's aversion to the New Deal persisted with little abatement as he dissented from various key liberal rulings: one that ratified taxes on Federal and state salaries and another that held that Communist Party membership was insufficient grounds for deportation of non-citizens. After the death of

Pierce Butler in November 1930, McReynolds was the sole remnant of the "nine old men" who had wreaked such havoc on Roosevelt's policies.

McReynolds retired from the court on January 31, 1941. He died in Washington, D.C., on August 24, 1946. ◆

Miller, Samuel

APRIL 5, 1816–OCTOBER 23, 1890 ● ASSOCIATE JUSTICE

Formal training as a physician followed by informal training as a lawyer might seem like an unlikely route to the Supreme Court of the United States, but it was the one traveled by Samuel Miller. A Kentucky native who moved to Iowa because of his opposition to slavery, Miller became a leading Republican and an ardent supporter of Abraham Lincoln, who eventually made Miller the first appointee to the high court from west of the Mississippi. Despite his lack of formal legal training, Miller served with distinction during his 28–year term on the Court, most notably in his efforts to stem the use of the Fourteenth Amendment as a shield against business regulation.

polemic: the art of political or adversarial conversation.

Samuel Miller

Both of Miller's parents—Frederick Miller, a Pennsylvanian of German descent, and Patsy Freeman, a North Carolinian—came to Kentucky early in the 19th century. Despite a spotty home education, Miller was admitted to the medical school at Transylvania University in Lexington, Kentucky, in 1836. After receiving his M.D. degree in 1838, he settled down to practice medicine for the next dozen years in the rural mountain community of Barboursville, where he married Lucy Ballinger.

In evenings spent at the town's debating society, Miller discovered a talent for political **polemic** that

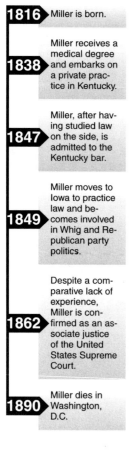

1816 ▶ Miller is born.

1838 ▶ Miller receives a medical degree and embarks on a private practice in Kentucky.

1847 ▶ Miller, after having studied law on the side, is admitted to the Kentucky bar.

1849 ▶ Miller moves to Iowa to practice law and becomes involved in Whig and Republican party politics.

1862 ▶ Despite a comparative lack of experience, Miller is confirmed as an associate justice of the United States Supreme Court.

1890 ▶ Miller dies in Washington, D.C.

helped to win him a seat as a local justice of the peace, an assignment that led him to take up law studies as a sideline. He was admitted to the bar in 1847, by which time he had become an activist in the antislavery Whig Party. When the slave-owning interests prevailed at the Democratic-controlled state convention of 1849, Miller packed up his family's belongings and set out for the free state of Iowa. He settled in Keokuk, where he set up a thriving law partnership, remarrying in 1857 after the death of his first wife. An activist in the fledgling Republican Party, Miller stood unsuccessfully for the party's nomination for governor in 1861.

As a longtime backer of Abraham Lincoln and a staunch opponent of slavery, Miller became a contender for a vacancy on the Supreme Court in 1862, when various Western politicians pressured Lincoln to appoint someone from their region. Despite Miller's spotty legal training, Lincoln's respect for his intellect, integrity, and political views led him to nominate Miller to become the Court's first justice from a state west of the Mississippi River.

Undaunted by the superior legal training of his colleagues from the East, Miller took pride in the independent spirit bred of his own more homespun self-education in the law. He later wrote of his belief that it was "from some western prairie town . . . that future Marshalls and Mansfields shall arise and give new impulses and add new honor to the profession of the law."

Miller soon established a distinctively progressive profile on the Court, usually defending the prerogatives of the federal government and its commercial regulatory powers. His adamantly pro-Union views were evident in his support for military trials for pro-Confederate civilians and in his endorsement of postwar loyalty oaths for teachers, attorneys, and clergy. In *Hepburn v. Griswold,* his dissent backed the idea of paper money as an emergency war measure, an opinion that became the Court's majority view a year later when its self-reversal paved the way for a regular paper currency in the United States.

Miller's most important legal legacy arose from his opinion in the *Slaughter-House Cases* (1873). After the carpet-bag government of Louisiana granted a monopoly on the livestock butchering trade to a single firm in Louisiana, a group of competing butchers brought suit against the law on the grounds that the Fourteenth Amendment's due process and equal protection provisions guaranteed their "privileges and immunities" as citizens to run their businesses without government interference.

The 5–4 majority opinion in this case, written by Miller, stated that the Fourteenth Amendment's rights applied only to federal citizenship, not state citizenship, and that while the Louisiana law might have encroached on the latter, there was no violation of the former. Any other interpretation, the Court held, "would constitute this court a perpetual censor upon all legislation of the States." The ruling went on to state that "we doubt very much whether any action of a state not directed by way of discrimination against the negroes as a class . . . will ever be held to come within the purview of this provision."

This interpretation was overturned in the 1890s, when the Court held that corporations were the legal equivalent of human beings and were thus entitled to the immunities and privileges specified in the Fourteenth Amendment.

Ironically, this decision, which sought to uphold the Fourteenth Amendment's original purpose of guaranteeing citizenship rights to African Americans, actually limited the federal government's purview over racial discrimination by consigning a wide swath of citizenship issues to the states. Nevertheless, Miller did later defend African Americans' rights to participate in congressional elections in *Ex parte Yarbrough* (1884).

Miller was one of the five justices who served on the electoral commission that broke the 1876 electoral deadlock in the presidential contest between the Democrat Samuel J. Tilden and the Republican Rutherford B. Hayes. Miller voted with the Republican majority to make Hayes the president.

Samuel Miller remained an active and productive member of the Supreme Court until his death in Washington, D.C. on October 13, 1890. ◆

Nevertheless, Miller did later defend African Americans' rights to participate in congressional elections in *Ex parte Yarbrough* (1884).

Minton, Sherman

OCTOBER 20, 1890–APRIL 9, 1965 ● ASSOCIATE JUSTICE

A New Deal liberal who evolved into a judicial conservative, Sherman Minton began life on a modest Indiana farm and ended it as an associate justice of the United States Supreme Court. In between he worked his way through college, distinguished himself as a brilliant student at the Yale School of Law, was elected to the U.S. Senate, and served as a federal circuit court judge.

Sherman Minton
testifies in front of
Congress in 1949.

Sherman Minton was born on October 30, 1890, in the farming village of Georgetown, Indiana, eight miles from New Albany, the town where he later settled as an adult. He was a strapping, athletic lad who starred at football, baseball, and track for the New Albany High School. But he was also an outstanding student who organized the school's first debating society. After graduating in 1910, he enrolled at Indiana University, where he maintained himself by waiting tables for his fraternity.

Here, too, Minton excelled both athletically and academically, complementing his LL.B. degree with an award as the school's outstanding public speaker along with a scholarship to attend the Yale School of Law. During his year of graduate work at Yale, he won top academic honors and wrote a thesis that was later reported to be "one of the best ever written at the university." He also helped to found the Yale Legal Aid Society.

After taking his LL.M. degree from Yale in 1916, Minton returned to New Albany to set up a private law practice, but his professional plans were put on hold by the outbreak of World War I. He enlisted in officer training school and served as a captain with the infantry on several European fronts. After his discharge in August 1919, Minton returned to New Albany to re-establish his law practice. In 1925 he joined a law firm in Miami, Florida, where he spent three years before returning to New Albany.

Minton was initiated into public service when his schoolmate, Paul V. McNutt, won a landslide election as governor of Indiana in 1933. McNutt appointed Minton counselor of the Public Service Commission, in which capacity he "was credited with writing many of the 'Little New Deal' laws in the first year of the McNutt Administration," according to *The New York Times*. He also oversaw a $3 million reduction in state utility rates, a record that helped catapult him to the Democratic nomination for—and ultimate victory in—the U.S. Senate race of 1934.

In the Senate, Minton, although temperamentally conservative, was swept up in the reformist spirit of the times. He became an effective champion of New Deal policies, including Roosevelt's controversial and ultimately unsuccessful plan to expand the Supreme Court to 15 justices to dilute the high bench's obstinate opposition to his social experiments.

In 1940 Minton, lost his reelection bid to Raymond E. Willis, a Republican swept into office on the coattails of Wendell Willkie's strong showing in the Indiana presidential contest. Roosevelt immediately snapped up Minton's services as a White House administrative assistant. After only four months in that position, Minton accepted Roosevelt's nomination to the United States Circuit Court of Appeals for the seventh circuit, covering Illinois, Wisconsin, and Indiana. Minton's support of the New Deal was evident in two key decisions: his support of the Federal Trade Commission's charge of collusive pricing against Standard Oil, and his ruling that the R. R. Donnelly Company intimidated its employees who sought to form a union. No reflexive liberal, Minton upheld the loyalty oaths required under the Taft-Hartley law and ruled that pensions are a legitimate component of collective bargaining.

Minton's hard-nosed, centrist brand of liberalism appealed to President Harry Truman, who nominated him to the Supreme Court on September 15, 1949. Citing his New Deal orthodoxy and his support for Rooselvelt's court packing scheme, some conservative Senators voiced reservations about his appointment. After extensive questioning by the Senate Judiciary Committee, however, Minton was approved by the Senate on October 3, 1949, and was sworn in by the Chief Justice nine days later at a White House ceremony.

1890 Minton is born in Georgetown, Indiana.

1916 Minton graduates from Yale University with a law degree.

1934 Minton wins a seat in the U.S. Senate representing Indiana.

1940 Minton is appointed to the federal bench on the Seventh Circuit Court of Appeals.

1949 Minton is confirmed an associate justice of the United States Supreme Court.

1956 Minton resigns from the Supreme Court due to poor health and dies in New Albany, Indiana, in 1965.

Minton's Republican critics needn't have worried. Once he ascended to the high bench, he took a decided turn away from judicial activism. Minton's newly conservative approach was evident in the case of Ellen Knauff, a German who married an American soldier during the war but was barred from entering the country for no announced reason, despite the contrary provisions of the War Brides Act. Minton wrote the majority opinion upholding the exclusion, even with the lack of a public reason for it. He wrote, "Whatever the procedure authorized by Congress is, it is due process as far as an alien denied entry is concerned."

Minton also wrote the majority opinion upholding New York State's Feinberg Law, which banned members of what were deemed "subversive" political groups from teaching in public schools. In 1953 he even cast the lone dissenting vote from the Court's ruling that a whites-only preprimary election by a Texas group—The Jaybird Democratic Association—was really a state activity and thus could not exclude blacks. Insisting that because the Jaybirds were a private group and thus exempt from constitutional constraints, Minton wrote: "I am not concerned in the least as to what happens to the Jaybirds or their unworthy scheme. I am concerned about what this court says is state action." Minton did, however, join the unanimous 1954 Court decision to outlaw public school desegregation, *Brown v. Board of Education.*

Minton resigned from the Supreme Court in 1956 because of poor health. He died in New Albany on April 9, 1965. ◆

Moody, William Henry

DECEMBER 23, 1853–JULY 2, 1917 ● ASSOCIATE JUSTICE

The roots of William Moody's family extend deep into the seed-time of colonial America, back to 1643, when the progenitor of his clan arrived in Ipswich, Massachusetts later to settle in Newbury, where William Henry Moody was born two centuries later. After turns as a private lawyer, city solicitor, district attorney, U. S. congressman, secretary of the navy, and U.S. attorney general, Moody was appointed to the Supreme Court by President Theodore Roosevelt in 1906 and served four years before illness forced him to retire.

William Henry Moody was born on December 23, 1853, in the Newbury house that his forebears had built 200 years earlier.

He attended elementary school in Danvers, where his family had moved in 1859, and eventually enrolled at the Phillips Andover Academy in Andover, Massachusetts, a distinguished private school—then exclusively male—for the offspring of the nation's social elite. After graduating cum laude from Harvard College in 1876, he entered Harvard Law School but left after one year to study law privately in the office of a distinguished local attorney, Richard H. Dana, Jr. After 18 months of study, he was granted **dispensation** from the normally required three-year course requirement and was allowed to take the bar exam, which he passed on his first try.

After his admission to the bar in 1878, Moody established a private practice in Haverhill, Massachusetts, where he partnered first with Edwin N. Hill and later with Joseph K. Jenness. Moody quickly established himself as one of the ablest lawyers in the area, attracting most of the major corporate clients in the region. His eminence drew the attention of the local Republican Party, under whose aegis he was elected Haverhill's city solicitor in 1888. In 1890 Moody was appointed district attorney for the eastern district of Massachusetts.

By now widely regarded as the state's leading trial lawyer, Moody was summoned to lead a prosecution outside his district: the notorious Lizzie Borden murder trial in Fall River, Massachussetts, in 1892. Despite the defendant's acquittal, Moody's involvement with the case enhanced his reputation with state Republican leaders, including Senator Henry Lodge, who helped him to secure the party's nomination for a seat in the U.S. Congress. Moody won the special election for the House in November 1893.

During his nine years in Congress, Moody proved an outstanding legislator, widely respected by both parties for his mastery of policy detail.

One friendship that Moody formed early in his congressional career—with the then-police commissioner of New York

William Moody

dispensation: exemption.

1853 Moody is born.

1878 Moody is admitted to the Massachusetts bar.

1890 Moody is appointed the district attorney for eastern Massachusetts.

1893 Moody wins a special election for a seat in the U.S. House of Representatives.

1904 President Theodore Roosevelt appoints Moody United States attorney general.

1906 Moody is confirmed as an associate justice of the United States Supreme Court.

1910 Moody retires from the Supreme Court and dies in 1917.

City, Theodore Roosevelt—bore political fruit years later, when Roosevelt became president after William McKinley's assassination. In 1902 Roosevelt appointed Moody secretary of the navy, in which capacity he maneuvered effectively to win increased funding to rebuild and expand the U.S. fleet, much to Roosevelt's delight.

When Attorney General Philander C. Knox resigned in 1904, Roosevelt named Moody to succeed him. As the nation's top prosecutor, Moody was a dedicated warrior in Roosevelt's antitrust crusade, most famously in his supervision of *Swift and Company v. United States*, known as the Beef Trust Case, in which the government prevailed against monopolistic restraint of competition in the meat industry. A wide range of industries felt the sting of Moody's trust-busting zeal: paper, fertilizer, salt, tobacco, oil, and lumber, among them. Roosevelt said, "His record as Attorney General can be compared without fear with the record of any other man who ever held that office."

Roosevelt's esteem for Moody—and his desire to have a political ally on the high bench—prompted him to nominate Moody for a seat on the Supreme Court on December 3, 1906. Despite Moody's reputation among some conservative senators as an anti-corporate radical, the nomination was confirmed within two weeks, and Moody took his seat on December 17, 1906.

Moody's four-year term on the court—truncated by illness—generally, but not always, reflected his Progressive affinity for federal action as a means of economic regulation. An important early signal of Moody's judicial posture was his dissent in the *First Employers Liability Case* (1908), in which the Court overturned the 1906 Employers' Liability Act, which held that common carriers involved in interstate commerce were responsible for their employees' injuries sustained on the job. In a 5–4 vote the Court judged the law as an infringement of the states' police power over interstate commerce. Moody's dissent relied on the interstate commerce clause of the Constitution. He wrote: "Its unchanging provisions are adaptable to the infinite variety of the changing conditions of our National life."

Moody did, however, recognize some legitimate limits on federal authority over the economy, acknowledging the states' police power over the economy and other aspects of everyday life in cases such as *Tilt v. Kelsey* (1907). In this case, Moody penned the Court's opinion that power over rules for bequest of property reside with the states. Moreover, in *Twining v. New Jersey* Moody wrote the majority opinion that the Fourteenth Amendment did not extend the bill of rights to the states. Hence, citizens who believed that a state government had violated their rights would be obliged to seek redress through the ballot box rather than the courts.

Moody's productivity on the bench trailed off in 1909 as he battled a crippling case of arthritis. Once Congress obliged him with a special retirement package, Moody retired in 1910. He died in his hometown of Haverhill on July 2, 1917. ◆

Moore, Alfred

MAY 21, 1755–OCTOBER 15, 1810 ● ASSOCIATE JUSTICE

Alfred Moore was born in Brunswick County (or, according to other sources, New Hanover County), North Carolina, in 1755. He was born into an illustrious family. His mother was Anne (Grange) Moore and his father, Judge Maurice Moore, was a North Carolina colonial judge. The family owned a large plantation. He was also related to Roger Moore, who was a major figure in the 1641 Irish Rebellion, and James Moore, a two-time governor of South Carolina. Because the schools in Moore's area weren't very good, he left home and attended school in Boston, Massachusetts. After school, Moore studied law under his father and received his law license in 1775. He was only 20.

Moore's career was quickly sidetracked when the Revolutionary War began. He was made a captain in the First North Carolina Continental Regiment when the Third Provincial Congress elected him to the post in 1775. The unit's leader was Moore's uncle, Colonel James Moore. Moore was strongly behind the cause of independence, but the war years took a large toll on the Moore family. In 1777, Moore's father died, James Moore died and Moore's brother was killed in a battle. Moore resigned his post and went back home to take care of his mother and the family's plantation. Moore stayed involved in wartime activities though. His actions with a militia and participation in raids on British troops in Wilmington were enough to merit retaliation from the British. The British destroyed his plantation and left Moore's finances in shambles.

1755 — Moore is born in Brunswick (or New Hanover County), North Carolina.

1775 — Moore receives his law license.

1782 — Moore is elected to the North Carolina legislature.

1799 — Moore is named to the Supreme Court by President John Adams.

1810 — Moore dies in Bladen County, North Carolina.

Moore never became the outstanding figure in history that he might have been.

Moore rebounded quickly. He soon became a prominent local figure and regained his fortune through his prosperous private law practice. He was known for his skill in criminal law, his keen perception, and strong powers of analysis. Moore's mind was more imposing than his personal appearance. He was a short, thin man with wide eyes and a large forehead, accentuated by his receding hairline. Moore married a local woman, Susanna Elizabeth Eagles, and was elected to the North Carolina General Assembly.

During the 1780s Moore's reputation spread. He and William R. Davie were known as the top legal minds in the state. In 1782, he was named North Carolina's Attorney General. His most notable trial as Attorney General was *Bayard v. Singleton* in 1787. The case had to do with the confiscated property of Tories who had left the state. The case was historic because it was an early discussion of the doctrine of judicial review. Moore served in this position for nine years until he resigned in protest of a new law that allowed for a new position of Solicitor General. Moore felt that the newly created position overlapped with his duties as Attorney General and called the law unconstitutional.

Despite the illustrious beginnings of his professional career, Moore never became the outstanding figure in history that he might have been. Although he rose to the top of his profession, his career was marked by missed opportunities and unfortunate absences. For example, Moore was a Federalist, supporting a strong, centralized federal government instead of less concentrated power spread among each of the states. So when the Annapolis Convention was arranged in 1786 to help strengthen the Confederation, Moore was the natural choice to attend as the delegate from North Carolina. But Moore was ill and unable to attend the meeting. When the next convention happened the following year, Moore was not chosen. His well-known political views also cost him support among North Carolina's pro-state farmers in a bid for a seat on the United States Senate. He lost by one vote in the legislature.

In the 1790s, Moore concentrated on his plantation and private practice, but in 1798, he was one of three people nominated by President John Adams to negotiate a treaty with the Cherokee Nation. But again, Moore missed his chance to make a bold impression on history. He left the negotiations before the treaty was signed.

In 1798, Moore was elected to the North Carolina superior court, and after less than a year on the bench, he was appointed by President Adams to fill James Iredell's vacated seat as associate justice on the United States Supreme Court. (Coincidentally, Moore had also replaced Iredell as Attorney General.) Reportedly, President Adams had actually wanted Davie but Davie had just been given a diplomatic position to France.

Becoming a Supreme Court Justice would seem like Moore's chance to make his mark on history, but Moore actually exerted less influence as associate justice than he had earlier in his career in private practice and fighting for his causes like Constitutional ratification. During his five-year tenure, Moore wrote only one opinion. The case, *Bas v. Tingy* (1800), came before the Court soon after Moore arrived. It concerned a 1799 law about what recaptors of ships seized by the French should receive as a bounty. Moore upheld the opinion that the United States was in an undeclared war with France, thus ships captured by France should be treated the same as those captured by an enemy nation. In a later case involving French armed ships, *United States v. Schooner Peggy* (1801), Moore was absent during the final arguments and the decision.

In 1804, Moore resigned from the Court. Like several of the judges before him, the rigors of having to travel around to the various circuit courts was too much for him. He became ill and returned to his plantation. In his later years, Moore was instrumental in establishing the University of North Carolina. In 1810, he died at his son-in-law's house. Since there is little record of his judicial life, perhaps his greatest legacy was his work in the establishment of the university. ◆

During his five-year tenure, Moore wrote only one opinion.

Murphy, Frank

APRIL 13, 1890–JULY 19, 1949 ● ASSOCIATE JUSTICE

William Francis "Frank" Murphy was born in Sand Beach (now Harbor Beach), Michigan, on April 13, 1890, the third of four children of John F. Murphy, a lawyer who was active in Democratic Party politics, and Mary Brennan. He received his law degree (with an undistinguished academic record) from the University of Michigan in 1914, then joined a Detroit law firm, where he practiced until the United States entered World War I in 1917. After training as an officer, he was commissioned as an infantry lieutenant and served briefly in Europe at the war's end.

Frank Murphy

Murphy began a career in public service shortly after his discharge from the army in 1919. He was appointed first assistant U.S. attorney for the Eastern District of Michigan. He returned to private law practice briefly in 1922 and 1923, but in 1924 he was appointed to the Recorder's Court, a criminal court in Detroit, where he served until 1930. During these years his judicial philosophy was already in evidence. A liberal Democrat, he consistently defended the rights of organized labor and the civil liberties of criminal defendants.

During the 1930s Murphy turned his attention to politics. In 1930 he was elected mayor of Detroit, devoting much of his energy to trying to help the city overcome the crushing unemployment caused by the onset of the Great Depression. In 1932 he vigorously supported Franklin D. Roosevelt in his successful bid for the presidency, and the president rewarded him by appointing him governor-general of the Philippine Islands. Later, when the Philippines were made a commonwealth in 1935, Murphy was appointed the islands' first high commissioner. In both capacities he tried to bring New Deal-type reforms to the islands.

When Roosevelt ran for reelection in 1936, Murphy returned to the United States to help the incumbent president carry Michigan. That year, too, he successfully ran for governor of Michigan and served a single two-year term. Perhaps his most noteworthy accomplishment as governor was helping to settle a sit-down strike at General Motors and forcing the company to recognize the workers' new union, the United Auto Workers. In 1938 he lost his bid for reelection in the largely Republican state.

Roosevelt called on Murphy again in 1939, appointing him the nation's attorney general. During the year that Murphy served in this capacity, he created the Civil Rights Division of the Department of Justice and led a crusade against corruption and organized crime. When U.S. Supreme Court Justice Pierce

Butler died in 1939, Murphy seemed the perfect candidate to replace him. Like Pierce, he was a Catholic from the Midwest. Further, he supported President Roosevelt's New Deal economic policies for dealing with the Depression, and he seemed likely to support the president's international goals as world war loomed again. Early in 1940 he was unanimously confirmed by the Senate, and he took his oath of office on February 5.

Murphy, though, was reluctant to take the position. He was not sure that he was qualified, nor that he wanted to trade an active life in politics for the more contemplative life of a jurist. When war broke out, for example, he wanted to return to military service, despite being in his early 50s, and in 1943 and 1944 he asked the president to send him back to the Philippines. The president refused, and Murphy had to settle for an appointment as chair of the Philippine War Relief committee and chair of the National Committee against Nazi Persecution and Extermination of the Jews.

Murphy sat on the high court until his death in 1949. At first he tended to vote with the Court's majority, but later he began to articulate a more pronounced individual view. To his way of thinking, a Supreme Court justice should not rely entirely on precedent. Rather, he believed a justice should rely at least as much on individual conscience and the public interest in upholding principles of justice and the freedom of the individual. Because he rejected precedent as his sole guide, he dissented from the Court majority 69 times, and in 25 cases in which the Court overturned precedent, he ruled with the majority 21 times. He once observed that being on the Supreme Court provides "the rarest of all opportunities to evangelize for tolerance and all things that are just, that sweeten this life for men." Colleagues often remarked, "The Court tempers justice with Murphy."

Murphy wrote numerous opinions in the areas of labor law, the rights of criminal defendants, and civil rights. Perhaps his most noteworthy labor law opinion was his very first, *Thornhill v. Alabama* (1940). Murphy ruled that peaceful picketing in a labor dispute fell under the umbrella of freedom of speech. After this decision states were no longer able to prohibit picketing in labor disputes, even if the economic interests of the company were harmed.

Murphy's most significant opinions in defense of the rights of criminal defendants were *Trupiano v. United States* (1948) and *Wolf v. Colorado* (1949). In *Trupiano* Murphy ruled that federal law enforcement officers needed a warrant to search or seize

"No other single member of the Court . . . approaches the consistent advocacy of civil liberties as did Murphy."
Vincent M. Barnett, Jr., *Cornell Law Quarterly*, 1946

Murphy ruled that peaceful picketing in a labor dispute fell under the umbrella of freedom of speech.

property. In *Wolf* he dissented, arguing that evidence obtained illegally in state cases should be excluded, just as it was in federal cases. In other cases he argued that defendants in state criminal cases were entitled to counsel, even in non-capital cases—a position the Court as a whole did not adopt until years later.

As a civil libertarian, Murphy was a strong advocate of First Amendment rights, but he tended to give precedence to freedom of religion. Thus, he defended the right of religious groups such as the Jehovah's Witnesses to practice their religion, including conscientious objection to military service. Six years before the important 1954 desegregation case *Brown v. Board of Education*, he opposed "separate-but-equal" schooling. He also dissented in *Korematsu v. United States*, a famous 1944 case concerning the internment of Japanese-Americans on the West Coast during World War II. Murphy wrote that the internment fell into "the ugly abyss of racism."

Murphy's health began to fail during his final three years on the Court, and he was hospitalized with a variety of illnesses. He died on July 19, 1949. ◆

Nelson, Samuel

NOVEMBER 10, 1792–DECEMBER 13, 1873 ● ASSOCIATE JUSTICE

Samuel Nelson was born November 10, 1792 in Hebron, New York. His grandparents were Scotch-Irish immigrants who arrived in the mid-1700s. His parents, John Rogers and Jean McArthur, raised him on a farm. Nelson attended local schools and did so well that he was pushed to go into the ministry. Nelson agreed with the plan and pursued a career as a minister by moving to Vermont at age 15 to attend Middlebury College. Academically, he started a year ahead of his peers who were entering as freshmen. After graduating, Nelson changed his plans and decided that he wanted to study law and took a clerkship with Judges Savage and Woods in Salem, New York.

Nelson began forging a professional and personal life on his own. He was admitted to the New York bar in 1817 and opened his own office in Cortland, New York. Two years later, Nelson married Pamela Woods, the daughter of his former boss, Judge Woods. During this time, Nelson also made a first **foray** into politics. In 1820, he was a presidential elector for James Monroe. His burgeoning political involvement led to an appointment to the post of local postmaster. In 1821, he attended the New York State Constitutional Convention as the delegate from Cortland County. Nelson was the youngest delegate there.

This time in Nelson's life was also marked by personal tragedy. In 1822, his wife died after bearing one son. In 1825, Nelson married his second wife, Catherine Ann Russell. The two would have two daughters and one son.

foray: journey.

1792 — Nelson is born in Hebron, New York.

1820 — Nelson is named postmaster of Cortland, New York.

1831 — Nelson is named to the New York Supreme Court.

1845 — Nelson is confirmed to the United States Supreme Court.

1873 — Nelson dies in Cooperstown, New York.

During these years on the bench, Nelson gained the solid reputation that would stay with him throughout his career.

Despite the upheaval in his personal life, Nelson's professional life flourished. In 1823, he was appointed a New York circuit judge. The appointment was the first of many and marked the beginning of a judicial career that would last nearly 50 years. Nelson was next named an associate justice of the New York Supreme Court in 1831. Five years later, he became chief justice of that court.

In 1845, President John Tyler nominated Nelson to fill the vacancy on the United States Supreme Court left by Justice Smith Thompson, who had died. Nelson was not Tyler's first choice; in fact, Nelson was very far down the list. Other choices ahead of him included Martin Van Buren (who Tyler chose to eliminate him from running for president), several judges who did not want the position, and several judges who were deemed unsuitable. Matters were complicated by the fact that impeachment proceedings against Tyler had been introduced in the House. Nelson was known as a Jacksonian Democrat, but when his name came before the Senate, he was quickly confirmed without any political wrangling. Despite this inauspicious start, it was soon recognized that Nelson was a good, sensible choice for the job.

During these years on the bench, Nelson gained the solid reputation that would stay with him throughout his career. He was known as a person who was more interested in following the law, rather than advancing a political cause. He was thought to follow his own conscience and did not vote according to any particular party lines. He was a very diligent worker who took his duties very seriously. Many of his biographers describe Nelson as a man with common sense.

Nelson's areas of expertise included admiralty, international and patent law. *Hotchkiss v. Greenwood* (1850) was a case involving patent law. The opinion written by Nelson was a leading one in applying the concept of nonobviousness of subject matter as one of the requirements for something to be patented. He used his background in admiralty law in deciding the cases of *Hough v. Western Transportation Co.* (1866) and *New Jersey Steam Navigation Co. v. Merchants' Bank* (1848). Both involved the jurisdiction of the federal court in matters of admiralty.

Nelson also presided over cases involving the ratios of power of states versus the federal government in regulating commerce. In the *Passengers Cases* (1847), he upheld the use of state powers. Nelson was not especially eager to take a proactive stance and decide on matters involving constitutional questions. He had been on the Court 10 years before he wrote his first majority opinion on a constitutional matter in *Pennsylvania v. Wheeling & Belmont Bridge Company* (1855). During his years on the court, he only wrote 22 majority opinions on cases involving constitutional matters. This was compared to the 307 he wrote in other cases.

Twice during Nelson's time on the bench he was mentioned as a possible presidential candidate, but he never ended up being seriously considered.

Nelson served almost 27 years in the United States Supreme Court. During these years, he always strived to look at each case on its own merits and approach it fairly, carefully and diligently. Because he did not make showy, groundbreaking decisions, his career did not make a big imprint upon history.

In 1871, Nelson was appointed by President Ulysses S. Grant as a United States representative to the Alabama Claims Commission. This committee was to help resolve the differences with England that had happened over the Civil War and issues of maritime law. Though successful in his endeavors, the strain of the job coupled with Nelson's age were too much for him. He resigned from the court in 1872 and died December 13, 1873 in Cooperstown, New York. ◆

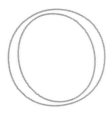

O'Connor, Sandra Day

MARCH 26, 1930– ● ASSOCIATE JUSTICE

Sandra Day O'Connor became the first woman associate justice of the United States Supreme Court in 1981, effectively ending the all-male hegemony that had begun with the Court's inception in the 18th century. O'Connor's position as a centrist on the Court has brought her praise from both conservatives and liberals, who recognize her for her integrity.

Sandra Day O'Connor

Sandra Day was born in El Paso, Texas, on March 26, 1930. The first of three children of Harry and Ada Mae Day, Sandra grew up on a 155,000-acre family ranch near Duncan, Arizona. Her grandfather, Henry Clay Day, had come West from Vermont in the late 1800s and began ranching in the rough region that later became part of the state of Arizona. The Lazy B ranch was far from any town or hospital, so Ada Mae Day stayed at her mother's home in El Paso before giving birth to Sandra.

As a child, Sandra spent her time at the Lazy B, where she learned to ride horses with cowboys, drive a truck, fire a gun, and mend fences. She lived at her grandmother's house in El Paso during the

In July 1981, President Ronald Reagan made good on a campaign promise to appoint a woman to the Supreme Court by picking O'Connor as his first appointee to the U.S. Supreme Court.

school term each year. A serious and high-achieving student, she skipped two grades and graduated from high school at 16.

Sandra went on to Stanford University near San Francisco. She graduated from Stanford in 1950 and Stanford Law School in 1952. She met John Jay O'Connor III, a fellow Stanford law student, and the couple married when she graduated. Coincidentally, at Stanford she also met William Rehnquist, later her colleague on the nation's highest court.

As a woman in a mainly male profession, O'Connor suffered a number of rejections from firms that did not hire women. She eventually found a job as deputy county attorney in San Mateo, California. She later said that this job taught her to love public service. John took a position with the United States Army that took the couple to Frankfort, Germany, for three years. In that time, O'Connor also worked as a lawyer for the military.

In 1957, the O'Connors settled in Phoenix, Arizona, and O'Connor stopped practicing law to stay home with the couple's three sons. O'Connor worked in many volunteer jobs before returning to work as soon as her sons were all in school. "I just never thought about living my life without being in the workforce," she said later. After pursuing private practice in Maryville, Arizona, she became an assistant attorney general for the state in 1965. Four years later, running as a Republican, she won a state Senate seat. O'Connor learned to be an insider, and after four years, she became the Senate majority leader, becoming the first woman in the United States to hold the position of majority leader.

In 1974, O'Connor won a race for the post of Maricopa county judge. In 1979, the governor appointed her to the Arizona Court of Appeals, the second highest court in the state. O'Connor's reputation as a careful jurist spread.

In July 1981, President Ronald Reagan made good on a campaign promise to appoint a woman to the Supreme Court by picking O'Connor as his first appointee to the U.S. Supreme Court. After her confirmation by the Senate, she was sworn in as an associate justice on September 25, 1981. She filled the vacancy created by the retirement of Justice Potter Stewart. O'Connor became the first woman to serve as an associate justice of the Supreme Court of the United States.

From the start of her tenure on the court, O'Connor aligned herself with conservative Rehnquist. However, in the late 1980s, O'Connor became more of a centrist on a court that was clearly divided between conservatives and liberals. Proving to be moderate and pragmatic, she sometimes sided with the court's liberal minority on social issues. It became common for 5-4 rulings by the Court's conservative bloc to be tempered by an O'Connor **concurrence.** Court observers began seeing O'Connor as the swing vote on a Court often divided over issues such as affirmative action, the death penalty, and abortion. "As O'Connor goes, so goes the Court," one observer would declare in 1990. When David Souter joined the Court in the fall of that year, O'Connor and he voted the same way in every decision during his first term.

Among O'Connor's noted opinions were those dealing with issues of religious freedom. A concurring opinion she wrote in *Lynch v. Donnelly* (1984) on the constitutionality of a government-sponsored nativity scene established the legal standard for determining when such displays violate the Constitution's prohibition on government involvement in religion. A year later, another O'Connor concurrence was important in outlining the constitutional bounds on a state-prescribed "voluntary moment of silence" for school children. According to O'Connor, the challenged law was unconstitutional in that its purpose was to encourage prayer. She said it favored "the child who chooses to pray . . . over the child who chooses to meditate or reflect."

In other opinions, O'Connor endorsed affirmative action for minorities if "narrowly tailored" to correct a clearly demonstrated wrong, but not otherwise. In a landmark 1989 opinion, *City of Richmond v. J. A. Croson Co.,* O'Connor's opinion for the Court concluded that government programs setting aside a fixed percentage of public contracts for minority businesses violated equal protection.

On the highly controversial issue of abortion, O'Connor searched for a middle ground in a series of decisions in the 1980s. In *Planned Parenthood of Southeastern Pennsylvania v. Casey* (1992), O'Connor and Justice Anthony Kennedy joined a controversial opinion by Justice Souter that criticized the constitutional foundation for the Court's original 1973 recognition of the right to abortion (*Roe v. Wade*). However, they upheld *Roe v. Wade.* O'Connor favored limiting intrusions by federal courts on state powers, especially in criminal matters. She took a similarly restrained view of federal judicial power with respect to the legislative and executive branches.

Many people wondered whether a woman Supreme Court justice would tend to issue opinions favorable to women, but

1930 O'Connor is born in El Paso, Texas.

1952 O'Connor graduates from Stanford University Law School.

1965 O'Connor becomes assistant attorney general for Arizona.

1979 O'Connor is appointed to the Arizona Court of Appeals.

1981 O'Connor is selected by President Ronald Reagan as the first woman Supreme Court justice.

2000 O'Connor votes with the majority in *Bush v. Gore.*

concurrence: a concurring opinion written by one or more of the justices which agrees with the majority opinion, but may differ with the reasoning in reaching that decision.

Meritor Savings Bank v. Vinson (1986)

In March of 1986, the Supreme Court of the United States heard arguments directed to the question: Did the Civil Rights Act of 1964 prohibit the creation of a "hostile workplace environment," or were its provisions limited to preventing direct economic discrimination such as paying lower salaries to women who did the same work as men?

After an employee of the Meritor Savings Bank, Mechelle Vinson, was dismissed from her job, she filed suit against the vice president of the bank, Sidney Taylor. Her suit charged that his constant sexual harassment created a hostile working environment in violation of Title VII of the Civil Rights Act. The court agreed with Vinson, and awarded both compensatory and punitive damages. The bank appealed the case to the Supreme Court. Robert Troll, Jr. argued the case for Meritor Savings Bank, claiming that the Civil Rights Act was not violated because Ms. Vinson had not been subject to economic discrimination, and that the Act did not apply to any other forms of discrimination.

On June 19, 1986, the Supreme Court found in favor of Ms. Vinson. In its opinion, it cited that, in drafting civil rights legislation, the intent of Congress was clearly "to strike at the entire spectrum of disparate treatment" between the sexes. The Court went on to say that the Equal Employment Opportunities Commission guidelines did indeed treat sexual harassment as a form of discrimination. The Court's decision made it far more difficult for employers to tolerate subtle forms of discriminatory practice in the workplace, and held the employer, not just the harassing employee, liable for such practices when they occurred.

observers saw little about O'Connor's decisions that were feminist. "I think the important fact about my appointment is not that I will decide cases as a woman," she said just after joining the Court, "but that I am a woman who will get to decide cases." In 1982, O'Connor wrote an opinion invalidating a women-only enrollment policy at a Mississippi state nursing school, saying it "tends to perpetuate the stereotyped view of nursing as an exclusively women's job."

In the 1999–2000 term, O'Connor voted in the majority in all but 4 of the 73 cases the Court decided. O'Connor's influence as a centrist became stronger than ever. She often limited the influence of the Court's right wing, namely Rehnquist, Antonin Scalia, and Clarence Thomas. In a 5–4 decision striking down state laws that banned a medical procedure that critics called "partial-birth" abortion, O'Connor was a key vote for the majority. But she offered a blueprint for states that still wanted to ban the controversial procedure. Typical of O'Connor, she steered a course down the middle of the Court's ideological spectrum but kept the door open for a similar case to come out differently.

The U.S. presidential elections of November 2000 drew the Court into a case unlike any it had dealt with in the past. In the nearly tied contest between Vice President Al Gore and Texas Governor George W. Bush, the state of Florida became the final battleground, as numerous disputes arose over how votes were counted. In one case, the Florida Supreme Court ruled that Florida's Secretary of State had set an unreasonable deadline for counties to turn in their vote tallies. Her deadline had prevented many votes from being recounted, allowing Bush to keep his slim lead.

On December 4 the Court issued an unusual unsigned decision that **remanded** the matter back to the Florida Supreme Court "for further consideration." By doing this, the Court declined to decide the merits of the case, saying they found "considerable uncertainty" in the Florida court's decision. Court observers commented that the nation's highest court had managed to save its image as a nonpartisan body by not siding with either political candidate.

O'Connor's self-discipline and drive became legendary. The usually tanned O'Connor liked to ski and play golf and tennis. Off the bench, she became a center of social events among her court colleagues. She organized parties, bridge games, and official trips for the justices. She helped Justice Harry Blackmun obtain a grand piano for the Court, and they began an annual spring musicale.

O'Connor kept her close ties with Rehnquist, and played bridge with Justices Kennedy and Stephen Breyer. She also shared an interest in international legal affairs with those two and Ruth Bader Ginsburg. As the two women justices on the Court, Ginsburg and O'Connor were not especially close, but they respected each other. Ginsburg, who joined the court in 1993, called O'Connor "the most helpful big sister anyone could have."

O'Connor was tall with sharp and clear eyes, while her voice was quiet and confidently authoritative. Her law clerks described her as intense and a perfectionist, but also warm and upbeat. O'Connor established a morning exercise class in the Court gym for the women employees. While she often worked long hours—sometimes seven day weeks—she treated her staff to popcorn, Mexican brunches, or outings to the Smithsonian Institution or white-water rafting.

In 1988, O'Connor was diagnosed with breast cancer. The day before her surgery, she kept a speaking engagement at Washington and Lee University. She returned to work ten days after the surgery, never missing an oral argument. ◆

O'Connor's self-discipline and drive became legendary.

remand: court order which refers a case back to the lower court from which it came, usually with instructions to proceed in a different manner.

Paterson, William

DECEMBER 24, 1745–SEPTEMBER 9, 1806 ● ASSOCIATE JUSTICE

William Paterson

William Paterson was born on Christmas Eve in County Antrim, Ireland. His parents, Richard and Mary Paterson, landed at New Castle, Delaware, in October, 1747. The family lived in various places, including several towns in Connecticut and Trenton, New Jersey, while Paterson's father traveled around selling tinware. In 1750, the family settled in Princeton, New Jersey, and Paterson's father got a job making and selling tinware. Paterson's father was a wise businessman who saved his money and made prudent real estate investments. By the time Paterson was old enough to go to college, his family had enough money to send him to the College of New Jersey (which later became Princeton University).

Paterson received his bachelor's degree in 1763 and three years later, he earned an M.A. degree. In college, Paterson already showed the energy and drive that would be a hallmark of the rest of his career. For example, even though he was busy getting his M.A. at the College of

231

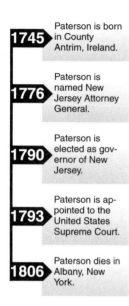

1745 — Paterson is born in County Antrim, Ireland.

1776 — Paterson is named New Jersey Attorney General.

1790 — Paterson is elected as governor of New Jersey.

1793 — Paterson is appointed to the United States Supreme Court.

1806 — Paterson dies in Albany, New York.

During his career Paterson became known for his belief in a strong national government.

New Jersey, Paterson found time to study law with Richard Stockton, a man who would later go on to sign the Declaration of Independence. Paterson was also involved in extracurricular activities. He was a co-founder of a club called "The Well-Meaning Society," in which students gathered to discuss politics and issues of the day. (The club would later become the long-running Cliosophic Club).

Paterson passed the bar in 1768 and began practicing law in New Bromley, New Jersey. But he found life to be dull in the town and soon returned to Princeton. Here his political career began. Paterson became known as a advocate for independence, so as the American Revolution began, Paterson was a natural choice to be a leader. In 1775, he went to the Provincial Congress of New Jersey and was quickly elected to be the assistant secretary. Paterson was deeply involved in local politics and served in many capacities, including stints on the legislative council and the council of safety. He was also instrumental in helping write the state's constitution. In 1779, Paterson married Cornelia Bell. He would go on to have three children with her.

From 1776 to 1783, he served as the state's attorney general. In 1783, Paterson's personal life suffered a setback when his wife died during childbirth. Despite this tragedy, his professional life kept up its frantic pace and Paterson managed to handle his thriving law practice. During these years, Paterson made a lot of money defending weathy men and creditors. In 1785, two years after his first wife's death, he married Euphemia White, who had been a close friend of his wife's.

During his career Paterson became known for his belief in a strong national government. He had very specific opinions about how the nation should be organized and showed no hesitation in speaking his beliefs. Paterson had a major influence on the Constitutional Convention of 1787. There was a dispute in how each state should be represented in the legislature. A "Virginia Plan" suggested that each state should be represented according to their population. Paterson's idea (commonly called the New Jersey Plan) suggested that each state should have the same amount of representation, regardless of size. The two plans were combined in what was called the Great Compromise. In this plan there would be two chambers in the legislature, an upper house and a lower house. One, the Senate, would have equal representation from each state. The other, the House of

Representatives, would have representation according to population.

In 1789, Paterson was elected as a Senator from New Jersey. He served for a short time, but cut his stay short when the governor of New Jersey died and Paterson was chosen to succeed him. Though Paterson did not serve in the Senate very long, he was characteristically productive during the time he was there. While there, he co-wrote the Judiciary Act of 1789. This document single-handedly laid out the organization of the federal courts. It invented the idea of a United States Supreme Court with a Chief Justice and five Associate Justices, developed the system of circuit and district courts and created the position of Attorney General. It also gave the federal courts the power to override state court decision when the Constitution or federal law was involved. This was a major step in giving the federal courts a large amount of power. During what little spare time he must have had, he also helped charter the town of Paterson, New Jersey, wrote the Laws of the State of New Jersey, and helped reorganize the local court system.

In 1793, President George Washington named Paterson to the Supreme Court to replace Thomas Johnson. Paterson became as involved in the Court as he had with all of his previous ventures. He was a major voice on the Court for the 15 years he served. In cases involving interpretations of the document, Paterson was able to speak to the intentions of the framers when writing it because he had been intregal in framing the Constitution.

Paterson held what most would take as an unreasonably hard line in fighting what he saw as **sedition,** that is, rebellion against the state. He advocated harsh punishment in cases against various writers who criticized the federal government. In a notorious case against newspaper publisher Matthew Lyon, Paterson earned a fair amount of enemies for his overbearing ruling.

Paterson spent much of his time traveling around to various courts, or "riding circuit." Traveling in those days was much more arduous than it is today and it began to adversely affect Paterson's health and in 1804, he was injured while traveling. In 1806, he headed to Ballston Springs, New York, in search of medical treatment, but only made it to his daughter's house in Albany, New York. He died September 9, 1806. ◆

Paterson became as involved in the Court as he had with all of his previous ventures.

sedition: incitement of resistance or the actual action of insurrection of an established authority.

Peckham, Rufus W.

NOVEMBER 8, 1838–OCTOBER 24, 1909 ● ASSOCIATE JUSTICE

The Peckham name was intimately connected with New York State politics throughout much of the 19th century. Rufus Wheeler Peckham, Sr., and his wife, Isabella Lacey, were descendants of prominent families whose roots in the state dated back to the 17th century. Peckham senior, whose name was highly regarded in political and judicial circles, served as the district attorney of Albany County and, later, as a judge on the New York Supreme Court (the state's lowest court) and on the state's highest court, the Court of Appeals. Peckham senior was lost at sea while traveling abroad in 1873.

Before his untimely death, he and Isabella had two sons. The elder, Wheeler Hazard Peckham, became a distinguished attorney who would play a prominent role in busting up the infamous Boss Tweed political machine, Tammany Hall, that bilked New York City taxpayers out of millions of dollars. The younger son, Rufus Wheeler Peckham, Jr., also became a lawyer and, eventually, a member of the U.S. Supreme Court.

Rufus Peckham

Peckham was born on November 8, 1838. He was educated at the Albany Boys Academy and later studied privately in Philadelphia. In 1856 he and Wheeler took a year-long tour of Europe, a common practice among privileged young Americans at the time. When he returned to the United States, he studied law for two years at his father's firm, Peckham & Tremain, where he practiced with his brother after passing the bar examination at age 21. That year, his father was elected to the state supreme court.

Peckham was a successful attorney. Among his clients was the Albany and Susquehanna Railroad, which he defended against the Erie

Railroad and its owners, the notorious financiers Jim Fiske and Jay Gould. He became a prominent member of Albany society and in 1866 married Harriette M. Arnold, the daughter of a wealthy New York City businessman. He also became active in politics, allying himself with the upstate wing of the Democratic Party. This alliance led to his election in 1869 as district attorney for Albany County. In this capacity he became friends with Grover Cleveland, who later became governor of New York and president of the United States.

Peckham served as district attorney for three years. He returned to private practice, but he entered public life again in 1881 when he became counsel to the city of Albany. Promotion came rapidly: In 1883 he became a judge on the New York Supreme Court, and in 1886 he was elected to the New York Court of Appeals. Amazingly, his career path—private practice, county district attorney, supreme court judge, and court of appeals justice—was precisely the same path his father had followed, and visitors to the court of appeals at the time noted the striking resemblance between Peckham and the portrait of his father that hung there.

Peckham served happily on the court of appeals until 1895. Although he was a partisan Democrat, he successfully kept his political opinions out of the courtroom—so much so that in 1891 he upheld the victories of Republican candidates in contested election cases. It was this nonpartisanship in the courtroom that made him a suitable candidate for elevation to the U.S. Supreme Court as a replacement for Justice Howell Jackson when he died in 1895.

Two years earlier, President Cleveland had attempted to fill the seat left vacant by the death of Justice Samuel Blatchford with Rufus's brother Wheeler, but Wheeler's nomination was blocked by New York senator David Hill because Wheeler, as chair of the New York State Bar Association, had ordered the investigation of one of Hill's political allies for election fraud. The protracted battle was part of an ongoing struggle between Cleveland and Hill for control of the state's Democratic Party. Thus, when Rufus's name was proposed in 1895, Cleveland contacted Hill to determine if the senator had any objection. Since Rufus had stayed out of party politics, Hill did not. Rufus Peckham was confirmed by the Senate late that year.

Peckham had little reaction to the appointment. He actually preferred being a trial court judge and worried that he would find the scholarly halls of the Supreme Court dull. He accepted the

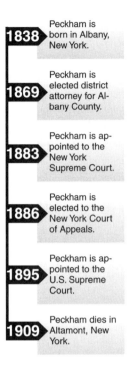

1838 Peckham is born in Albany, New York.

1869 Peckham is elected district attorney for Albany County.

1883 Peckham is appointed to the New York Supreme Court.

1886 Peckham is elected to the New York Court of Appeals.

1895 Peckham is appointed to the U.S. Supreme Court.

1909 Peckham dies in Altamont, New York.

Peckham devoted the rest of his life to his work as a Supreme Court justice.

position, though, commenting to a friend, "If I have got to be put away on the shelf I suppose I might as well be on the top shelf."

Peckham devoted the rest of his life to his work as a Supreme Court justice. He stayed out of politics even though his name was mentioned as a possible candidate for state governor in 1907. His tenure coincided with a period of extraordinarily rapid business expansion, years during which the Court struggled with new and evolving concepts of the proper role of government in regulating the affairs of business.

The Court often stood in opposition to the Progressive and Populist movements, which wanted government to restrain what they saw as the excesses of corporations and business trusts. As a justice, Peckham believed that his primary duty was to draw—and police—sharp lines between the powers of the state governments, those of the federal government, and the rights of individuals. Thus, for example, he believed that government had the power to regulate business, but only when interstate commerce was directly and significantly affected. He also believed in the right of the individual to enter freely into contracts and to be free of government interference in the process.

These views led to what may have been Peckham's most significant decision, in *Lochner v. New York* (1905). In this case, a baker in Utica, New York, was convicted of violating state laws regulating maximum working hours. The baker appealed to the Supreme Court, arguing that the state's need to protect public health had nothing to do with the number of hours his employees worked. Peckham agreed and found the New York statute unconstitutional, writing, "Clean and wholesome bread does not depend upon whether the baker works ten hours per day or 60 hours per week."

Peckham's majority opinion drew sharp dissents from Oliver Wendell Holmes, Jr., and others—dissents that may have influenced Peckham three years later when he joined a unanimous Court in upholding a similar law in Oregon. In the view of many constitutional scholars, the *Lochner* decision represents the high-water mark of the Court's tendency to judge cases on the basis of abstract principles and precedents rather than social and economic changes that may have left those principles and precedents outdated.

Rufus W. Peckham died while still in office on October 24, 1909, in Altamont, New York. ◆

Pitney, Mahlon

FEBRUARY 5, 1858–DECEMBER 9, 1924 ● ASSOCIATE JUSTICE

Mahlon Pitney was born in Morristown, New Jersey, on February 5, 1858, the second of three sons of Henry Cooper Pitney, a prominent attorney, and Sarah Louisa Halsted. He attended private schools in Morristown, then enrolled in the College of New Jersey (now Princeton University), where future president Woodrow Wilson was a classmate. During his college years he showed athletic ability and managed the school's baseball team during his senior year; he also persuaded a major league player from Philadelphia to coach the team, marking what may have been the first time any college hired a professional baseball coach.

Pitney showed aptitude as a debater in college, so when he graduated in 1879, his father convinced him that he could suc-

Mahlon Pitney

ceed as an attorney. He read law in his father's office and gained admission to the state bar association in 1882. That year, too, he completed a master's degree at Princeton. When he became a Supreme Court justice years later, he was the only member of the Court without a law degree.

Pitney set up a private practice in Dover, New Jersey, where he also worked as a director and officer of an iron company. Seven years later, though, his father was appointed vice chancellor of the state court system, so Pitney returned to Morristown to manage the family law practice. In 1891 he married Florence Shelton, and in time the couple had three children.

In the early 1890s Pitney rose to prominence in politics. He was a Republican, but in 1894 he won a seat in the U.S. House of Representatives in the largely Democratic Fourth Congressional District. In his

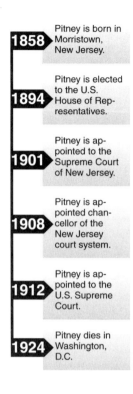

1858 ▶ Pitney is born in Morristown, New Jersey.

1894 ▶ Pitney is elected to the U.S. House of Representatives.

1901 ▶ Pitney is appointed to the Supreme Court of New Jersey.

1908 ▶ Pitney is appointed chancellor of the New Jersey court system.

1912 ▶ Pitney is appointed to the U.S. Supreme Court.

1924 ▶ Pitney dies in Washington, D.C.

two terms in Congress he was a member of the House Appropriations Committee and the Committee to Reform the Civil Service. Pitney, though, wanted to be governor of New Jersey, so in 1899 he resigned from Congress to win a seat in the state senate, a stepping-stone to the governor's mansion.

His political ambitions were derailed when the current governor, who had in mind his own candidate to succeed him, got Pitney out of the way by appointing him as an associate justice of the Supreme Court of New Jersey. Pitney put aside his political ambitions, and in six years on the court, the Court of Errors and Appeals, the state's highest court, reversed only 4 of his 166 opinions. In 1908 the governor appointed him chancellor of the state's court system, where his father had served as vice chancellor.

Pitney was surprised by his appointment to the U.S. Supreme Court in 1912. He had met with President William Howard Taft to discuss over lunch another candidate for the seat left vacant by the death of Justice John Harlan. Pitney, though, apparently impressed the president, who was in a fierce struggle with Theodore Roosevelt for the Republican presidential nomination and wanted to shore up his support with the Republican Party in New Jersey. A week later Pitney was playing golf in Atlantic City when word of his nomination reached him.

Pitney faced a difficult confirmation battle in the U.S. Senate. In the late 19th and early 20th centuries, conservatives and progressives were locked in a fierce battle over the direction the country would take. Progressives were ardent supporters of organized labor and fought what they saw as the excesses of large corporations and business trusts. Conservatives were more inclined to protect the property rights of capitalists and often thought of unions as mobs of rabble-rousers.

Pitney was perceived as conservative, and in particular an opponent of organized labor. Progressives in the Senate, led by the firebrand Robert M. La Follette, pointed to a decision Pitney had reached in 1908 in *Jonas Glass Co. v. Glass Bottle Blowers Association*. In this case, Pitney upheld a lower court order stopping a boycott by a labor association that was trying to unionize a plant. But with the support of his old college classmate, New Jersey governor Woodrow Wilson, Pitney was finally confirmed in March 1912.

Pitney served on the high court for 11 years and earned a reputation for durability. Of the Court's 2,412 decisions during his tenure, he participated in all but 19, and seven of those were during his final illness. He was particularly important for his opinions having to do with taxation. In *Eisner v. Macomber* (1920), for example, he defined "income" under the Sixteenth Amendment and established the principle that income resulting from the increase in value of an investment was not taxable until the investment was sold and the income actually pocketed.

But the issue of his attitude to organized labor continued to dog him. Although he had said in his Senate confirmation hearings, "I am not an enemy to labor," Pitney issued a number of rulings that seemed hostile to unions. Perhaps the most significant was a 1915 case, *Coppage v. Kansas*. Kansas had passed a state law that forbade so-called yellow-dog contracts. These were agreements between workers and management that prohibited workers from joining a labor union as a condition of employment. In invalidating the law, Pitney argued that a worker had no inherent right to join a labor union. Similarly, in *Hitchman Coal & Coke Co. v. Mitchell* (1917), he upheld a company's request for an injunction against the United Mine Workers, a union attempting to organize the company's nonunion workforce.

To label Pitney a reactionary, though, tells only part of the story, for Pitney was opposed to monopoly power—a favorite issue of progressives—and highly supportive of the rights of nonunion workers. In a number of cases that arose under the Federal Employers' Liability Act, he ruled in favor of rail employees injured on the job. He also joined progressives in supporting state workers' compensation laws, and he wrote the Court's opinions affirming the constitutionality of such laws in *New York Central Railroad v. White* (1917) and *Mountain Timber Co. v. Washington* (1917). Similarly, in cases that challenged the Interstate Commerce Commission and rules and rates governing the rail industry, Pitney showed little sympathy for the railroad companies.

Pitney was an active man who loved to hunt, sail on the Atlantic Coast, and play golf. He was also an accomplished chess player and in fact reached draws in two matches with world champion Emanuel Lasker. But overwork on the Court caught up with him in 1922, when a stroke in August forced his retirement at the end of the year. He died in his home in Washington, D.C, on December 9, 1924. ◆

In invalidating the law, Pitney argued that a worker had no inherent right to join a labor union.

Pitney showed little sympathy for the railroad companies.

Powell, Lewis F., Jr.

SEPTEMBER 19, 1907– AUGUST 25, 1998 ● ASSOCIATE JUSTICE

L ewis Franklin Powell, Jr., was born September 19, 1907, in Suffolk, Virginia. His family had deep roots in the region. One of his ancestors was an original Jamestown settler and governor. Powell's mother, Mary Lewis Gwathmey Powell, was raised on a Virginia plantation by an uncle who had been with the Confederate forces at their surrender at Appomatox.

Powell grew up in Richmond where his father, Lewis Franklin Powell, managed a Richmond company that manufactured boxes and furniture. The family prospered, and Powell's mother was a homemaker. Powell was the oldest of four children, and he attended a local private academy that aimed at preparing boys for the University of Virginia. However, Powell went instead to Washington and Lee University in Lexington, Virginia, where he achieved academic success.

Lewis F. Powell, Jr.

Powell graduated from Washington and Lee in 1929 and obtained his law degree from that institution in 1931. He then earned a master's degree in law from the Harvard Law School in 1932. Rejecting a high-paying position in New York, Powell chose instead to return to his hometown, earning a third of the New York offer. He joined a leading Richmond law firm, Christian, Barton, and Parker, that same year. In 1934, he left to join Richmond's largest firm, Hunton, Williams, Anderson, Gay, and Moor. Two years later, Powell married Josephine Rucker, the daughter of a prominent Richmond doctor. In 1938, Powell became a partner in the firm, and soon came to be regarded as one of the state's most distinguished lawyers.

When World War II broke out in 1939, Powell was exempt from the draft because he and his wife had two daughters. However, he enlisted and joined the Army Air Corps intelligence unit. He became chief of a very important intelligence operation, called the ULTRA project, which interpreted German code and learned what their military plans were. Powell felt proud of saving many lives in the war through his efforts.

Returning to his law practice after the war, Powell and his wife had another daughter and a son. He became involved in local politics and served in several civic posts. In 1954, the U.S. Supreme Court declared segregated schools illegal (*Brown v. Board of Education of Topeka*), which caused opposition in the South. As chairman of the public school board in Richmond (1952–61), Powell became largely responsible for that city's eventual peaceful integration of the public schools, while other school districts underwent bitter conflicts.

During the 1960s, Powell served as president of three American legal associations. He served as president of the American Bar Association from 1964 to 1965. In that position, he proposed various improvements in court procedures and in legal aid to the poor. In Powell's many years of legal services, he earned respect among colleagues as being thoughtful, practical, and good at reconciling opposing parties.

When Justice Hugo L. Black retired, President Richard M. Nixon nominated the greatly respected Powell for a seat on the Supreme Court on October 22, 1971. Powell was 64 years old, and at first he declined the nomination, thinking he was too old. However, Nixon appealed to him, and his family and friends encouraged him. The Senate quickly confirmed Powell in December, with only one senator voting against him. He took his seat on the court in January of 1972.

Soon Powell made his mark. In *United States v. United States District Court* (1972) Powell wrote the opinion that limited the power of the president to authorize searches to protect national security. In *San Antonio Independent School District v. Rodriguez* (1973), Powell wrote an opinion that gave broad authority to state and local officials in administering public schools.

Nixon had chosen Powell to be a Southern conservative, and he was one of the more conservative members of the court during the 1970s and early 1980s. But Powell's service far outlived the political aims of Nixon's strategy. Powell took a moderate-to-liberal stance on such issues as legalized abortion, separation of church and state, and civil rights questions. He was a strong defender of free speech rights and other civil liberties. In 1986, he cast the deciding vote in two major court rulings

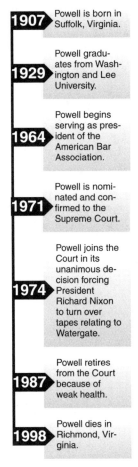

1907 Powell is born in Suffolk, Virginia.

1929 Powell graduates from Washington and Lee University.

1964 Powell begins serving as president of the American Bar Association.

1971 Powell is nominated and confirmed to the Supreme Court.

1974 Powell joins the Court in its unanimous decision forcing President Richard Nixon to turn over tapes relating to Watergate.

1987 Powell retires from the Court because of weak health.

1998 Powell dies in Richmond, Virginia.

"For over 15 years on the Supreme Court, he approached each case without an ideological agenda, carefully applying the Constitution, the law and Supreme Court precedent regardless of his own personal views about the case. His opinions were a model of balance and judiciousness."

President Bill Clinton, August 25, 1998, on Powell

executive privelege an exception for the executive in a branch of government from the disclosure of communications in spite of legal requirements to do so; rationalized by the threat of an adverse affect on the functions of the executive.

affirmative action: government policy which encourages institutions of various kinds to focus on hiring minorities such as women, African Americans, Hispanics, etc.

petitioner: individual or group bringing suit in a court case

viewed as victories for liberals. One of these decisions—*Wygant v. Jackson Board of Education*—supported affirmative action programs, and the other—*Thornburgh v. American College of Obstetricians & Gynecologists*—upheld the Court's previous ruling establishing a woman's right to have an abortion, *Roe v. Wade* (1973).

Powell also played a critical role in the court's unanimous 1974 decision forcing Nixon to turn over White House tapes relating to Watergate but ensuring that the president's claim of **executive privilege** not be rejected completely. Powell believed in a strong executive and did not want one difficult case to undermine the power of future presidents.

He took a special pride in one of his greatest balancing acts—his controlling opinion in the landmark case, *Regents of the University of California v. Bakke* (1977). The Court and country were acutely divided over this first great test of "**affirmative action.**" Allan Bakke, a white male, claimed that minority quotas set aside at a branch of the University of California medical school denied him equal protection of the law by admitting less qualified students in his place. Powell wrote the majority opinion allowing colleges and universities to consider race among other factors when deciding which students to admit. He found the middle ground that allowed schools to take race into account for diversity, but also forbidding schools to set aside a specific number of slots for racial minorities.

When the Court appointments of President Ronald Reagan began, Powell became an important centrist judge. He often provided the decisive "swing vote" in the Court's 5–4 decisions. However, Powell remained conservative on issues of crime and law enforcement, especially in cases involving criminal justice. For example, he supported state laws imposing the death penalty.

Powell later regretted two decisions he made. He had voted with the majority in the Georgia anti-sodomy law case known as *Bowers v. Hardwick* (1986) when the Court ruled that consenting adults have no constitutional right of privacy that allows them to engage in homosexual acts. Powell also regretted authoring a 1987 decision, *McCleskey v. Kemp*. The **petitioner,** a black man, had been convicted in a Georgia trial court of armed robbery and murder after a white police officer died during a store robbery. His petition included a claim that, in Georgia, courts sentenced defendants to capital punishment in a racially discriminatory way that violated the Eighth and Four-teenth Amendments. Powell's opinion said that Georgia's capital punishment was not discriminatory just because statistics showed that blacks were more likely to receive the death penalty than whites.

Powell earned the affection and respect of his fellow justices, who found him to be friendly, courteous, and hardworking. He was considered a soft-spoken Southern gentleman. He was a good listener and respectful of the views of others. Chief Justice Rehnquist, who joined the Court on the same January day in 1972 that Powell did, said in a statement after Powell's death, "He was the very embodiment of 'judicial temperament'; receptive to the ideas of his colleagues, fair to the parties to the case, but ultimately relying on his own seasoned judgment."

Powell retired in 1987 because of his poor health. Two years earlier, he had nearly died of uncontrolled bleeding after prostate cancer surgery and had not regained his energy.

After his relatively quiet service on the court, Powell's retirement set off a political storm of protest concerning his replacement, Robert H. Bork, a judge chosen by Reagan. The Senate held heated debates on Bork's conservative ideology and judicial philosophy and then rejected Bork as a high court candidate. Reagan's second choice, Douglas H. Ginsburg, withdrew after news of his possible drug use surfaced. In 1988, after the highly contested and unsuccessful nominations of Bork and Ginsburg, Reagan nominated Anthony M. Kennedy to the U.S. Supreme Court, finally replacing Powell.

Until 1996, Powell sat as a judge on the Fourth Circuit Court of Appeals in Richmond. He also taught at his alma mater, Washington and Lee University, and at the University of Virginia. Powell and his wife kept homes in both Washington, D.C., and Richmond.

Powell died in his sleep of pneumonia at his home on August 25, 1998, in Richmond, Virginia. Josephine Powell had died in 1996. ◆

Reed, Stanley

DECEMBER 31, 1884–APRIL 2, 1980 ● ASSOCIATE JUSTICE

Stanley Forman Reed was born in Minerva, Kentucky, on the last day of 1884. His father, John Reed, was a doctor; his mother was Frances Forman. Reed grew up in comfortable circumstances and was able to attend school at private academies. He graduated from Kentucky Wesleyan College in 1902, then received a second bachelor's degree in 1906 from Yale, where he won the Bennett American History Prize.

Reed spent a year at the University of Virginia law school, but he returned to Kentucky to marry Winifred Elgin in 1908. That fall he enrolled at the Columbia University law school but did not complete his degree. Instead he traveled with his wife to France to complete a year studying civil and international law at the Sorbonne in Paris. After returning to the United States, he was admitted to the Kentucky bar in 1910 and opened a private practice in Maysville.

Reed also became active in politics. Running as a Democrat, he was elected to the Kentucky General

Stanley Reed

1884 Reed is born in Minerva, Kentucky.

1935 Reed is appointed U.S. solicitor general.

1938 Reed is appointed to the U.S. Supreme Court.

1957 Reed retires from the Supreme Court.

1980 Reed dies in New York.

Many Court observers saw Reed as a liberal, but in reality he was a centrist.

Assembly in 1912, where he served for two terms until 1916. He returned to private practice but closed his office to serve in an army intelligence unit during the final year of World War I.

After the war Reed returned to private practice until 1929, when he was appointed general counsel of the Federal Farm Board, an agency created to help alleviate some of the effects of the Great Depression on agriculture. Then in 1932 President Herbert Hoover appointed him general counsel for the Reconstruction Finance Corporation, an agency that loaned money to banks, businesses, and farms—again to combat the Depression. Reed caught the attention of President Franklin D. Roosevelt, who in 1935 appointed him solicitor general, a job in which his primary task was to defend the president's New Deal legislation against challenges to its constitutionality before the U.S. Supreme Court.

Initially, Reed did not have much success, for the Supreme Court struck down such initiatives as the National Industrial Recovery Act and the Agricultural Adjustment Act. Later, perhaps because the president had threatened to "pack" the Court with justices more sympathetic to his programs, Reed enjoyed more success when the Court upheld the National Labor Relations Board and the Tennessee Valley Authority Act.

Reed ascended to the high court in 1938, when Roosevelt appointed him to replace Justice George Sutherland. Unlike Roosevelt's first appointee, Hugo Black, Reed was noncontroversial—though to some observers his large jowls and stern demeanor negated his friendliness and civility—and just 10 days after his nomination he was confirmed unanimously in the Senate. Reed went on to serve on the Court for 19 years, writing 339 opinions, including 88 dissents.

Many Court observers saw Reed as a liberal, but in reality he was a centrist—somewhat liberal on economic issues, somewhat conservative on civil liberties. In general he paid a great deal of deference to Congress and the president. In 1952, for example, he dissented when the Court majority, in *Youngstown Sheet & Tube Co. v. Sawyer*, struck down President Harry Truman's seizure of the steel industry during the Korean War. In a later case, *Peters v. Hobby* (1955), he dissented when the Court overturned executive authority in a loyalty review board case.

Reed also supported the government's actions against subversives in the highly charged anticommunist era of the late 1940s and 1950s. In 1952, for example, he wrote for the majority in *Carlson v. Landon*, upholding the jailing of alien communists while the attorney general dealt with procedures for their deportation. In decisions such as these, he exercised the principle of judicial restraint, the view that the Court should not formulate policy or question the wisdom of laws passed by the legislative branch of government.

In economic matters, Reed believed in big government, and he supported both social welfare programs and the federal government's right to regulate business. In 1939, for example, he and the Court upheld the constitutionality of the Agricultural Marketing Act—giving him some satisfaction, since the ruling in effect overturned the Court's ruling against the Agricultural Adjustment Act when Reed was solicitor general. In *United States v. Appalachian Electric Power Co.* (1940), he wrote an opinion that expanded the federal government's authority over inland waterways.

In civil liberties cases, Reed took a narrow view of the Constitution and refused to see freedoms granted by the Bill of Rights as absolute. In criminal cases, for example, he wrote that he was "opposed to broadening the possibilities of defendants escaping punishment by . . . more rigorous technical requirements in the administration of justice." He took a similar position in cases involving freedom of speech. In *United Public Workers v. Mitchell* (1947), he rejected arguments by federal employees that the Hatch Act (prohibiting political speech) violated their civil rights, writing: "It is accepted constitutional doctrine that fundamental human rights are not absolute. This court must balance the extent of the guarantees of freedom against Congressional enactment to protect a democratic society against the supposed evil of political partisanship by employees of the government."

Having served under four chief justices, Reed retired from the Supreme Court in 1957, though he remained active until he was well into his 80s. He maintained an office in the Supreme Court building and often engaged in judicial affairs. He served briefly as chair of the Civil Rights Commission, established under the Civil Rights Act of 1957. He also accepted several hundred assignments to hear cases on the Court of Claims and the Court of Appeals of the District of Columbia—a statutory right of retired Supreme Court justices. When he retired in 1970 he had written more than 40 majority opinions for these courts.

Late in life Reed moved to a nursing home in New York, where he remained until his death on April 2, 1980. Throughout his life he had visited his farm in Maysville, which became his final resting place. ◆

> *"How sure I was in the innocent days when law to a country lawyer seemed automatic—no two sides to any legal issue."*
> Handwritten note from Stanley Reed to Justice Felix Frankfurter

In civil liberties cases, Reed took a narrow view of the Constitution.

Rehnquist, William H.

OCTOBER 1, 1924– ● CHIEF JUSTICE

As 16th chief justice of the Supreme Court, William Rehnquist reigned over one of the most conservative courts the nation had ever known.

William Hubbs Rehnquist was born October 1, 1924, in Milwaukee, Wisconsin. He showed an early love of learning as a schoolboy in affluent Shorewood, a Milwaukee suburb. His father, William Benjamin Rehnquist, was not a college graduate, but he ran a successful wholesale paper business. Rehnquist's mother, Margery Peck Rehnquist, had attended the University of Wisconsin. She spoke French and Spanish, and was president of the Milwaukee Great Books Club.

From 1943 to 1946, Rehnquist served in the United States Army Air Corps at home and overseas. Upon his discharge, he ranked as sergeant. Rehnquist attended Stanford University near San Francisco, receiving a bachelor's degree and then a master's in 1948. He then earned a master's at Harvard University in 1950. Returning to Stanford, he attended law school, where he graduated first in his class in 1952. That year, U.S. Supreme Court Justice Robert H. Jackson appointed Rehnquist his law clerk in Washington, D.C., where he served for a year.

In 1953, already married to CIA employee Natalie "Nan" Cornell, of San Diego, California, Rehnquist began the private practice of law with a partner in Phoenix, Arizona. The firm performed mainly real estate law, wills, and contracts. He continued in this practice until 1969, meanwhile becoming active in the conservative wing of the Republican Party.

In 1969, President Richard M. Nixon appointed Rehnquist assistant attorney general of the Office of

William H. Rehnquist

Legal Counsel for the Department of Justice in Washington, D.C. In that post, Rehnquist became known for his support of increased police powers and did not generally support civil rights legislation.

Admiring Rehnquist's conservatism, Nixon nominated him as an associate justice of the U.S. Supreme Court on October 21, 1971. Rehnquist was only 47 years old and had never served as a judge. The nomination set off a debate in the Senate centering on Rehnquist's philosophy, which his opponents termed "ultraconservative." During Senate hearings on the nomination, several civil rights groups and liberals objected to positions Rehnquist had taken on such issues as school desegregation and police surveillance. After extended hearings, the Senate finally confirmed Rehnquist by a vote of 68–26 on December 10, 1971. He took his seat on the court in January 7, 1972.

In the liberal Court of the 1970s and early 1980s, the vigorous and articulate Rehnquist became the core judge in the Court's conservative minority bloc. As an associate justice, Rehnquist continued to reflect his conservative viewpoint on almost every issue and was the most conservative justice on the court. (Conservatism is an attitude or philosophy that emphasizes tradition. Conservatives want to conserve traditional institutions, values, and ideas, seeing them as guides to right behavior and decisions.)

On June 17, 1986, when Warren Burger retired as chief justice, President Ronald Reagan named Rehnquist to the post. The nomination set off debate in the Senate again over Rehnquist's conservatism. Many liberals protested Rehnquist's nomination. Among the controversies were reports that contracts on his house in Phoenix and a vacation home in Vermont prohibited them from being resold to racial or ethnic minorities. Rehnquist claimed he had been unaware of these sections on his contracts. Some critics accused Rehnquist of intimidating blacks and Hispanics to keep them from voting during the 1960s when he was a Republican Party official in Arizona. Rehnquist said that he had simply been settling disputes.

The Senate confirmed Rehnquist later in 1986, and he was sworn in on September 26, 1986. Rehnquist led a group of conservative Supreme Court justices whose numbers increased with appointments made by Reagan and Reagan's successor, President George Bush. The Court issued many conservative rulings under Rehnquist, especially regarding criminal procedures—

1924 Rehnquist is born in Milwaukee, Wisconsin.

1952 Rehnquist graduates first in his class from Stanford Law School.

1969 Rehnquist is appointed assistant attorney general for the Department of Justice in Washington, D.C.

1971 Rehnquist is nominated as an associate justice of the U.S. Supreme Court.

1972 Rehnquist takes his seat on the Supreme Court.

1986 Rehnquist is nominated and confirmed as chief justice by President Ronald Reagan.

2000 Rehnquist votes with the majority in *Bush v. Gore.*

"I have difficulty in concluding, as the Court does, that the right of 'privacy' is involved in this case. Nor is the 'privacy' that the Court finds here even a distant relative of the freedom from searches and seizures protected by the Fourth Amendment to the Constitution, which the Court has referred to as embodying a right to privacy."

William Rehnquist, dissenting opinion in *Roe v. Wade* (1973), which held that Texas could not outlaw abortions

methods for arresting, prosecuting, and punishing people accused of crimes. He helped restrict the federal courts' power of *habeas corpus*. This Constitutional right protects citizens against arrest and detention without good reason. Rehnquist also curbed the ability of Congress to expand federal authority.

The death penalty, abortion, and affirmative action also received conservative opinions from Rehnquist. Affirmative action refers to policies aimed at increasing the numbers of minorities and women in employment, education, business, government, and other areas. Affirmative action is intended to help groups that have suffered from discrimination, but critics argue that the benefits are not fairly handed out.

In the early 1990s, however, several of the Court's conservatives broke with Rehnquist to uphold some earlier Supreme Court rulings that many conservatives felt had been too liberal on abortion and other issues. Rehnquist was on the dissenting side of the court's affirmation of abortion rights and its protection of gay rights, two of the most publicized decisions of his tenure as chief justice.

In early 1999, Rehnquist, as is dictated by the Constitution, presided over the Senate's impeachment trial of President Bill Clinton. Clinton was impeached by the House for giving false statements to a federal grand jury during a deposition in a civil suit against him. The Senate heard the case and voted to acquit the president on all articles of impeachment. Rehnquist was recognized by Senators Trent Lott and Tom Daschle for his handling of the trial.

The U.S. presidential elections of November 2000 drew the Court into a case unlike any it had dealt with in the past. In the nearly tied contest between Vice President Al Gore and Texas Governor George W. Bush, the state of Florida became the final battleground, as numerous disputes arose over how votes were counted. The Florida Supreme Court ruled that Florida' Secretary of State had set an unreasonable deadline for counties to turn in their vote tallies, prevented many votes from being recounted, allowing Bush to keep his slim lead.

On December 4 the Court issued an unusual unsigned decision that sent the matter back to the Florida Supreme Court "for further consideration." By doing this, the Court declined to decide the merits of the case, saying they found "considerable uncertainty" in the Florida court's decision. Court observers commented that the nation's highest court had managed to

U.S. Term Limits v. Thornton (1995)

The early 1990s saw widespread support for the imposition of term limits on political office, and in 1992 voters in the state of Arkansas elected to impose them on all their elected officials, including those serving in the U.S. Congress. The constitutionality of this new law, however, was challenged, in the courts.

Attorneys arguing for the state of Arkansas, along with attorneys representing other states that had passed similar term–limit laws, argued that the people of the individual states had a right to choose whomever they pleased to govern them. However, the new term–limit laws raised a conflict with the U.S. Constitution, which specifically set forth the qualifications for service in the U.S. Congress.

The Supreme Court decided 5–4 that the term limits were unconstitutional as they applied to federal office. Justices Thomas, Rehnquist, O'Connor, and Scalia joined in a minority opinion. They affirmed that the people of the individual states did indeed have the right to choose whomever they wished, according to their own, locally devised standards. The majority, however, disagreed. Justices Stevens, Kennedy, Souter, Ginsberg, and Breyer, stated that "allowing individual states to craft their own congressional qualifications would erode the structure designed by the Framers [of the Constitution] for a 'more perfect union.' "

save its image as a nonpartisan body by not siding with either political candidate.

Rehnquist became known for his informal manner on the Court, sometimes wearing desert boots under his robes. He became friendly with liberal colleagues such as William Brennan and Thurgood Marshall. He amazed his law clerks and others with his brilliance. "He's so smart it's scary," said Charles Cooper, an attorney who clerked for Rehnquist. "His memory and his intellect are so large that it doesn't take him nearly as long to do things or to know things as it does everyone around him." Rehnquist dramatically reduced the Court's caseload and improved its efficiency.

Rehnquist, though, could sharply interrupt lawyers when their time had expired and scold those who were ignorant or disrespectful of the rules. He began insisting that lawyers call the Supreme Court judges "Mr. Justice" or "Madam Justice" rather than the more common "Judge."

One night each month, Rehnquist would gather with a group of friends to play poker. Regulars included Associate Justice Antonin Scalia, author William Bennett, and other high-level Washington friends. Rehnquist was known for making the group stick to the rules and avoid unnecessary chatter. Rehnquist also enjoyed bridge, oil painting, choral singing, stamp collecting, and theater. He swam regularly and played a weekly game of doubles tennis with his law clerks. He was also an author, publishing *Grand Inquests: The Historic Impeachments of Justice Samuel Chase and President Andrew Johnson* (1992), a history of the 19th century impeachment trials of Justice Samuel Chase and President Andrew Johnson. His other works include *All the Laws but One: Civil Liberties in Wartime* (2000) and *The Supreme Court: A History* (2001).

In 1991, Rehnquist became broken hearted by his wife Nan's death from ovarian cancer after 38 years of marriage. According to acquaintances, they had been a remarkably devoted couple. After her death, Rehnquist found consolation in the company of the couple's three grown children: James, a lawyer in Boston; Janet, a federal prosecutor in Virginia; and Nancy, who lived with her family in Vermont. Rehnquist and his family were longtime members of Emmanuel Lutheran Church, Bethesda, Maryland. ◆

Roberts, Owen

MAY 2, 1875–MAY 17, 1955 ● ASSOCIATE JUSTICE

Owen Josephus Roberts was born in Philadelphia, Pennsylvania, on May 2, 1875, the only son of Josephus Roberts, a successful hardware and wagon merchant, and Emma Laferty. As a youngster he attended Germantown Academy, where he excelled on the debate team, and at age 16 he enrolled at the University of Pennsylvania. At Penn he majored in Greek and Latin, and early on he considered a career teaching Greek. But after graduating Phi Beta Kappa at age 20 in 1895, he enrolled in the university's law school, where he was an editor of the *American Law Register* and graduated with highest honors in 1898.

Roberts joined a law firm in Philadelphia, but he also accepted a part-time appointment at the Penn law school, where he taught business-related law courses for 22 years, rising from the rank of instructor to full professor. In the meantime he was appointed first assistant district attorney for Philadelphia in 1903, a position he held until 1906, when he returned to private practice.

In the years that followed Roberts built his private law practice until the U.S. attorney general appointed him as special deputy attorney general to prosecute violations of the Espionage Act in 1917. In 1904 he had married Elizabeth Rogers, and the two had one daughter.

Roberts surfaced again in 1924, when President Calvin Coolidge appointed him special counsel for the United States. His job was to prosecute wrongdoers in the infamous Teapot Dome scandal that had scuttled the presidential administration of Warren Harding. The U.S. Navy had succeeded in leasing oil reserves (one of which was located in Teapot Dome, Wyoming) from the government by bribing Secretary of the Interior Albert B. Fall. The prosecution took six years, but Roberts was able to cancel the Navy lease and convict Fall and other key figures in the scandal.

Owen J. Roberts

In 1930 Supreme Court Justice Edward Sanford died. President Herbert Hoover's first choice to replace him drew opposition because he was seen as anti-labor and opposed to the participation of African Americans in the political process. When the Senate rejected him, Hoover turned to Roberts. The unions had no objection, and he won the support of the black community because he had been a trustee of historically black Lincoln University. With no opposition, the Senate confirmed him unanimously in May 1930.

Roberts joined a Court that was sharply divided. One faction consisted of liberal justices—Oliver Wendell Holmes, Jr. (later replaced by Benjamin Cardozo), Louis Brandeis, and Harlan Stone—who believed that the Constitution permitted government to regulate business and enact experimental social legislation. Arrayed against them were the "Four Horsemen," conservative justices Willis Van Devanter, James McReynolds, George Sutherland, and Pierce Butler, who wanted to keep government's hands off business and believed that much of the

Roberts joined a Court that was sharply divided.

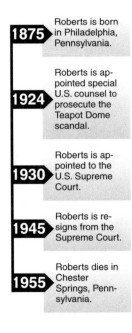

Roberts is born in Philadelphia, Pennsylvania.

1924 Roberts is appointed special U.S. counsel to prosecute the Teapot Dome scandal.

1930 Roberts is appointed to the U.S. Supreme Court.

1945 Roberts is resigns from the Supreme Court.

1955 Roberts dies in Chester Springs, Pennsylvania.

social legislation of the early 20th century was unconstitutional. Roberts, along with Chief Justice Charles Evans Hughes, was regarded as a crucial swing vote, sometimes giving the conservatives a majority, sometimes the liberals.

In the area of civil liberties, Roberts tilted the Court in a decidedly liberal direction. Two 1931 cases were significant: *Stromberg v. California* and *Near v. Minnesota*. In both cases Roberts cited the Fourteenth Amendment to the Constitution to rule that federal guarantees of freedom of speech and of the press were protected from interference by the states as well. He applied the same principle in a 1940 freedom of religion case, *Cantwell v. Connecticut*.

Roberts also voted with the liberal bloc in cases involving criminal procedure. In *Powell v. Alabama* (1932) he ruled that the Fourteenth Amendment guaranteed indigent defendants the right to counsel both in state trials for capital crimes and in non-capital crimes if the result would otherwise be an unfair trial. In *Brown v. Mississippi* (1936) the Court for the first time said that coerced confessions in state trials violated defendants' right to due process.

In economic matters, Roberts initially seemed again to lean toward the liberals when he upheld state laws passed to alleviate the effects of the Great Depression. He joined the Court majority, for example, in upholding the validity of New York laws designed to help the state's dairy farmers by regulating the price of milk and in upholding a Minnesota law that would grant extensions to property owners struggling to pay off mortgages.

After Franklin D. Roosevelt was elected president, however, the Court tacked in a more conservative direction in response to the president's sweeping New Deal federal legislation. Roberts wrote for the majority in invalidating the Railroad Retirement Act of 1933. Then, in *Schechter Poultry Corp. v. United States* (1935), he joined a unanimous Court in invalidating the National Industrial Recovery Act of 1933, arguing that Congress had exceeded its power to regulate commerce. The Court struck a further blow to Roosevelt in 1936, when it found the Agricultural Adjustment Act of 1933 unconstitutional, saying that agriculture was a local matter and that Congress had no authority to pay farmers to reduce their acreage in an effort to bolster farm prices.

By 1937 Roosevelt had had enough. To circumvent an uncooperative Supreme Court, he proposed to Congress what people called a "court-packing" plan that would have increased the number of seats on the Court, enabling him to appoint justices sympathetic to his initiatives. The plan seemed to lose steam when Roberts reversed his position in an earlier case and voted to support minimum wage laws in New York—though the Court's vote had already been taken when Roosevelt announced his proposal. But in the years that followed Roberts and Hughes shifted to the liberal bloc and upheld the president's New Deal programs, including the National Labor Relations Act of 1935, the Social Security Act of 1935, the Fair Labor Standards Act of 1938, and the reenacted Agriculture Adjustment Act of 1942.

In many instances, Roberts reversed positions he had taken just a few years earlier. In doing so, he expanded his interpretation of the Constitution's commerce clause to give the federal government broad authority to exercise its taxing, spending, and regulatory authority.

Roberts resigned from the high court in July 1945 to pursue other interests. In 1948 he accepted without pay the deanship of the University of Pennsylvania Law School, a position he held for three years. He died on his farm in Chester Springs, Pennsylvania, on May 17, 1955. ◆

"We will make haste, but we will make haste slowly."
Owen Roberts, beginning his six–year prosecution of wrongdoers in the Teapot Dome scandal, 1924

Rutledge, John

SEPTEMBER 1739–JULY 18, 1800 ● CHIEF JUSTICE

John Rutledge was born in September 1739 near Charleston, South Carolina, to a wealthy 15-year-old heiress, Sarah Hext Rutledge. His father, Dr. John Rutledge, was a physician who had emigrated from Ireland. Dr. Rutledge died in 1750, leaving his wife, age 26, with seven children. Young Rutledge studied with a local clergyman before attending a school in Charleston. As many wealthy South Carolinians did, Rutledge undertook his higher education in London, where he studied law for three years before being admitted to the English bar in February 1760.

Returning to South Carolina, Rutledge began practicing law in Charleston in 1761. His family connections and wealth allowed him to work on very profitable cases. In 1763, he married Elizabeth Grimke, of a respected Charleston family. Her nieces, Angelina and Sarah Grimke, became famous abolitionists and

John Rutledge

feminists in the 1800s. The Rutledges had ten children, one of whom—John Rutledge, Jr.—later served in the United States House of Representatives. They lived in a Charleston townhouse, where Rutledge resided most of the rest of his life.

Rutledge became the attorney general for the colony of South Carolina in 1764, under the British governor of the colony. However, troubles with Great Britain intensified about the time of the Stamp Act in 1765. The British Parliament passed the Stamp Act to raise funds to support the British army stationed in America. The act specified that Americans must buy stamps for deeds, mortgages, liquor licenses, law licenses, playing cards, and almanacs. The colonies reacted to the Stamp Act by convening a general congress.

South Carolina sent Rutledge as one of their delegates to the Stamp Act Congress, which met in New York in October 1765. Rutledge hoped to ensure continued self-government for the colonies, without breaking from the British. He did, however, chair a committee of the congress that drew up a petition to the British House of Lords declaring that stamp taxes could not be collected without the people's consent. American resistance forced the British Parliament to repeal the Stamp Act in 1766.

South Carolina sent Rutledge to represent the state in the First Continental Congress in 1774. The Continental Congress was a convention of delegates from the American colonies that met in Philadelphia to unify the colonies and which became the ruling body of the newly forming nation. Rutledge joined with other conservatives who did not seek complete independence from Britain, but sought fair treatment for the colonies. The congress set forth a Declaration of Rights, adopted on October 14, 1774.

The following year, Rutledge served on the Second Continental Congress, which met in Philadelphia on May 10, 1775. This congress organized an army and appointed George Washington commander in chief. With the outbreak of the Revolutionary War, the Second Continental Congress encouraged the colonies to adopt new republican governments. On July 4, 1776, the congress approved the Declaration of Independence.

Rutledge returned to help his colony draft a new state constitution allowing for an independent government. When the state convened their first assembly in 1776, they elected Rutledge as South Carolina's first executive, with the title of president. He served this position for two years. He resigned briefly in opposition to the new South Carolina constitution, which changed several things including his title from president to governor.

However, Rutledge took up his post again quickly when the British began invading South Carolina and the military situation grew desperate. In 1780, the British captured Charleston and confiscated Rutledge's property. Rutledge and his government fled to the North Carolina border. After the British surrendered, Rutledge returned to establish order in the state. His reign as governor ended in 1782.

From May 1782 to September 1783, Rutledge served in the Congress of the Confederation, the national legislature established by the Articles of Confederation, which operated the U.S. government from March 1, 1781, to March 4, 1789. The Congress of the Confederation was later replaced by the congress established by the U.S. Constitution. From 1784 to 1790, Rutledge served in the South Carolina House of Representatives.

Meanwhile, South Carolina sent Rutledge to the constitutional convention of 1787, along with several other delegates. The constitutional convention wrote an entirely new document to replace the Articles of Confederation—the Constitution of the United States.

Rutledge spoke at the convention as an aristocrat and wealthy landowner, favoring a strong national government and discouraging too much control by citizens. He also helped convince Northern delegates that the Southern states would pull out of the United States if the Constitution did not allow slavery. Rutledge considered slavery important to commerce, and not a moral issue. Rutledge endorsed the final draft, and the Constitution was ratified in June 1788.

President Washington appointed Rutledge as one of five associate justices of the U.S. Supreme Court in 1789. The chief justice was John Jay. Rutledge took office February 15, 1790.

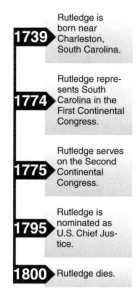

1739 Rutledge is born near Charleston, South Carolina.

1774 Rutledge represents South Carolina in the First Continental Congress.

1775 Rutledge serves on the Second Continental Congress.

1795 Rutledge is nominated as U.S. Chief Justice.

1800 Rutledge dies.

Sick from gout, though, Rutledge did not attend the first sessions in New York. Dissatisfied with the position, Rutledge soon resigned, and in 1791 became chief justice of South Carolina.

As the status of the Supreme Court increased, Rutledge regretted his resignation. His finances had never recovered from the war, then his wife died in 1792, leaving Rutledge with fewer ties to home. Rutledge wrote a personal letter to Washington asking if he could replace Jay when he left the chief justice position. Washington agreed.

In 1795, Washington nominated Rutledge as U.S. Chief Justice. However, Rutledge only served part of one term. The U.S. Senate did not confirm his appointment because he openly opposed the popular Jay's Treaty. John Jay, the nation's first chief justice, negotiated this agreement with Great Britain in 1794 to help end British-American political differences. This proved to be a major political blunder for Rutledge. He was in Charleston when the news of the Senate rejection reached him. He was so distraught that he jumped into the bay and had to be pulled out by two slaves.

Rutledge became a recluse and suffered lapses in sanity. He died in July 18, 1800, at the age of 60 and was buried at St. Michael's Episcopal Church in Charleston.

Rutledge's younger brother, Edward, born 1749, was also an important lawyer and statesman of the young United States. He became a South Carolina signer of the Declaration of Independence, and also represented South Carolina in the First and Second Continental Congresses. When Edward was a captain of artillery in the Revolutionary War, the British captured him when Charleston fell and held him prisoner for about a year. Edward served in the South Carolina Senate from 1796 to 1798 and was governor of South Carolina from 1798 to 1800. ◆

Rutledge, Wiley

JULY 20, 1894–SEPTEMBER 10, 1949 ● ASSOCIATE JUSTICE

Wiley Blount Rutledge, Jr., was born in Cloverport, Kentucky, on July 20, 1894. His father, Wiley B. Rutledge, Sr., was a Baptist minister. His mother, Mary Louise Wigginton, contracted tuberculosis in 1901, and the family moved about looking for a more healthful climate.

When she died of the disease in 1903, the family settled in Marysville, a town not far from Knoxville, Tennessee. Rutledge enrolled in Marysville College, then transferred to the University of Wisconsin, where he majored in ancient languages and graduated in 1914.

With an eye to a career in law, he enrolled in the law school at Indiana University, supporting himself by teaching high school in Bloomington. Before he completed his studies, though, he was struck with the disease that had killed his mother and entered a sanitarium in North Carolina. When he largely recovered in 1917 he married Annabel Person, his Greek teacher at Marysville College, and the couple had three children.

Wiley Rutledge

To overcome lingering effects of the tuberculosis, Rutledge moved to the dry air of Albuquerque, New Mexico, where again he taught high school. Finally cured of the disease, he moved to Boulder, Colorado, in 1920 and enrolled in the University of Colorado law school, once again teaching high school to support himself and his family. He graduated in 1922, worked in private practice in Boulder, then returned to the university to teach in 1924. Later he taught for nine years (1926–35) at the Washington University law school in St. Louis, five of them as dean, and from 1935 to 1939 he was dean of the law school at the University of Iowa.

In the 1930s Rutledge was a vocal supporter of the New Deal economic policies of President Franklin D. Roosevelt. He also supported the president's 1937 "court-packing" plan that would have increased the number of justices on a Supreme Court that was refusing to uphold the constitutionality of many of his initiatives. At one point Rutledge even offered to resign from the University of Iowa faculty when the Republican state legislature, which opposed the court-packing plan, threatened to withhold faculty salary increases if Rutledge testified in support of it.

Roosevelt appreciated Rutledge's support and in 1938 considered him for a seat on the Supreme Court. The appointment

1894 — Rutledge is born in Cloverport, Kentucky.

1938 — Rutledge is appointed to the U.S. Court of Appeals for the District of Columbia.

1943 — Rutledge is appointed to the U.S. Supreme Court.

1949 — Rutledge dies in York, Maine.

Rutledge was known primarily for his expansive view of individual constitutional rights.

went to Felix Frankfurter, but Rutledge received second prize, a seat on the U.S. Court of Appeals for the District of Columbia, where he served with future Chief Justice Fred Vinson. He remained at the top of Roosevelt's short list, and when James Byrnes resigned from the Court in 1942, the president appointed Rutledge to replace him. The last of Roosevelt's eight appointees, Rutledge was confirmed in February 1943.

Rutledge served on the Court for just six years, but in those years he made a major impact, helping to tilt the Court away from the conservatism of the Taft Court of the 1930s. Among his majority opinions were 11 upholding the expansion of federal regulatory power under the New Deal. He also joined the majority in *Korematsu v. United States* in upholding the internment of Japanese Americans on the West Coast. Though he bore no hostility to Japanese Americans, he, like many Americans, believed that the war effort required his unqualified support.

Despite his position in *Korematsu*, Rutledge was known primarily for his expansive view of individual constitutional rights. In *Schneiderman v. United States* (1943), for example, he joined the Court majority in overturning the decision of a lower court revoking the naturalized citizenship of the plaintiff because he was a communist. In *Thomas v. Collins* (1945), he wrote for the Court in support of the rights of labor and struck down a Texas law that required union organizers to obtain an "organizer's card" from the Texas secretary of state.

Most of Rutledge's opinions in support of individual rights, however, were in the form of powerful dissents—dissents in which he was often joined by Justice Frank Murphy. A key dissent was in *Everson v. Board of Education*, a 1947 case that had to do with the religious establishment clause of the First Amendment. The Court majority upheld the policy of a New Jersey school district of providing bus transportation to parochial school children. In dissenting, Rutledge cited Thomas Jefferson and James Madison to argue that the policy was unconstitutional because it breached the wall separating church and state. Fifteen years later, William O. Douglas, who had voted with the majority in *Everson*, conceded that Rutledge was right, and his *Everson* dissent remains one of the key texts in the constitutional issue of church and state.

Rutledge wrote key dissents in a number of other cases. He dissented in *Goesart v. Cleary* (1948) when the majority found constitutional a state law that said that a woman could not work as a barmaid unless her husband or father owned the bar—presumably to protect the woman's moral character. He also dissented in the 1946 case *In re Yamashita*. Yamashita was a Japanese general who commanded troops in the Philippines during World War II. After the war he was tried by a military court for war crimes committed by his troops. His case reached the Supreme Court after he was tried and sentenced to death. The petition alleged that his trial failed to adhere to the most minimal standards of fair procedure. Under Chief Justice Harlan Stone, the Court refused to hear the petition. Rutledge (with Murphy) strongly dissented. "More is at stake than General Yamashita's fate," he wrote. "There could be no possible sympathy for him if he is guilty of the atrocities for which his death is sought. But there can be and should be justice administered according to law. . . . It is not too early, it is never too early, for the nation steadfastly to follow its great constitutional traditions, none older or more universally protective against unbridled power than due process of law in the trial and punishment of men, that is, of all men. . . . It can become too late." For Rutledge, even the most despised criminal was entitled to equal justice under the law.

The dissenting voices of what was by now the Vinson court were silenced within two months of one another. In July 1949 Justice Frank Murphy died. On September 10 of that year Rutledge suffered a massive stroke and died in York, Maine. ◆

> *"If it can be done for Schneiderman, it can be done for thousands or tens of thousands of others."*
> Wiley Rutledge, *Schneiderman v. United States* (1943)

Sanford, Edward

JULY 23, 1865–MARCH 8, 1930 ● ASSOCIATE JUSTICE

E dward Terry Sanford was born in Knoxville, Tennessee, on July 23, 1865, just three months after the end of the Civil War. The oldest of six children, he grew up in comfortable circumstances. His father, Edward Sanford, Sr., had left Connecticut in the early 1850s and amassed a fortune in the lumber and construction business in Knoxville. His mother, Emma Chavannes, was a refined woman of French-Swiss descent.

Edward Sanford

The Sanford family attached a great deal of value to education, so as a child Edward attended private schools before enrolling at the University of Tennessee, where in 1883 he graduated at age 18 at the head of his class. He then went to Harvard University, where two years later he received another bachelor's degree and was the class orator on graduation day. His education, though, was by no means done. He entered Harvard Law School in 1886, and before graduating three years later with a master's degree and a law degree, he was one of the first editors of the prestigious *Harvard Law Review*. By the time he graduated he had already passed the Tennessee bar

1865 — Sanford is born in Knoxville, Tennessee.

1907 — Sanford is appointed assistant U.S. attorney general.

1908 — Sanford is appointed to the district court of eastern and central Tennessee.

1924 — Sanford is appointed to the U.S. Supreme Court.

1930 — Sanford dies in Washington, D.C.

examination, but when he left Harvard he did postgraduate study in languages in France and Germany.

Sanford was still a young man when he returned to Knoxville to begin nearly two decades of private law practice at the prestigious firm of Andrews & Thornburgh. Just a few months after he joined the firm, partner George Andrews died. Andrews had been scheduled to argue a number of cases before the Tennessee Supreme Court, whose new term was convening shortly. Sanford stepped into the breach, took over all of Andrews's cases, and with little preparation was able to argue them successfully. For the remainder of his time at Andrews & Thornburgh he specialized in civil and appellate work, earning a reputation as an extraordinarily diligent lawyer who was without exception meticulously prepared when he entered the courtroom.

Sanford was as active at home as he was at the office. In 1891 he married Lutie Mallory Woodruff, and the couple had two daughters. Among other civic, charitable, professional, and educational activities, he was a trustee of the University of Tennessee, a charter member of the board of governors of the Kentucky General Hospital, a member of the board of directors of two colleges, vice president of the Tennessee Historical Society, and vice president of the American Bar Association. In his limited free time, he enjoyed playing golf.

Sanford's ascent to the U.S. Supreme Court began in 1905. That year he was invited to Washington, D.C., to help U.S. attorney general (and future Supreme Court justice) William Moody prosecute a fertilizer monopoly—much of whose activity was in Tennessee—under the 1890 Sherman Antitrust Act. In 1907 he applied for and received a position as assistant attorney general when it was suggested to him that such a position could help him fulfill his ambition of becoming a federal judge. Sanford served in this post for 17 months, frequently arguing cases before the Supreme Court. Then in 1908 President Theodore Roosevelt persuaded him to fill a vacancy on the district court in eastern and central Tennessee. Sanford remained in this post for 15 years, where he continued to earn a reputation for diligence—but also one for lenience when it was time to sentence criminals.

In late 1922 Justice Mahlon Pitney retired, and President Warren Harding had the rare opportunity as president to appoint a fourth Supreme Court justice. With the backing of the Tennessee Republican governor, the Democratic legislature,

Chief Justice William Howard Taft, and virtually everyone who knew him, Sanford received the appointment and was confirmed in the Senate in January 1923. In just seven years on the high court, he delivered the opinion of the Court in 130 cases, many having to do with admiralty law, taxation, bankruptcy law, and patents.

Sanford was involved in a number of important cases. In one, the *Pocket Veto Case* (1929), he resolved a constitutional issue that had bedeviled the nation from its beginning by giving a definitive interpretation of the "pocket veto." This is a provision in the Constitution by which a bill becomes law if the president has not signed it "unless the Congress by their Adjournment prevent its Return." In general he supported federal and state regulation of business, so that in cases like *Tagg Bros. & Moorhead v. U.S.* (1930) he supported federal control of grain exchanges and stockyards.

In the area of civil rights, Sanford's record was mixed. In a number of cases he recognized the existence of non-economic rights under the due process clause of the Fourteenth Amendment. He voted, for example, to invalidate all-white primary elections in Texas, but he also voted to uphold school segregation and wrote an opinion upholding racially restrictive covenants, or agreements by property owners not to sell their property to non-Caucasians.

The most important civil liberties case in which Sanford was involved was *Gitlow v. New York* (1925). Benjamin Gitlow, an avowed communist who later ran for president, was convicted under a New York criminal anarchy statute because his pamphlet, *The Left Wing Manifesto*, urged violent overthrow of the government. At issue was freedom of speech and of the press as well as the Fourteenth Amendment's due process clause. Writing for the Court, Sanford sustained the conviction, referring to the "bad tendency" of such speech and saying that authorities might extinguish a revolutionary "spark without waiting until it has enkindled the flame or blazed into the conflagration." But the case was important for another reason. It established the principle "that freedom of speech and of the press . . . are among the fundamental personal rights and 'liberties' protected by the due process clause of the Fourteenth Amendment." The Court served notice that it would apply the Bill of Rights not just to federal questions but to state questions.

Sanford was on his way to a birthday celebration for Oliver Wendell Holmes in Washington, D.C., when he stopped to

"He was pleasing in address, quick in his mental processes, ready at repartee, forceful in discussing questions of both fact and law, and he impressed both Courts and Juries with his fairness and sincerity."
James A. Fowler in the *American Bar Association Journal*, 1931, on Sanford

have a tooth pulled. Almost immediately he fell victim to uremic poisoning and died on March 8, 1930. His passing went almost unnoticed, for William Howard Taft died the same day and it was his name, not Sanford's, that dominated the headlines. ◆

Scalia, Antonin

MARCH 11, 1936– ● ASSOCIATE JUSTICE

law review: a journal published by a law school containing scholarly articles by prominent figures in academia, usually edited by superior students.

Antonin Scalia

Antonin Scalia, the high court's first justice of Italian American descent, was born in Trenton, New Jersey, on March 11, 1936. His father was S. Eugene Scalia, a professor of Romance languages who had emigrated from Sicily. His mother, Catherine, was a schoolteacher born to Italian immigrant parents. When "Nino," their only child, was five years old, the elder Scalia took a teaching position at Brooklyn College and the family moved to Elmhurst, a section of Queens in New York City.

As a child, Scalia showed an early talent for music. He played the French horn in the school band, and music became a lifelong interest. In addition to enjoying classical music, especially opera, he played the piano and sang tenor. His education began in the public schools of Queens, but later he enrolled in St. Francis Xavier, a military prep school in Manhattan. After graduating first in his class, he attended Georgetown University, where he graduated as valedictorian with a degree in history in 1957. He went on to attend the Harvard Law School, where he graduated magna cum laude and served as an editor on the university's prestigious **law review.** As a Harvard postgraduate fellow in 1960–1961, he traveled in Europe for a year. He married Maureen Mc-

Carthy in 1960, and the two, sustained by their deep Catholic faith and commitment to community service, eventually had nine children.

Scalia's law career began in 1961 when he joined a firm in Cleveland, Ohio. There he specialized in real estate, corporate finance, labor, and antitrust law. In 1967, though, he concluded that he would make a better teacher than lawyer, so he joined the faculty of the law school at the University of Virginia. In both of these positions he showed a kind of brash contentiousness—a love of spirited debate about legal issues and the ability to ask probing questions—that would serve as a hallmark of his legal career.

In 1971, public service lured Scalia away from teaching. From 1971 to 1972 he served as general counsel for the Office of Telecommunications Policy in the Nixon administration. Here he helped competing industry groups negotiate a framework for the growing cable television industry. From 1972 to 1974 he chaired the Administrative Conference of the United States, an agency whose task was to reform the process of administrative law. From 1974 to 1977 he was an assistant attorney general in the Department of Justice's Office of Legal Counsel in the Ford administration. But in 1977 he returned to academic life when he accepted a position on the faculty at the University of Chicago law school.

By this time Scalia had cemented his conservative reputation. As a scholar-in-residence at the American Enterprise Institute in Washington, D.C., and in numerous law review articles, he articulated positions that would later underpin his conservative judicial opinions.

Scalia began to gain national prominence in 1982, when President Ronald Reagan appointed him to the U.S. Court of Appeals for the District of Columbia—a court generally regarded as second in importance only to the Supreme Court. Scalia was reluctant to leave the University of Chicago, which made it a policy to pay the college expenses of faculty members' children—a benefit of great value in Scalia's large family at the time. He accepted the appointment, though, and served on the bench for four years.

One of Scalia's most visible cases arose in 1985, when he was a member of a three-judge panel that ruled on the Gramm-Rudman-Hollings budget-balancing law. The court ruled that the law was invalid because it violated the constitutional separation of powers between the legislative and executive

"Both for those who agree and those who disagree with them, the Scalia opinions should provide grist for the academic mills for years to come."
Bernard Schwartz, *A History of the Supreme Court,* 1993

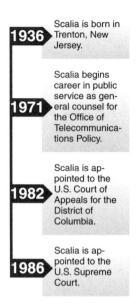

1936 Scalia is born in Trenton, New Jersey.

1971 Scalia begins career in public service as general counsel for the Office of Telecommunications Policy.

1982 Scalia is appointed to the U.S. Court of Appeals for the District of Columbia.

1986 Scalia is appointed to the U.S. Supreme Court.

On the bench Scalia was guided by a number of relatively clear-cut positions.

branches. The case later reached the Supreme Court, where the lower court's decision was affirmed.

In 1986 Chief Justice Warren Burger retired from the U.S. Supreme Court. President Ronald Reagan, wanting to strengthen the conservative wing of the Court, appointed Justice William Rehnquist to replace Burger as chief justice. To take Rehnquist's seat, the president nominated Scalia. In testimony before the Senate in his confirmation hearings, Scalia articulated his judicial philosophy: that the most important part of the Constitution was its system of "checks and balances among the three branches, . . . so that no one of them is able to run roughshod over the liberties of the people." Although Scalia proved to be a somewhat controversial justice, he gained unanimous approval by the Senate in September of that year.

On the bench Scalia was guided by a number of relatively clear-cut positions. First, he believed that the court system has limited powers and that one of the primary roles of the Supreme Court is to ensure that power is allocated among the three branches of government in a way that the framers of the Constitution intended. Thus, in *Morrison v. Olson* (1988) the Court upheld the constitutionality of the office of special prosecutor—an official appointed to investigate possible wrongdoing by members of the executive branch. Scalia dissented from the majority opinion, arguing that the Constitution did not permit Congress to give authority to prosecute to someone not under the control of the executive branch.

A second position Scalia took is that the Court cannot create "rights" that are not enumerated in the Constitution. For example, in a pair of early cases, *Webster v. Reproductive Health Services* (1989) and *Cruzan v. Director, Missouri Department of Health* (1990), he rejected the notion that the Constitution provided a right to an abortion or a right to refuse life-prolonging medical treatment. He argued, characteristically, that these were political issues that should be decided not by the courts but by legislators.

Most importantly, Scalia was guided by the principle of "textualism." According to this view, a justice is required to interpret the law based on the actual text of the Constitution. This contrasts with the view of other jurists who believe that the Constitution is a "living document" that needs to be reinterpreted in the context of the times. Scalia applied the same approach to his interpretation of laws and statutes. When other

2000 Presidential Election

The 2000 presidential election was one of the most remarkable political contests in United States history. Ultimately, Texas governor George W. Bush defeated Vice President Al Gore in a struggle that came down to the 25 decisive Electoral College votes in the state of Florida, and a voting margin and process so slim and subjective that the United States Supreme Court was forced to make two decisions that affected the election's outcome.

On November 7, 2000, American voters went to the polls to cast their ballots, and millions watched the election returns on television. The voting was close between Bush and Gore. At one point, the news media, relying on exit polling data and other projections, declared Gore the winner in Florida, even before all of the polls closed in that state. This turned out to be premature and the media outlets later reversed themselves and eventually declared Bush the winner in Florida and President–elect early the next day. Gore even phoned Bush and conceded. However, Gore later called the governor back and retracted his concession, an unprecedented act in presidential elections. The election was over, but there was no clear winner.

Gore retracted his concession due to reported claims of voter difficulty in various Florida counties and the fact that because the margin was so close in the state, Florida law provided for an automatic recount of the votes. In the meantime, a horde of lawsuits were filed in Florida. The Gore campaign filed lawsuits to declare so–called "butterfly ballots" in Palm Beach County illegal, and also filed suit to initiate more recounts following the automatic recount, but only in selected counties. The Bush campaign filed countersuits to stop the additional recounts once the mandated recounts were finished. The Florida secretary of state, on the basis of regulations guiding voter recounts, certified the election for Governor Bush after the mandated recount showed him ahead in the vote. Gore filed suit and appealed to the Florida Supreme Court, which said the secretary of state acted too hastily and that manual recounts in counties—selected by Gore—should continue. Bush appealed to the U.S. Supreme Court, which agreed to hear the case.

The Supreme Court, in a 5–4 decision halted the manual recounts going on in the state of Florida and set a hearing. Lawyers for Gore argued that all of the votes cast in Florida were not being counted, and lawyers for Bush argued that there had been numerous recounts over and above what the law required, and that Gore was mining for votes to overtake Bush's lead in the Florida vote. The Court, in a 5–4 decision, reversed the decision of the Florida Supreme Court, effectively stopping the recount in Florida and allowing the certification of Governor Bush as the winner of Florida. This gave Bush 271 electoral votes to Gore's 267, and the presidency.

In its opinion, the Court said that deciding the case involving an election was their "unsought responsibility," but when the election shifted from the vote of the people into the court room, the Court had to act and resolve the issue.

jurists broadly interpreted a possibly ambiguous law and wanted to bring in outside evidence (for example, remarks made by legislators during debates over the law), Scalia insisted that jurists were bound by the actual words of the law that was passed.

Scalia's views often placed him at odds with other members of the Court.

Scalia's limited, textualist approach played a role in numerous decisions involving social issues. In *R.A.V. v. City of St. Paul* (1992), for example, he argued that laws against so-called hate speech were unconstitutional, noting that "special hostility towards the particular biases thus singled out . . . is precisely what the First Amendment forbids." That same year, he reacted with hostility to the Court's opinion in *Lee v. Wiseman.* The majority ruled that reciting nondenominational prayers in public schools was unconstitutional, but in his dissent, Scalia called the majority opinion "nothing short of ludicrous." While he personally abhorred flag burners, he upheld the right of protestors to burn flags. He also believed that mandatory drug testing in the workplace was a violation of the Fourth Amendment's stricture against unreasonable searches and seizures.

In 1996 Scalia dissented from the Court's ruling that the men-only policy of the Virginia Military Institute was a violation of the equal rights of women. Finally, in *Romer v. Evans*, a 1996 case involving gay rights, the majority ruled that a Colorado constitutional amendment denying legal redress for discrimination based on homosexuality was unconstitutional. Never one to avoid controversy, Scalia scoffed at the majority opinion.

Scalia's views often placed him at odds with other members of the Court—and indeed, with some of the public who saw him as hostile to the kind of judicial activism that characterized, for example, the Court under the leadership of Chief Justice Earl Warren. Scalia was often the lone dissenting voice on cases, though sometimes he had an ally in Justice Clarence Thomas. Often called "The Terminator" by liberals, he wrote withering dissents that were often referred to as "verbal hand grenades," although they were well written and made for engaging reading. Some observers may have rejected his views, but most agreed that his disarming personality, wit, and strong convictions made those views impossible to ignore. ◆

Shiras, George, Jr.

JANUARY 26, 1832–AUGUST 2, 1924 ● ASSOCIATE JUSTICE

George Shiras, Jr., holds the distinction of being the only U.S. Supreme Court justice in history to have had neither judicial nor political experience. He was born in

Pittsburgh, Pennsylvania, on January 26, 1832, the descendant of a Scottish family that had settled in America in the mid-18th century. His grandfather had migrated to western Pennsylvania as a member of the militia that put down the 1794 Whiskey Rebellion. His father, George Shiras, Sr., purchased the grandfather's brewery and accumulated enough money to buy a farm on the bank of the Ohio River near Pittsburgh. His mother, Eliza Harron, was the daughter of a minister.

In 1849 Shiras enrolled at Ohio University in Athens. He transferred to Yale University in 1851, where he took a particular interest in the study of Greek. After graduating Phi Beta Kappa in 1853, he attended the law school at Yale, but he did not take his degree (although Yale awarded him its first honorary doctorate of law in 1883). He read law in the Pittsburgh office of Judge Hopewell Hepburn and was admitted to the bar association in 1855. He then practiced law briefly with his brother in Dubuque, Iowa, but after marrying Lillie Kennedy in 1857, he returned to Pittsburgh to become Hepburn's law partner.

After Hepburn died in 1862, Shiras maintained the practice himself for the next 30 years. The practice was lucrative because of the explosive growth of the mining and steel industries in Pennsylvania at that time, and Shiras counted among his clients a number of the era's steel barons and large corporations, including the Baltimore and Ohio Railroad. Oddly, though, he was indifferent to wealth and frequently failed to follow up on unpaid legal bills.

Shiras was a moderate Republican, but he stayed out of party politics. His sole political involvement was serving as a presidential elector in 1888. But when Supreme Court Justice Joseph Bradley died in 1892, Shiras's cousin, Secretary of State James Blaine, recommended him to President Benjamin Harrison, who made the nomination. Shiras's appointment was opposed by Pennsylvania's two U.S. senators, members of the Republican Party establishment. They were insulted that Harrison had not asked for their advice. But when Shiras received widespread support from the press, the state bar association, and prominent business leaders, the senators withdrew their opposition and Shiras was confirmed in the Senate. He served on the Court for 11 years, writing 259 majority opinions and only 14 dissents, believing that for the good of the country the Court should be unanimous as often as possible.

The major issues facing the Court during those years were the constitutionality of social reform laws and the extent to

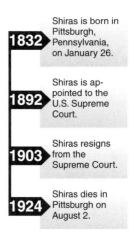

1832 Shiras is born in Pittsburgh, Pennsylvania, on January 26.

1892 Shiras is appointed to the U.S. Supreme Court.

1903 Shiras resigns from the Supreme Court.

1924 Shiras dies in Pittsburgh on August 2.

which the state could regulate business. Conservatives wanted the Court to protect private property interests and strike down reform and regulatory laws passed under increasing pressure from populists and progressives, including minimum wages, the eight-hour workday, and the nationalization of progressives' most hated target, the railroads. In the 1890s the Court began to evolve from a staunchly conservative stance to one that was at least slightly more progressive, and Shiras joined the Court in following this trend. Thus, in *Brass v. North Dakota* (1894) he joined the majority in upholding a North Dakota act setting maximum prices for grain storage, in effect sustaining an earlier ruling in a similar case, *Munn v. Illinois* (1877), that had rankled conservatives for nearly two decades. In *Holden v. Hardy* (1898) he voted with the Court to uphold a Utah law setting maximum working hours for miners. And in *Knoxville Iron Co. v. Harbison* (1901) he wrote the majority opinion striking down the validity of "scrip acts," the exploitative practice of paying workers in company towns with "scrip" they could use to buy goods at the company store. But in cases involving federal regulatory power, Shiras was decidedly more conservative, voting, for example, with the majority to restrict the Sherman Antitrust Act in *United States v. E. C. Knight Co.* (1895).

Shiras was one of eight justices who voted to establish the "separate-but-equal" doctrine of racial segregation in the infamous 1896 case *Plessy v. Ferguson*. Despite this vote, his record on civil liberties was relatively moderate. In *Swearington v. United States* (1896) he overturned the conviction of a Populist newspaper editor for publishing "obscenity" in a sharp, but clearly not obscene, attack on a Republican. That same year in *Wong Wing v. United States*, he found a law prescribing severe penalties for illegal Chinese aliens, passed under pressure from organized labor, unconstitutional. And in a 1901 dissent in *De-Lima v. Bidwell*, he maintained that full constitutional rights should be extended to citizens in American territories.

Despite his 11 years as a reasonably competent justice, Shiras is remembered primarily for two oddities. One was his role in the 1895 case *Pollock v. Farmers' Loan & Co.*, usually referred to as the *Income Tax Case*, for it involved the question of whether a personal income tax, a favorite proposal of progressives, was constitutional. The case was decided on April 8, but Justice Howell Jackson was absent and the Court split 4–4. After re-arguments the Court voted again and the tax was found unconstitutional by a 5–4 vote. But Jackson voted with the minority, meaning that one of the justices changed his earlier vote. Many historians believe that either Horace Gray or David Brewer changed his vote, but for many years Shiras was believed to have been the culprit. He was briefly in the public eye again in 1913 when the Sixteenth Amendment, creating the income tax, was passed.

Shiras is also remembered for having lived a long time after leaving the Court. For a century most justices had remained on the Court until they died or were too ill to carry out their duties. Shiras vowed to remain on the Court only 10 years. True to his word, he resigned in 1903 and divided the next 21 years between his home in Florida and a summer home on Lake Michigan.

He died in Pittsburgh on August 2, 1924, at the age of 92, leaving behind a legacy as one of the most personable, even whimsical, Supreme Court justices—by one account, "the liveliest spirit on the bench." ◆

Souter, David H.

SEPTEMBER 17, 1939– ● ASSOCIATE JUSTICE

When he was appointed as the nation's 105th U.S. Supreme Court justice in 1990, David Hackett Souter was an unknown figure, and neither conservatives nor liberals could predict in which direction he might tilt the Court. As a judge he hadn't ruled on many of the major issues of the day, and this lack of a "paper trail" led some to dub him the "Stealth candidate," after the Air Force plane that evades detection by radar. In an effort to understand him, Court observers searched for clues in his small-town Yankee roots.

Souter was born in Melrose, Massachusetts, on September 17, 1939. He spent much of his childhood, though, on his grandparents' farm in Weare, a small town near Concord, New Hampshire. His father, Joseph A. Souter, was a banker; his mother, Helen Hackett, worked as a store clerk. David was their only child. Joseph Souter suffered from a heart condition, so when David's grandparents died, the family moved to the farm and its slower-paced way of life.

Weare was a typical small New England town. Neighbors knew one another—sometimes too well—and governed themselves through town meetings, a vestige of true participatory

"If you screwed up, David took the blame. If you did well, you got the credit."
Bill Glahn, quoted in *Time*, August 6, 1990, referring to Souter's tenure as attorney general of New Hampshire

David H. Souter

democracy that fascinated Souter as he watched from the back bench of the meeting hall. He was an excellent student, and when he graduated from Concord High School in 1957, his classmates voted him "most sophisticated" and "most likely to succeed." He considered a career in the ministry, and throughout his life remained deeply committed to the Episcopal Church, but instead he attended Harvard University, where he majored in philosophy and wrote a senior thesis on the jurisprudence of Justice Oliver Wendell Holmes, Jr.

When Souter graduated magna cum laude in 1961, his friends gave him a scrapbook with fictitious newspaper clippings. One of those clippings was headlined, "David Souter Nominated to the Supreme Court."

Souter won a Rhodes scholarship and studied at Oxford University in England for two years, receiving bachelor's and master's degrees in jurisprudence. He then returned to Harvard to study law. After graduating in 1966, he stayed in New Hampshire to join Orr & Reno, a prestigious Concord law firm. Even his colleagues recognized that this scholarly young attorney would make a natural judge, so when the state attorney general offered him a job in 1968, he accepted, launching his career in public service as an assistant attorney general in the state's criminal division. Three years later, Warren Rudman, who later would become a U.S. senator, was appointed state attorney general, and he chose Souter as his deputy. Souter continued his ascent in 1976 when Governor Meldrin Thompson appointed him to succeed Rudman, who had decided to return to private practice.

Perhaps one of Souter's most controversial acts as attorney general was the prosecution and jailing of over 1,000 protesters at the Seabrook nuclear power plant in 1977. Additionally, he defended the governor's desire to fly the flag at half-mast on Good Friday and the state's efforts to prosecute drivers who, for religious reasons, covered up the state motto, Live Free or Die, on their license plates.

Souter's next move came in 1978, when he was appointed to the New Hampshire Superior Court. In this capacity he "rode the circuit," traveling to New Hampshire's 10 counties to hear both original jurisdiction and appellate cases ranging from international litigation to child custody disputes. He also heard numerous criminal cases and gained a reputation as tough when it came time to issue sentences. During these years he developed the practice of meeting with the jury after their verdict to discuss the case with them so that he could gain insight into their thinking. He later commented that his experience as a courtroom judge taught him that "at the end of our task some human being is going to be affected."

After five years on the superior court, Souter was rewarded when Governor John Sununu appointed him an associate justice of the Supreme Court of New Hampshire, where he served for seven years. Perhaps his most noteworthy decision was in *State v. Koppel*, a 1987 case in which he dissented from the court's holding that random sobriety checkpoints were unconstitutional.

Souter's elevation to the U.S. Supreme Court was rapid and unexpected. In 1990 President George Bush appointed him to the U.S. Court of Appeals for the First Circuit in Boston. Souter served in this capacity for just three months. He had not written an opinion—nor even been assigned an office—when Justice William Brennan retired from the high court. President Bush had already assembled a list of candidates for the position, so just three days later he was able to place Souter's name in nomination for the vacancy.

Given Souter's relative obscurity, interest groups scrambled to learn what they could of him. The press nosed around for scandal, but all they could find was that Souter was a hardworking bachelor who enjoyed classical music, collecting art and antiques, reading, and climbing the mountains in his home state. He had served on the board of trustees of Concord Hospital, and he was chairman of the board from 1978 to 1984. He was also an ardent student of history and served as vice president of the New Hampshire Historical Society.

During his Senate confirmation hearings, Souter's obscurity actually worked in his favor, particularly after the contentiousness that had marked the confirmation hearings of Robert Bork, whose nomination the Senate failed to approve in light of Bork's well-documented conservative views. Conservatives still

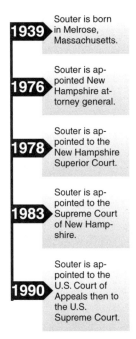

1939 Souter is born in Melrose, Massachusetts.

1976 Souter is appointed New Hampshire attorney general.

1978 Souter is appointed to the New Hampshire Superior Court.

1983 Souter is appointed to the Supreme Court of New Hampshire.

1990 Souter is appointed to the U.S. Court of Appeals then to the U.S. Supreme Court.

Souter's elevation to the U.S. Supreme Court was rapid and unexpected.

Washington v. Glucksberg (1997)

In the state of Washington, as in most of the United States, there are laws that define assisted suicide as a crime. On January 8, 1997, the Senior Assistant Attorney General of the state of Washington appeared before the United States Supreme Court to argue on behalf of Dr. Harold Glucksberg and several other parties, including three terminally ill patients, claiming that such laws are unconstitutional. Glucksberg argued that the Washington law violated the Fourteenth Amendment by denying mentally competent, terminally ill individuals the right to choose to end their lives.

The Supreme Court disagreed. In the opinion of the Court, the Justices stated that there is no constitutionally guaranteed right to suicide, and gave two main reasons for this position. First, they argued that suicide is "offensive to national traditions and practices," citing the fact that nearly every state treated suicide, and assisting a suicide, as criminal acts. Second, they noted that, in this case, the state had interests that were more compelling than the rights of individuals. In particular, the state's interest in protecting a certain standard of medical ethics, in protecting disabled people from being pressured into choosing suicide, and was preserving human life were all more important than the individual's right to commit suicide. However, the Court did make a distinction between suicide and the choice to refuse medication or forced feeding. The latter remains outside the definition of "suicide" or "assisted suicide."

thought that they had an ally in Souter, particularly in light of a 1986 opinion in which Souter had rejected judicial activism. At that time Souter had written that "the court's interpretive task is to determine the meaning of" of the language of the Constitution "as it was understood when the framers proposed it."

Liberals were worried about his position on abortion because he had opposed the New Hampshire legislature's effort to include in a bill a provision that would allow judges to give teenagers consent to an abortion when teenagers were unable to get their parents' consent. In fact, abortion was very much a **"litmus test"** issue in the early 1990s. Brennan was seen as the last liberal stalwart on the Court, in contrast to more recent appointees, who were tilting the Court in a conservative direction. Some observers believed that one more conservative justice would create a majority that would overturn *Roe v. Wade*, the 1973 case in which the Court permitted abortion. They believed, too, that a more conservative Court would roll back other civil rights gains made over the previous decades.

Souter, though, avoided these and other minefields by insisting that his mind was open to all views. About the key issue of abortion, he responded to a question from Senator Ted Kennedy by saying, "Whether or not I find [abortion] moral or immoral will play no role in any decision I make." The Senate responded

litmus test: term used in reference to Supreme Court appointees' views on particularly controversial issues which may come before the Court.

favorably to Souter's poise, knowledge, moderation, and sense of humor and confirmed him on October 2, 1990, by a 90–9 vote.

During the 1990s, the conservative majority that some observers anticipated did not take shape, for the Court's more conservative wing split into two groups. One group, consisting of Chief Justice William Rehnquist and Justices Antonin Scalia and Clarence Thomas, was strongly conservative. These justices wanted to overturn what they considered to be the "excesses" of the liberal Warren court. A more moderate, "centrist" core included Souter along with Justices Sandra Day O'Connor and Anthony Kennedy. Thus, when *Roe v. Wade* faced a stiff challenge in *Planned Parenthood of Southeastern Pennsylvania v. Casey* (1992), Souter, O'Connor, and Kennedy jointly wrote the Court's opinion declining to overturn the earlier case, though the Court did permit some state regulation of abortion.

Souter wrote other significant opinions, particularly in the areas of free speech and the separation of church and state. In *Cohen v. Cowles Media Co.* (1991), he argued in a dissent that the public's right to free and unfettered information outweighed a newspaper's promise of confidentiality to a source. In *Lee v. Weisman* (1992), he concurred with the majority in holding that prayer in public schools—even nonsectarian prayer—was unconstitutional. In *Rosenberger v. University of Virginia* (1995), he dissented from a majority opinion that a student-run Christian newspaper was entitled to funds from the state university.

David Souter was a small, slightly built man who dressed so frugally that his friend Warren Rudman once remarked that judicial robes might "jazz up his wardrobe." A rugged New Englander, he refused to wear an overcoat, even on the coldest days, and he carried his lunch—usually an apple and some yogurt—with him to work each day. When the Court was not in session, he returned to his beloved New Hampshire to hike its mountains and visit his mother, who lived in a nursing home near Weare. ◆

Stevens, John Paul

APRIL 20, 1920– ● ASSOCIATE JUSTICE

The youngest of four sons, John Paul Stevens was born in Chicago, Illinois, on April 20, 1920, to Ernest Stevens and Elizabeth Street. He grew up in comfortable circumstances, for his father had amassed a fortune in the hotel

John Paul Stevens

and insurance businesses. The Chicago Hilton hotel, formerly called the Stevens Hotel, was owned and managed by Stevens's father.

As a child, Stevens lived near the University of Chicago, his father's alma mater. He attended high school at the university's laboratory school, and when it came time to move on to college, he matriculated at the university, where he majored in English and edited the school newspaper. He was an outstanding student, graduating Phi Beta Kappa in 1941. In 1942 he married Elizabeth Jane Sheeren, and the couple eventually had four children before divorcing in 1979. In 1980 he married Maryan Simon.

Like many young men and women at the time, Stevens interrupted his education to contribute to the war effort. From 1942 to 1945 he served as a naval officer assigned to a code-breaking team, and he was a recipient of the Bronze Star. After the war one of his brothers encouraged him to study law, so he enrolled in the law school at Northwestern University. There he served as editor of the school's law review and graduated in 1947 first in his class with the highest grades in the law school's history. With this type of record he was able to clerk for liberal Supreme Court justice Wiley Rutledge in 1947–1948.

Stevens returned to Chicago and entered private practice with a firm that specialized in antitrust law. Later, in 1951, he formed his own law firm specializing in antitrust litigation. Because of his expertise in antitrust law, he was named to serve for a year (1951–1952) as an associate counsel for a U.S. House of Representatives subcommittee investigating monopolies. From 1953 to 1955 he also served on the Attorney General's National Committee to Study the Antitrust Laws. During the mid-1950s he also taught antitrust at the law schools at Northwestern and the University of Chicago. He remained in private practice until 1970, when President Richard Nixon appointed him to the U.S. Court of Appeals for the Seventh Circuit.

Throughout his judicial career Stevens was known as an independent-minded judge who did not always behave in predictable ways. He demonstrated this by defying convention and dissenting in his first judicial opinion on the court of appeals—one that foreshadowed his abiding concern with individual rights. The case, *Groppi v. Leslie,* involved a political demonstrator who was summarily imprisoned by the Wisconsin legislature. A local district court judge found the imprisonment unconstitutional, but the court of appeals reversed that ruling. Stevens dissented, noting that there have to be constitutional restraints on the control of disorderly conduct. When the case reached the U.S. Supreme Court the following year, the Court unanimously adopted Stevens's view.

After becoming president in 1974 in the wake of the Watergate scandals and the resignation of President Nixon, Gerald R. Ford was determined to restore integrity to the Department of Justice. To that end he appointed as attorney general the highly regarded Edward Levi, formerly the president of the University of Chicago. During his presidency, Ford had the opportunity to appoint one Supreme Court justice when William O. Douglas retired from the bench in 1975. Ford asked Levi to submit a list of candidates who, like Levi himself, would help restore the American public's faith in government. At the top of Levi's list was Stevens, who had earned high marks from the American Bar Association's Standing Committee on Federal Judiciary, which found Stevens's circuit court opinions models of excellence.

Ford made the appointment, and in late 1975 the Senate unanimously confirmed Stevens. He took the oath of office on December 19.

Once again, Stevens defied convention. Typically, new Supreme Court justices during their first few terms tend to join with other justices either in concurring with the majority or in dissenting. During his first full term (1976–1977), though, Stevens wrote 17 separate concurrences and 27 separate dissents—an unheard-of number of separate opinions for a new justice. Stevens had signaled his intention to operate in this way during his confirmation hearings, when he noted that litigants had a right to know the thinking of members of the Court, and that a record of the justices' views should be preserved if the case ever came up for reexamination. Many observers, however, noted that Stevens's frequent dissents and even his concurrences—which often pointed to flaws in majority opinions—

Once again, Stevens defied convention.

1920 Stevens is born in Chicago, Illinois.

1951 Stevens is appointed as associate counsel of the U.S. House of Representatives committee to study monopolies.

1970 Stevens is appointed to the U.S. Court of Appeals for the Seventh Circuit.

1975 Stevens is appointed to the U.S. Supreme Court.

fragmented the Court and left the public uncertain about what the Court was really saying.

Stevens's voting record also tended to defy classification. When he was appointed to the high court, he was perceived as a moderate, and during his early years on the Court he voted with the conservative bloc almost as often as he did with the liberal bloc. But in the view of many observers he drifted toward a more liberal position later in his tenure, at least in contrast to the more conservative trend exhibited by Chief Justice William Rehnquist and Justices Antonin Scalia and Clarence Thomas.

Initially, women's rights organizations were opposed to his nomination, but Stevens demonstrated a sensitivity to the rights not only women but of African Americans, children, prisoners, aliens, and other vulnerable members of society that earned him praise from liberal constituencies.

Perhaps the major reason that Stevens seemed unpredictable was his insistence on forging opinions that were based not on political ideology nor entirely on precedent, but rather on an exploration of the facts of individual cases and how those facts intersected with prevailing social and cultural values. A good example was his majority opinion in *Federal Communications Commission v. Pacifica Foundation*, a 1978 freedom of speech case. The case involved comedian George Carlin, whose racy monologue, "The Seven Words You Can't Say on TV," was broadcast during an afternoon radio show. The father of a child who inadvertently heard the broadcast filed a complaint with the Federal Communications Commission, which ruled against the radio station. The Supreme Court upheld the decision.

A "conservative" justice might simply have ruled against the station; a "liberal" justice might simply have concluded that the station's right to freedom of speech was in question. Stevens, though, explored the full context in which the case arose. He noted, for example, that offensive language in a book might deserve more protection than that in a radio broadcast, because the radio broadcast intrudes on privacy in the home while the book is less accessible. The monologue was broadcast during the afternoon, when it was more likely that a child might hear it. The audience for the broadcast was different from the audience for, say, a theatrical production in which offensive language is used. Based on lines of reasoning such as these, Stevens was unwilling to grant First Amendment protection to the broadcast—but equally unwilling to write a broad opinion in defense of an unfettered right to free speech.

Clinton v. Jones (1997)

In 1997, Paula Corbin Jones, a former Arkansas state employee, brought a civil lawsuit against President Bill Clinton charging that he had committed "abhorrent acts" of sexual harassment against her while he was Governor of Arkansas. She further charged that when she refused Clinton's advances, he caused her to be penalized at work. President Clinton responded to the lawsuit by claiming presidential immunity from prosecution, and the court suspended hearings in the case until the question of immunity could be resolved. At first, it was decided that the lawsuit would have to wait until Clinton was no longer in office, but Jones appealed that decision to the Eighth Circuit Court of Appeals, which decided that waiting until the end of Clinton's term in office was the same thing as granting immunity, at least temporarily, and ordered that the trial continue. President Clinton took his case to the Supreme Court, arguing that this decision violated the constitutional principle of separation of powers, for the Judiciary was interfering with the conduct of his responsibilities as chief executive of the country.

The Supreme Court was thus faced with resolving the question: Is a sitting president entitled to immunity from prosecution for crimes claimed to have taken place prior to his taking office? The Court responded with a unanimous "no." Justice John Paul Stevens delivered the Court's opinion, in which he stated that while the office of the president deserves the highest respect, this was no justification for blanket immunity. The opinion specifically stated that it was not concerned about the possibility of lawsuits being used for partisan political purposes, affirming the Court's belief that the legal system possessed sufficient safeguards against such a thing happening.

Stevens was similarly hard to predict in matters of criminal law. The more conservative wing of the Court during Stevens's tenure wanted to restrict the rights of criminals, for example by overturning decisions that excluded illegally obtained evidence or insisted that a suspect receive **Miranda warnings**. The more liberal wing wanted to expand rights for criminal defendants. In a number of cases, Stevens joined the more conservative wing in circumscribing those rights'for example, in allowing a search without warrant of an impounded vehicle. In a number of others, though, he seemed more inclined to broaden criminal defendants' rights. Thus, for example, in *Brewer v. Williams* (1977) he ruled that a defendant's right to counsel had been violated when the police elicited from him a confession during a lengthy car ride to the jailhouse. While the dissenting justices argued that the public should not be punished for the mistakes of law enforcement officers, Stevens took the position that enforcing strict rules for the treatment of criminal suspects was necessary for a well-ordered legal system.

Stevens was a quiet, mild-mannered justice with a **puckish** smile and a love of wearing bow ties. He enjoyed playing squash,

Miranda warning: warning given by arresting law enforcement officers notifying suspects of their lawful rights, as commanded by the decision in *Miranda v. Arizona*.

puckish: impish, whimsical.

tennis, bridge, and golf, and he flew his own small airplane. Among his colleagues on the Court, he was valued for his ability to write strong, elegant decisions and to stimulate thought-provoking legal debate. ◆

Stewart, Potter

JANUARY 23, 1915–DECEMBER 7, 1985 ● ASSOCIATE JUSTICE

Although he was born in Jackson, Michigan, on January 23, 1915, Potter Stewart grew up in Cincinnati, Ohio, where he was the second of three children of a well-to-do family. His father, James Garfield Stewart, was a lawyer who served as a city councilman, mayor, and a justice on the Ohio Supreme Court. His mother, Harriet Loomis, was president of the League of Women Voters and campaigned actively for reform in city government.

Stewart was a good student, and his classmates and friends liked him for his wit and love of practical jokes. After graduating from the Hotchkiss School in Connecticut in 1933, he enrolled at Yale University, where he was editor of the student newspaper (surprising his Republican father by endorsing Democrat Franklin D. Roosevelt for president) and graduated Phi Beta Kappa in 1937 with a major in English literature. After a year of study at England's Cambridge University, he enrolled in law school at Yale, where he served as editor of the prestigious *Yale Law Journal* and graduated with honors in 1941.

Stewart joined a law firm in New York City, but his career was interrupted almost immediately by World War II. He served as a naval officer, and in 1943, while his ship was briefly docked in Virginia, he married Mary Ann Bertles. After the war he returned to New York,

Potter Stewart

but he soon took a job with a law firm in Cincinnati, where he earned a reputation as a skilled trial lawyer. Like his father, he ran for a seat on the city council, winning two-year terms in 1949 and 1951.

Stewart began his ascent to the U.S. Supreme Court in 1954, when the Republican senator from Ohio recommended him for a federal judgeship. President Dwight D. Eisenhower agreed and appointed Stewart to the Sixth Circuit Court of Appeals, making him at age 39 the youngest judge in the federal judiciary system. Here he began to earn a lifelong reputation for elegant opinions graced by pithy aphorisms. In arguing, for example, to set aside the conviction of a man who was arrested, tried, and sentenced in one day, he wrote that "swift justice demands more than just swiftness."

Potter served on the court of appeals until he was called to Washington in 1958. He had no inkling why and was surprised to learn that the president was nominating him to fill the seat on the Supreme Court left vacant by the retirement of Harold Burton. Although he took his seat in October, the Senate was in recess and he was not confirmed until May 1959. The confirmation vote was 70–17, with all the "nays" cast by Democrats from the South who wanted a justice who would overturn the Court's ruling in the landmark 1954 desegregation case, *Brown v. Board of Education*.

Stewart joined a Court that was sharply divided between liberals, who saw the Court as the guardian of individual liberties, and conservatives, who deferred to other branches of government. Despite his Republican roots, he quickly emerged as a centrist judge and a crucial "swing vote" in close cases, sometimes giving the majority to one bloc, sometimes to the other. Stewart endeavored to rule on questions as narrowly as possible and to keep his personal values and beliefs out of his rulings. Thus, for example, while he personally opposed the death penalty, he upheld its constitutionality, though he insisted on the strictest procedural safeguards. In *Furman v. Georgia* (1972) he wrote that in some cases the death penalty was "cruel and unusual in the same way that being struck by lightning is cruel and unusual." In 1965 he dissented when the Court, in *Griswold v. Connecticut*, overturned a state law banning contraceptives, writing that personally he found the law "uncommonly silly" but not unconstitutional.

Stewart is best known for his rulings in several specific cases that demonstrate his approach to questions involving civil

"I know it when I see it."
Potter Stewart's classic remark on obscenity in *Jacobellis v. Ohio* (1964)

Stewart endeavored to rule on questions as narrowly as possible and to keep his personal values and beliefs out of his rulings.

Gregg v. Georgia (1976)

In the mid–1970s, Troy Gregg and a companion were hitchhiking in Georgia. They were eventually given a ride in a car that was carrying Fred Simmons and Bob Moore. Shortly afterwards, the bodies of Simmons and Moore were found on the side of the road, and Gregg was picked up by the police. He was later convicted of armed robbery and murder, and sentenced to death.

Gregg appealed his conviction to the Supreme Court, where his court–appointed counsel, G. Hughel Harrison argued that the death penalty constituted "cruel and unusual punishment," which is specifically prohibited by the Eighth Amendment of the Constitution.

In a 7–2 decision (Justices Stewart, Powell, Stevens, Rehnquist, White, and Blackmun, along with Chief Justice Burger, in the majority; Justices Brennan and Marshall dissenting) the Supreme Court upheld the conviction of the lower courts, and affirmed the death penalty for Troy Gregg. The Court's majority opinion held that "cruel and unusual" referred to punishment that was arbitrarily applied, or that caused unnecessary pain, or that was disproportionately severe in comparison to the crime. It stated that none of these considerations were at issue in Gregg's case. The Court specifically noted that, since the "judgment phase" of the trial was separate from the "penalty phase," and that the penalty was consistent with punishments meted out in similar cases, there was no violation of the Eighth Amendment. In addition, the Court affirmed the claim that the death penalty was a legitimate way for states to try to deter others from committing similar crimes.

liberties. *Shelton v. Tucker* (1962) involved an Arkansas statute that required public school teachers to list all of the organizations to which they belonged or contributed money. The goal was to inquire into their fitness for their jobs. Stewart, however, ruled that the statute was too broad. In his decision he did not strike down such a requirement, but he did maintain that Arkansas could accomplish its stated purpose with narrower disclosure requirements. This principle of "least restraint" was one that the Court relied on in later cases.

Regarding the difficult issue of church and state, Stewart briefly dissented from the Court's landmark ruling in *Engle v. Vitale* (1962) that prayer in public schools was unconstitutional. In a similar case, *Abington School District v. Schempp* (1962), he outlined his views in more detail. His dissent argued that the Establishment Clause and the Free Exercise Clause of the First Amendment sometimes came into "irreconcilable conflict" and that "separation of church and state" was an elusive goal because "religion and government must necessarily interact in countless ways."

Stewart is perhaps best known for a statement he made in *Jacobellis v. Ohio*, another 1962 case that had to do with the issue of pornography. Showing again his gift for the well-turned phrase, he gave the classic answer to the question "What is pornography?" when he wrote: "I shall not today attempt further to define [it]. . . . But I know it when I see it."

Finally, Stewart was a defender of the Fourth Amendment and wrote the opinion in the landmark case *Katz v. United States* (1967). This was one of several opinions in which he redefined legal police searches. He ruled that tapping a phone in a phone booth to record a conversation invaded a defendant's right to privacy and was an "unreasonable search and seizure," even though no "search" of the phone booth had taken place.

In 1968 President Richard Nixon considered elevating Stewart to Chief Justice when Earl Warren announced his retirement. In characteristically self-effacing fashion, Stewart met with the president and withdrew his name from consideration. In July 1981 he retired to spend more time with his family, though he remained busy, serving on presidential commissions, as chair of an international arbitration commission, and as a court of appeals judge on select cases. He also put his mellifluous voice to work recording legal texts for the blind. In 1985 he suffered a stroke while visiting his daughter in Vermont. He died on December 7 in Hanover, New Hampshire. ◆

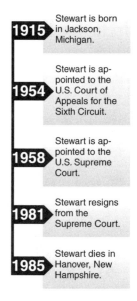

1915 Stewart is born in Jackson, Michigan.

1954 Stewart is appointed to the U.S. Court of Appeals for the Sixth Circuit.

1958 Stewart is appointed to the U.S. Supreme Court.

1981 Stewart resigns from the Supreme Court.

1985 Stewart dies in Hanover, New Hampshire.

Stone, Harlan Fiske

OCTOBER 11, 1872–APRIL 22, 1946 ● ASSOCIATE JUSTICE

Harlan Fiske Stone, the first U.S. Supreme Court justice to occupy all nine seats (based on seniority) on the bench, was born on October 11, 1872, in Chesterfield, New Hampshire. His father, Frederick Lauson Stone, was a farmer; his mother, Anne Butler, had been a schoolteacher. Stone was the descendant of a family that had settled in Massachusetts in 1635, and a number of his ancestors had served as selectmen in their small New England communities.

When Stone was two years old, the family moved to Mill Valley, a town near Amherst, Massachusetts, where the four children would have greater educational opportunities. In 1888 Stone enrolled at the Massachusetts Agricultural College (now the University of Massachusetts), but he was expelled as a result of a prank. In 1890, though, he was admitted to

Harlan Fiske Stone

Amherst College, where he played football, served as class president, and graduated Phi Beta Kappa in 1894. He remained at the college to earn a master's degree three years later. Initially, he wanted to be a teacher, and in fact taught science and coached football at a high school in Newburyport, Massachusetts. But after attending sessions of the local superior court, where he was befriended by district attorney and future Supreme Court justice William Moody, he decided that he wanted a career in law.

Stone enrolled at the Columbia University Law School, working part-time as a history teacher at a local academy to finance his studies. After graduating in 1898, he worked for a prestigious Wall Street law firm while remaining at the Columbia Law School to teach part-time. In 1899 he married accomplished landscape painter Agnes Harvey, a childhood sweetheart to whom he had been engaged for nine years, and the two eventually had two sons. In 1905 he resigned his position at Columbia because of differences with the university's president and became a full partner in another Wall Street firm, Wilmer, Canfield & Stone. Stone enjoyed teaching, though, so five years later the president of Columbia was able to lure him back. From 1910 to 1923 Stone was a popular teacher and dean at the law school, where he was an advocate of an approach to law called legal realism—an approach that subordinated fixed rules and precedents to the study of the evolution of law as a living human institution. But he continued to have differences with the university president, who resented Stone's support of dissenters and conscientious objectors during World War I. (Stone's essay "The Conscientious Objector" is considered a classic defense of nonconformity.) These differences, plus the low pay, led Stone to resign in early 1923 to take a well-paid position as head of the litigation department at the law firm of Sullivan & Cromwell. Finally, he could afford a box at New York City's Metropolitan Opera.

It was not to last. President Calvin Coolidge, who assumed office in the wake of the scandals surrounding the administration of his predecessor, Warren Harding, was looking for an attorney general who was beyond reproach. He turned to his Amherst classmate, Harlan Fiske Stone. Stone accepted the position in April 1924—at one-eighth the salary he had been earning at the firm.

Stone served as U.S. attorney general for less than a year—a year during which he cleaned up the Justice Department and hired J. Edgar Hoover to head the FBI. Shortly after Coolidge was reelected, Supreme Court Justice Joseph McKenna resigned, and Coolidge once again called on his college classmate to fill the vacancy. Stone was the first Supreme Court nominee ever to testify before the Senate Judiciary Committee, and after he was overwhelmingly confirmed by the Senate in February 1925, he took the oath of office in March. A large and robust man, he took long walks each day and later was a member of President Herbert Hoover's "medicine ball cabinet," meeting with the president at 6:30 in the morning to exercise on the White House lawn.

Stone sat on the Supreme Court during one of its more turbulent periods as the nation attempted to cope with the massive economic and social problems caused by the Great Depression. Stone's predecessors on the Court had limited the powers of Congress and the states to regulate economic and social ills. They had also resisted federal efforts to regulate such industries as manufacturing and agriculture because, in the Court's view, they were local and state, not federal, interests. Many observers at the time feared that Stone would follow in this tradition— that he was another conservative Wall Street lawyer who would defend corporate interests over the needs of the people. Stone, however, proved them wrong. He frequently found himself allied with Justices Louis Brandeis and Benjamin Cardozo in urging judicial restraint, or deference to the legislative powers of Congress. Thus, while the Court majority repeatedly struck down many of President Franklin Roosevelt's New Deal initiatives, such as the Agricultural Adjustment Act of 1936, Stone usually dissented, arguing that "Courts are not the only agency of government that must be assumed to have capacity to govern." By 1937 the majority of the Court had come to agree with this view, and the Court began to uphold the president's and Congress's New Deal legislation.

In the area of civil rights and individual liberties, however, Stone was much less likely to assume that legislators were acting

"Had I realized what I'd be doing later in my career, I'd have hung on to that pitchfork." Stone, referring to the pitchfork he was using to shovel manure when he received word that he had been admitted to Amherst College

1872 Stone is born in Chesterfield, New Hampshire, on October 11.

1923 Stone is appointed U.S. attorney general.

1925 Stone is appointed to the U.S. Supreme Court.

1941 Stone is appointed Chief Justice of the Supreme Court.

1946 Stone dies in Washington, D.C., on April 22.

Stone found the demands of being Chief Justice overwhelming.

within the scope of the Constitution, and many of his rulings (and dissents) during this period widened the scope of civil liberties. He announced this view, oddly enough, in a footnote in *United States v. Carolene Products Co.* (1938), a note that has been called "the most celebrated footnote in constitutional law." One of the most significant cases in which he attempted to expand civil liberties was *Minersville School District v. Gobitis,* a 1940 case that involved the children of Jehovah's Witnesses, who refused on religious grounds to salute the flag in school. The Court majority ruled that the requirement was within the scope of the authority of the state legislature. Stone, however, forcefully dissented, and his position was upheld by the Court in a similar case three years later, *West Virginia State Board of Education v. Barnette.*

In 1930 Chief Justice William Howard Taft had resigned from the Court, and many expected that Stone would replace him. Taft, however, did not believe that Stone had the ability to, in Taft's terms, "mass the court," meaning to impose some sort of unanimity on the justices. For this reason, Charles Evans Hughes was appointed Chief Justice. Stone finally got his chance, though, when Hughes retired in 1941 and President Roosevelt, wanting to reward Stone for his support of New Deal initiatives, nominated him as Chief Justice. The Senate unanimously approved the nomination, and Stone served as Chief Justice until his death five years later.

World War II posed particular problems for the Supreme Court. Stone continued to believe that civil liberties were more important than property rights. However, the demands of wartime forced him and many of his colleagues to accept the view that civil liberties might sometimes have to be curtailed for the greater good during a national crisis. Thus, for example, he supported the internment of Japanese Americans on the West Coast in *Hirabayashi v. United States* in 1943, and he deferred to military courts and tribunals in espionage cases. A further problem was Stone's lack of administrative ability, and Taft's view that he was unable to "mass the court" proved to be prophetic. The Court under Stone was marked by divided opinions, split votes, and numerous dissents, and conferences among the justices were allowed to spin off into fruitless talk.

Stone found the demands of being Chief Justice overwhelming, saying in 1945 that he felt "tied to my oar like a galley slave and pulling for dear life." Nonetheless, he denied rumors that he would retire. On April 22, 1946, he delivered a dissent in *Girouard v. United States* regarding Congress's power to deny citizenship to conscientious objectors. He concluded with the words "It is not the function of this Court to disregard the will of Congress in the exercise of its constitutional power." Moments later he collapsed from a stroke and died later that day. ◆

Story, Joseph

SEPTEMBER 18, 1779–SEPTEMBER 10, 1845 ● ASSOCIATE JUSTICE

E ven if he had not served for over three decades on the U.S. Supreme Court, Joseph Story would still be remembered as one of the leading constitutional scholars of the 19th century.

Story was born in Marblehead, Massachusetts, on September 18, 1779, and during his youth he was surrounded by tales of the American Revolution. His father, Elisha Story, was a prominent doctor who had served in the Continental Army and was one of the Sons of Liberty responsible for the Boston Tea Party. His maternal grandfather had foiled a British raid on the colonial arsenal in Salem, Massachusetts. Elisha Story had seven children by a first marriage, and Joseph was the oldest of 11 children born to his second wife, Mehitable Pedrick.

Story enrolled at Harvard in 1795 and graduated second in his class three years later. Back in Marblehead he read law with a future chief justice of the state supreme court and was admitted to the bar in 1801. What he really wanted to be, though, was a poet, and in 1805 he published a long poem entitled *The Power of Solitude*. Sadly, the effort was pronounced a failure (Story later bought up and burned any copies of the poem he could find).

Joseph Story

When both his father and his wife died that same year, Story overcame his grief and disappointment by setting his sights on a legal career and burying himself in work. Active in Democratic-Republican Party politics, he was elected in 1805 to the first of three terms in the Massachusetts House of Representatives, and in 1808 he was elected to finish out a term in the U.S. House of Representatives. In 1810 he achieved a measure of national prominence when he was retained in a major land-fraud case and persuaded the U.S. Supreme Court to use for the first time its power to overturn a state law.

In 1808 Story married Sarah Waldo Wetmore, the daughter of a Boston Court of Common Pleas judge. Their son, William Wetmore Story, became a world-renowned artist and sculptor.

In 1810 Supreme Court Justice William Cushing died. President James Madison's first two choices to replace him, including John Quincy Adams, turned the post down, and his third was rejected by the Senate. In November 1811 Madison finally turned to Story, who was confirmed three days later. He took his seat in February 1812, at age 32 the youngest Supreme Court justice in the nation's history.

During the early 19th century the overriding issue facing the Court was the relative power of the federal government and the states. Under the leadership of Chief Justice John Marshall, the Court greatly expanded the power of the federal government and established the Supreme Court as a co-equal branch of government. Throughout his 33-year tenure on the Court, Story supported Marshall in this goal, often referred to as "judicial nationalism." He argued, for example, that federal common law should apply in criminal matters and repeatedly urged Congress to pass laws to "give the Judicial Courts of the United States power to punish all crimes and offenses against the Government, as at common law."

In a landmark case, *Swift v. Tyson* (1842), Story persuaded the Court to join him in creating a federal common law for civil procedure. The ruling contributed greatly to the development of corporations in the late 19th century, for it created uniform and predictable national rules applying to business and commerce.

While arguing for the supremacy of the national government, Story, conversely, denounced states' rights. He launched his assault on states' rights in *Fairfax's Devisee v. Hunter's Lessee* (1813). With Story writing for the majority, the Court overturned a decision by the Virginia courts upholding the confiscation of land owned by British subjects during the American Revolution, arguing that the state court had violated the 1783 peace treaty with Great Britain. The Virginia courts denied that the Supreme Court had jurisdiction, and when the case came back to the Supreme Court as *Martin v. Hunter's Lessee* in 1816, Story forcefully asserted the power of the federal courts to review the actions of the states. He wrote that the Constitution was not created "by the states in their sovereign capacities, but emphatically, as the preamble of the constitution declared, by 'the people of the United States.'" It is difficult to overstate the importance of this decision in tilting the balance of power from the states to the federal government, with the Supreme Court as the final arbiter.

On the issue of slavery, Story was personally opposed to the practice. He did write the opinion of the Court in *Prigg v. Pennsylvania* (1842), an important case upholding the constitutionality of the fugitive slave laws, but he did so not because he supported slavery but because he was trying to wrest control of the slave trade away from the states. He often used his position on the bench to denounce slavery, and in the celebrated case *United States v. Amistad* (1841) he freed a boatload of Africans, the "Amistads," who had been illegally transported to Cuba before revolting against their captors. Their story is told in a 1997 major motion picture, *Amistad*.

While away from the bench, Story had what would constitute a full career for most people, and any list of his activities seems endless. He was a confidant of politicians, advising, for example, Daniel Webster on international law after Webster became secretary of state. He proposed legislation to Congress. In 1820 he was a member of the Massachusetts Constitutional Convention, and in 1836–1837 he served on a commission to codify Massachusetts law. He was on the board of Harvard University, and after joining its law school faculty in 1829, he was instrumental in turning the school into one of the nation's best. He was president of the Merchant's Bank of Salem for 20 years and vice president of the Salem Savings Banks for 12. Most importantly, he was a dedicated legal scholar and prolific writer, publishing nine works about the law. His three-volume *Commentaries on the Constitution* (1833) became an important text in law schools.

In the 1830s President Andrew Jackson replaced many of Story's colleagues on the Court. With the death of Marshall in

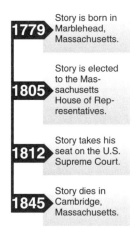

1779 Story is born in Marblehead, Massachusetts.

1805 Story is elected to the Massachusetts House of Representatives.

1812 Story takes his seat on the U.S. Supreme Court.

1845 Story dies in Cambridge, Massachusetts.

On the issue of slavery, Story was personally opposed to the practice.

1835, Story was virtually alone in defending the judicial nationalism of the Marshall court. Frequently he found himself in the role of dissenter as the Court under Roger Taney tilted back in the direction of states' rights—though Taney respected Story and regarded him as the Court's scholar. In the 1840s Story's health began to fail, but before he could resign he died in Cambridge, Massachusetts, on September 10, 1845. ◆

Strong, William

MAY 6, 1808–AUGUST 19, 1895 ● ASSOCIATE JUSTICE

William Strong was born on a small family farm in Somers, Connecticut, on May 6, 1808, to William Lighthouse Strong, a minister, and Harriet Deming. In 1630 his ancestors had emigrated from England to Massachusetts, where Strong's grandfather had been a prominent lawyer. As a child Strong attended the local public schools while his father tutored him in classical languages and mathematics.

After a year at private academies Strong enrolled at age 15 at Yale, where he graduated in 1828 with the help of a loan from several Yale faculty members. To pay off the debt, he worked for three years as a schoolteacher in New Jersey while reading law with a local attorney. He then returned to Yale, where he completed a master's degree in law in 1832. That year he was admitted to the state bar associations in both Connecticut and Pennsylvania.

Strong settled into the growing community of Reading, Pennsylvania, where he opened a flourishing practice. Active in the community, he served on the city council and the board of education, was a director of the Farmer's Bank and the Lebanon Valley Railroad, and was counsel to the Philadelphia and Reading Railroad Company. In 1836

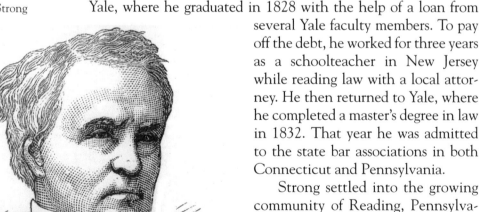

William Strong

he married Priscilla Mallery, but she died prematurely in 1844. He married Rachel Bull in 1850.

Running as a Democrat, Strong was elected to the U.S. Congress on an antislavery platform in 1846. He was reelected in 1848, but he declined to run for a third term and returned to private law practice in Pennsylvania. Then in 1857 he was appointed to the Pennsylvania Supreme Court, where he continued to oppose slavery. Now a Republican, he supported the Union government during the Civil War. When Supreme Court Chief Justice Roger Taney died in 1864, President Abraham Lincoln considered appointing Strong to fill the vacant seat, but for political reasons he instead appointed Salmon Chase.

After 11 years on the state supreme court, Strong resigned to return to private practice. But in 1869 his name came up again when Supreme Court Justice Robert Grier submitted his resignation. President Ulysses S. Grant considered him again for the post, but Congress overwhelmingly supported Edwin Stanton, and Grant, bowing to pressure, appointed the former secretary of war. In an odd turn of events, Stanton died just four days later, so in February 1870, after Grier's official retirement, Grant appointed Strong, who was confirmed on February 18.

Strong's appointment to the Supreme Court, however, was surrounded with controversy. The roots of the controversy extended back to the Civil War and the Legal Tender Act of 1862. This act authorized the federal government to issue paper currency (printed with green ink, hence the name "greenbacks" for paper currency) to pay off debts incurred during the war. The validity of paper currency, though, was challenged in the courts. At issue was nothing less than the economic future of a nation that was outgrowing its reliance on silver and gold coins.

As a justice on the Pennsylvania Supreme Court, Strong had upheld the constitutionality of paper currency as legal tender, but the issue was by no means settled. Salmon Chase got his appointment from Lincoln largely because as secretary of the treasury he had secured passage of the Legal Tender Act, so he was expected to uphold the act. But when a key case, *Hepburn v. Griswold*, came before the Court in 1869, Chase surprised everyone and joined the majority in ruling the Legal Tender Act unconstitutional. Right in the middle of this controversy, Strong, along with Joseph P. Bradley, joined the Court, leading to charges that Grant was trying to "pack" the Court with justices who would uphold the Legal Tender Act. The charge was unfair, for the Court had already made its decision before Strong was appointed, but the

"Nothing he did on the Court became him like the leaving of it."
Charles Fairman, *Mr. Justice Miller and the Supreme Court, 1862–1890,* 1939

Strong's appointment to the Supreme Court, however, was surrounded with controversy.

1808 Strong is born in Somers, Connecticut.

1846 Strong is elected to the U.S. House of Representatives.

1847 Strong is appointed to the Pennsylvania Supreme Court.

1870 Strong is appointed to the U.S. Supreme Court.

1880 Strong resigns from the Supreme Court.

1895 Strong dies in Lake Minnewaska, New York.

charge was renewed in 1871 when the Court again ruled on the issue and, with Strong writing the majority opinion, upheld the constitutionality of paper money as legal currency.

During his 11 years on the high court, Strong was an able justice, writing most of his opinions in mundane cases involving such matters as patents, taxes, and shipping rights. A conservative, he generally sided with the pro-business faction of the Court, opposing government regulation of business and commerce. But the Court also heard several important cases that had a bearing on the civil rights in the post-Civil War period, and in this area Strong's record was mixed. One the one hand, he restricted civil rights laws in *Blyew v. United States* (1872), a notorious case that arose after a Kentucky court found a man not guilty of the murder of three African Americans. The man was then indicted under the Civil Rights Act of 1866, which gave the federal government jurisdiction over cases involving civil rights. Strong, however, ruled that the Court did not have jurisdiction because the act referred to "persons in existence" and the African Americans no longer existed.

On the other hand, Strong advanced the cause of civil rights in at least two important cases. In *Stauder v. West Virginia* (1880) he found a state law excluding blacks from jury duty unconstitutional. And in *Ex parte Virginia* (1880) he found that a state judge who had excluded blacks from jury duty had violated the Civil Rights Act of 1875.

Although Strong tried to avoid politics, he was a reluctant member of the commission formed in 1877 to settle the disputed presidential election between Rutherford B. Hayes and Samuel Tilden. Still a Republican, he cast his support to Hayes, and while he was charged with partisanship, every member of the commission was subject to the same charge, for the commission voted along strict party lines.

Unlike many Supreme Court justices in the 19th century, Strong resigned from the Court while he was still healthy. Some historians have suggested that he did so as a way of persuading Nathan Clifford, Ward Hunt, and Noah Swayne—all frequently absent because of illness and infirmity—to step aside. In his retirement, Strong continued to live in the nation's capital, where he was very active in religious affairs. He also wrote an important article that led to the establishment of courts of appeals to alleviate some of the burden on the Supreme Court.

After a brief illness, Strong died in Lake Minnewaska, New York, on August 19, 1895. ◆

Sutherland, George

MARCH 25, 1862–JULY 18, 1942 ● ASSOCIATE JUSTICE

George Sutherland, the only U.S. Supreme Court justice from Utah, was born in Buckinghamshire, England, on March 25, 1862, to Alexander George Sutherland and Frances Slater. That year Sutherland's father converted to the Mormon faith, and in 1863 he moved his family to Springville, Utah, to be near the church. Soon, however, he renounced the Mormon faith and moved his family to Montana. But in 1869 the Sutherlands returned to Utah and settled in Provo, where the elder Sutherland worked as a miner, a postmaster, a justice of the peace, and eventually a lawyer.

As a child George earned money for college by working in a mining recorder's office, a clothing store, and at the Wells Fargo Company. In 1879 he enrolled at Brigham Young Academy (now University), and after graduating in 1881, he entered law school at the University of Michigan. He did not obtain his degree, however, and in 1883 he returned to Provo to join his father's law practice and marry Rosamond Lee. The couple had three children, and their marriage lasted nearly 60 years.

In the 1880s Sutherland embarked on a political career. Although he maintained good relations with the Mormon Church, he believed that its practice of polygamy was wrong and campaigned against admission of Utah to the Union until the practice was stopped. As a member of the Liberal Party, he ran for mayor of Provo in 1890, but he was soundly defeated. After the Mormon Church renounced polygamy, the Liberal Party disbanded. Sutherland became a Republican, and in 1892 he mounted an unsuccessful bid for his party's nomination as territorial representative to Congress.

Sutherland finally tasted success in 1896 when Utah was admitted to the Union and he was elected to the state's first senate. Then in 1900 he was elected as the state's only member of the U.S. House of Representatives, and to reward him for his ardent defense of Utah's interests in the House, the state legislature appointed him to the U.S. Senate in 1905 (in the days before senators were popularly elected). In two terms as a senator Sutherland was a vigorous proponent of worker's compensation and the right of women to vote. When he introduced the Nineteenth Amendment to the Senate, he said, "Any

"My Dear Sutherland: This is perhaps the finest opinion in the history of American constitutional law. Regretfully, I adhere to my error. Brandeis."

Note from Justice Louis Brandeis attached to a dissent written and circulated by Sutherland in 1934

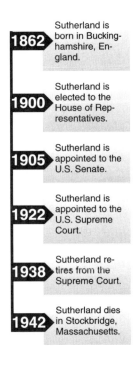

1862   Sutherland is born in Buckinghamshire, England.

1900   Sutherland is elected to the House of Representatives.

1905   Sutherland is appointed to the U.S. Senate.

1922   Sutherland is appointed to the U.S. Supreme Court.

1938   Sutherland retires from the Supreme Court.

1942   Sutherland dies in Stockbridge, Massachusetts.

argument which I may use to justify my own right to vote justifies . . . the right of my wife, sister, mother, and daughter to exercise the same right."

By 1916 senators were elected by popular vote, and Sutherland failed to win a third term. He remained in the nation's capital to practice law, and that year he was elected president of the American Bar Association. His name was first mentioned for a seat on the Supreme Court in 1921 when Chief Justice Edward White died, but President Warren Harding gave the post to former president William Howard Taft instead. But when Justice John Clarke announced his retirement in 1922, Harding nominated Sutherland to fill the vacant seat. The Senate confirmed him without discussion the same day.

During his nearly 16 years on the bench, Sutherland may have often disagreed with his "brethren," but he always enjoyed warm and congenial relations with them and was regarded as a powerful and articulate voice on the Court.

Sutherland had announced his judicial philosophy in a speech to the Utah Bar Association in 1895: "Judges do not make laws, but declare them; the rules which govern their deliberations and decisions are to a large extent fixed and permanent . . . [not] to be controlled by temporary considerations or policies."

On this basis Sutherland believed that much of the social and economic legislation passed during his tenure on the Court was unconstitutional—that it violated the Fifth and Fourteenth Amendments of the Constitution by interfering with the individual liberties of the people, especially their right to enter freely into contracts. Thus, for example, in a 1923 case, *Adkins v. Children's Hospital*, he joined the Court in ruling that a minimum wage law for women working in Washington, D.C., hospitals was unconstitutional. Sutherland called the law "a naked, arbitrary exercise of power."

No one should have been surprised, then, that during the New Deal era of the 1930s, Sutherland was one of the conservative "Four Horseman"—joining Justices Willis Van Devanter, James McReynolds, and Pierce Butler. These justices usually voted as a bloc to strike down the sweeping regulatory and social legislation passed by Congress and President Franklin D. Roosevelt to combat the Great Depression. In all, Sutherland joined the Court nearly every time in ruling 18 acts of Congress and 185 state laws or local ordinances unconstitutional.

A good example was a 1936 case, *Carter v. Carter Coal Co.* The case arose in connection with the Bituminous Coal Act of

1935, an effort to impose order on the chaotic and unsafe coal mining industry. The act established minimum and maximum prices and imposed a 15 percent sales tax that would be returned to firms that cooperated with the government in carrying out the aims of the act. Predictably, Sutherland found the act unconstitutional, saying that the tax was in reality a penalty and that the "beneficent aims" of any legislation "can never serve in lieu of constitutional power."

Yet to simply label Sutherland a conservative tells only part of the story, for his strong advocacy of individual liberty and restraint of government power led to rulings that might be classified as liberal. In *Powell v. Alabama* (1932), for example, he wrote the Court's majority opinion setting aside the conviction of one of the "Scottsboro Nine," a group of black youths convicted of raping two white girls in a notorious case. Sutherland argued that the youths had not received a fair trial because they had been convicted in a mob atmosphere and denied the right to counsel. Similarly, in *Grosjean v. American Press Co.* (1936) he defended the freedom of the press in ruling that a state tax on newspaper advertising was in effect a form of unconstitutional prior restraint of the press.

When President Roosevelt, frustrated by an uncooperative Supreme Court, announced his "court-packing" plan to increase the number of justices in 1937, Sutherland steadfastly refused to retire, despite his failing health. After the plan was defeated, he retired in January 1938 and died four years later in Stockbridge, Massachusetts, on July 18, 1942. ◆

Swayne, Noah

DECEMBER 7, 1804–JUNE 8, 1884 ● ASSOCIATE JUSTICE

Noah Haynes Swayne was born in Frederick County, Virginia, on December 7, 1804, the youngest of nine children. His parents, Joshua Swayne and Rebecca Smith, were farmers and staunch Quakers whose opposition to slavery undoubtedly influenced the future Supreme Court justice. As a child Swayne attended the local public schools, then a Quaker academy in Waterford, Virginia, before moving to Alexandria to study medicine. His medical career, though, was interrupted by the death of his instructor, so he turned to the

Noah Swayne

law. He read law at an attorney's office in Warrenton, Virginia, and was admitted at age 19 to the state bar.

Driven by his hatred of slavery, Swayne moved to the free state of Ohio and settled in Coshocton in 1825. There, over the next 35 years, he built a successful legal and political career. In addition to the private practice of law, he held a variety of posts. In 1826 he was appointed county prosecuting attorney. In 1829 he was elected to the state legislature. In 1830 President Andrew Jackson appointed him U.S. attorney for the District of Ohio. In the state capital, Columbus, he was elected to the city council in 1834. In 1836 he was elected again to the state legislature, where he remained until 1841. In the meantime he had married Sarah Ann Wager of Virginia in 1832, and the couple had five children.

Somehow Swayne also found time to provide unpaid service to his adopted state. In 1837 he was appointed to a three-member commission formed to straighten out the state's finances in the wake of that year's financial panic. In 1840 he served on another commission that surveyed the condition of the blind throughout the state, an effort that was later extended to the deaf and the mentally impaired. Additionally, he served as a trustee for several similar organizations.

Politically, Swayne had been a Jacksonian Democrat, but he became increasingly disenchanted with the party because of its pro-slavery stance. In the 1850s he joined the fledgling Republican Party. In 1856 he backed the party's first presidential candidate, John C. Fremont, whose platform included supporting Congress in its efforts to exclude slavery from new territories. When the Civil War broke out, Swayne stoutly supported President Abraham Lincoln and the Union effort.

Swayne was working as an aide to Ohio's governor when his friend and fellow Ohioan, Supreme Court Justice John McClean, suddenly died in early 1862. Swayne, contrary to the usual practice, immediately orchestrated a campaign to secure an appointment to the vacant seat, enlisting the Ohio congressional delegation, the governor, Treasury Secretary Salmon Chase, and New York lawyer and future presidential candidate Samuel Tilden. Since McClean had told the president that he wanted Swayne to succeed him, the president made the appointment, his first to the high court. Despite his lack of judicial experience, Swayne was confirmed in the Senate with only one "nay" vote.

Swayne was a friendly, good-humored man who easily made friends. He was also popular among attorneys and with the press throughout the Sixth Circuit, to which he was assigned. But the unhappy fact is that the Court breathed a bit of a sigh of relief when he resigned 19 years later. Historians have been less than kind to him, for his impact on the Court and on constitutional history was minimal.

During the Civil War Swayne proved a useful ally to the president by upholding executive war powers. In the 1863 *Prize Cases,* for example, he supported the president's seizure of Confederate ships and use of blockades before Congress had explicitly given him the power to prosecute war. He later upheld the federal government's issuance of paper currency to pay war debts, though he ducked the issue of whether that currency would be legal tender in peacetime. And in *Ex parte Vallandigham* (1864) he upheld the authority of military tribunals and courts to arrest and try civilians accused of impeding the war effort. No blind patriot, though, he intervened with the president to stop the execution of a Confederate spy, and he himself freed a man accused of treason, saying that the evidence was insufficient. Swayne wrote that "causeless and wicked as this rebellion is . . . it is not the less our duty to hold the scales of justice . . . with a firm and steady hand."

Swayne's greatest impact may have been in supporting the "Reconstruction amendments," the Thirteenth, Fourteenth, and Fifteenth. Consistent with his Quaker roots, he ardently supported passage of the Thirteenth Amendment, which abolished slavery. His support of the intent of the Fourteenth Amendment, which tried to put teeth into the Thirteenth by guaranteeing citizens "due process of law," "equal protection," and the "privileges and immunities" of citizenship, came primarily in a dissent in the landmark *Slaughter House Cases* of 1873. The majority Court restricted the application and scope of the amendment, paving the way for states to restrict the civil liberties of African Americans. In later years, those who wanted to extend the amendment's scope often relied on Swayne's

"Fairly construed these amendments may be said to rise to the dignity of a new Magna Carta."
Noah Swayne, in his dissent in the *Slaughter House Cases* (1873), commenting on the Thirteenth, Fourteenth, and Fifteenth Amendments

During the Civil War Swayne proved a useful ally to the president by upholding executive war powers.

1804 ▸ Swayne is born in Frederick County, Virginia.

1830 ▸ Swayne is appointed U.S. attorney for the District of Ohio.

1862 ▸ Swayne is appointed to the U.S. Supreme Court.

1881 ▸ Swayne resigns from the Supreme Court.

1884 ▸ Swayne dies in New York City.

dissent. When states were considering the Fifteenth Amendment, granting the right to vote regardless of race, color, or "previous condition of servitude," Swayne played a major role in getting the amendment ratified in his home state of Ohio.

When Chief Justice Roger Taney died in 1864, Swayne again violated convention by campaigning vigorously to replace him. Despite some support from his colleagues and others who feared that the president would appoint a radical Republican, the post went instead to Salmon Chase. Swayne tried again in 1873 when Chase died. According to his colleague, Justice Samuel Miller, he wanted the post so much that he "artfully beslobbered the President." Again he was disappointed when the center seat went to Morrison Waite.

In the late 1870s Swayne's mental faculties were clearly deserting him, but he refused to resign. Only when President Rutherford B. Hayes assured him in 1881 that he would appoint fellow Ohioan and close friend Stanley Matthews to the bench did he submit his resignation. He died in New York City on June 8, 1884. ◆

Taft, William Howard

SEPTEMBER 15, 1857–MARCH 8, 1930 ● CHIEF JUSTICE

William Howard Taft holds the distinction of being the only person in the nation's history to serve as both President of the United States and Chief Justice of the Supreme Court.

William Howard Taft

Although he was born in Cincinnati, Ohio, on September 15, 1857, Taft's roots were in New England, where his ancestors had settled in the late 17th century. Taft inherited from his forbears a desire for public service. His grandfather had been a judge in the probate and county courts in Vermont, and his father, Alphonso Taft, had gained national prominence as a two-term member of the Ohio Supreme Court, as attorney general in the administration of President Ulysses S. Grant, and as an ambassador under President Chester A. Arthur. William was the oldest surviving child of Alphonso and his second wife, Louisa Maria Torrey.

Taft attended Yale University, where his amiability and popularity were a source of concern to his father—concerns that proved to be unfounded, though, when Taft graduated second in his class in 1878. That year he entered the Cincinnati Law School, financing his studies by working as a legal affairs reporter for a local newspaper. After graduating in 1880 and passing the bar examination, he began his career in public service as an assistant prosecuting attorney in Hamilton County, Ohio, later as assistant county solicitor. During these years he became active in Republican party politics. In 1886 he married Helen Herron, and one of their three children, Robert Taft, would later serve several terms as a U.S. senator from Ohio. Helen Taft played an important role in her husband's career, for while he was more interested in the judiciary, she urged him to pursue politics.

For a number of years, Taft got his way. In 1887 he was appointed to the superior court of Ohio and won election to the post in his own right in 1888. In 1890 President Benjamin Harrison named him solicitor general, a position that required him to argue cases before the U.S. Supreme Court. Two years later he was appointed to the U.S. District Court for the Sixth Circuit, a position in which he served happily for eight years. At the same time he taught law and served as dean at the Cincinnati Law School. Although he was a conservative, he surprised observers by writing opinions during these years upholding the right of labor to organize and strike.

In 1901 Helen Taft's political ambitions for her husband began to be fulfilled. That year President William McKinley appointed him governor general of the Philippines, a **protectorate** the United States had acquired as a result of the Spanish American War. Taft proved an able administrator, and during his four years in the Philippines he introduced numerous political reforms and economic improvements. After becoming president in 1901, Theodore Roosevelt offered Taft a seat on the Supreme Court, but Taft declined because he felt committed to his post in the Philippines. In 1904, though, he joined the Roosevelt administration as secretary of war. He also served the president as a roving ambassador in such places as Cuba and the Far East, and he supervised the construction of the Panama Canal.

After Roosevelt indicated that he would not run for reelection in 1908, Taft's name was mentioned as his successor, and with Roosevelt's help and the financial backing of his half-brother, he defeated William Jennings Bryan for the presidency. As president, he continued many of the reform policies that Roosevelt had begun, particularly antitrust suits against business monopolies. He was also able to appoint six justices to the

protectorate: a nation under the military protection and governmental control of another.

History of the Supreme Court Building

When the Supreme Court was established in 1789, no provision was made to provide it with a permanent physical home. At the time the capital of the United States was New York City, and the Supreme Court worked out of the Merchants Exchange Building in the lower part of Manhattan. When the capital city was moved to Philadelphia, the Court moved as well, taking up quarters first in Independence Hall and later in City Hall.

Even after the nation's capital was moved to Washington, D.C., the Supreme Court remained without a building of its own. The Court spent many years making do with temporary quarters in the Capitol Building and elsewhere in the city, including, briefly, in a private home. In 1929, however, former president and then Supreme Court Justice William Howard Taft decided that the time had come to find quarters that reflected the dignity and integrity of the Court. Under his urging, Congress charged architect Cass Gilbert to design a suitable building. When Gilbert died before completing his task, the job was taken up by his son, Cass Gilbert Jr., and architect John R. Rockart. After Congress allocated $9.74 million for the task, work began on the building in 1932. It was completed in 1935.

The current Supreme Court Building, located on First Street in Washington, D.C., is 385 feet wide and 304 feet deep, and at its tallest point it reaches four stories above the ground floor. The architectural style used is classic Corinthian, so that it would fit in well with the nearby congressional buildings. The exterior is made of Vermont marble, while inside the builders used marble from Georgia and Alabama, and American white oak was used for the window and door casings, wainscoting, and other details.

Supreme Court, the first president since Andrew Jackson to appoint a Court majority.

Rifts began to develop between Roosevelt and Taft, however. Roosevelt was a progressive president who expanded the power of the executive branch. Taft, in contrast, believed that the Constitution restricted the president's powers. Further, he replaced many of Roosevelt's appointees and failed to carry through on other Roosevelt initiatives, including conservation and protection of federal lands. Relations between the two men noticeably cooled, and when Taft ran for reelection in 1912, Roosevelt split and ran for the presidency under the banner of the Bull Moose Party, the progressive wing of the Republican Party. The split Republican vote gave the election to Democrat Woodrow Wilson, and Taft was out of a job.

During the Wilson administration, Taft was a professor of constitutional law at Yale University, but he remained active in public affairs. He served for a year as president of the American Bar Association and in 1915 was elected president of the League to Enforce Peace. He also served as joint chair of the National War Labor Board and actively campaigned for U.S.

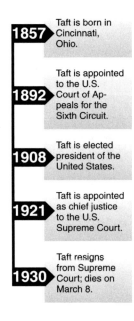

1857 Taft is born in Cincinnati, Ohio.

1892 Taft is appointed to the U.S. Court of Appeals for the Sixth Circuit.

1908 Taft is elected president of the United States.

1921 Taft is appointed as chief justice to the U.S. Supreme Court.

1930 Taft resigns from Supreme Court; dies on March 8.

entry into the League of Nations. His 1916 book, *Our Chief Magistrate and His Powers*, examined the scope of presidential powers.

Taft, though, had never lost the desire to be Chief Justice of the Supreme Court, but with a Democratic president, the outlook was bleak. His break came in 1920 when a Republican, Warren G. Harding, was elected president. Harding was willing to appoint Taft to replace the ailing Edward D. White—Taft even went so far as to visit White to persuade him to retire. White refused, but when he died less than a year later, Harding made the appointment, and Taft was confirmed in the Senate on June 30, 1921.

Two major accomplishments marked Taft's nine years as Chief Justice. One was the construction of new quarters for the Supreme Court, which previously had occupied cramped space in the Capitol Building. Work began in 1929, but Taft did not live to see its completion in 1935. His other, perhaps more important accomplishment was improving the efficiency of the Court. Taft inherited a badly divided Court with a huge backlog of cases. He introduced a number of reforms that improved the efficiency not only of the Supreme Court, but also of the entire federal judicial system. In particular he secured passage of the 1925 Judiciary Act, which gave the Court more control over the cases it would hear and expedite its consideration of important constitutional questions.

Taft came of age during a period of great economic turmoil in the United States. Corporations were becoming more powerful, business trusts were driving out competition, and large personal fortunes were being amassed. In response there was a great deal of popular unrest, including strikes, boycotts, and the formation of Populist and Progressive parties and organizations such as the Knights of Labor, the Greenbackers, and the Grangers. Socialist candidates were winning more votes in presidential elections than they had before or since. Many people feared popular revolution.

It was against this backdrop that Taft formed his essentially conservative views—views that led some observers to see him as just another bloated capitalist. He was, for example, hesitant to restrict property rights in favor of social experimentation. He articulated this view in his majority opinion in *Bailey v. Drexel Furniture Company* (1922). In an effort to curb child labor abuses, the Revenue Act of 1919 imposed a tax on profits made by firms engaged in interstate commerce that used child labor.

The furniture company, which employed a 14-year-old boy, sued to recover the tax. At issue was the question was whether the taxing power of the federal government could be used to correct a social ill. The Taft Court ruled that it could not, arguing that the "tax" was a penalty and that it invaded the powers of the states reserved under the Tenth Amendment to the Constitution.

At the same time, though, Taft issued some opinions that were relatively progressive. In *Stafford v. Wallace* (1922), for example, he upheld the Packers and Stockyards Act of 1921, expanding both the definition of interstate commerce and the power of the federal government to regulate it. Similarly, he dissented in *Adkins v. Children's Hospital* (1923) when the Court invalidated a congressional act that set minimum wage standards for women and minority workers in the District of Columbia. He wrote: "It is not the function of this court to hold congressional acts invalid simply because they are passed to carry out economic views which the court believes to be unwise or unsound."

Taft was a large man whose weight often reached 300 pounds. By 1930 his health began to fail. He had high blood pressure and hardening of the arteries, which caused a series of strokes. Recognizing that he was unable to carry out his duties, he resigned on February 3. He spent his final weeks confined to a bed in Washington, D.C., where he died on March 8, 1930. ◆

Taft issued some opinions that were relatively progressive.

Taney, Roger B.

MARCH 17, 1777–OCTOBER 12, 1864 ● CHIEF JUSTICE

Roger Brooke Taney—best known for presiding over the U.S. Supreme Court when it issued its decision in the landmark *Dred Scott* case—was born in Calvert County, Maryland, on March 17, 1777, to a prominent Anglo-Catholic family that had settled in the area in the mid-17th century. His father, Michael Taney, owned a tobacco plantation; his mother was Monica Brooke.

As a child Taney was educated at the village school and privately tutored at home. At age 15 he enrolled at Carlisle College in Pennsylvania, where he graduated in 1795 as class valedictorian. Taney was a second son, so without prospect of

Roger B. Taney

insurrection an act of resistance or rebellion against an established civil authority or government.

inheriting his father's plantation, he read law for three years with Judge Jeremiah Chase in Annapolis, Maryland. There he befriended Francis Scott Key, the attorney who wrote the words to "The Star-Spangled Banner," and in 1806 he married Key's sister, Anne.

After being admitted to the bar in 1799 Taney set up a private law practice and was elected to the Maryland House of Delegates, where he served for just a single year before losing his bid for reelection. He then moved to Frederick, Maryland, where he practiced law for more than two decades.

Taney enjoyed considerable success as an attorney, despite his shyness, poor health, and a gaunt, unattractive appearance. In one highly charged case in 1819, he successfully defended a preacher who had been charged with inciting slaves to **insurrection** with an antislavery sermon. Taney told the jury, "A hard necessity indeed compels us to endure the evil of slavery for a time. . . . Yet while it continues, it is a blot on our national character; and every real lover of freedom . . . hopes it will . . . be . . . gradually wiped away."

Taney himself had freed slaves he inherited, but his position was that slavery was an issue to be decided not by the federal government but by the states. He also took a paternalistic attitude toward slaves, believing that they were a lower order of people who should be freed out of benevolence, not as a matter of right.

Taney never lost his interest in politics. A Federalist, he led a faction of the party that supported the War of 1812, earning him the disfavor of antiwar Federalists. By 1816 he was the acknowledged leader of the Maryland Federalist Party, and that year he was elected to the Maryland Senate, serving a five-year term. After moving to Baltimore in 1823 he continued to practice law and was elected the state's attorney general in 1827. In the meantime he had broken with the Federalist Party and supported Andrew Jackson in 1824 in his hotly contested bid for the presidency.

Taney had come to view the Federalists as outmoded and, with Jackson, believed that expansion and economic growth would occur most rapidly in semi-autonomous states and even neighborhood centers of influence. While Jackson lost in 1824, he won in 1828, and to reward Taney for his efforts on his behalf, Jackson appointed him attorney general in 1831 after his entire cabinet had to resign in the wake of scandals. Taney had not been interested in federal office, but he took the post, despite its huge cut in pay.

As attorney general Taney became embroiled in a dispute, the so-called Bank War, over the nation's central bank, the Second Bank of the United States. Jackson vehemently opposed the monopolistic power inherent in such a bank, and when the U.S. Congress re-chartered it in 1832, the president ordered the secretary of the treasury to withdraw all federal funds from it. The secretary refused, so Jackson dismissed him and appointed Taney to his post. After withdrawing the funds (causing a financial panic as Second Bank officers called in loans), Taney set to work establishing a series of smaller banks, called "pet banks," to replace the national bank. But he had never been confirmed as treasury secretary by the Senate, which finally rejected his nomination months later in 1834.

Taney returned to private practice, but in 1835 Jackson nominated him to replace Gabriel Duvall on the Supreme Court. The Senate again rejected him. Jackson tried yet again, nominating him to replace Chief Justice John Marshall on the high court. Many Whig members of Congress believed that Taney was a **hack** being repaid for his actions in the Bank War, but Marshall's earlier support of him to replace Duvall tipped the scales in his favor. He was confirmed in the Senate by a vote of 29–15 in March 1836. Taney thus became the first Catholic and the first non-Protestant to serve on the high court.

In a historical footnote, Taney introduced two innovations to the Court. One was the custom of wearing ordinary pants rather than the traditional knee breeches under their robes, symbolizing a change from the aristocratic Revolutionary War era to a new, more modern vision of change and expansion. The other was to assign opinions to individual justices rather than, as Chief Justice, writing all of the opinions himself.

Taney served as Chief Justice for 28 years. His reputation suffered for two reasons. First, he had to fill the shoes of John Marshall, perhaps the most influential Chief Justice in the nation's history. Second, he was the architect of the Court's

"No wonder that the Chief Justice should have sunk his voice to a whisper . . . knowing that he was engaged in a pitiful attempt to impose upon the public."
New York Tribune, in response to Taney's *Dred Scott* opinion, quoted in Bernard Schwartz, *A History of the Supreme Court,* 1993

hack: derisive terms used to describe a politician or political appointee as entirely beholden to the party he or she represents.

Dred Scott v. Sandford (1857)

Dred Scott was a Missouri slave who, in 1833, fled from his owner to Illinois, which had outlawed slavery. From Illinois he eventually made his way to the Louisiana Territory, where slavery was also forbidden, and lived there until 1843. On the urging of abolitionists, Scott eventually returned to Missouri and sued for his freedom in the state courts, claiming that 10 years as a citizen of free territories were enough to change his status. When the Missouri courts ruled against him, he appealed to the Supreme Court.

Sanford (spelled Sandford in court documents) was the man who claimed to own Scott, and he argued that "no pure blooded Negro descended from slaves could be a citizen" of a state or of the United States, and therefore Scott's claim to freedom was unfounded. The Supreme Court agreed with Sandford.

Chief Justice Roger B. Taney wrote the opinion of the court, which raised two important points. First, Taney argued that only a citizen of the United States could be a citizen of any of the individual states. Second, Taney wrote that only Congress could confer national citizenship to a person who could not claim citizenship status by birth. Since Scott was born a slave, and therefore not a natural citizen, and since Congress had never granted him citizenship status, Dred Scott remained a slave regardless of how long he lived in free territory. The decision went even further, and declared the Missouri Compromise, which balanced the proportion of slave and free states, unconstitutional. This decision touched off an uproar in the abolitionist states, and was an important contributor to the eventual outbreak of the Civil War.

decision in *Dred Scott v. Sandford*. In the view of many constitutional scholars, this judgment is unfair, for Taney was an effective Chief Justice whose rulings in a number of important cases shifted American jurisprudence in a more progressive direction.

One of these cases was *Charles River Bridge v. Warren Bridge Company* (1837). The dispute was between two companies that operated bridges over the Charles River in Massachusetts. The Charles River Bridge Company believed that the state had granted it a permanent monopoly to operate a toll bridge. Warren Bridge had later been authorized by the state to build a second bridge, which in time passengers could use for free. Writing for the majority, Taney ruled in favor of Warren Bridge, arguing that because Charles Bridge's contract with the state did not explicitly say that the company had monopoly control, it did not. Further, he pointed to the burgeoning population of the Boston-Cambridge area, which required a second bridge for economic growth. This manifest need for a second bridge prompted him to go on to say that private companies had a social responsibility, and that in the future, in disputes of this type, the Court would decided in favor of the public interest.

"The object and end of all government is to promote the happiness and prosperity of the community by which it is established," Taney noted. This was a modern perspective taken for granted today, but it was controversial in the 1830s.

The issue that dominated the Court's attention during the 1850s, of course, was slavery, culminating in the 1857 case *Dred Scott v. Sandford*. (The defendant's name was really Sanford, but the misspelling of a New York court reporter has become enshrined.) Dred Scott was a self-emancipated slave who sued for his freedom in 1846. In 1850 the Missouri Circuit Court granted him standing and declared him free. His "owner" appealed to the Missouri Supreme Court, which overturned the circuit court ruling and declared him a slave. With the help of abolitionists, Scott filed suit in federal court, and eventually the case reached the Supreme Court in 1856.

With the nation watching, the Court heard arguments in February and again in December. Taney was hoping to skirt the constitutional issues, but President James Buchanan met with him and pressured him to settle once and for all the question of whether slavery was constitutional or not.

On March 6 and 7, 1857, the nine Supreme Court justices handed down their separate opinions. In his 55-page opinion, Taney argued that the framers of the Constitution considered slaves property with no legal rights; hence, they were not citizens of the United States, and as non-citizens, they could not sue in federal court. Taney also declared the 1820 Missouri Compromise unconstitutional, saying that Article V of the Constitution protected private property, and since slaves were property, Congress was obligated to protect slavery in new U.S. territories. As the enfeebled Taney, now nearly 80 years old, delivered his opinion, his voice broke and he fell into a whisper that could barely be heard.

Taney had hoped that the decision would put the issue to rest and reduce the threat of sectional division in the country. Instead it had the opposite effect, causing deep divisions in the Court (Justice Benjamin Curtis resigned in protest) and indeed throughout the nation. He was bitterly denounced for his decision—while being cheered by most Southern Democrats.

In the final years of his life Taney became increasingly embittered toward the North and antislavery forces. He regarded Abraham Lincoln as a **despot,** even while administering to him the oath of office in 1861. During the Civil War he took an enjoyment in curtailing the president's wartime powers. Broken in

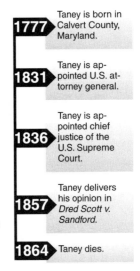

1777 Taney is born in Calvert County, Maryland.

1831 Taney is appointed U.S. attorney general.

1836 Taney is appointed chief justice of the U.S. Supreme Court.

1857 Taney delivers his opinion in *Dred Scott v. Sandford.*

1864 Taney dies.

Taney had hoped that the decision would put the issue to rest and reduce the threat of sectional division in the country.

despot: a tyrannical leader exercising an abuse of power.

health and in spirit, he spent his final weeks at home and died at age 87 on October 12, 1864. ◆

Thomas, Clarence

JUNE 23, 1948– ● ASSOCIATE JUSTICE

Among the most controversial Supreme Court appointees of the 20th century, Clarence Thomas was born in Pin Point, Georgia, a small community near Savannah, on June 23, 1948. He was the second child of Leola Williams and M. C. Thomas. His early life was one of extreme hardship. Pin Point lacked even the most basic services, and as a small child he lived in a shack with dirt floors and no plumbing. When he was two years old, his father abandoned him, an older sister, and their pregnant mother, who then supported the family by working as a maid. Later, their house burned down, so Thomas and his younger brother were sent to Savannah to live with their grandparents, Myers and Christine Anderson. Myers Anderson, an ardent Democrat and member of the National Association for the Advancement of Colored People (NAACP) had a major impact on Thomas's upbringing.

Clarence Thomas

Anderson was also a devout Catholic, and he believed that the best way for Thomas to escape poverty was through a demanding parochial-school education. He sent Thomas to an all-black Catholic elementary school, to an all-black Catholic high school, then, for his final two years of high school, to St. John Vianney Minor Seminary outside Savannah, where Thomas was the only African American.

With a view to becoming a priest, Thomas enrolled at Immaculate Conception Seminary in Missouri in 1967, but he dropped out and abandoned the idea of the priesthood after encountering racist remarks in the wake of the assassination of Martin Luther King, Jr. In 1968 he made his way to Holy Cross College in Worcester, Massachusetts, which was actively recruiting black students, and graduated in 1971 with honors in English. At Holy Cross he volunteered in a breakfast program for children and helped found the college's Black Student Union. He began to demonstrate his views on race relations when he dissented from a decision by the BSU to live in an all-black dormitory, preferring, he said, to live with and try to understand the white majority. The day after graduation, he married Kathy Ambush, and the couple had one son. Thomas retained custody of the son after the two were divorced in 1984.

Under an affirmative action program designed to attract minorities, Thomas attended law school at Yale, where, he said later, he felt rage at being looked upon as an affirmative action "token," not only by classmates but by law firms that interviewed him for jobs. After graduating in 1974, he decided to take a position on the staff of Missouri attorney general John Danforth, who became his political mentor. Danforth, though, was elected to the U.S. Senate in 1977, so Thomas took a job at the Monsanto Company in St. Louis, where he shepherded pesticides through the government-approval process. In 1979 he moved to Washington, D.C., where he became a legislative assistant for Danforth—but only on the condition that he not be assigned to civil rights work.

By this time, Thomas was an opponent of affirmative action, as well as busing, welfare, and government set-asides for minorities, believing that programs like these undermined self-reliance and promoted dependency on government. Instead, he worked on energy and environmental projects.

Despite his resistance to civil rights work, in 1981 Thomas accepted a position as assistant secretary for civil rights in the Reagan administration's Department of Education. Then in 1982 he was appointed chair of the U.S. Equal Employment Opportunity Commission, a position he held for eight years. His conservative views informed his work at the EEOC. Previously, the agency had relied on class-action lawsuits to correct patterns of racial discrimination at corporations and other organizations. Thomas, instead, focused on individual cases of discrimination and rejected numerical goals and timetables for racial integration. In 1986 he met Virginia Lamp, a fellow conservative and lawyer, and the two were married in 1987.

"I cannot do to white people what an elite group of whites did to black people.... If I write racism into law, then I am in God's eyes no better than they are."
Clarence Thomas, quoted on University of Pennsylvania Web site www.law.upenn.edu

Nominating and Approval Process for Supreme Court Justices

When an opening on the Supreme Court occurs due to the retirement, death, or resignation of a sitting Justice, the President of the United States selects a potential replacement, usually drawn from the ranks of higher–court justices, those sitting on such tribunals as district or state supreme courts. The President bases his choice on a number of factors, not least of which may be questions of judicial philosophy. Prior to announcing the nominee, the President's staff researches the life and judicial history of possible candidates in order to discover any issues that might block the approval process. The name is then submitted to Congress, which must approve the choice.

Once a nominee to the Supreme Court has been named, the Senate Judiciary Committee meets to review the candidate. A part of this review process involves hearings in which the nominee is questioned closely about his or her judicial decisions and general philosophy. Approval of the presidential nominee is by no means certain, and controversial nominees undergo particularly grueling questioning. This occurred, for example, when a largely Democratic Senate refused to approve Ronald Reagan's nomination of Judge Robert Bork to the Court. The hearings can be wide–ranging and extremely tough, and a nominee is judged on his or her personal life as well as judicial actions. When President George Bush's nomination Justice Clarence Thomas was under review, the Senate Judiciary Committee questioned him closely about allegations of sexual harassment alleged by a former colleague, Anita Hill. While Thomas did receive Senate approval in the end, the resulting 52-48 vote was the closest in the history of Supreme Court appointments.

Thomas's ascent to the Supreme Court began in 1990, when he attracted the attention of President George Bush, who appointed him to the U.S. Circuit Court of Appeals for the District of Columbia—perhaps the most visible judicial post outside the high court. Thomas had served for just 18 months on the court when Bush nominated him to the Supreme Court to replace the Court's first black justice, Thurgood Marshall.

The confirmation process proved to be a long and difficult one for Thomas. Immediately, groups such as the NAACP and the Congressional Black Caucus announced that they would oppose the nomination because of Thomas's conservative views. During the confirmation hearings, the Senate Judiciary Committee tried to pin him down on hot-button issues such as abortion, but he managed to sidestep these questions, insisting that answering them would undermine his judicial impartiality.

Then, on October 8, 1991, Anita Hill, a law professor at the University of Oklahoma, dropped a bombshell by confirming statements that had appeared in an FBI report on Thomas. In a televised press conference, she alleged that Thomas had sexually harassed her when she worked under him first at the Department of Education, then at the EEOC. The Judiciary Committee was determined to give her charges a public hearing. With the nation tethered to its television sets, Hill offered sometimes lurid testimony to the committee. She alleged, among other things, that Thomas in her presence had bragged about his sexual prowess and talked about scenes from pornographic movies.

Thomas indignantly denied the charges, calling the hearings a "high-tech lynching." Feminists were outraged, while others simply did not believe Hill, asking why, if his conduct was so objectionable, she followed him from the Department of Education to the EEOC. Amid the controversy, Thomas was confirmed in the Senate by a vote of 52 to 48, the closest Supreme Court confirmation vote in the 20th century. At age 43, he became the youngest member of the Court.

Thomas quickly took his place as a mainstay of the Court's conservative wing, joining Chief Justice William Rehnquist and Justice Antonin Scalia. He voted with Scalia over 90 percent of the time. Because of his conservative views, he continued to act as a lightning rod for controversy. The NAACP condemned his decisions on, for example, school desegregation. An invitation to speak at a school awards ceremony sparked protests and was withdrawn; a similar invitation to address a youth camp was withdrawn. Thomas, though, clung to his belief that the proper role of a Supreme Court justice was to interpret the original intent of the framers of the Constitution and to follow strictly the text of the Constitution without regard to personal or societal attitudes.

Thomas articulated his view that the Court's role should be limited in a number of cases. In an early one, *Hudson v. McMillian* (1992), he dissented from the Court's ruling that excessive force by a prison guard may violate the Eighth Amendment's prohibition against cruel and unusual punishment, even if the prisoner is not injured. Thomas wrote that the Eighth Amendment "should not be turned into a national code of prison regulation" and that the majority's view was "yet another manifestation of the pervasive view that the federal constitution must address all ills in our society."

Similarly, in *Lewis v. Casey* (1996) he joined the Court majority in ruling that the issue of access to the courts for prisoners was a state issue, not one for the federal courts. He wrote: "It is a bedrock principle of judicial restraint that a right be lodged firmly in the text or tradition of a specific constitutional

1948 Thomas is born in Pin Point, Georgia.

1981 Thomas is appointed assistant secretary for civil rights in the Department of Education.

1982 Thomas is appointed chair of the Equal Employment Opportunity Commission.

1990 Thomas is appointed to the U.S. Court of Appeals for the District of Columbia.

1991 Thomas is appointed to the U.S. Supreme Court.

Thomas articulated his view that the Court's role should be limited in a number of cases.

provision before we will recognize it as fundamental. Strict adherence to this approach is essential if we are to fulfill our constitutionally assigned role of giving full effect to the mandate of the Framers without infusing the constitutional fabric with our own political views."

Thomas continued to oppose affirmative action and similar programs designed to aid minorities. In a concurring opinion he wrote for *Adarand Constructors, Inc. v. Pena* (1995), he referred to affirmative action as "government sponsored discrimination" and said that even though it was based on "benign prejudice," it was "just as noxious as discrimination inspired by malicious prejudice." He firmly rejected the use of sociological data and statistics in settling constitutional issues in *Missouri v. Jenkins* (1995), preferring to focus on specific discriminatory practices rather than on large-scale patterns of discrimination.

After a decade on the high court, some of the controversy surrounding Thomas's appointment receded to the background, but Court observers continued to view him through the lens of their political views. To some, he remained a throwback; to others he represented the virtues of self-reliance and tenacity in the face of racial discrimination. ◆

Thompson, Smith

JANUARY 17, 1768–DECEMBER 18, 1843 ● ASSOCIATE JUSTICE

Smith Thompson was born January 17, 1768, in Dutchess County, New York. He came from a family of nine children. His father was Ezra Thompson and his mother was Rachel (Smith) Thompson. The family came from New Englanders, including Anthony Thompson, who came to Boston in 1637.

Thompson's father was a well-off farmer, who was also an anti-federalist involved with state and local politics. Thompson attended the local school before heading off to the College of New Jersey (which would later become Princeton University). He graduated in 1788.

After college, Thompson earned money by working as a schoolteacher. He also started studying law with Gilbert Livingston and James Kent. Livingston was part of a prominent and influential family, although his particular branch of the

family was considered to be less notable. Like Thompson and Thompson's father, Livingston was an anti-
federalist. Kent, a noted attorney
who would go on to reach greater
political heights, held more conservative views. Thompson passed the
bar in 1792, and in 1795 took over
Kent's place as Livingston's partner.

In 1794, Thompson married
Livingston's daughter, Sarah. The
couple would have two sons and two
daughters. The marriage had the
benefit, whether intentional or un-
intentional, of putting his career on
a faster track. In 1800, soon after
marrying into the Livingston family,
Thompson was elected to the New
York legislature. In 1801, he was a
delegate to the state constitutional
convention.

Smith Thompson

Thompson's career on the bench began in 1802. At first he
was appointed to be district attorney but was unable to take the
job when he was offered a seat on the New York Supreme Court.
During the years he served, the New York Supreme Court was
known for its activism. In 1814, he became chief justice, replacing his old mentor Kent, who left to become chancellor.

Thompson's career took a bit of a detour in 1818 when President James Monroe invited Thompson into his cabinet to serve
as his Secretary of the Navy. Before being asked, he had not
been a personal friend of Monroe's or expressed any particular
interest in the position, but Thompson was an extremely ambitious man and was happy to take the post.

Thompson's stint in the cabinet failed to be especially noteworthy, but it ended up being a worthwhile appointment. Becoming an ally of Monroe's paid off for Thompson in 1823 after
Justice Brockholst Livingston died and a seat became open on
the United States Supreme Court. Monroe nominated Thompson, choosing him over another candidate, who, ironically, was
Thompson's former mentor James Kent.

The seat on the bench would seem to be a great opportunity, but Thompson almost declined. He harbored ambitions to
become the Republican nominee for president in 1824 and did

1768 Thompson is born in Dutchess County, New York.

1802 Thompson joins the New Jersey Supreme Court.

1823 Thompson is named to the United States Supreme Court by James Monroe.

1831 Thompson rules in *Cherokee Nation v. Georgia*.

1843 Thompson dies in Poughkeepsie, New York.

not want to spoil his chances. Thompson, showing the kind of political maneuvering that would be a mark of his career, decided to take the appointment to the Supreme Court only after it became obvious that John Quincy Adams was going to get the nomination for president.

During his 20 years on in the Court, Thompson was part of a group of justices that were starting to disagree with the trends of the federalist Marshall court. Thompson disagreed with Marshall's ideas about a strong federal government. In *Ogden v. Saunders* (1827), a case involving the validity of a state's bankruptcy law, Thompson was one of the justices making up a 4–3 majority that forced Marshall into his only constitutional dissent.

Thompson was an involved justice. He wrote opinions for the court for 85 cases, concurred five times and dissented 11 times.

Despite his obvious talent on the bench, Thompson—or his ego—did not seem to find it completely satisfying. In 1828, he again sought to take his career in a more political, less judicial direction. That year he accepted a nomination for the governor of New York. It was a political mistake. In his bitter and contentious race against Martin Van Buren,

Thompson was criticized for not resigning from the bench and keeping his position as a backup in case he lost the race. As it turned out, he did need that backup job because he went on to lose the election.

In 1836, Thompson—who had become a widower—married his first wife's cousin, Eliza Livingston. The couple had one son and two daughters. Besides his duties on the bench, Thompson was involved with other activities. A deeply religious man, he was the vice-president of the American Bible Society. He was also awarded several honorary degrees and an appointment to the state Board of Regents.

Despite his tendency towards political wrangling and backbiting in his political life, Thompson was known for his humanitarian leanings on the bench. *The United States v. The Schooner Amistad* (1841), concerned an illegal ship filled with African slaves. The slaves rebelled and took over the ship but had in turn been captured. Although Thompson did not rule in the case, he wrote that he thought that the slaves should be returned to Africa and freed.

In *Cherokee Nation v. Georgia* (1831), Thompson dissented, asserting that the Native Americans were separate sovereigns, even though they had been conquered militarily. This decision is considered to be the best of Thompson's career.

After serving 40 years on various courts, Thompson left the bench and became ill. Thompson died at his house, "Rust Plaetz" (Resting Place) in Poughkeepsie, New York, on December 18, 1843. He was 76. ◆

Todd, Thomas

JANUARY 23, 1765–FEBRUARY 7, 1826 ● ASSOCIATE JUSTICE

Thomas Todd, the first Supreme Court justice from west of the Appalachians and the brother-in-law of First Lady Dolley Madison, was born in King and Queen County, Virginia, on January 23, 1765. His grandfather, a wealthy Virginia landowner, had passed his estate down to Todd's father, Richard Todd. Richard, though, died when Thomas was just 18 months old, and when the estate passed to Richard's older brother, Thomas and his mother, Elizabeth Richards, moved to Manchester, Virginia. Before her death when Thomas was just 11 years old, Elizabeth had managed to save enough money running a boarding house to pay for her son's education.

When the British army invaded Virginia during the Revolutionary War, Todd enlisted as a private in the Continental Army. After the war he enrolled at Liberty Hall, which later became Washington and Lee University, where he graduated in 1783. He then moved in with Harry Innes, his mother's cousin, and in exchange for a legal education, he tutored Innes's daughters.

Innes also introduced Todd to politics. During the 1780s Kentucky was trying to become a state separate from Virginia, and in 1784 Innes

Thomas Todd

Although Todd was respected by his colleagues, his impact on the Court was minimal.

moved the family to Danville, Kentucky, when he was asked to set up a district court. In the years that followed he chaired five conventions that petitioned the federal government for statehood, and Todd served as the conventions' secretary and clerk. He was admitted to the bar association in 1788 and quickly developed a thriving legal practice specializing in the many disputed land and title claims that necessarily arose as a result of western migration. That year, too, he married Elizabeth Harris.

Kentucky was admitted to the Union in 1792, and Todd served as secretary of the state's new legislature. The state's constitution is in Todd's handwriting. He was then appointed chief clerk of the state supreme court, the Kentucky Court of Appeals, in 1799. When the legislature added a fourth seat to the bench in 1801, the governor appointed Todd to the post, and five years later, he was elevated to chief justice, where he acquired a reputation for fairness and was rarely overturned by higher courts. When the retiring chief justice failed to receive the pension promised him by the state, Todd took him in and cared for him until his death. In gratitude, he willed Todd his extensive estates.

Todd's appointment to the U.S. Supreme Court came in 1807 after Congress amended the 1789 Judiciary Act to add a seventh federal circuit, including Tennessee, Kentucky, and Ohio. This action added a seventh seat to the Supreme Court. In filling the position, President Thomas Jefferson consulted with the congressional delegations from those states. They recommended Todd for the position. Without even meeting Todd, Jefferson made the appointment, and Todd was confirmed in the Senate in March.

Although Todd was respected by his colleagues, his impact on the Court was minimal. The life of a Supreme Court justice in the early 19th century could be precarious. Todd missed the entire 1809 term, for example, because travel conditions were poor and many of the bridges on the way to Washington, D.C., were washed out. He also missed several entire terms because of illness, the demands of riding through a frontier circuit court, and the need to oversee a number of investments in toll bridges, canals, and turnpikes. At the end of his 19 years, the Court had delivered 644 opinions, but Todd had written only 14, most of them having to do with land disputes. His only dissent was five lines long.

Also minimizing Todd's impact was the dominance of Chief Justice John Marshall, perhaps the most influential chief justice in the Court's history. When Jefferson appointed Todd, he probably hoped that Todd would join the president's other two appointees, Justices William Johnson and Brockholst Livingston, in opposing Marshall's sweeping efforts to strengthen the power of the federal government. Occasionally the others dissented from Marshall's views, but Marshall was adept at getting the Court to rule unanimously, and Todd was unable or unwilling to oppose the chief justice and joined with him in most of the great constitutional questions of the day. Thus, for example, he joined the Court in such cases as *Martin v. Hunter's Lessee* (1816), which confirmed the Court's right to overturn the decisions of state courts, and *Gibbons v. Ogden* (1824), which established the power of the federal government to regulate business and commerce.

Todd's most significant opinion was probably *Preston v. Browder,* an 1816 case in which he affirmed the right of the North Carolina legislature to maintain the sanctity of Indian treaties by restricting land claims within Indian territories.

In 1811 Todd's wife Elizabeth died. A year later he married Lucy Payne, Dolley Madison's sister. Lucy initially rejected Todd's marriage proposal, but when Todd left for Kentucky, she had a change of heart and dispatched a messenger who caught up with him in Pennsylvania with a note consenting "to be a second prey." The wedding took place in the East Room of the White House, the first marriage to take place in the executive mansion.

By the end of his life Todd had amassed an extensive estate and invested much of his wealth in public improvements, including the Kentucky River Company, the Kentucky Turnpike (one of the first publicly improved highways west of the Alleghenies), and the Frankfort toll bridge. When he died on February 7, 1826, in Frankfort, Kentucky, he had to provided amply for his eight children. ◆

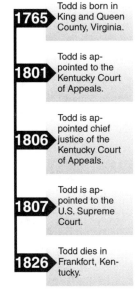

1765 Todd is born in King and Queen County, Virginia.

1801 Todd is appointed to the Kentucky Court of Appeals.

1806 Todd is appointed chief justice of the Kentucky Court of Appeals.

1807 Todd is appointed to the U.S. Supreme Court.

1826 Todd dies in Frankfort, Kentucky.

Trimble, Robert

NOVEMBER 17, 1776–AUGUST 25, 1828 ● ASSOCIATE JUSTICE

Robert Trimble was born on November 17, 1776, in Augusta County (or, according to other sources, Berkeley County), Virginia. He was raised in Kentucky where his

Robert Trimble

father, William Trimble, was an early settler. The elder Trimble made his money by acquiring land. At the time, Kentucky was sparsely populated—there were only a few scattered settlements—so Trimble did not have very many amenities (or neighbors, even) growing up. As a boy, he worked the land and hunted. The details of his early education are somewhat sketchy but it is generally accepted that Trimble went to a local school. He also worked on educating himself and had a well-rounded group of interests. He was a good athlete as well as a good student, and was considered to be a leader even as a youth.

In the 1790s, Trimble probably attended Bourbon Academy in Bourbon County and Kentucky Academy (later Transylvania University) in Woodford County. Some accounts report that Trimble also spent some time teaching while completing his own education. After finishing school, Trimble had the good fortune to study law with two illustrious figures: James Brown, who would later go on to become the Minister to France; and George Nicholas, who was the main writer of the first Kentucky constitution and the first professor of law at Transylvania.

Trimble set out to start his own practice in 1800. He worked in Paris, a very small town in Kentucky. Even though his town only had about 500 citizens, Trimble became a successful attorney, and word of his legal skills spread. In 1802, his reputation helped him earn a seat in the Kentucky House of Representatives. He was only 26 years old.

Trimble only served one term and in 1803 married Nancy Timberlake. He worked on expanding his lucrative private practice until 1807, when he accepted an appointment to be a justice on the Kentucky Court of Appeals. He served for only two years, then resigned, citing financial hardships. He and his wife had at least 10 children, and the position as judge paid only $1000 a year. Trimble said that he could not afford to keep the job. The poor pay also caused Trimble to turn down a position of Chief Justice of Kentucky in 1810 and a seat on the Court of

Appeals in 1813. In 1812, he turned down a seat in the United States Senate.

Trimble stuck with his prosperous practice to earn enough to feed his growing family. His reputation grew further, and he served on most of the big local trials of the day. Though he declined political appointments, he remained active in political life. He was a presidential elector in 1808, 1812 and 1816 and was a trustee of Transylvania University.

The decision to concentrate on his private practice eventually paid off for Trimble financially. Even though he was known for his fair and moderate fees, he soon amassed enough money (and cows and pigs, which were also sometimes used as payment) to lessen the financial pressure he had felt earlier in his career. In 1817, he accepted a nomination from President James Madison to become the federal district judge for Kentucky, succeeding Harry Innes.

Trimble's eight years of service as the federal district judge was marked by some controversy over the virulent cases involving state versus federal rights. Trimble took some positions asserting the superiority of federal powers that greatly angered some of his fellow Kentuckians. The same controversy that made Trimble unpopular in Kentucky was what caught the ear of President John Quincy Adams, who nominated him for a position on the United States Supreme Court in 1826. It was thought that Trimble's opinions on the supremacy of the federal government might cause his nomination to be rejected by the United States Senate, but when the final vote tallies came in, only five senators voted against Trimble. He was confirmed by the Senate on May 9, 1826, to fill the seat left vacant by his friend and fellow Kentuckian, Thomas Todd.

Trimble's career on the Supreme Court would last only two years before being abruptly cut short by his sudden death from what was termed a "malignant bilious fever." In the short time that Trimble served, he exhibited the kind of judicial powers that showed that he had the potential to be one of the great justices. Before his death, he wrote 16 opinions.

During his service, Trimble often sided with Chief Justice John Marshall, supporting the rights of the federal government over the rights of the state governments. At the time, when the Court was often referred to as "the Marshall Court," Marshall was a very strong force, writing most of the opinions and influencing most of the Court's decisions. Only a few times did

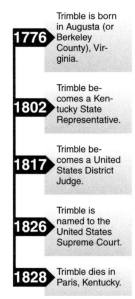

1776 — Trimble is born in Augusta (or Berkeley County), Virginia.

1802 — Trimble becomes a Kentucky State Representative.

1817 — Trimble becomes a United States District Judge.

1826 — Trimble is named to the United States Supreme Court.

1828 — Trimble dies in Paris, Kentucky.

Trimble disagree with Marshall. The biggest case on which Trimble disagreed with Marshall was *Ogden v. Saunders*, which concerned state bankruptcy laws. Trimble agreed with the 4–3 majority in voting to support state bankruptcy laws. That case was Marshall's sole constitutional dissent.

Trimble died in 1828 in Paris, Kentucky. ◆

Van Devanter, Willis

APRIL 17, 1859–FEBRUARY 8, 1941 ● ASSOCIATE JUSTICE

Willis Van Devanter, whose name is associated as much with the untamed Wyoming frontier as with the hushed halls of the Supreme Court, was born in Marion, Indiana, on April 17, 1859, to Isaac Van Devanter, a lawyer, and Violetta Spencer. Willis was the oldest of their eight children. As a youngster, he liked the life of a farmer, but at the urging of his father he pursued an education. In 1875 he enrolled at Indiana Asbury University (now DePauw), but he had to withdraw after two years to help his father recuperate from an illness. He returned to school, though, and after graduating second in his class from the Cincinnati Law School in 1881, he joined his father's law firm, Lacey & Van Devanter.

In 1883 Van Devanter married Dellice Burhams, and the following year—after his father retired—he carted her off to the Wyoming Territory, following his father's partner, John Lacey, who had been appointed to the territorial supreme court. There he set up a lucrative

Willis Van Devanter

323

private law practice, profiting from the innumerable disputes that arose over cattle rustling, land claims, and water rights. In 1892, for example, he played a major role in the infamous Johnson County War, a dispute that arose between rival "cattlemen's associations." After the U.S. Cavalry arrested the members of a raiding party that tried to lay claim a disputed cattle herd, Van Devanter won their acquittal in court. He also allied himself with the increasingly powerful railroad companies, often defending his biggest client, Union Pacific, during congressional inquiries into its land acquisition activities.

During the 1880s Van Devanter also became active in Republican Party politics, and in time he was the most influential member of the Wyoming party establishment. In 1887 he was appointed city attorney for Cheyenne, and in 1888 he was elected to the territorial House of Representatives. Among his accomplishments as a state legislator was an appropriations bill that funded construction of the University of Wyoming at Laramie. He also codified territorial law, and the legal codes he wrote formed the basis of the Wyoming's constitution when the territory was made a state in 1890.

In the meantime Van Devanter supported the presidential campaign of Benjamin Harrison, who in 1889 rewarded him with an appointment as chief justice of the territorial supreme court. During his years as chief justice, none of his rulings in criminal cases was ever appealed, and none of his civil decisions was ever overturned. After Wyoming was admitted to the Union, he was elected to the state's new supreme court, but within days he resigned and returned to private practice.

Illness prevented Van Devanter from campaigning for the Republican ticket in 1896, but the new president, William McKinley, knew that Van Devanter had served his party well and brought him to Washington, D.C., in 1897 to serve as assistant attorney general in the Department of the Interior. There Van Devanter was valuable because of his knowledge of the law that pertained to public lands and Indian affairs. In 1903 President Theodore Roosevelt elevated him to the U.S. Court of Appeals for the Eighth Circuit, where over a period of seven years he gained a reputation for his ability to settle complex technical and jurisdictional questions.

When Justice Edward White was elevated to chief justice in 1910 to replace the recently deceased Melville Fuller, President William Howard Taft nominated Van Devanter to the vacant Supreme Court seat. Van Devanter encountered some resistance from liberals and progressives concerned about his ties to the railroad industry. Nonetheless he won confirmation in the Senate, becoming the only justice from Wyoming in Supreme Court history.

Van Devanter's name is not as well known as that of many other Supreme Court justices. Rather than shaping great constitutional issues, he was the Court's "technician." In his 26 years on the bench, he wrote majority opinions in only 346 cases, and most of those dealt with complex jurisdictional issues—water and land rights, admiralty law, and Indian affairs. He was particularly valuable to the Court in conferences, where he showed skill as a negotiator and often provided information on procedural issues. Justice Louis Brandeis called him a "master of formulas that decided cases without creating precedents."

Despite his reputation as a conservative, Van Devanter leaned toward progressivism early in his term. In *Kieran v. Portland* (1911), for example, he upheld the Employees Liability Act of 1908, which required companies to compensate employees injured on the job. In *Southern Railway Company v. United States* (1911), he upheld the constitutionality of the Safety Appliances Act of 1893, a law that regulated the safety of railroad cars. And in several decisions he expanded the concept of "commerce," in effect helping to turn commerce into a national issue (and thus within the scope of the U.S. Constitution) rather than strictly a state issue.

Perhaps Van Devanter's most significant decision came in *McGrain v. Daugherty* (1927), a case that arose out of the Teapot Dome oil-lease scandal during the Harding administration. When Congress subpoenaed the brother of the corrupt attorney general at the center of the scandal, he ignored the subpoenas, arguing that Congress had exceeded its authority. Van Devanter ruled that Congress does have the right to compel witnesses to testify, even when its purpose is not to legislate.

Van Devanter was one of the "Four Horsemen," a bloc of conservative justices that included Pierce Butler, James McReynolds, and George Sutherland. During the 1930s the Court heard numerous cases that arose from the New Deal initiatives of President Franklin D. Roosevelt and the Democratic Congress to combat the Great Depression. Repeatedly, the Four Horseman struck down these programs when they believed the programs were unconstitutional and a dangerous extension of federal authority. In fact, Van Devanter was ready to retire from the Court in 1932, but he stayed until 1937 primarily to oppose

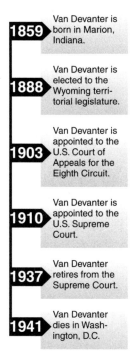

1859 Van Devanter is born in Marion, Indiana.

1888 Van Devanter is elected to the Wyoming territorial legislature.

1903 Van Devanter is appointed to the U.S. Court of Appeals for the Eighth Circuit.

1910 Van Devanter is appointed to the U.S. Supreme Court.

1937 Van Devanter retires from the Supreme Court.

1941 Van Devanter dies in Washington, D.C.

Van Devanter ruled that Congress does have the right to compel witnesses to testify, even when its purpose is not to legislate.

the New Deal. He finally retired when the president signed a bill that increased retirement benefits for justices over age 70.

After his retirement Van Devanter moved to New York, where he heard cases in the U.S. District Court, often working until well past midnight to prepare for court the following morning. He died in Washington, D.C., on February 8, 1941. ◆

Vinson, Fred

JANUARY 22, 1890–SEPTEMBER 8, 1953 ● CHIEF JUSTICE

Frederick Moore Vinson, the only member of the Supreme Court to have served in all three branches of government, was born in Louisa, Kentucky, on January 22, 1890. Through much of his career he tried to portray himself as a poor boy from the hills, but in fact his circumstances were relatively comfortable. His father, James Vinson, was the jailer for both the town and the county, often prompting Vinson to joke that he was born in jail. His mother was Virginia Ferguson, who supplemented the family income by taking in boarders. Vinson was their second son.

From an early age Vinson displayed a remarkable intellect. He graduated at the top of his class from Kentucky Normal College in 1908. His professors, recognizing his potential, arranged for him to enroll at Centre College as a senior, and he earned a second degree in 1909. He remained at Centre College to attend law school, graduating in 1911 with the highest scores in the school's history.

Vinson's classmates at Centre recalled his ability to memorize textbooks and add in his head columns of six-digit numbers. He also showed talent as a baseball player, starring on the Centre College team and playing **semiprofessional** ball in the Kentucky Blue Grass League. He actually gave some thought to a career as a professional baseball player, but when the Cincinnati Reds turned him down, he decided to stick with the law.

Vinson returned to Louisiana, where he settled into the role of small-town lawyer and, in 1923, married a hometown woman, Roberta Dixson. He won his first elective office in 1921 as commonwealth attorney for the 32nd judicial district of Kentucky. Then, three years, later, he won a special election to complete an unexpired term in the U.S. House of Representatives.

> "[Vinson] seems to me to have the confident air of a man who does not see the complexities of problems and blithely hits the obvious points."
>
> Diary entry, Justice Felix Frankfurter

semiprofessional: an athlete paid to play a sport for an organized team, though not as a full-time occupation.

Except for the years 1928–1930, Vinson served in the House until he resigned in 1938. During these years he quietly rose through the ranks to become a member of the powerful House Ways and Means Committee, where he became an expert in tax issues and government finance and pushed through reforms in the American tax structure. He was also a major architect of the Social Security system.

For his support of New Deal programs designed to combat the effects of the Great Depression, Vinson was rewarded by President Franklin D. Roosevelt in 1937 with an appointment to the U.S. District Court of Appeals for the District of Columbia. He took his seat on the bench in 1938. He later assumed additional responsibilities as chief judge of the Emergency Court of Appeals, which heard claims arising from the government's efforts to stabilize prices during World War II.

As a circuit court judge, Vinson adopted the judicial philosophy that would guide him later on the Supreme Court. Essentially conservative, he held strictly to precedent and did not believe that courts should make laws. He believed in a strong federal government, and he showed little sympathy for individuals who claimed that their civil liberties had been violated.

Vinson began serving in the executive branch of government in 1943, when he resigned from the court and became director of the Office of Economic Stabilization. There his chief task was controlling inflation during the war by fighting off requests from business for price increases and from organized labor for wage increases. Other posts in the executive branch soon followed. In March 1945 he became administrator of the Federal Loan Agency, but a month later he was appointed director of the Office of War Mobilization and Reconversion, overseeing the smooth conversion from a wartime to a peacetime economy.

When Harry S. Truman became president, he recognized Vinson's immense skills as a fiscal manager and in July 1945 appointed him secretary of the Treasury. In this post he played a major role in creating the International Bank for Reconstruction and Development and the International Monetary Fund.

Vinson, though, did not serve for long as Treasury secretary. In April 1946 Supreme Court Chief Justice Harlan Stone died. Truman hoped that by appointing the right person to replace him, he could reduce some of the bickering that had badly divided the Stone court, so in June he nominated Vinson rather than one of the associate justices as Stone's successor. Vinson was confirmed in the Senate two weeks later, and he took his

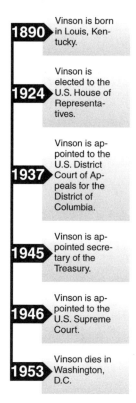

1890 Vinson is born in Louis, Kentucky.

1924 Vinson is elected to the U.S. House of Representatives.

1937 Vinson is appointed to the U.S. District Court of Appeals for the District of Columbia.

1945 Vinson is appointed secretary of the Treasury.

1946 Vinson is appointed to the U.S. Supreme Court.

1953 Vinson dies in Washington, D.C.

In cases having to do with civil liberties, particularly the First Amendment right of free speech, Vinson took a different tack.

seat on the bench on June 24. Vinson's success in reducing tension on the Court was at best modest (in his last term only 19 percent of the Court's opinions were unanimous, a record low). This, combined with his relatively brief tenure as Chief Justice, has led historians to give him somewhat low marks.

Prior to World War II, the Supreme Court was occupied primarily with economic and property rights cases. After the war, in contrast, the Court's most significant decisions were in the areas of civil rights and civil liberties. In these types of cases, Vinson's record was mixed. One the one hand, he wrote three unanimous opinions that undermined the "separate but equal" doctrine laid out in the 1896 landmark racial segregation case, *Plessy v. Ferguson*. The first of these was in *Shelley v. Kraemer*, a 1948 case in which the Court struck down restrictive racial covenants in housing—agreements that homeowners would not sell their homes to non-Caucasians. Vinson wrote that such covenants violated the equal protection clause of the Fourteenth Amendment of the Constitution.

In 1950, the Court attacked segregation directly in *McLaurin v. Oklahoma State Regents*, ruling that African Americans admitted to a state university had to be granted full access to its facilities. That same year, in *Sweatt v. Painter*, the Court held that a separate law school for blacks in Texas was not equal to the all-white University of Texas law school. This case would set the stage for *Brown v. Board of Education*, the 1954 landmark desegregation case in which the Court struck down the separate but equal doctrine.

In cases having to do with civil liberties, particularly the First Amendment right of free speech, Vinson took a different tack. His tenure as Chief Justice coincided with the Cold War, and Vinson supported the right of the federal government to legislate against groups that advocated the overthrow of the American system. In a 1950 case, *American Communications Association v. Douds*, he upheld the Taft-Hartley Act, which required union officials to sign affidavits saying that they had never been communists or members of any subversive organization. In the most significant of these kinds of cases, *Dennis v. United States* (1951), he upheld the 1940 Smith Act, under which 12 members of the Communist Party were convicted for conspiring to overthrow the American government. In his decision Vinson wrote: "No one could conceive that it is not within the power or Congress to prohibit acts intended to overthrow the government by force or violence."

Later, in 1953, Vinson called the Court back to Washington from its summer recess to overturn the stay of execution that Justice William Douglas had granted to Julius and Ethel Rosenberg, a married couple who had been convicted of spying for the Soviet Union.

As he was on the circuit court, Vinson was deferential to executive and legislative authority, upholding, for example, President Truman's emergency seizure of the coal mines following a nationwide strike in 1946. The most prominent case involving executive authority, though, was *Youngstown Sheet & Tube Co. v. Sawyer* (1952). During the Korean War, the United Steel Workers labor union had threatened to strike when the Wage Stabilization Board failed to work out a contract agreement with the steel companies. Truman ordered government seizure of the steel mills, claiming wartime executive power. A 6–3 Court majority ruled that the president had exceeded his constitutional authority. Vinson dissented, writing that the president, as commander-in-chief, could take any action that was not specifically prohibited by the Constitution. Truman thought highly of Vinson and mentioned his name as a possible successor to him in the White House.

Vinson died of a heart attack in his Washington apartment on September 8, 1953. Having devoted virtually his entire career to modestly paid public service, he left behind an estate worth less than $1,000. ◆

Waite, Morrison

NOVEMBER 27, 1816–MARCH 23, 1888 ● CHIEF JUSTICE

Morrison Remick Waite was born on November 27, 1816, in Lyme, Connecticut. His ancestors had settled in the state in the early 17th century, and several had fought in the Continental Army during the American Revolution. The family had also produced a number of judges and lawyers, including Waite's father, Henry Waite, who served as chief justice of the Connecticut Supreme Court. Henry Waite's wife was Marie Selden, and Morrison was their eldest son.

Morrison R. Waite

Waite attended nearby Bacon Academy before enrolling, as many of his forbears had, at Yale University, where he graduated in 1837. He then struck out for the western frontier and landed in Maumee City, Ohio, to study law with Samuel Young. Waite eventually became Young's partner. In 1840 he married Amelia Warner, and the couple had five children. In 1848 Waite moved his family to nearby Toledo, Ohio, where he established a successful corporate and business law practice with his younger brother.

Waite's appointment as Chief Justice of the U.S. Supreme Court came as a surprise to everyone—including Waite—in light of his

Waite got off to a rocky start on the high court.

relative lack of prominence in public affairs. He sat briefly on the Toledo City Council and served a single term (1849–1850) in the Ohio state legislature. Twice, in 1846 and 1862, he ran for Congress, but he was unsuccessful both times. He was active in Republican Party politics, and during the Civil War he made speeches and wrote petitions in support of the Union. In 1863 he was appointed to the Ohio Supreme Court, but he turned the appointment down.

Waite's only notable public service was in 1871, when President Ulysses S. Grant appointed him to a three-member delegation to the Geneva Arbitration in Europe. The goal of this body was to settle compensation claims between Great Britain and the United States arising out of the Civil War and to support the U.S. claim that Great Britain had violated neutrality by accepting Confederate ships in its ports. Waite and his colleagues won a $15.5 million award for the U.S. government.

Waite was serving as president of the Ohio Constitutional Convention in 1873 when word reached him that Grant had appointed him Chief Justice of the Supreme Court to fill the vacancy left by Salmon Chase. By no means, however, was Waite at the top of Grant's list. The president's first choice declined the offer after his involvement in a major financial scandal became known, another candidate was deemed too old, and two other nominees were rejected by the Senate. In desperation Grant, whose administration was marred by charges of corruption, turned to Waite, a fresh face in Washington, D.C., who did not carry the political baggage of many of Grant's cronies. Waite was confirmed unanimously in the Senate in January 1874.

Waite got off to a rocky start on the high court. He had never been a judge, nor had he ever argued a case before the Court. Because of his inexperience and complete lack of knowledge of Court procedures, many of his colleagues on the Court openly patronized him. But he went on to a relatively successful 14-year tenure as Chief Justice on the strength of his personality. In time his colleagues recognized his essential friendliness, good humor, and humility. Even Justice Samuel Miller, known for his critical nature, said that Waite had "a kindliness of heart rarely if ever excelled."

Waite was also a good manager and an extraordinarily hard worker. Under his leadership the Court decided nearly 3,500 cases, and Waite himself wrote 872 opinions. He was able to impose a measure of unanimity on the Court, and among his opinions, only a few were dissents from the majority.

Given this large number of cases, the Waite court ruled on nearly every issue imaginable. Two areas stand out for their significance in constitutional history. One concerned the Court's role in economic and business regulation; the other was Reconstruction of the South, in particular interpretation of the so-called Reconstruction amendments—the Thirteenth, Fourteenth, and Fifteenth.

After the Civil War the United States underwent a period of enormous business expansion marked by the development of large corporations and business trusts. During these years the Court grappled repeatedly with the question of who, if anyone, had the power to regulate these businesses. Some Supreme Court justices believed that businesses were private property and that, as such, the government should keep its hands off them. Others believed that the public interest demanded that businesses and corporations be regulated—though that raised the further question of whether this power lay in the hands of the federal government or in those of the individual states. Waite believed that government did have the power to regulate, and in a series of cases he decided that that power should be lodged with the states.

Among the most important of these were the so-called *Granger Cases*. These cases began with a series of laws passed primarily in the Midwest to protect the interests of farmers against big business, particularly the railroads (a common whipping boy for populist agitators) and related enterprises. The most important of the Granger cases was *Munn v. Illinois* (1876). Munn operated a grain elevator in Chicago. He was convicted for operating without a license and charging rates higher than those set by the state legislature under the 1871 Illinois Warehouse Act. Munn argued that by setting rates, the state was diminishing the value of his property, thus violating the due process clause of the Fourteenth Amendment. Writing for the Court, Waite rejected this view, arguing that the state had the power to regulate private property and commerce when that commerce was "affected with a public interest."

Similarly, in *Railroad Company v. Richmond* (1878) Waite ruled that regulation "is not 'taking' property within the meaning of the constitutional prohibition." Waite, though, did not believe that the state's power to regulate was absolute and maintained that corporations themselves were protected by due process. In later years a more business-friendly Supreme Court used this principle to invalidate some of the regulation that the

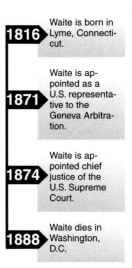

1816 Waite is born in Lyme, Connecticut.

1871 Waite is appointed as a U.S. representative to the Geneva Arbitration.

1874 Waite is appointed chief justice of the U.S. Supreme Court.

1888 Waite dies in Washington, D.C.

Waite continued to carry a crushing workload to the end of his life.

Waite court upheld. Nonetheless, in *Munn*, Waite almost single-handedly altered the course of business regulation in the United States.

A second major issue the Waite court had to grapple with was Reconstruction and the application of the Reconstruction amendments as they affected freed slaves. The Thirteenth Amendment granted political, social, and legal rights to three million African Americans in the South. The Fourteenth Amendment tried to give teeth to the Thirteenth by forbidding the states to deprive citizens of life or liberty without "due process of law" and requiring the states to grant all citizens "equal protection of the laws" and the "privileges and immunities" of citizenship. The Fifteenth Amendment dealt with the narrower issue of voting rights and protected the right to vote regardless of "race, color, or previous condition of servitude." These amendments, though, failed to stamp out harassment of African Americans who attempted to vote or take part in politics, so Congress passed the Enforcement Acts of 1870–1871, marking as crimes certain specified behavior toward potential voters.

Against this backdrop, Waite ruled in two important cases. One was *United States v. Cruikshank* (1876), in which the Court overturned the conviction in Louisiana of three men accused of using violence and fraud to deny African Americans the right to vote. Waite's reasoning was that fraud and violence were not federal offenses, and that the indictment did not charge the men with racial discrimination. The other case was *United States v. Reese* (1876), in which the Court declared portions of the Enforcement Acts unconstitutional because they did not require proof that the reason for denying voting rights was race.

While these decisions were setbacks for civil rights, it should be emphasized that Waite was not hostile to African Americans. He believed that racial divisions in the post-Civil War South would recede as blacks gained further education, and to this end he was an active supporter of **philanthropic** organizations that funded colleges for blacks in the South and lobbied Congress to provide additional funds. Further, in other cases involving civil rights he showed a more progressive attitude. In *Strauder v. West Virginia* (1879), for example, he struck down all-white juries, and in the same year in *Neal v. Delaware* he ruled that state judges could not exclude African Americans from juries.

Waite continued to carry a crushing workload to the end of his life. He was also nearly bankrupt. Exhausted and ill, he in-

philanthropic: charitable.

sisted on appearing in court on March 20, 1888, to read an opinion he had drafted in a complicated and hotly disputed patent claim. He was unable to do so and died on March 23. ◆

Warren, Earl

MARCH 19, 1891–JULY 9, 1974 ● CHIEF JUSTICE

It is customary to refer to the U.S. Supreme Court by the name of its Chief Justice: the Taney court, the Chase court, the Taft court, and so on. The implication is that the Chief Justice, whether through superior legal craftsmanship or force of personality, is able to impose a judicial philosophy on the Court and shape the direction it takes. Two Chief Justices' names have been particularly enshrined in this way: Under John Marshall, "the Marshall court" took bold and decisive steps to increase the authority of the nation's young federal government. Under Earl Warren, "the Warren court" was an activist, liberal court that strove to overturn racial segregation and defend the personal liberties of the people.

Earl Warren

Earl Warren was born in Los Angeles, California, on March 19, 1891, to Scandinavian immigrants Methias Warren and Chrystal Hernlund. Methias worked as a railroad repairman and moved the family to Bakersfield, California, so that he could work at the Southern Pacific rail yards there. The family had so little money that the elder Warren joked that he was too poor to give his son a middle name. Working as a "call boy" for the railroad as a youngster, Warren came to despise corporations that laid men off without notice, refused to compensate injured employees, and exploited minorities.

"One look at you and he said, 'I quit.'"
Warren's friends, teasing him about Justice Oliver Wendell Holmes, Jr.'s resignation from the U.S. Supreme Court

When Warren graduated from the University of California at Berkeley in 1912, he was one of the first students from his high school to receive a college degree. He remained at Berkeley to attend law school and was awarded his degree in 1914. He worked briefly for a law firm and for an oil company until the United States entered World War I, then he enlisted in the Army. He had hoped to see action overseas, but instead he remained stateside at various training camps.

After the war Warren began a long and distinguished career in public service. In 1918 he took a position as a legal and municipal aide. In 1920 he became deputy district attorney for Alameda County. Then in 1925 he became district attorney, a position he held until 1938. In a 1931 survey he was named "the best district attorney in the United States." In the meantime he had married Nina Palmquist Meyers in 1925. The couple had six children, and some historians believe that Warren's extraordinarily attractive family helped boost his political career.

In a historical footnote, Justice Oliver Wendell Holmes, Jr., resigned from the U.S. Supreme Court the day after Warren first argued before it.

After 13 years as a district attorney, Warren turned to statewide politics. In 1938 he was elected attorney general of California—after having been nominated by both the Democratic Party and his own Republican Party. In 1942 he was elected to the first of three terms as governor of the state, and his success in hospital modernization, prison reform, highway development, and other initiatives led his successor, Edmund Brown, to call Warren the best governor the state ever had.

The next logical step for Warren was national politics. In 1948 he was the Republican candidate for vice president on the ticket with Thomas Dewey, and in 1952 he made a strong bid for the Republican presidential nomination. He later gave his support to Dwight D. Eisenhower, who then promised him an appointment to the Supreme Court.

Warren did not have to wait long. In September 1953 Chief Justice Fred Vinson died, and Warren took his seat as Chief Justice at the beginning of the 1953 term. He was officially confirmed by the Senate in March 1954.

During his 16 years as Chief Justice, no one ever accused Warren of being an expert legal technician. Rather, he was a leader who, in weekly conferences with his colleagues, was able to frame issues in a way that went right to the heart of fundamental principles of justice and fairness. During oral arguments

Roth v. United States (1991)

A New York bookseller, Roth was arrested for shipping "obscene circulars and an obscene book" out of state, in violation of federal anti–obscenity laws. When his appeal was taken up by the Supreme Court, it was combined with a similar case, *Alberts v. California*. At issue in both cases was whether or not obscenity was protected by the First Amendment guarantee of freedom of speech.

    The Supreme Court voted 6–3 to uphold the *Alberts* decision, but 7–2 against Roth. In both cases, the Supreme Court determined that obscenity was not protected if it was "utterly without redeeming social importance" according to the contemporary community standards as understood by the average person, and if the dominant theme was an appeal to "prurient interest." The Court went on to define prurient interest as "having a tendency to incite lustful thoughts."

    The opinion of the Court, delivered by Justice William Brennan, reasoned that the Constitution's protection of free speech was intended to assure the free expression of political and social ideas, and was never intended to cover obscenity. Justice John Harlan, who voted with the majority in *Alberts*, dissented on *Roth* because the first case involved state law (the materials in question were not shipped across state lines), while the second had to do with federal law. Harlan argued that the states had greater freedom in regulating obscenity, since it was easier to ascertain what "community standards" would allow, but that federal law had greater problems in doing so, and he feared the imposition of bland conformity on the exchange of ideas. Justice Brennan would later come to reverse his opinion on this issue, in the 1973 case of *Miller v. California*.

he frequently interrupted attorneys with the question, "But was it fair?" In his written opinions he avoided legal jargon and technicalities in favor of a simple, direct style that examined the human issues surrounding a case in a way that non-lawyers could understand. Put simply, he wrote ethical opinions, not legal opinions, and to Warren's supporters, it was this moral vision that formed the essence of "the Warren Court." To his detractors, though—and there were legions of them who called vocally for his impeachment—he legislated from the bench and was an enemy of law and order.

Earlier Courts had focused on constitutional questions having to do with the regulation of business and commerce or the apportionment of power between the states and the federal government—important issues, but ones that today may seem a little dry. The Warren court, however, sat during a period of unprecedented social turmoil, and it was the Court's decisions on dramatic social issues for which it remains best known.

Warren had an almost immediate opportunity to place his stamp on the Court in 1954 in the landmark *Brown v. Board of*

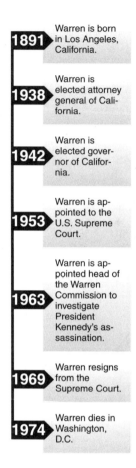

1891 Warren is born in Los Angeles, California.

1938 Warren is elected attorney general of California.

1942 Warren is elected governor of California.

1953 Warren is appointed to the U.S. Supreme Court.

1963 Warren is appointed head of the Warren Commission to investigate President Kennedy's assassination.

1969 Warren resigns from the Supreme Court.

1974 Warren dies in Washington, D.C.

Education decision. The case involved Linda Brown, a nine-year-old whose father filed suit claiming that racially segregated schools in Topeka, Kansas, were inherently discriminatory. The case—which actually consolidated a number of cases in South Carolina, Virginia, Delaware, and Kansas—was first heard in 1952 under Warren's predecessor, Fred Vinson, but the justices were divided and some seemed reluctant to overturn laws and precedents that allowed "separate but equal" schooling. After hearing oral arguments again in late 1953 (arguments presented by future Supreme Court justice Thurgood Marshall), Warren argued in conference that those laws and precedents could be upheld only if one believed that blacks were inferior. His viewpoint prevailed, and in a show of unity the Court ruled unanimously that school segregation was impermissible.

The *Brown* case began an era of important civil rights gains, in particular stamping out state-sanctioned segregation in the South. A decade later, in *Johnson v. Virginia*, the Court was able to write, "It is no longer open to question that a State may not constitutionally require segregation of public facilities."

While *Brown* was the Warren court's most important ruling, it was by no means the only one that had far-reaching consequences. In the landmark 1961 case *Mapp v. Ohio*, the Court ruled that illegally obtained evidence could not be used at trial. In *Gideon v. Wainwright* (1963), the Court ruled that indigent defendants were entitled to court-appointed counsel. In 1965 the Court established a right of privacy in *Griswold v. Connecticut* when it overturned a state ban on birth-control devices and pills. In *Tinker v. Des Moines School District* (1969) the Court upheld the right of high school students to engage in peaceful, non-disruptive protest against the war in Vietnam, giving students the right to free speech.

Anyone who watches police dramas on television sees the effects of *Miranda v. Arizona*, a 1966 case in which the Court ruled that criminal suspects must be informed of their rights ("You have the right to remain silent. . . .") And in at least three opinions the Warren court overturned the convictions of communists and radicals, arguing that their rights to freedom of speech had been violated.

In light of his civil rights and civil liberties record, it is ironic that as a district attorney Warren had vigorously prosecuted "radicals" and had used anticommunist tactics and possibly illegally obtained evidence to prosecute union members charged with murder. It is a further irony that as attorney general of California he supported the internment of Japanese Americans on the West Coast—though he later profoundly regretted that decision.

Warren's name is also linked in the public mind with the assassination of President John F. Kennedy. In the days that followed the tragedy, rumors spread that the assassination was the end result of a massive conspiracy. President Lyndon Johnson wanted to quell such rumors, so he appointed a commission to investigate the assassination, with Warren as its head. In its final report, the Warren Commission concluded that Lee Harvey Oswald had acted alone. But because of problems with the investigation—in particular lack of time and lack of cooperation on the part of the FBI and the CIA, many Americans refused to accept the commission's conclusion and continued to believe that a conspiracy lay behind the president's death.

Warren resigned from the Supreme Court in June 1969 after President Richard Nixon named his successor, Warren E. Burger. Nixon was opposed to the liberalism of the Warren court and believed that Burger would reverse many of its rulings. He was disappointed, for in many respects the Burger court extended the legacy of the Warren court, particularly in the area of privacy rights.

In 1974 Warren suffered a series of heart attacks and died in Washington, D.C., on July 9. ◆

In its final report, the Warren Commission concluded that Lee Harvey Oswald had acted alone.

Washington, Bushrod

JUNE 5, 1762–NOVEMBER 26, 1829 ● ASSOCIATE JUSTICE

Bushrod Washington was born to a prominent family in Westmoreland County, Virginia, on June 5, 1762. His father, John Augustine Washington, was a planter. His mother had been Hannah Bushrod, the daughter of a well-to-do Virginia family. Present at Bushrod's birth was his father's favorite brother, George Washington, who would play a major role in Bushrod's career.

Washington was educated in the classics, then sent to the College of William and Mary, where he graduated in 1778 at age 16. Two years later he returned to the college to attend the law lectures of George Wythe, the nation's first law professor. There he met future Chief Justice John Marshall, and the two became lifelong friends.

Bushrod Washington

In the late stages of the Revolutionary War, Washington was a member of the Continental Army and was present at Yorktown when the British surrendered. With the financial backing of his uncle, he resumed his legal studies in 1782 at the Philadelphia office of James Wilson, a prominent attorney, a signer of the Declaration of Independence, and, later, an associate justice of the Supreme Court.

At age 21 Washington launched a private law practice. One of his first clients was his famous uncle, and he handled George and Martha Washington's legal affairs for the rest of their lives. Initially he set up shop in Westmoreland County, but he later moved to Alexandria, Virginia, and then to Richmond. In 1785 he met and married Julia Ann Blackburn, the daughter of General Washington's aide-de-camp. At the urging of his uncle, he ran successfully for a seat in the Virginia General Assembly in 1787, and in 1788 he was a member of the convention called to consider ratification of the U.S. Constitution. He served in both of these bodies with his old friend, John Marshall.

Back in his Richmond law practice Washington was involved in nearly a quarter of the cases argued before the Virginia Court of Appeals, where his opponent was often Marshall. The publication of his meticulous notes on these cases was important, for at that time the Virginia Court of Appeals was the most influential court in the nation.

Washington rose to the Supreme Court after the death of his old law mentor, Justice James Wilson, in 1798. President John Adams was determined to appoint a Virginian to the Court, and the two leading candidates were Washington and Marshall. Adams offered the post to Marshall, but Marshall was running for Congress. Washington was, too, but by this time he greatly preferred the law to politics, so he gladly accepted the appointment when Marshall turned it down. He joined the Court while Congress was in recess and was easily confirmed later by the Senate in December 1798.

In addition to serving on the high court, Washington rode circuit in Trenton and Newark, New Jersey, and in Philadelphia, where he may have heard his most noteworthy case, *United States v. Bright* (1809). The case involved a direct conflict between the federal government and the state government of Pennsylvania. The dispute, which dated back to the Revolutionary War, was over a ship Pennsylvania had seized as a war prize. The federal government, though, laid claim to the ship. When the Supreme Court ruled against Pennsylvania, General Michael Bright assembled armed troops to prevent officials from delivering the Court's writ. For his efforts he was brought to trial and convicted for resisting the process of a court of the United States. Washington's words at sentencing still apply: "A state has no constitutional power . . . to employ force to resist the execution of a decree of a federal court."

Like many Supreme Court justices in its early years, Washington is not well known, because the Court was dominated by John Marshall, who was appointed Chief Justice in 1801. After Joseph Story joined the Court in 1811, these two, backed by Washington, were the dominant voices for the next 18 years, forging decisions that granted broad powers to the federal government. Deferring to Marshall, who wrote most of the Court's majority opinions, Washington wrote only 70 opinions in 31 years on the bench—and just a single dissent. Nonetheless, he was influential on the Court, and his relative paucity of written opinions disguises the depth of his legal insight.

Washington played a role in at least three major cases that had a bearing on the powers of the states versus those of the federal government. One was *Dartmouth College v. Woodward*, an 1819 case in which the Court brought all corporations under the contracts clause of the Constitution. Although he joined the majority, Washington wrote a concurrence that tried to rein in the effects of the Court's sweeping ruling. A second was *Ogden v. Saunders* (1827), a landmark case having to do with bankruptcy laws but more generally having a significant bearing on how the Constitution applied to business in the states. With Marshall dissenting, Washington wrote part of the majority opinion deferring to New York State's bankruptcy laws. The third was *Green v. Biddle* (1823), in which the Court ruled unconstitutional a Kentucky law passed to settle conflicting land claims. Writing for the majority, Washington maintained that the state had violated an agreement between Kentucky and Virginia made when Kentucky became a state.

"I have heard a favourable acct. of Bushrod, and doubt not but his prudence will direct him to a proper line of Conduct. I have given him my sentiments on his head, and persuade myself that . . . he will stand as good a chance as most youth of his age to avoid the Vices of large Cities. . . ."
George Washington, in a 1783 letter to Bushrod's father

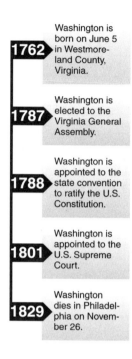

1762 ▶ Washington is born on June 5 in Westmoreland County, Virginia.

1787 ▶ Washington is elected to the Virginia General Assembly.

1788 ▶ Washington is appointed to the state convention to ratify the U.S. Constitution.

1801 ▶ Washington is appointed to the U.S. Supreme Court.

1829 ▶ Washington dies in Philadelphia on November 26.

Rulings such as these show that Washington tried to defer to the states when he could, but like Marshall and Story he did not hesitate to invoke the Supreme Court's growing power to review—and strike down if necessary—the acts of state legislatures and courts.

In 1802 Martha Washington died and Bushrod, his uncle's favorite nephew, inherited the estate, Mount Vernon. By this time the home was in some disrepair, but Washington and his wife moved in and restored it. Under the terms of George Washington's will, he freed the slaves working on the estate, but in an attempt to bring it back to profitability, Bushrod Washington brought in more slaves, outraging abolitionists. Washington, though, believed that slavery would gradually be eliminated, and to that end he was lifelong president of the American Colonization Society, which supported the emancipation of slaves and their return to Africa.

While he was on circuit court business in Philadelphia, Washington died on November 26, 1829. His wife was so heartbroken that she died three days later while bringing his body back to Mount Vernon for burial. ◆

Wayne, James

1790–JULY 5, 1867 ● ASSOCIATE JUSTICE

James Moore Wayne, who served on the Supreme Court for over three decades, was born in 1790 (the exact date is uncertain) in Savannah, Georgia. His father had emigrated to the United States from England in 1759 and settled in Charleston, South Carolina, where he married Elizabeth Clifford. After the Revolutionary War he moved to Savannah. Soon he was socially prominent, and his various business ventures prospered—with the aid of nearly 100 slaves.

As a child, Wayne was tutored at home until he enrolled at the College of New Jersey (now Princeton) in 1804. He was not a particularly good student and was even expelled for a time for taking part in a student rebellion. But he graduated in 1808 and returned to Savannah, where he read law under a local attorney. Later, in New Haven, Connecticut, he read law under the distinguished judge Charles Chauncy.

After his father died in 1810, Wayne returned to Savannah and completed his legal education in the office of his brother-in-law. He was admitted to the bar in 1811 and entered private practice.

The 1810s and 1820s were a busy time for Wayne. When the War of 1812 broke out, he enlisted in a cavalry company, eventually becoming its captain. In 1813 he married Mary Johnson Campbell; one of their three children, Henry C. Wayne, was later a general in the Confederate army and commanded the troops that offered the last resistance to General William Sherman in his decisive march to the sea near the end of the Civil War. There followed a series of elective posts: in 1815, to the Georgia legislature; in 1817, mayor of Savannah; in 1819, to the city's court of common pleas; in 1822, judge of the eastern circuit of the state superior court. Then in 1828 he left the bench to run successfully for Congress, where he served four two-year terms.

James Wayne

As a member of Congress, Wayne was a staunch supporter of President Andrew Jackson. He backed Jackson, for example, when the president refused to create a separate Cherokee Indian nation within Georgia, and, like Jackson, he was opposed to a centralized national bank. Further, he was the only Georgian in Congress to support Jackson during an 1828 dispute with South Carolina. The state blamed Jackson for its economic depression, citing the president's high tariffs, the so-called "tariff of abomination," on imported goods. Resistance to the tariffs was so intense that the state not only refused to collect them but also threatened to secede from the Union. When a bill gave Jackson authority to intervene with federal troops, Wayne worked tirelessly to negotiate a compromise and to allay South Carolina's growing dissatisfaction with the federal government.

Wayne rose to the Supreme Court after Justice William Johnson died in 1834. Jackson wanted to appoint another

Wayne was a proponent of slavery, yet he took positions that seemed inconsistent with a pro-slavery stance.

Southerner, so he turned to Wayne in early 1835. Wayne's tenure on the Court, while 32 years long, was relatively undistinguished. He wrote only 180 opinions, and most involved cases that were not particularly important. Moreover, his opinions were often regarded as long-winded and sometimes even incoherent.

Nonetheless, Wayne was an important force in upholding and extending the power of the federal government—an unusual position for a Southerner to take in the years prior to the Civil War, when "states' rights" was almost a battle cry in the South. Thus, in the *Passenger Cases* of 1849, he opposed state power to regulate immigration by taxing immigrants, arguing that it invaded the power of Congress under the commerce clause of the Constitution. In a dissent in an 1852 case, *Cooley v. Board of Wardens of the Port of Philadelphia*, he argued that the federal government had exclusive jurisdiction over international commerce. And in *Louisville Railroad Company v. Letson* (1844) he expanded the jurisdiction of the federal courts in cases involving corporations.

During the Civil War, Wayne continued to be a strong supporter of the national government. Rather than withdrawing to Georgia, he remained in Washington, D.C., to give the Court "a judicial voice in behalf of the South and her Constitutional rights." His loyalty to the federal government, though, came at considerable personal cost, for a Georgia court declared him an "enemy alien," and the state confiscated his property in Savannah. He supported President Abraham Lincoln's blockade of Southern ports in the 1863 *Prize Cases*, and in *Ex parte Vallandigham* (1864), he wrote the majority opinion refusing to interfere with a military tribunal that had arrested a civilian for supporting the rebellion.

Wayne was a proponent of slavery, yet he took positions that seemed inconsistent with a pro-slavery stance. In an 1835 case, for example, he ruled that the right of a slave freed under the terms of its owner's will took precedence over the claim of a creditor to the slave owner's estate. He supported the enforcement of laws banning the slave trade, and in *Prigg v. Pennsylvania* (1842) he joined with Justice Joseph Story in arguing that the slave trade was a national issue, not a states' rights issue. His goal in these rulings, however, was not to oppose slavery but to bring it under federal control. His motivation was similar in the notorious 1857 case *Dred Scott v. Sandford*, in which he supported Chief Justice Roger Taney's argument that free blacks were not citizens of the United States and were therefore not entitled to sue in federal court. Wayne hoped that the decision, which also found unconstitutional the 1820 Missouri Compromise giving Congress authority to ban slavery in new U.S. territories, would settle the slavery question once and for all. His hope was wishful thinking.

Following the Civil War, Wayne refused to back punitive federal Reconstruction efforts. For example, he joined the Court majority in striking down loyalty oaths in the South. He obtained a pardon for the judge who had declared him an enemy alien. He also refused to ride his circuit in states that were under military rule.

In the summer of 1867 Wayne contracted typhoid fever and died on July 5 in Washington, D.C. ◆

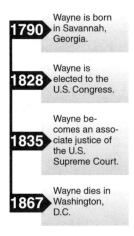

1790 Wayne is born in Savannah, Georgia.

1828 Wayne is elected to the U.S. Congress.

1835 Wayne becomes an associate justice of the U.S. Supreme Court.

1867 Wayne dies in Washington, D.C.

White, Byron

JUNE 8, 1917– ● ASSOCIATE JUSTICE

Byron Raymond White was born in Fort Collins, Colorado, on June 8, 1917, although he grew up in the northern Colorado farming community of Wellington. His father, A. Albert White, managed a lumber supply company outlet, and during the summers and after school Byron labored in the area's sugar beet fields and for the Colorado and Southern Railroad.

Neither of White's parents attended high school, but they valued education, and their offspring had outstanding academic records. White often said that one of the greatest influences on his life was his brother, Clayton "Sam" White, who graduated first in his high school class. At that time Colorado automatically awarded scholarships to high school valedictorians, so Sam went on to the University of Colorado, where he starred in football, won a prestigious Rhodes scholarship to study at Oxford University in England, and studied medicine.

Byron followed closely in his footsteps. He, too, graduated first in his high school class and attended the University of Colorado. Nicknamed "Whizzer," he was a sports standout, winning letters in football, basketball, and baseball, and he was a football All-American on the university's 1937 Cotton Bowl team. Graduating Phi Beta Kappa and first in his class in 1938, he,

Byron R. White

too, won a Rhodes scholarship, although he delayed his entry at Oxford to play for the Pittsburgh Pirates (now the Steelers) as the highest paid professional football player at the time. As rookie of the year he led the league in rushing, and in 1954 he was named to the National Football League Hall of Fame.

In early 1939 White finally made it to Oxford, where he met John F. Kennedy, whose father was the American ambassador to Great Britain. White remained in England for only nine months, though, because American students were sent home at the outbreak of World War II. Back home he enrolled at the Yale University law school, though for financial reasons he continued to play professional football for the Detroit Lions on the weekends during the 1940 and 1941 seasons. After the United States entered the war, he won two Bronze Stars as a Navy intelligence officer in the Pacific. He also renewed his acquaintance with John Kennedy and in fact prepared the report on the sinking of Kennedy's ship, the PT-109.

After the war White married his college sweetheart, Marion Stearns, and returned to Yale, graduating near the top of his class in 1946. He clerked for a year for U.S. Supreme Court Justice Fred Vinson, then returned to Colorado to practice law for 14 years with a Denver law firm. During these years he enjoyed the solitude of the West, often fly-fishing in western Montana and skiing the Colorado mountains.

White also began to achieve prominence in statewide Democratic politics. An ardent supporter of his old acquaintance, John Kennedy, during the 1960 presidential race he organized the Colorado Committee for Kennedy. After Kennedy was nominated, White headed up the National Citizens for Kennedy Committee. For his support, the new president named him deputy attorney general under Robert Kennedy.

At the Justice Department White received high marks for his role in the civil rights struggles of the early 1960s, particularly during the 1961 "freedom rides" in Alabama when he supervised the deputies and marshals dispatched to Montgomery after violence erupted. But he was also criticized for failing to block the nominations of numerous federal court judges who proved to be obstacles to civil rights progress. In retrospect, this criticism is unfair in light of the fact that White had to investigate the professional qualifications of candidates for over 1,000 such appointments.

White rose to the high court in 1962 after the resignation of Justice Charles Whittaker. White was not at the top of Kennedy's list, but the president was hesitant to appoint yet another Ivy Leaguer to his administration, and he wanted to keep another leading candidate, Arthur Goldberg, in his administration as secretary of labor. At the suggestion of Nicholas Katzenbach at the Justice Department, he turned to White, despite White's lack of judicial experience and the fact that he had never held elective office. White was confirmed in April 1962 and five days later began his 31-year tenure as an associate justice.

White joined the Court during a time of great turbulence. In 1962 the Court was sharply divided between a liberal, activist bloc led by Chief Justice Earl Warren and a more conservative bloc, which advocated judicial restraint, led by Whittaker and Felix Frankfurter. But that fall Frankfurter retired and was replaced by Arthur Goldberg, giving the Warren court a solid liberal majority.

White tended to be more conservative, though Court historians have often been perplexed by his voting record and have recognized that he took a pragmatic rather than an ideological position on most issues. Nonetheless, in the early years, White and Goldberg often found themselves on opposite sides of issues, and White often dissented from the opinion of the majority Court.

One of the first opinions that signaled White's jurisprudence was a dissent he wrote in *Robinson v. California* (1962). The Court majority struck down a state law that made narcotics addiction a crime, saying that the law inflicted "cruel and unusual punishment" in violation of the Eighth Amendment. In his dissent, White advocated judicial restraint in interfering with state laws. He wrote: "I deem this application of 'cruel and unusual punishment' so novel that I suspect the Court was hard

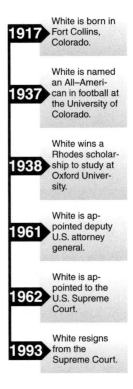

1917 White is born in Fort Collins, Colorado.

1937 White is named an All–American in football at the University of Colorado.

1938 White wins a Rhodes scholarship to study at Oxford University.

1961 White is appointed deputy U.S. attorney general.

1962 White is appointed to the U.S. Supreme Court.

1993 White resigns from the Supreme Court.

South Dakota v. Dole (1987)

In the late 1980s, Congress enacted legislation intended to reduce highway deaths due to drunk drivers by establishing a uniform drinking age. The new law directed the Secretary of Transportation to withhold a percentage of federal highway funds from any state that permitted "the purchase or public possession of any alcoholic beverage by a person who is less than 21 years of age." The state of South Dakota had a legal drinking age of 19, but did not want to give up its full share of federal funds for highway repair and construction, so it petitioned the Supreme Court to challenge the law.

Roger A. Tellinghuisen, who represented South Dakota, argued that the law, by withholding funds from a state that refused to go along with the federally established drinking age, was essentially interfering with the states' right to run its own affairs, and that it violated the Twenty–first Amendment to the Constitution, which repealed Prohibition. When the case reached the Supreme Court, the justices voted 7–2 to uphold the Congressional legislation (Justices White, Marshall, Blackmun, Powell, Stevens, and Scalia, along with Chief Justice Rehnquist voted in the majority; Justices O'Connor and Brennan dissented). The Court, found that the new law did not violate the Twenty–first Amendment, for it did not seek to ban the sale of alcohol in general, merely to encourage limits to its consumption. This, the Court held, advanced the general welfare of the nation. The Court also found that the legislation did not violate the principle of states' rights, because it did not force any state to adopt a federally mandated drinking age; rather, it simply provided a financial incentive to do so.

put to find a way to ascribe to the Framers of the Constitution the result reached today rather than to its own notions of ordered liberty."

Similarly, White took a conservative position in matters of criminal procedure, particularly in the landmark 1966 case *Miranda v. Arizona*. Ernesto Miranda was convicted of kidnapping and rape after confessing while in police custody. In overturning the conviction, the Court held that Miranda's right against self-incrimination had been violated, and in the process the Court laid down new rules for advising criminal suspects of their rights at the time of arrest (the familiar words known to anyone who watches television police dramas, "You have the right to remain silent. . . ."). Writing that the effect of the ruling on criminal law would be "corrosive," White sharply dissented. "I have no desire whatsoever to share the responsibility for any such impact on the present criminal process," he declared. " . . . In some unknown number of cases, the Court's rule will return a killer, a rapist or other criminal to the streets and to the environment which produced him, to repeat his crime whenever it pleases him." The result, White wrote, was "not a gain, but a loss, in human dignity."

Despite his conservatism and law-and-order stance, White issued rulings that expanded civil rights and liberties in at least two noteworthy cases. Writing for the majority in *Reitman v. Mulkey* (1967), he struck down a California ballot proposition that in effect allowed property owners to discriminate when selling or renting property. The decision was far-reaching, for it applied the equal protection clause of the Fourteenth Amendment to the states, even in cases when discrimination was private rather than state action. The other decision, *Camara v. Municipal Court* (1967), had to do with property inspections by municipal housing authorities. In ruling that even municipal inspectors (as well as the police) needed search warrants to inspect property, White greatly strengthened the Fourth Amendment's protection against "unreasonable searches and seizures."

In 1969 Chief Justice Earl Warren was replaced by Chief Justice Warren Burger. Possibly the most difficult and contentious case the Burger court decided was *Roe v. Wade*, the 1973 abortion rights case. The groundwork for *Roe v. Wade* had been forged in a 1965 case, *Griswold v. Connecticut*, in which the Court established a broad right to privacy in striking down a state law against the use of contraceptives and even against giving medical advice on their use. When *Roe v. Wade* (and a companion case, *Doe v. Bolton*) came before the Court, the justices wrestled with the issue of privacy rights in a protracted series of oral arguments, memoranda, conferences, and drafts of opinions. When the Court finally struck down laws in Texas and Georgia banning abortions, White issued a withering dissent, arguing that the "right" to privacy was not enumerated in the Constitution and that the Court had been guilty of wielding "raw judicial power."

Through his years on the Supreme Court White was known for his brusque manner and aggressive questioning of counsel in oral arguments. He also found it difficult to shed the image of being the "jock justice" on the Court, not only because of his athletic accomplishments but also because of his intense competitiveness.

Byron White retired from the Court at the end of the 1993 term. ◆

Despite his conservatism and law-and-order stance, White issued rulings that expanded civil rights and liberties in at least two noteworthy cases.

White, Edward Douglass

NOVEMBER 3, 1845–MAY 19, 1921 ● CHIEF JUSTICE

dward Douglass White, the first associate justice of the Supreme Court to be elevated to Chief Justice, was born in Lafourche Parish, Louisiana, on November 3, 1845, to a prominent Irish Catholic family. His great-grandfather had been a prosperous businessman in Philadelphia. His grandfather had been a doctor and a territorial representative to Congress before settling in Louisiana, where he was later appointed as a U.S. district judge. His father, for whom White was named, had been a leading figure in Louisiana politics: city judge, five-term member of Congress, and governor of the state. The elder White died shortly after Edward junior was born, but the income from his large sugar-beet plantation gave White's mother, Catherine Ringgold, and their five children financial security.

White received a Catholic education, and Catholicism remained important to him throughout his life. As a child he attended a convent school in New Orleans, but at age 11 he was sent to a Jesuit boarding school in Maryland. In 1858 he enrolled at Georgetown College (now University), but he returned home without a degree in 1861 at the outbreak of the Civil War.

During the war he enlisted in the Confederate Army and in 1863 was one of a large number of troops captured during the Union siege of Port Hudson, Louisiana. He was shortly released and spent the remainder of the war on the family plantation. After the war he continued his law studies and was admitted to the bar in 1868.

Like his father before him, White became a prominent figure—both figuratively and literally, for he weighed over 250 pounds—in state politics. In 1874 he was elected to the Louisiana Senate. Five years later, at age 34, he was appointed to

Edward Douglass White

the state supreme court, but he resigned his position as a result of a political dispute that led to a state constitutional provision setting a minimum age for supreme court judges. He spent much of the next decade practicing law and enjoying life as a wealthy, cultured resident of the elegant French Quarter of New Orleans.

White entered the political fray again in 1888 by managing the campaign of Francis Nicholls for governor, and as governor Nicholls rewarded him in 1891 with an appointment to fill a vacancy in the U.S. Senate. Though he served only three years in the Senate, White was popular and influential among his colleagues. He was a staunch defender of the rights of the states against intrusions by the federal government, and while he generally supported President Grover Cleveland, he vigorously opposed Cleveland's efforts to lower tariffs on imported sugar. This measure would have hurt the interests of White's constituents on the sugar-beet plantations by lowering the price of imported sugar.

While the Senate was debating the issue in February 1894, the president summoned the senator to the White House. White girded himself for a debate over the tariff bill—and was astonished to learn that Cleveland was nominating him for a seat on the Supreme Court to replace the recently deceased Samuel Blatchford. Some historians suggest that because White was a major roadblock to his tariff bill, Cleveland appointed him to the Court to get him out of the way. If true, the plan did not work very well. Although he was unanimously confirmed the next day, White remained in the Senate for three weeks, working to defeat the president's bill and actually raising protective tariffs on many imported goods, including sugar. White won another victory that year when he finally persuaded Leita Montgomery Kent, who had rebuffed him 20 years earlier, to marry him.

White served as an associate justice on the high court for nearly 17 years. Then, in 1910, Chief Justice Melville Fuller died. President William Howard Taft's first choice to fill the center seat was Charles Evans Hughes, who had joined the Court just months earlier. But Taft himself had always wanted to be Chief Justice—more so than president—and he looked ahead to his judicial career after leaving the White House. Hughes was only 48 years old, while White was 65. Many historians speculate that Taft appointed the older White knowing that his tenure as Chief Justice would likely be much shorter that Hughes's would have been.

> *"I think a jowl also helps a Justice of the Supreme Court, and White had an impressive jowl."*
> Felix Frankfurter, quoted in *Felix Frankfurter on the Supreme Court*, ed. Philip B. Kurland, 1970

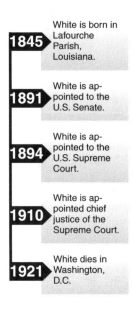

1845 White is born in Lafourche Parish, Louisiana.

1891 White is appointed to the U.S. Senate.

1894 White is appointed to the U.S. Supreme Court.

1910 White is appointed chief justice of the Supreme Court.

1921 White dies in Washington, D.C.

Thus, on December 12, 1910, Taft gave the appointment to White, who was confirmed in the Senate the same day. The plan worked, for Taft succeeded White as Chief Justice in 1921, and Hughes got his chance later when he succeeded Taft. White thus became the first associate justice to be confirmed as Chief Justice. (George Washington tried to elevate John Rutledge in 1795, but the Senate refused to confirm him.)

During his 27 years on the high court, White was conservative. He defended the interests of big business while opposing organized labor, free speech, progressive reform legislation, racial desegregation, and intrusions of the federal government in the affairs of the states. A case in point is his attitude toward antitrust legislation, specifically the Sherman Antitrust Act of 1890. The act had been an important piece of progressive reform legislation. It was a direct assault on the power of the massive corporations that had formed in the aftermath of the Civil War. White, however, refused to interpret the act literally. Rather, he advocated what he called the "rule of reason," arguing that the act prohibited only those monopolies that "unreasonably" restrained competition. In a series of antitrust cases in the 1890s and the early 20th century, he voted against efforts to break up monopolies. As Chief Justice he did write the majority opinion in *Standard Oil Company v. United States* (1911), a decision that broke up the Standard Oil monopoly. He made it clear in his opinion, however, that in the future the Court would apply the rule of reason and that the Sherman act was applicable to only a very small number of monopolies.

Like many conservatives of his time, White was opposed to organized labor, which he saw as interfering with the property rights of business owners and with the right of freedom of contract. In what came to be known as the *Employers' Liability Cases*, he wrote the majority opinion striking down a federal law requiring the railroad companies to compensate employees for their injuries. Similarly, in *Adair v. United States* (1908) he rejected a federal law that prohibited "yellow dog contracts"—agreements by workers not to join unions—in the railroad industry. He also struck down federal restrictions on child labor in *Hammer v. Dagenhart* (1918).

Characteristically, though, White upheld state regulation in these matters, believing that the states had the right to police business and commerce within their own borders. Thus, he dissented when the Court struck down a New York law limiting the number of hours that bakers could work in the landmark case *Lochner v. New York* (1905), and he joined a unanimous Court in upholding an Oregon law that limited working hours for women in laundries in *Muller v. Oregon* (1908).

While opposing federal intervention in the economic affairs of states, White granted broad power to the federal government to suppress radicalism and sedition. In *Toledo Newspapers v. United States* (1918) he wrote a majority opinion that upheld a contempt citation issued against a newspaper for criticizing a federal district court. It would take Oliver Wendell Holmes, Jr. and Louis Brandeis—later justices—to develop views regarding freedom of the press that are taken for granted today. In *Gilbert v. Minnesota* (1920) White dissented when the Court upheld the conviction of a political radical, but his dissent was based not on a belief in free speech but on his belief that the federal government, not the states, should have jurisdiction in these kinds of cases.

White generally supported segregation and joined the Court majority in establishing the "separate but equal" doctrine in *Plessy v. Ferguson* in 1896. However, he did vote to strike down some of the worst violations of the Thirteenth, Fourteenth, and Fifteenth Amendments. For example, he voted against "peonage," or the practice of forced servitude in repayment of debt that in effect left some Southern blacks in a condition akin to slavery. He also struck down laws that prevented blacks from voting and joined a unanimous Court that struck down laws prohibiting nonwhites from living in certain neighborhoods.

By 1920 White's health was beginning to fail, and he was under pressure to retire from the bench. He resisted until he became ill in May 1921, and he died in Washington, D.C, on May 19 after unsuccessful surgery. He was remembered as a hard-working justice who wrote 590 majority opinions, 16 concurrences, and just 53 dissents. He was also remembered as a charming, genial, and even lovable man who carried candy in his pockets for children. He was very much a product of his time and resisted many of the changes in jurisprudence and social attitudes that took root during his tenure but would not find expression on the Court until he and his generation passed. ◆

White granted broad power to the federal government to suppress radicalism and sedition.

Whittaker, Charles

FEBRUARY 22, 1901–NOVEMBER 26, 1973 ● ASSOCIATE JUSTICE

Charles Evans Whittaker was born on a farm near Troy, Kansas, on February 22, 1901. As a child he attended a small schoolhouse near the farm, then rode a pony to attend high school in Troy. But after his mother, Ida Miller, died on his 16th birthday, he dropped out of high school to work on the family farm with his father, Charles Whittaker. He supplemented the family income by trapping game and selling the pelts.

Even as a teenager, Whittaker knew that he wanted to be a lawyer, so at age 19 he set out for Kansas City, Missouri, with $700 in his pocket. There he found a job as an office boy at a law firm. He was also admitted to the unaccredited Kansas City School of Law on the condition that he simultaneously finish his high school studies. For three years he worked during the day and studied at night, and in 1923 he graduated from law school, passed the bar examination, and took a job as an attorney at the firm where he had been an office boy. Over the next 30 years he gained a reputation as a hard-working perfectionist, first as a trial lawyer, then in corporate and business law. In 1928 he married Winifred Pugh, and the couple had three sons.

Charles Whittaker

It would be an understatement to say that Whittaker's rise through the federal judiciary system was rapid. He took his first step in 1954, when a vacancy opened in the federal district court for the western district of Missouri. Whittaker wanted the job, so he put in a call to his friend and client, Roy Roberts, the owner of the *Kansas City Star* newspaper and a confidant of President Dwight D. Eisenhower. Roberts enthusiastically recommended Whittaker to the president, who made the appointment. Whittaker later said that his two years as a district court judge were the happiest of his life.

The next step came in 1955, when a seat opened on the federal Court of Appeals for the Eighth Circuit. Eisenhower wanted to appoint a Missourian to the post, and Whittaker was the only federal judge from the state. Eisenhower made the appointment, and Whittaker joined the court in 1956. After the excitement of trial work as a district court judge, however, he found appellate court work dreary. Fortunately, the position lasted only nine months.

In 1957 Justice Stanley Reed retired from the U.S. Supreme Court. Again, geography played a role in Eisenhower's choice of a replacement. He wanted a Republican from the Midwest with federal judicial experience, and Whittaker was one of the few judges who fit the bill. The president nominated Whittaker in March, and 17 days later he was confirmed unanimously in the Senate.

In just three years Whittaker had risen from an unknown Midwestern lawyer to a seat on the high court, prompting Justice Felix Frankfurter to joke that the Supreme Court could get a judge from the district court faster than it could get a case.

Whittaker joined a Court that was evenly divided between a liberal wing led by Chief Justice Earl Warren and a conservative wing. In conferences, the Court often split 4–4 on votes, and Whittaker, as the junior justice and the last to vote, cast the deciding fifth vote in a remarkable number of cases. He thus was the crucial "swing vote," sometimes giving the majority to the liberals, sometimes to the conservatives, though eventually he became a moderate conservative.

In cases involving individual liberties, Whittaker tended to side with the liberals. Thus, in *Green v. United States* (1957), he provided the fifth vote when the Court ruled that a man tried for first-degree murder but found guilty of second-degree murder could not be tried again for first-degree murder without violating the constitutional prohibition against double jeopardy. In *Moore v. Michigan* (1957) he joined the liberals in ruling that a poor, uneducated man had not known what he was doing when he waived his right to an attorney. And in *Trop v. Dulles* (1958) he cast the deciding vote that struck down the Nationality Act of 1940, which said that wartime deserters could be stripped of their U.S. citizenship.

Frequently, though, Whittaker joined the conservatives. He cast the fifth vote in another case called *Green v. United States* (1958) when the Court upheld a contempt citation issued against two members of the Communist Party who had refused

"You know Charlie had gone to night law school, and he began as an office boy and he'd been a farm boy and he had inside him an inferiority complex, which . . . showed and he'd say, 'Felix [Frankfurter] used words in there that I'd never heard of.' " Quoted by Bernard Schwartz in *A History of the Supreme Court*, 1993

1901 Whittaker is born in Troy, Kansas.

1954 Whittaker is appointed to the Federal District Court for western Missouri.

1956 Whittaker is appointed to the U.S. Court of Appeals for the Eighth Circuit.

1957 Whittaker is appointed to the U.S. Supreme Court.

1962 Whittaker resigns from the Supreme Court.

1973 Whittaker dies in Kansas City.

to surrender to federal marshals. In two 1958 cases, *Thomas v. Arizona* and *Crooker v. California*, he joined the conservatives in upholding the convictions of men who claimed that they had confessed to crimes only because they had been coerced. And in *Beilan v. Board of Education* (1958) he cast the deciding vote with the conservatives to rule that a public school teacher could be fired for not answering questions about possible communist affiliations.

Whittaker spent only five years on the Court, and they were not happy ones. As a jurist he had always been driven to master the facts of a case, then apply those facts to existing law. He soon found that Supreme Court cases were too complex and involved too many issues for him to do this to his satisfaction. Always a bit of a nervous, impatient man, with something of an inferiority complex because of his academic credentials, he soon found the job overwhelming and fell into a deep depression. In March 1962 he entered the Walter Reed Army Medical Center because of a nervous breakdown. Following his doctors' advice, he resigned from the Supreme Court shortly thereafter.

After regaining his health, Whittaker worked as an arbitrator for General Motors. He also wrote a code for the ethical conduct of senators at the request of the Senate Committee on Standards and Conduct. He died of an aneurysm in Kansas City on November 26, 1973. Despite his lack of distinction as a Supreme Court justice, he deserves admiration for a life that mirrored the "rags-to-riches" stories of Horatio Alger that he loved to read as a child. ◆

Wilson, James

SEPTEMBER 14, 1742–AUGUST 21, 1798 ● ASSOCIATE JUSTICE

James Wilson was born on September 14, 1742, in the small town of Carskerdo, Scotland, which is near the famous village of St. Andrews. His parents, William and Aleson Wilson, expected their son to become a minister, and initially he followed that path. At age 15, he enrolled in the University of St. Andrews, where he studied religion before a family crisis forced him to leave school in 1759 after just two years. When the crisis passed, Wilson continued his higher education first at the University of Glasgow from 1759 to 1763, and then at the

University of Edinburgh from 1763 to 1765. Despite all those years spent in college, it appears that Wilson never earned a bachelor's degree.

After leaving the University of Edinburgh, Wilson tried his hand at becoming an accountant, studying the profession on his own. After a brief attempt at that profession, Wilson again changed his mind, this time setting sail for the British colony that would become the United States. Arriving in late 1765, Wilson landed New York City and settled in Philadelphia. Using letters of introduction that he carried with him, Wilson met several prominent people in the Philadelphia community. One of those people was Richard Peters, who was a high-ranking official at the College of Philadelphia. He offered Wilson a job teaching Latin, which Wilson accepted in February 1766.

James Wilson

While teaching, Wilson finally realized which career path he wanted to follow, choosing to study law under the tutelage of Philadelphia attorney John Dickson. In late 1767, after reading all he could on British law, Wilson was admitted to the Pennsylvania bar. Approximately six months later, he moved to Reading, Pennsylvania and opened his own law office.

In Reading, Wilson's hard work paid off when his law office did quite well; however, his practice really flourished when he moved to nearby Carlisle, where the Scottish and Irish immigrants who lived in the area trusted him with their legal situations. By 1774, his office received more than half of all legal work in the county in which he lived, and he also took cases from the surrounding seven counties. During that time, he used his success to become a wealthy landowner, and in 1771, he married Rachel Bird, who he had been seeing for a number of years. While his practice did provide a substantial amount of money, Wilson never had as much money as he represented to the public because he was a near-compulsive real estate speculator, often borrowing money to buy and sell land and bank shares.

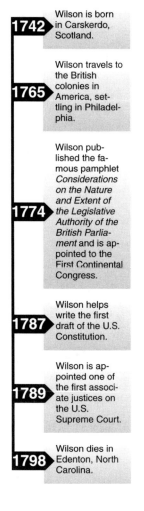

1742
Wilson is born in Carskerdo, Scotland.

1765
Wilson travels to the British colonies in America, settling in Philadelphia.

1774
Wilson published the famous pamphlet *Considerations on the Nature and Extent of the Legislative Authority of the British Parliament* and is appointed to the First Continental Congress.

1787
Wilson helps write the first draft of the U.S. Constitution.

1789
Wilson is appointed one of the first associate justices on the U.S. Supreme Court.

1798
Wilson dies in Edenton, North Carolina.

In 1774, Wilson's career took another shift when he entered politics for the first time. He first headed an important committee in Carlisle, from which he was selected as a delegate to the First Continental Congress, which was held in 1775 in Philadelphia. Before attending the Congress, Wilson published a pamphlet called *Considerations on the Nature and Extent of the Legislative Authority of the British Parliament* in which he became one of the first politicians in America to suggest that England had no power over the colonies and that the states should form their own nation. The pamphlet was a very popular reading item that was extremely influential in starting the move for American independence.

Wilson, who was one of the signers of the Declaration of Independence, also served as a delegate to the Second Continental Congress and to the Constitutional Convention; the latter event was held in 1787 in Philadelphia. At the convention, Wilson served on the committee that created the first draft of the U.S. Constitution. When the war with Great Britain broke out in 1776, Wilson served in the military, acting as a colonel of a militia battalion that fought in New Jersey. From 1779 to 1783, he served as the Advocate General for France in America, ruling on commercial and maritime issues.

Wilson kept busy while he was the Advocate General, wearing several other hats at the same time. For instance, in 1781 he was named a director of the first-ever Bank of North America. In 1782, Wilson was again elected to the Continental Congress as a representative of Pennsylvania, a position he held until 1787.

Once the federal government was fully established, Wilson made it clear that his real goal was to be considered for the position of Chief Justice of the newly formed U.S. Supreme Court. However, on September 24, 1789, he was named one of the Court's inaugural group of associate justices instead, a situation he tried to make the best of. In his written opinions, Wilson regularly took positions that upheld the power of the U.S. federal government in the face of challenges from the individual states. For example, in *Chisholm v. Georgia*, Wilson wrote that the states were to be treated no differently from an individual person. Just as each person in the new country had to follow federal laws issued by the U.S. Congress, so too did each state have to recognize the "controlling judiciary" that the Supreme Court represented.

At the same time that he served on the Supreme Court, Wilson also worked as a law professor at the College of

Philadelphia; in fact, he was the first to teach law in the school's history. In 1793, Wilson remarried, taking Hannah Grey as his bride. Wilson first wife had died seven years earlier and left him with six children.

During Wilson's eight-year stay on the Supreme Court, his financial condition continued to worsen. While still putting up a front of great wealth, Wilson was in fact going deeper and deeper into trouble, continuing to borrow money to speculate on land deals that he eventually lost out on, making it impossible to repay the loans. In the winter of 1796, he fled his home in an attempt to escape imprisonment for bad debts, but he could not outrun the law. He was caught and sentenced to prison because he owed his creditors more than $197,000, a staggering sum for that time. When first imprisoned, he was still a member of the Supreme Court. His health failed rapidly in prison, and on August 21, 1798, Wilson died in a seedy hotel adjacent to the court house in the city of Edenton, North Carolina. ◆

> *"All men are by nature, equal and free. No one has a right to any authority over another without his consent . . . The consequence is, that the happiness of the society is the first law of every government."*
>
> James Wilson in *Considerations on the Nature and Extent of the Legislative Authority of the British Parliament,* 1774

Woodbury, Levi

DECEMBER 22, 1789–SEPTEMBER 4, 1851 ● ASSOCIATE JUSTICE

Levi Woodbury was born on December 22, 1789, in Francestown, New Hampshire. He was the second of ten children born to Peter and Mary Woodbury. The Woodbury family had been in America since 1623 and was fairly well off. Woodbury would go on to have a distinguished and varied career in government service that took him from the New Hampshire state capital to Washington, D.C.

As a child, Woodbury first attended the village school in Francestown and then moved on to the Atkinson Academy. A bright student, Woodbury had no trouble being admitted to prestigious Dartmouth University, where he graduated with Phi Beta Kappa honors in 1808. Upon graduation, Woodbury decided that he wanted to have a career in law, so he took up private studies with Judge Jeremiah Smith; he also took classes at the Litchfield Law School in Connecticut. It was not uncommon at that time for law students to study privately instead of attending a full course of law school, so Woodbury had no problem being admitted to the bar in 1812. He opened his own

Levi Woodbury

practice that served Francestown and the surrounding area, and he became a popular speaker and writer. In 1819, he married Elizabeth Williams Clapp and moved to Portsmouth, New Hampshire. The couple had five children together.

With his law practice doing very well, Woodbury decided to branch out into politics. In 1816, he was named to fill a clerk position in the New Hampshire Senate. Just one year later, at the young age of 26, Woodbury was one of three men named to be associate justices on the New Hampshire State Supreme Court. He received the appointment as a result of his friendship with New Hampshire governor William Plumer, who recognized that Woodbury had a brilliant grasp of legal matters.

Woodbury remained on the court for six years until he made an even bigger jump up the political ladder. With the support of a section of the Democratic party known as the "Young America" faction, as well as bipartisan support from the Federalist party, Woodbury was elected governor of New Hampshire; he was only 32 years old at the time. While Woodbury had a reputation as a fairly conservative judge, some of the things he proposed when he took office seem almost progressive for the time, such as more educational opportunities for women and the use of new mechanical devices in agriculture. After serving one term as governor, Woodbury was unable to maintain the cross-party support that had earned him the office in the first place, and he was defeated in his bid for re-election in 1825.

Woodbury refused to let the defeat slow him down; the same year he was defeated, he simply switched gears and was elected to the state legislature, where he was named Speaker of the House. A popular politician, it did not come as a surprise when he was selected to represent New Hampshire in the U.S. Senate. His term as a senator was longer than his stay in the governor's mansion—he stayed in Congress from 1825 until 1831. In the Senate, he was called the "Rock of New England Democracy" and was considered to be one of the most powerful senators, a fact reinforced by all of the important committees he served on, such as Commerce, and Agriculture.

Once he reached Washington, D.C., Woodbury showed that he intended to stay there, and he proved to be an outstanding politician who served his country in many ways. After his term in the Senate ended, he was named Secretary of the Navy, a position he held for three years. His three years were quiet ones, although he did oversee a major expansion of the Navy.

Woodbury's next assignment was as Secretary of the U.S. Treasury, a position he held from 1834 until 1841. The seven years that Woodbury was in office were tumultuous ones, as important questions regarding the role of the Bank of the United States needed to be resolved. Still a strong conservative, Woodbury felt that the federal bank was not needed and that it did not have the authority to conduct business that could be handled by the state banks. He felt that the Treasury should remain independent, and that it did not need a bank to manage the government's money; he also felt strongly that Congress did not have the authority to recharter the bank. When a cash crisis called the Panic of 1837 hit, Woodbury did an excellent job of easing the public's fears, making sure that those who held paper currency would not lose their money. Woodbury also encouraged the use of surplus funds to improve the nation's infrastructure, and he is the last Secretary of the Treasury to leave office with no national debt outstanding.

Near the end of his term as secretary, Woodbury turned down an offer to become Chief Justice of the New Hampshire Supreme Court, and it appeared his political career might be drawing to a close. However, upon his retirement in 1841, he decided to resume his career in the Senate, easily winning the election. He spent four more years in the Senate, firmly defending his Democratic principles. In 1845, his career took one final unexpected turn. Late that year, President James Polk approached Woodbury and asked him to serve as associate justice on the U.S. Supreme Court. Woodbury agreed and was confirmed by the Senate in January 1846.

Just by accepting the nomination, Woodbury established one first in Supreme Court history—he was the first justice to have attended law school. As a justice, Woodbury held firm to his conservative views that strongly favored states' rights over the power of the federal government. He was often in the minority on cases involving states' rights, but that did not bother him in the least. Examples of his favoring the states includes a

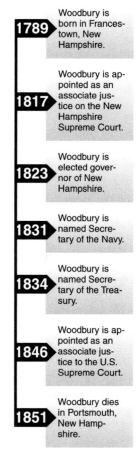

1789 Woodbury is born in Francestown, New Hampshire.

1817 Woodbury is appointed as an associate justice on the New Hampshire Supreme Court.

1823 Woodbury is elected governor of New Hampshire.

1831 Woodbury is named Secretary of the Navy.

1834 Woodbury is named Secretary of the Treasury.

1846 Woodbury is appointed as an associate justice to the U.S. Supreme Court.

1851 Woodbury dies in Portsmouth, New Hampshire.

Woodbury established one first in Supreme Court history— he was the first justice to have attended law school.

case in which the court ruled that it was constitutional for the states to pass prohibitionist laws that made liquor illegal. In *Jones v. Van Zandt*, a more important case that involved slavery, Woodbury again ruled in favor of the states, ruling that slavery was "a political question, settled by each state for itself."

While satisfied with his seat on the Supreme Court, Woodbury had higher aspirations. He had been under consideration for the Democratic presidential nomination in 1848, but when he was passed over that year, he was considered a lock to receive the bid in 1852. Unfortunately, Woodbury never made it to that nomination, as he died unexpectedly while at home in Portsmouth on September 4, 1851. ◆

Woods, William B.

AUGUST 3, 1824–MAY 14, 1887 ● ASSOCIATE JUSTICE

William B. Woods was born on August 3, 1824, in Newark, Ohio. His parents, Ezekiel and Sarah Woods owned a farm, and his father also worked as a merchant. After graduating from high school, Woods received enough financial support from his parents to go to college, first attending Western Reserve College in Hudson, Ohio, for three years before transferring to Yale University. There, he graduated with honors in 1845.

Upon graduation, Woods chose to go into law as a career. As was the common practice at the time, he did not attend law school, but instead studied law privately while working for attorney S. D. King in Newark. In 1847, he was admitted to the bar and opened up a new practice with King as his partner. The two were in practice together for more than a decade, closing only when the Civil War broke out. In addition to his law practice, Woods

Willam B. Woods

entered the local political arena in Newark, successfully running for mayor in 1856. One year later, he was elected to the General Assembly of Ohio, where he was quickly named Speaker of the House.

As the conflict between the North and the South grew larger, Woods underwent an evolution in his opinion about the war. At first, he was strongly opposed to both the war and President Abraham Lincoln. He even tried to delay passage of a financial bill that would have prepared the state of Ohio to defend itself if attacked. In time, however, he concluded that the North's cause was a just one and urged Ohio residents to fully support the Union; in the state's General Assembly, he even fought for passage of a bill that would exempt men who volunteered for service in the military from losing their property due to bad debts or back taxes owed.

In 1862, he took his support to a higher level when he enrolled in the Union army, where he served until 1866. Nearly his entire four years was spent in the field, often in battle. He participated in some of the war's biggest battles, including Shiloh and Vicksburg, and he served with General Sherman as the latter marched across the South. By the time he was discharged in February 1866, he had risen from lieutenant-colonel to the rank of brigadier-general and brevet major general. After the war, he decided to remain in the South, opening a law office in the town of Bentonville, Alabama.

Like most Union leaders, Woods was a strong supporter of the Republican party, which meant that he helped enact the party's Reconstruction plan for the South after the war and also that he was in line to receive a reward from the party in exchange for his loyalty. That reward came in 1869 when President Ulysses S. Grant appointed Woods to be a judge of the Fifth Circuit Court, which served Georgia and the states bordering the Gulf of Mexico. After he was appointed, he moved to Atlanta, Georgia, where he lived for 11 years. Because so many of the states—especially the Southern ones—were in complete disarray and were largely unable to hear cases, the burden on the federal circuit courts was extremely heavy. Woods performed well as circuit judge and remained in that office for 11 years.

In 1880, President Rutherford B. Hayes was faced with making a nomination to fill a vacant seat on the Supreme Court. It was widely agreed that the next justice should be from the South, since no one from that region was on the court at the

"It is undoubtedly true that all citizens capable of bearing arms constitute the reserved military force or reserve militia of the United States as well as of the States, and in view of this prerogative of the general government, as well as of its general powers, the States cannot, even laying the constitutional provision in question out of view, prohibit the people from keeping and bearing arms, so as to deprive the United States of their rightful resource for maintaining public security, and disable the people from performing their duty to the general government."

William B. Woods in his opinion for *Presser v. Illinois,* an 1886 case involving the Second Amendment

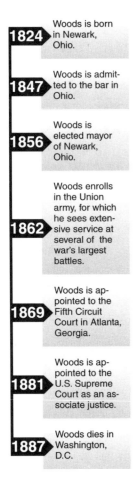

1824 — Woods is born in Newark, Ohio.

1847 — Woods is admitted to the bar in Ohio.

1856 — Woods is elected mayor of Newark, Ohio.

1862 — Woods enrolls in the Union army, for which he sees extensive service at several of the war's largest battles.

1869 — Woods is appointed to the Fifth Circuit Court in Atlanta, Georgia.

1881 — Woods is appointed to the U.S. Supreme Court as an associate justice.

1887 — Woods dies in Washington, D.C.

time, thus no one was surprised when the nomination went to Woods, who accepted and was sworn in January 5, 1881.

Woods, who would end up serving only six years on the high court, wrote more than 200 opinions in that short time. Many of his opinions were written for intricate patent law cases, but perhaps his two most memorable opinions each involved a government rights issue. In *United States v. Harris*, the Court struck down the Ku Klux Klan Act, stating that the federal government had no authority, under the Fourteenth Amendment, to regulate the activities of individuals. In *Presser v. Illinois*, Woods wrote the lead opinion, which stated the Court's position that the Bill of Rights, in this case the Second Amendment and the right to bear arms, limited the powers of the federal government only and in no way affected the powers of the state government. Both cases were important at the time, but neither of them stood the test of time, as both were overturned in later court decisions.

After six years on the court, Woods unexpectedly took ill and died on May 14, 1887, in Washington, D.C. He was survived by his wife Anne, to whom he had been married for 32 years, and by one son and one daughter. ◆

Time Line of Events Surrounding Justices of the Supreme Court

1775-83

The American Revolution is fought, beginning at Lexington, and Concord, Massachusetts, on April 19, 1775

1776

The Continental Congress receives and adopts the Declaration of Independence, written by Thomas Jefferson.

1777

The Articles of Confederation are approved by the Continental Congress; though it establishes a weak central government, the Articles do not provide for a uniform monetary system, and do not protect the personal freedom of all American citizens.

1783

The Treaty of Paris, which officially recognizes the United States of America in the international community, is signed.

1786

Shays' Rebellion, an uprising involving farmers in western Massachusetts, begins. The revolt is brought down, but exposes the weaknesses of the central government's ability to enforce the law under the Articles of Confederation.

1787

A Constitutional Convention is held in Philadelphia to consider a replacement for the Articles of Confederation; a Constitution is written with seven articles, the first three of which outline the duties and obligations of the legislative, executive, and judicial branches of the federal government.

1788

The Constitution is ratified by 11 of the 13 states as several of the individual states propose amendments to the Constitution which would later become the Bill of Rights; George Washington is chosen as the first president of the United States, and the first Congress meets in New York City.

1789

Following Washington's inauguration as president, John Jay is named as the first chief justice of the U.S. Supreme Court; the ten amendments that will be known as the Bill of Rights are formally proposed to the states by Congress.

1790

The District of Columbia is created and serves as the United States capital city; Philadelphia will serve as the capital until 1800.

John Rutledge is confirmed as an associate justice of the Supreme Court.

1791

The first ten amendments to the United States Constitution—collectively known as the Bill of Rights—are ratified.

1792

Thomas Johnson is confirmed as an associate justice of the Supreme Court.

1793

Supreme Court justice John Blair rules against Georgia in *Chisholm v. Georgia*.

William Paterson is confirmed as an associate justice of the Supreme Court.

1795

The Eleventh Amendment to the Constitution is ratified, overruling *Chisolm v. Georgia*, limiting lawsuits against the states.

The United States Senate denies confirmation of John Rutledge as chief justice of the Supreme Court.

1796

Oliver Ellsworth is appointed chief justice of the Supreme Court after William Cushing declines his confirmation due to ill health.

In *Ware v. Hylton*, the Court rules that a treaty made by the United States supercedes a state statute.

1800

Alfred Moore is confirmed as an associate justice of the Supreme Court.

1801

John Marshall is appointed and confirmed chief justice of the Supreme Court.

Bushrod Washington is confirmed as an associate justice of the Supreme Court.

1803

Marshall writes the opinion in *Marbury v. Madison*, establishing the Supreme Court's power to review and reject acts of Congress as unconstitutional.

1804

The Twelfth Amendment to the Constitution is ratified, providing for distinct ballots for president and vice president.

William Johnson is confirmed as an associate justice of the Supreme Court.

1805

Supreme Court justice Samuel Chase is impeached by the House of Representatives for various instances of attempting to let political influences affect judicial decisions; Chase is acquitted in the Senate.

1807

Henry Livingston is confirmed as an associate justice of the Supreme Court.

Thomas Todd is confirmed as an associate justice of the Supreme Court.

1811

Gabriel Duvall is confirmed an associate justice of the Supreme Court.

1812

Joseph Story is confirmed as an associate justice of the Supreme Court.

1816

Justice Story's majority opinion in *Martin v. Hunter's Lessee* establishes the supremacy of federal courts over state courts concerning the interpretation of federal laws and treaties.

1819

Chief Justice Marshall writes the majority opinion in *McCulloch v. Maryland*, which finds that the Necessary and Proper clause of the Constitution enabled Congress to expand its ability to execute its powers under Article I.

1823

Chief Justice Marshall's opinion in *Gibbons v. Ogden* gives a broad interpretation of the Commerce Clause in the Constitution, which in turn opens the door to federal regulation of interstate commerce.

Smith Thompson is confirmed as an associate justice of the Supreme Court.

1826

Robert Trimble is confirmed as an associate justice of the Supreme Court.

1830

John McLean is confirmed as an associate justice of the Supreme Court.

1831

The Supreme Court rules in *Cheroke Nation v. Georgia* that the Cherokee tribe was a dependent nation—as opposed to a foreign nation—under the Constitution, establishing the groundwork for the relocation of the Cherokee and other tribes.

1832

In *Worcester v. Georgia*, the Supreme Court rules that Indian nations have the right to retain independent communities; the state of Georgia ignores the ruling and President Andrew Jackson decides against enforcing it in support of relocation.

1835

James Wayne is confirmed as an associate justice of the Supreme Court.

1836

Roger B. Taney is confirmed the chief justice of the Supreme Court.

Philip B. Barbour joins the Supreme Court as an associate justice.

1837

Supreme Court justice Henry Baldwin publishes *A General View of the Origin and Nature of the Constitution and Government of the United States*.

John Catron is confirmed as an associate justice of the Supreme Court.

1838

Alexis de Tocqueville publishes his masterpiece, *Democracy in America*, following his tour of the United States.

John McKinley is confirmed as an associate justice of the Supreme Court.

1841

Peter Daniel is confirmed as an associate justice of the Supreme Court.

1842

The Supreme Court upholds the Fugitive Slave Act of 1793 and also invalidates Pennsylvania's personal liberty law, under which a state official did not comply with a professional slave catcher.

1845

Samuel Nelson is confirmed as an associate justice of the Supreme Court.

1846

Robert C. Grier is confirmed as an associate justice of the Supreme Court.

1847

Dred Scott files his first lawsuit in an attempt to gain his freedom in Missouri.

1857

The Supreme Court issues its opinion in *Dred Scott v. Sanford* that a slave does not gain freedom upon entering a free state because, the Court rules, slaves are not citizens; the Court also declares that Congress cannot bar slavery from a territory, which invalidates the Missouri Compromise. Justice Benjamin Curtis writes the dissenting opinion in the case and later resigns from the Court to protest what he thought were political influences on the majority opinion in the *Dred Scott* case.

1858

Nathan Clifford is confirmed as an associate justice of the Supreme Court.

1859

Justice Roger B. Taney writes a Court opinion upholding the Fugitive Slave Act of 1850.

1861-65

The American Civil War is fought.

1862

David Davis is confirmed as an associate justice of the Supreme Court.

Samuel F. Miller is confirmed as an associate justice of the Supreme Court.

Noah Swayne is confirmed as an associate justice of the Supreme Court.

1863

Stephen J. Field is confirmed as an associate justice of the Supreme Court.

1865

The Thirteenth Amendment to the Constitution is ratified, specifically prohibiting slavery in the United States.

Supreme Court justice John Campbell is arrested after the assassination of President Lincoln on suspicion that he believed in the establishment of a legislature independent of the Congress; Campbell spent four months in prison before being released and resuming his seat on the Court.

Mississippi is the first state in the newly reunified nation to pass "Black Codes," which restrict the liberties of newly freed slaves and legalize segregation.

1868

The Fourteenth Amendment to the Constitution is ratified, giving U.S. citizenship to freed slaves and extending equal protection and due process to them.

The House of Representatives impeaches President Andrew Johnson, but he is acquitted in the Senate trial.

1870

The Fifteenth Amendment to the Constitution is ratified, making it unlawful to deny qualified citizens the right to vote based on their race.

William Strong is confirmed as an associate justice of the Supreme Court.

1871

The Supreme Court rules that federal murder suits are impermissible in *U.S. v. Cruikshank*, thus invalidating federal indictments for the murders of over 100 black men in an election dispute.

1873

Ward Hunt is confirmed as an associate justice of the Supreme Court.

1874

Morrison Waite is confirmed as the chief justice of the Supreme Court.

1875

The Supreme Court rules in *Minor v. Happersett* that limiting the right to vote to men does not violate women's rights under the Fourteenth Amendment.

1876

In *U.S. v. Reese*, the Court interprets the Fifteenth Amendment very narrowly, allowing states to conceive various methods of disenfranchising black voters.

Associate Justice Ward Hunt dissents in *United States v. Reese* and argues that all citizens of legal age should be allowed to vote.

1877

Supreme Court justice Joseph P. Bradley casts the deciding vote on a committee which makes Rutherford B. Hayes president.

John Marshall Harlan I is confirmed as an associate justice of the Supreme Court.

1878

The Court holds that bigamy is not protected under the First Amendment's religious freedoms clause in *Reynolds v. United States*.

1879

A West Virginia law limiting jury service to white males is struck down by the Supreme Court in *Strauder v. West Virginia*.

1881

Horace Gray is confirmed as an associate justice of the Supreme Court.

Stanley Matthews is confirmed as an associate justice of the Supreme Court by one vote.

1883

The Supreme Court decides the *Civil Rights Cases*, striking down parts of the Civil Rights Acts of 1875 as unconstitutional, saying that the Fourteenth Amendment forbids states—not individual citizens—from discriminating against others.

1884

According to the Supreme Court in *Elk v. Watkins*, American Indians are not citizens and the Fourteenth Amendment does not apply to them; Congress overrides this decision.

1886

In *Boyd v. United States*, the Supreme Court holds that protections against unreasonable searches and seizures as outlined in the Fourth and Fifth Amendments apply to civil matters as well as criminal cases.

The Supreme Court invalidates a zoning law being selectively applied against Chinese immigrants in violation of the Fourteenth Amendment in *Yick Wo v. Hopkins*.

1888

Lucius Lamar is confirmed as an associate justice of the Supreme Court.

1890

Supreme Court justice Samuel Blatchford writes the opinion for *Chicago, Milwaukee and St. Paul Railway Co. v. Minnesota*, which struck down a provision allowing an independent commission to decide if railroad rates were fair.

1893

Howell Jackson is confirmed as an associate justice of the Supreme Court.

1895

Justice David J. Brewer speaks for the majority in *In re Debs*, upholding the government's use of the injunction against unlawful strikes.

1896

The Supreme Court decides *Plessy v. Ferguson* and upholds legal segregation by stipulating that the government must provide "separate but equal" public facilities for blacks and whites. Justice Henry B. Brown writes the majority opinion.

Rufus Peckham is confirmed as an associate justice of the Supreme Court.

1898

In *Williams v. Mississippi*, the Supreme Court rejects the claim of a black man who argued that a death sentence by a white jury violated the equal protection clause of the Fourteenth Amendment.

Individuals of Chinese descent are citizens of the United States under the Fourteenth Amendment according to the Supreme Court in *United States v. Wonk Kim Ark*.

Joseph McKenna is confirmed as an associate justice of the Supreme Court.

1902

President Theodore Roosevelt appoints Oliver Wendell Holmes, Jr. as an associate justice of the Supreme Court; Holmes is confirmed by the Senate.

1903

In *Lone Wolf v. Hitchcock*, the Supreme Court declares that the "plenary powers" of Congress in Indian affairs are not subject to review by the courts.

William R. Day is confirmed as an associate justice of the Supreme Court.

1905

The Supreme Court decides in *Lochner v. New York* that state maximum hours laws for bakers imposed by a state are unconstitutional.

1906

William H. Moody is confirmed as an associate justice of the Supreme Court.

1908

An Oregon law limiting the amount of working hours for women is ruled unconstitutional by the Supreme Court in *Muller v. Oregon*. Justice David J. Brewer writes the opinion for the Court.

The Supreme Court rules that the Fifth Amendment's self incrimination clause does not apply to the states in *Twining v. New Jersey*.

1910

Horace Lurton is confirmed as an associate justice of the Supreme Court.

Edward White is confirmed as an associate justice of the Supreme Court.

Willis Van Devanter is confirmed as an associate justice of the Supreme Court.

1911

The Supreme Court holds in *Bailey v. Alabama* that southern statutes which criminalize breach of tenant farmer contracts amount to unlawful servitude, also called peonage.

Joseph R. Lamar is confirmed as an associate justice of the Supreme Court.

1912

Mahlon Pitney is confirmed as an associate justice of the Supreme Court.

1914

The Supreme Court establishes the exclusionary rule in their opinion in the case *Weeks v. United States*; the exclusionary rule governs evidence obtained in violation of the Fourth Amendment that is inadmissible in a trial.

James C. McReynolds is confirmed as an associate justice of the Supreme Court.

1915

In *Guinn v. Oklahoma*, the Supreme Court voids an Oklahoma grandfather clause, which allowed white citizens to avoid voting tests while forcing black citizens to take them, a violation of the Fifth Amendment.

1916

Louis Brandeis is confirmed by the Senate as an associate justice of the Supreme Court, the first person of the Jewish faith to become a justice.

Former Supreme Court justice Charles Evans Hughes is the Republican Party nominee for the presidency of the United States; he loses the election to Woodrow Wilson.

1917-18

The United States sends armed forces to Europe to fight with the Allied forces in World War I, which ends with the Versailles Treaty.

1919

The Eighteenth Amendment is ratified, outlawing the sale, distribution, importing, exporting, and manufacture of alcoholic beverages within the United States.

1920

The Nineteenth Amendment is ratified, granting the right to vote to women in the United States.

1921

Former president William Howard Taft is appointed and confirmed chief justice of the Supreme Court.

1922

Pierce Butler is appointed to the U.S. Supreme Court by President Warren G. Harding.

1922

In *United States v. Lanza*, the Supreme Court upholds state and federal prosecutions for violations of Prohibition laws. The Court denies the double jeopardy defense of the Fifth Amendment.

Supreme Court justice John Clarke resigns from the Court to head the movement for the establishment of the League of Nations.

George Sutherland is confirmed as an associate justice of the Supreme Court.

1923

The Supreme Court deems a state law prohibiting teaching in any language other than English as unconstitutional in *Meyer v. Nebraska*.

In *Moore v. Dempsey*, Justice Holmes writes the Court's majority opinion providing for strict review under habeus corpus of judicial proceedings in the states which violate due process.

The Supreme Court voids a minimum wage law for women in Washington, D.C., in *Adkins v. Children's Hospital*, reasoning that the law is a violation of contract.

1924

Edward Sandford is confirmed as an associate justice of the Supreme Court.

1927

The Supreme Court rules a Texas law prohibiting black citizens from voting in the Democratic primary elections as unconstitutional in *Nixon v. Herndon*.

Justice Holmes writes a concurring opinion in *Whitney v. California* which proposes a "clear and present danger" test for legislation which suppresses particular groups; the Court later adopts this test.

1928

Justice Brandeis writes the dissenting opinion in *Olmstead v. United States* in which he states that "the right to be left alone is the most comprehensive of rights" of American citizenship.

1930

Charles Evans Hughes is named chief justice of the Supreme Court.

Owen J. Roberts is confirmed as an associate justice of the Supreme Court.

The Supreme Court rules that *An American Tragedy* by Theodore Dreiser is obscene and not protected under the First Amendment.

1931

According to the Supreme Court in *Stromberg v. California*, First Amendment freedoms of speech and the press do apply to the states through the Fourteenth Amendment.

In *Near v. Minnesota*, the Supreme Court rules a Minnesota state law is a prior restraint to First Amendment freedoms, and therefore unconstitutional.

1932

The Supreme Court holds in *Powell v. Alabama* that the Due Process Clause of the Fourteenth Amendment required counsel appointments for nine indigent black youths, known as the "Scottsboro boys," accused of raping a white woman.

1933

The Twentieth Amendment is ratified, establishing a shortened period of time of inauguration for executive and congressional offices; the amendment also provides for the replacement of a president-elect who dies before assuming office.

The Twenty-first Amendment is ratified, repealing the Eighteenth Amendment and ending Prohibition.

1935

In another case involving the "Scottsboro boys," *Norris v. Alabama*, the Supreme Court overturns a conviction due to the exclusion of black citizens from grand juries and trials in violation of the Equal Protection Clause.

1936

The Supreme Court rules that confessions obtained through violent police measures violate the Due Process Clause of the Fourteenth Amendment in *Brown v. Mississippi*.

1937

President Franklin Roosevelt proposes a controversial plan to add justices to an overworked Supreme Court; the plan fails largely because it is believed Roosevelt would appoint justices who would look favorably on his New Deal agenda.

In *Palko v. Connecticut*, the Supreme Court rules against applying the Fifth Amendment's protection against double jeopardy in state court proceedings.

The Supreme Court decides in *De Jonge v. Oregon* that an Oregon criminal syndicalism law is unconstitutional in being used to arrest participants of a peaceful protest.

1938

Stanley Reed is confirmed as an associate justice of the Supreme Court.

1939

In *United States v. Miller*, the Supreme Court holds that the National Firearms Act is constitutional, and that the Second Amendment protects the right of citizens to bear arms only in the context of a militia.

Felix Frankfurter is confirmed as an associate justice of the Supreme Court.

William O. Douglas is confirmed as an associate justice of the Supreme Court.

1940

The Supreme Court rules a law requiring state approval for religious advocacy as unconstitutional in *Cantwell v. Connecticut*; the Court stipulates that states may only regulate "the time, place, and manner" of religious activity, but not declare an outright ban.

In *Minersville School District v. Gobitis*, the Supreme Court rules that a school district could legally expel a student of the Jehovah's Witness faith for refusing to salute the American flag on religious grounds.

Frank Murphy is confirmed as an associate justice of the Supreme Court.

1941

Harry Byrnes is confirmed as an associate justice of the Supreme Court.

Robert Jackson is confirmed as an associate justice of the Supreme Cour.

The Empire of Japan attacks United States naval forces at Pearl Harbor, Hawaii. The United States declares war on Japan, entering World War II.

The Supreme Court declares that "fighting words" have no redeeming social value in *Chaplinsky v. New Hampshire* and are not protected by the First Amendment.

1943

The Supreme Court reverses its ruling of *Minserville School Distric v. Gobitis* in *West Virginia Board of Education v. Barnette*.

The Supreme Court decides in *McNabb v. United States* that a defendant's incriminating statements may not be used in court if the defendant was unlawfully detained.

Wiley B. Rutledge is confirmed as an associate justice of the Supreme Court.

1944

In two separate cases, *Hirabayashi v. United States* and *Korematsu v. United States*, the Supreme Court upholds the government's detainment and relocation of Japanese Americans living on the West Coast during World War II.

1945

The United States ends World War II by bombing Hiroshima and Nagasaki, Japan, after having won the European front.

1946

Fred M. Vinson is confirmed as an associate justice of the Supreme Court.

1947

In *Everson v. Board of Education*, the Supreme Court upholds a law requiring bus fare reimbursement for school children, including those attending parochial schools; the Court states that the First Amendment requires that the states neither favor nor disfavor religion.

1948

The Supreme Court prohibits states from enforcing discriminatory agreements which interfere with property transfer and ownership in *Shelly v. Kraemer*.

1949

In *Wolf v. Colorado*, the Supreme Court rules that the Fourth Amendment's protections against unlawful search and seizure are applicable to the states through the Fourteenth Amendment.

Thomas Clark is confirmed as an associate justice to the Supreme Court.

Sherman Minton is confirmed as an associate justice of the Supreme Court.

1950

The Supreme Court requires the University of Texas Law School to admit a qualified black applicant under the Equal Protection Clause of the Fourteenth Amendment in *Sweatt v. Painter*.

1951

The Twenty-second Amendment is ratified, limiting the terms a president of the United States may serve to two.

In *Dennis v. United States*, the Supreme Court upholds the constitutionality of the Smith Act, which forbade the advocacy of the overthrow of the federal government.

The United States becomes involved in the Korean War.

1952

President Truman seizes the steel mills shut down by striking workers during the Korean War, but the Supreme Court declares his actions unconstitutional; Justice Harold Burton, who was appointed by Truman, writes the majority opinion.

1953

Earl Warren is appointed and confirmed the chief justice of the Supreme Court.

1954

The Supreme Court overrules *Plessy v. Ferguson* and rejects segregation in public schools in the landmark *Brown v. Board of Education* decision.

1955

In a follow-up to the *Brown* case, the Supreme Court rules that public schools be desegregated "with all deliberate speed."

John Marshall Harlan II, the grandson of John Marshall Harlan, is confirmed an associate justice of the Supreme Court.

1956

The Supreme Court overturns a state conviction of sedition in *Pennsylvania v. Nelson*, ruling that only federal law may address an attempted overthrow of the United States government.

1957

Charles Whittaker is confirmed as an associate justice of the Supreme Court.

1958

In *NAACP v. Alabama*, the Supreme Court rules that the National Association for the Advancement of Colored People (NAACP) may continue keeping their membership lists secret in accordance with the group's right to assemble peacefully.

1959

A University of Michigan student's refusal to testify before Congress regarding his membership in the Communist Party is upheld by the Supreme Court in *Barenblatt v. United States.*

Potter Stewart is confirmed as an associate justice of the Supreme Court.

1960

The Supreme Court rules in *Gomillion v. Lightfoot* that a city may not change its borders to exclude black voters.

1961

The Twenty-third Amendment is ratified, giving residents of the District of Columbia the right to vote for president and vice president.

1962

The Supreme Court rules that a state may not compose official prayers, even if they are nondenominational, as in the case of *Engel v. Vitale.*

Arthur J. Goldberg is confirmed as an associate justice of the Supreme Court.

1964

The Twenty-fourth Amendment is ratified, prohibiting the use of a poll tax during elections.

1965

Abe Fortas is confirmed as an associate justice of the Supreme Court.

1966

The Supreme Court upholds the Voting Rights Act of 1965 in *South Carolina v. Katzenbach.*

In *Miranda v. Arizona,* the Supreme Court rules that the Fifth Amendment's self-incrimination clause invalidates confessions by suspects unless a series of steps have been taken informing suspects of their rights under the law at the time of arrest.

1967

The Twenty-fifth Amendment is ratified, providing for the succession of the vice president to the presidency should the executive be removed from office or become incapacitated.

Thurgood Marshall is appointed and confirmed an associate justice of the Supreme Court; he is the first black member of the Court.

1969

In *Tinker v. Des Moines Independent School District*, the Supreme Court rules that a junior high student may wear a black armband to school to protest the Vietnam War in accordance with the First Amendment freedom of speech clause.

Associate Justice Abe Fortas resigns from the Supreme Court due to allegations of an improper financial arrangement with a corrupt stock broker.

1971

The Twenty-sixth Amendment is ratified, reducing the legal voting age from 21 to 18.

The Supreme Court allows the publication of classified documents known as the Pentagon Papers under the First Amendment in *New York Times v. United States*.

1972

In *Wisconsin v. Yoder*, the Supreme Court throws out the conviction of a married Amish couple fined for violating compulsory school attendance laws, which abridged the free exercise of the parents' religion.

Lewis Powell is confirmed as an associate justice of the Supreme Court.

1973

The Supreme Court rules in *Roe v. Wade* that the right to privacy includes the right to an abortion in the first trimester of pregnancy.

1974

An effort to integrate urban schools with suburban schools is defeated by the Supreme Court in *Milliken v. Bradley*.

1975

John Paul Stevens is confirmed as an associate justice of the Supreme Court.

1976

Campaign expenditure limits are ruled unconstitutional and a violation of First Amendment rights by the Supreme Court in *Buckley v. Valeo*.

In *Craig v. Boren*, the Supreme Court rules that classifications based on sex are subject to stricter review than other legislative classifications under the Equal Protection Clause.

1978

The Supreme Court limits affirmative action and quota systems in admission policies by ruling that laws may not discriminate against whites in order to further minority enrollment in *Regents of the University of California v. Bakke.*

1980

In *Fullilove v. Klutznick* the Supreme Court upholds a federal funded program which set aside 10 percent of government contracts for minority-owned businesses.

1981

Sandra Day O'Connor is appointed and confirmed as an associate justice of the Supreme Court, the first woman on the Court.

1983

The Supreme Court holds in *Lynch v. Donnelly* that a nativity scene displayed on government property does not violate the Establishment Clause if other religious and non-religious symbols are displayed.

1984

The Supreme Court creates an exception to the guidelines of arresting officers in *Miranda v. Arizona* to take into account the threat of a law enforcement officer's safety when making an arrest.

1985

In *Wallace v. Jaffree,* the Supreme Court rules that silent meditation in a public place is for the purpose of prayer.

In *Aguilar v. Felton,* the Supreme Court forbids public school teachers from teaching special education courses to parochial school students at parochial schools.

1986

Associate Justice William Rehnquist, who had served on the Court since 1972, is confirmed chief justice of the Supreme Court.

Antonin Scalia is confirmed as an associate justice of the Supreme Court.

1988

Anthony Kennedy is confirmed as an associate justice of the Supreme Court.

1989

The Supreme Court decides in *Webster v. Reproductive Health Services* that certain restrictions on abortions within the framework of *Roe v. Wade* are permitted.

1990

The Supreme Court rejects a defense from two Native Americans fired from their jobs for the use of the drug peyote in *Employment Division v. Smith*. The two Native Americans claimed they used the drug for religious purposes.

David Souter is confirmed as an associate justice of the Supreme Court.

1991

Clarence Thomas is confirmed by a 52-48 vote as an associate justice of the Supreme Court following contentious Senate hearings during which Thomas was accused of sexual harassment by a former associate; Thomas is the second African American justice of the Supreme Court.

1992

The Twenty-seventh Amendment is ratified, mandating an intervening election before congressional pay raises may take effect.

1993

The Supreme Court rules in *Shaw v. Reno* that congressional districts drawn by state legislatures in abnormal ways and only explainable on racial reasoning are unconstitutional.

1994

Random drug tests given to student athletes are upheld by the Supreme Court.

1997

The Supreme Court rules that the Religious Freedom Restoration Act of 1993 is unconstitutional; Congress attemped to outline various forms of permitted and acceptable public religious practices.

1998

In *Knowles v. Iowa*, the Supreme Court holds that a police officer is prohibited from searching a motorist's vehicle when the driver was merely stopped for a traffic violation.

1999

Chief Justice William Rehnquist presides over the impeachment trial of President William Jefferson Clinton; the president is acquitted by the Senate.

In *Cedar Rapids Community School District v. Garret F.*, the Supreme Court rules that state must provide medical assistance necessary for disabled youngsters to attend class under the Individuals with Disabilities Education Act.

In *Chicago v. Morales*, the Supreme Court rules that a gang loitering ordinance is a violation of the Due Process Clause of the Fourteenth Amendment and gives police too much discretion in law enforcement.

2000

The Supreme Court agrees to hear a suit brought in relation to the disputed presidential election in Florida, *Bush v. Palm Beach County Board of Canvassing*; in an unsigned opinion, the Court vacated the decision of the Florida Supreme Court to extend the deadline for the election certification, holding the Florida court overstepped its boundaries.

The Florida Supreme Court decides 4–3 to allow particular Florida counties to begin recounting ballots in the presidential election there. On appeal, the United States Supreme Court issues a stay of the recount and, by a 5–4 decision, rules that the Florida court's opinion and order was unconstitutional, and that the recounting cease. As the vote stood, Governor George W. Bush won the state of Florida, which gave him the necessary 270 Electoral College votes to win the presidency of the United States.

The College of William and Mary Law School dedicates a statue of Chief Justice John Marshall to honor its most distinguished alumnus. The statue is crafted by Gordon Kray.

 # Article Sources

The following authors contributed the new articles for **Macmillan Profiles:** *Justices of the United States Supreme Court:*

Mary Carvlin
Jill Hamilton
William Kaufman
Mike O'Neal
Jeff Turner

Photo Credits

Photographs appearing in *Justices of the United States Supreme Court* are from the following sources:

Baldwin, Henry (page 1): Corbis
Black, Hugo (page 7): Library of Congress
Blackmun, Harry (page 12): Archive Photos
Blair, John (page 17): Corbis
Bradley, Joseph (page 22): Archive Photos
Brandeis, Louis (page 25): Library of Congress
Brennan, William (page 29): Supreme Court Historical Society
Breyer, Steven (page 35): Archive Photos
Brown, Henry B. (page 40): Granger Collection
Burger, Warren (page 43): Library of Congress
Burton, Harold (page 48): Corbis
Byrnes, James (page 53): Archive Photos
Campbell John A. (page 57) Granger Collection
Cardozo, Benjamin (page 60): Corbis
Catron, John (page 64): Granger Collection
Chase, Salmon P. (page 67): Library of Congress
Chase, Samuel (page 71): Public Domain
Clark, Tom C. (page 75): Supreme Court Historical Society
Clarke, John H. (page 78): AP/Wide World Photos
Clifford, Nathan (page 81): Corbis
Curtis, Benjamin (page 83): Archive Photos
Cushing, William (page 86): Granger Collection
Daniel, Peter (page 89): Corbis
Davis, David (page 92): Granger Collection
Day, William (page 95): Granger Collection

Douglas, Willam (page 98): Archive Photos
Duvall, Gabriel (page 101): Granger Collection
Ellsworth, Oliver (page 105): Granger Collection
Field, Stephen (page 109): Library of Congress
Fortas, Abe (page 112): Archive Photos
Frankfurter, Felix (page 116): Supreme Court of the United States
Fuller, Melville (page 119): Corbis
Ginsburg, Ruth Bader (page 123): Corbis
Goldberg, Arthur (page 128): Library of Congress
Gray, Horace (page 131): Archive Photos
Grier, Robert C. (page 133): Granger Collection
Harlan, John Marshall (page 137): Public Domain
Holmes, Oliver Wendell Jr. (page 143): Library of Congress
Hughes, Charles Evans (page 147): Supreme Court of the United States
Iredell, James (page 153): Corbis
Jackson, Robert H. (page 160): Library of Congress
Jay, John (page 163): Library of Congress
Johnson, Thomas (page 166): Granger Collection
Kennedy, Anthony (page 171): Archive Photos
Lamar, Joseph R. (no photo): Supreme Court Historical Society
Lamar, Lucius Q.C. (page 178): Library of Congress
Livingston, Henry Brockholst (page 180): Corbis
Lurton, Horace (page 182): Corbis
Marshall, John (page 185): National Portrait Gallery
Marshall, Thurgood (page 190): Library of Congress
Matthews, Stanley (page 195): Granger Collection
McKinley, John (page 199): Archive Photos
McLean, John (page 201): Archive Photos
McReynolds, James (page 204): Corbis
Miller, Samuel (page 207): Corbis
Minton, Sherman (page 210): Corbis
Moody, William (page 213): Corbis
Moore, Alfred (no photo): Supreme Court Historical Society
Murphy, Frank (page 218): Library of Congress
O'Connor, Sandra Day (page 225): Corbis
Paterson, William (page 231): Library of Congress
Peckham, Rufus (page 234): Corbis
Pitney, Mahlon (page 237): Corbis
Powell, Lewis F. (page 240): Archive Photos
Reed, Stanley (page 245): Corbis
Rehnquist, William H. (page 248): Supreme Court of the United States
Roberts, Owen (page 253): Supreme Court of the United States
Rutledge, John (page 256): Library of Congress

Rutledge, Wiley (page 259): Corbis
Sanford, Edward (page 263): Supreme Court of the United States
Scalia, Antonin (page 266): Archive Photos
Souter, David (page 274): Supreme Court Historical Society
Stevens, John Paul (page 278): Archive Photos
Stewart, Potter (page 282): Public Domain
Stone, Harlan Fiske (page 286): Library of Congress
Story, Joseph (page 289): Library of Congress
Strong, William (page 292): Granger Collection
Swayne, Noah (page 298): Archive Photos
Taft, William Howard (page 301): Library of Congress
Taney, Roger B. (page 306): Corbis
Thomas, Clarence (page 310): AP/Wide World Photos
Thompson, Smith (page 315): Corbis
Todd, Thomas (page 317): Granger Collection
Trimble, Robert (page 320): Granger Collection
Van Devanter, Willis (page 323): Corbis
Waite, Morrison R. (page 331): Archive Photos
Warren, Earl (page 335): Library of Congress
Washington, Bushrod (page 340): Granger Collection
Wayne, James (page 343): Archive Photos
White, Byron R. (page 346): Library of Congress
White, Edward D. (page 350): Corbis
Whittaker, Charles E. (page 354): AP/Wide World Photos
Wilson, James (page 357): Archive Photos
Woodbury, Levi (page 360): Archive Photos
Woods, William B. (page 362): Granger Collection

Additional Resources

GENERAL SOURCES

BOOKS

Aaseng, Nathan. *You Are the Supreme Court Justice*. Oliver Press, 1994.

Barrett, Paul, et. al. *A Year in the Life of the Supreme Court*. Duke University Press, 1995.

Blandford, Linda A, and Evans, Patricia, eds. *Supreme Court of the United States 1789-1980: An Index to Opinions Arranged by Justice*. Kraus Publications, 1983.

Bladford Linda A. *Supreme Court of the United States 1789-1980: An Index to Opinions Arranged by Justice: First Supplement, 1981-1991*.

Champion, Dean J. *Dictionary of American Criminal Justice: Key Terms and Major Supreme Court Cases*. Fitzroy Dearborn Publishers, 1998.

Cushman, Claire, ed. *The Supreme Court Justices: Illustrated Biographies, 1789-1995*. Congressional Quarterly, 1995.

Estreicher, Samuel, and John Sexton. *Redefining the Supreme Court's Role: A Theory of Managing the Federal Judicial Process*. Yale University Press, 1986.

Galloway, Russell W. *Justice for All?: The Rich and Poor in Supreme Court History, 1790-1990*. Carolina Academic Press, 1991.

Hall, Kermit, ed. *The Least Dangerous Branch: The Supreme Court and the Separation of Powers (Equal Justice Under Law, Vol. 3)*. Carlson Publications, 1997.

Hall, Kermit, ed.. *Liberty and Justice for All: The Supreme Court and Freedom and Equality (Equal Justice Under Law, Vol. 6)*. Carlson Publications, 1997.

Hall, Kermit, ed. *A Nation of States: Federalism at the Bar of the Supreme Court (Equal Justice Under Law, Vol. 4)*. Carlson Publications, 1997.

Hall, Kermit, ed. *The Path to the Supreme Court: Nomination, Confirmation and Appointment (Equal Justice Under Law, Vol. 7)*. Carlson Publications, 1997.

Hall, Kermit, ed. *Private Profit and Public Interest: The Supreme Court and the Economy (Equal Justice Under Law, Vol. 5)* Carlson Publications, 1996.

Hall, Kermit, ed. *The Rights of the Accused: The Justices and Criminal Justice (Supreme Court in American Society, Vol 10).* Garland Publishers, 2000.

Hall, Kermit, ed. *The Supreme Court in American Society Reader: Equal Justice Under Law.* Garland Publishing, 2001.

Harrell, Mary Ann. *Equal Justice Under the Law: The Supreme Court in American Life.* Foundation of the Federal Bar Associations, 1975.

Harrison, Maureen. *Criminal Justice Decisions of the Supreme Court.* Excellent Books, 2002.

Kairys, David. *With Liberty and Justice for Some: A Critique of the Conservative Supreme Court.* New Press, 1993.

Martin, F.S., and R.U. Goehlert. *How to Research the Supreme Court.* Congressional Quarterly, 1992.

Manfredi, Christopher P. *The Supreme Court and Juvenile Justice.* Kansas University Press, 1998.

Maroon, Suzy. *The Supreme Court of the United States.* Licke Publishing, 1996.

Schwartz, Bernard. *Decision: How the Supreme Court Decides Cases.* Oxford University Press, 1996.

Schwartz, Bernard. *A History of the Supreme Court.* Oxford University Press, 1993.

Shnayerson, Robert. *The Illustrated History of the Supreme Court of the United States.* Harry N. Abrams, 1986.

State of the Judiciary: Annual Reports of the Chief Justice of the United States. William S. Hein, 2000.

The Supreme Court of the United States: Its Beginnings and Its Justices 1790-1991. U.S. Commission on the Bicentennial of the United States Constitution, 1992.

Urofsky, M.I. ed. *The Supreme Court Justices: A Biographical Dictionary.* Garland Publishing, 1994.

VIDEORECORDINGS

Best of Nightline - Judge O'Connor Nominated for Supreme Court (1981), MPI Home Video.

Interpreting the Law: The Role of the Supreme Court, 1990.

The Presidency and The Constitution: The Making of A Justice, PBS Video, 1987.

Search and Seizure: The Supreme Court and the Police, Film Odyssey, Inc., 1992.

The Supreme Court of the United States, Supreme Court Historical Society,

The Supreme Court's Holy Battles, PBS Video, 1989.

This Honorable Court, WETA/PBS, 1988.

WEBSITES

Annotated Bibliography on the Supreme Court and Constitutional Politics, http://ps.ucdavis.edu/classes/pol150/annote.htm

Federal Judges Biographical Database, http://air.fjc.gov/history/jabout_frm.html

Findlaw Constitutional Law Center: Supreme Court Justices, http://conlaw.usatoday.findlaw.com/supreme_court/justices/

Legal Information Institute: Historic Supreme Court Decisions - by Justice, http://supct.law.cornell.edu/supct/cases/judges.htm

Legal Information Institute: Justices of the Supreme Court, http://www2.law .cornell.edu/cgi-bin/foliocgi.exe/Justices/query=?realquerydlg

Members of the Supreme Court of the United States, http://www.infoplease.com/ipa/A0101281.html

The Oyez Project, http://oyez.northwestern.edu/

Supreme Court Historical Society, http://www.supremecourthistory.org/myweb/ justice/breyer.htm

Supreme Court of the United States, http://www.supremecourtus.gov/

JUSTICES

BALDWIN, HENRY

Legal Information Institute: Biographies of the Justicies—Henry Baldwin, http://www2.law.cornell.edu/cgi-bin/foliocgi.exe/justices/query=*/doc/{t70}

The Oyez Project—Henry Baldwin, http://oyez.northwestern.edu/justices/justices.cgi?justice_id=22

Henry Baldwin in *The Supreme Court of the United States: Its Beginnings and Its Justices 1790-1991*, pp. 94-95. U.S. Commission on the Bicentennial of the United States Constitution, 1992.

BARBOUR, PHILIP P.

Legal Information Institute: Biographies of the Justicies—Philip P. Barbour, http://www2.law.cornell.edu/cgi-bin/foliocgi.exe/justices/query=*/doc/{t74}

The Oyez Project—Philip P. Barbour, http://oyez.northwestern.edu/justices/justices.cgi?justice_id=25

Philip P. Barbour in *The Supreme Court of the United States: Its Beginnings and Its Justices 1790-1991*, pp. 98-99. U.S. Commission on the Bicentennial of the United States Constitution, 1992.

BLACK, HUGO L.

Black, Hugo L. *Mr. Justice and Mrs. Black :The Memoirs of Hugo L. Black and Elizabeth Black*. Random House, 1986.

Freyer, Tony, ed. *Justice Hugo Black and Modern America*. University of Alabama Press, 1990.

Legal Information Institute: Biographies of the Justicies—Hugo Black, http://www2.law.cornell.edu/cgi-bin/foliocgi.exe/justices/query=*/doc/{t162}

Newman, Roger. *Hugo Black: A Biography.* Pantheon Books, 1997.

The Oyez Project—Hugo L. Black, http://oyez.northwestern.edu/justices/justices.cgi?justice_id=76

Silverstein, Mark. *Constitutional Faiths: Felix Frankfurter, Hugo Black, and the Process of Judicial Decision Making.* Cornell University Press, 1984.

Hugo L. Black in *The Supreme Court of the United States: Its Beginnings and Its Justices 1790-1991,* pp. 186-187. U.S. Commission on the Bicentennial of the United States Constitution, 1992.

BLACKMUN, HARRY A.

Legal Information Institute: Biographies of the Justicies—Harry A. Blackmun, http://www2.law.cornell.edu/cgi-bin/foliocgi.exe/justices/query=*/doc/{t200}

The Oyez Project—Harry A. Blackmun, http://oyez.northwestern.edu/justices/justices.cgi?justice_id=98

Harry A. Blackmun in *The Supreme Court of the United States: Its Beginnings and Its Justices 1790-1991,* pp.224-225. U.S. Commission on the Bicentennial of the United States Constitution, 1992.

BLAIR, JOHN

Legal Information Institute: Biographies of the Justicies—John Blair, http://www2.law.cornell.edu/cgi-bin/foliocgi.exe/justices/query=*/doc/{t40}

The Oyez Project—John Blair, http://oyez.northwestern.edu/justices/justices.cgi?justice_id=5

John Blair in *The Supreme Court of the United States: Its Beginnings and Its Justices 1790-1991,* pp. 64-65. U.S. Commission on the Bicentennial of the United States Constitution, 1992.

BLATCHFORD, SAMUEL

Legal Information Institute: Biographies of the Justicies—Samuel Blatchford, http://www2.law.cornell.edu/cgi-bin/foliocgi.exe/justices/query=*/doc/{t116}

The Oyez Project—Samuel Blatchford, http://oyez.northwestern.edu/justices/justices.cgi?justice_id=48

Samuel Blatchford in *The Supreme Court of the United States: Its Beginnings and Its Justices 1790-1991,* pp. 140-141. U.S. Commission on the Bicentennial of the United States Constitution, 1992.

BRADLEY, JOSEPH P.

Bradley, Joseph P. *Miscellaneous Writings of the Late Hon. Joseph P. Bradley, Associate Justice of the Supreme Court of the United States.* F.B. Rothman, 1986.

Legal Information Institute: Biographies of the Justicies—Joseph P. Bradley, http://www2.law.cornell.edu/cgi-bin/foliocgi.exe/justices/query=*/doc/{t104}

The Oyez Project—Joseph P. Bradley,
http://oyez.northwestern.edu/justices/justices.cgi?justice_id=41

Joseph P. Bradley in *The Supreme Court of the United States: Its Beginnings and Its Justices 1790-1991*, pp. 128-129. U.S. Commission on the Bicentennial of the United States Constitution, 1992.

BRANDEIS, LOUIS D.

Freedman, Suzanne. *Louis Brandeis: The People's Justice*. Enslow Publishers, 1996 [young adult].

Legal Information Institute: Biographies of the Justicies—Louis D. Brandeis,
http://www2.law.cornell.edu/cgi-bin/foliocgi.exe/justices/query=*/doc/{t148}

Murphy, Bruce Allen. *The Brandeis/Frankfurter Connection: The Secret Political Activities of Two Supreme Court Justices*. Oxford University Press, 1982.

The Oyez Project—Louis D. Brandeis,
http://oyez.northwestern.edu/justices/justices.cgi?justice_id=67

Strum, Philippa. *Louis D. Brandeis: Justice for the People*. Harvard University Press, 1984.

Louis D. Brandeis in *The Supreme Court of the United States: Its Beginnings and Its Justices 1790-1991*, pp. 172-173. U.S. Commission on the Bicentennial of the United States Constitution, 1992.

Teitelbaum, Gene. *Justice Louis D. Brandeis: A Bibliography of Writings and Other Materials on the Justice*. Fred B. Rothman & Co., 1988.

BRENNAN, WILLIAM J., JR.

Clark, Hunter R. *Justice Brennan : The Great Conciliator*. Birch Lane Press, 1995.

Grodin, Joseph R., and William J. Brennan. *In Pursuit of Justice: Reflections of a State Supreme Court Justice*. University of California Press, 1989.

Legal Information Institute: Biographies of the Justicies—William J. Brennan, Jr.,
http://www2.law.cornell.edu/cgi-bin/foliocgi.exe/justices/query=*/doc/{t186}

Marion, David E. *The Jurisprudence of Justice William J. Brennan, Jr : The Law and Politics of 'Libertarian Dignity.'* Rowman & Littlefield, 1997.

Mr. Justice Brennan, PBS Video, 1996.

The Oyez Project—William J. Brennan, Jr.,
http://oyez.northwestern.edu/justices/justices.cgi?justice_id=90

Rosenkranz, E. Joshua, and Bernard Schwartz, eds. *Reason and Passion: Justice Brennan's Enduring Influence*. W.W. Norton, 1997.

William J. Brennan, Jr. in *The Supreme Court of the United States: Its Beginnings and Its Justices 1790-1991*, pp. 210-211. U.S. Commission on the Bicentennial of the United States Constitution, 1992.

BREWER, DAVID J.

Brodhead, Michael J. *David J. Brewer: The Life of a Supreme Court Justice 1837-1910*. Southern Illinois University Press, 1994.

Legal Information Institute: Biographies of the Justices—David J. Brewer, http://www2.law.cornell.edu/cgi-bin/foliocgi.exe/justices/query=*/doc/{t120}

The Oyez Project—David J. Brewer, http://oyez.northwestern.edu/justices/justices.cgi?justice_id=51

David J. Brewer in *The Supreme Court of the United States: Its Beginnings and Its Justices 1790-1991*, pp. 144-145. U.S. Commission on the Bicentennial of the United States Constitution, 1992.

BREYER, STEPHEN G.

Breyer, Stephen G. *Supreme Court of the U.S. Hearings and Reports on Successful and Unsuccessful Nominations of Supreme Court Justices by the Judiciary*. William S. Hein & Co., 1996.

Breyer, Stephen G. et. al. *Administrative Law and Regulatory Policy: Problems, Text, and Cases*. Aspen Publications, 1998.

Legal Information Institute: Biographies of the Justices—Stephen Breyer, http://www2.law.cornell.edu/cgi-bin/foliocgi.exe/justices/query=*/doc/{t216}

The Oyez Project—Stephen G. Breyer, http://oyez.northwestern.edu/justices/justices.cgi?justice_id=108

Supreme Court Historical Society—Steven G. Breyer, http://www.supremecourthistory.org/myweb/justice/breyer.htm

BROWN, HENRY B.

Legal Information Institute: Biographies of the Justices—Henry B. Brown, http://www2.law.cornell.edu/cgi-bin/foliocgi.exe/justices/query=*/doc/{t122}

The Oyez Project—Henry B. Brown, http://oyez.northwestern.edu/justices/justices.cgi?justice_id=52

Henry B. Brown in *The Supreme Court of the United States: Its Beginnings and Its Justices 1790-1991*, pp. 146-147. U.S. Commission on the Bicentennial of the United States Constitution, 1992.

BURGER, WARREN E.

Biasi, Vincent, ed. *The Burger Court: The Counter-Revolution that Wasn't*. Yale University Press, 1983.

Galloway, John, ed. *Criminal Justice and the Burger Court*. Facts on File, 1978.

Legal Information Institute: Biographies of the Justices—Warren E. Burger, http://www2.law.cornell.edu/cgi-bin/foliocgi.exe/justices/query=*/doc/{t31}

Maltz, Earl M. *The Chief Justiceship of Warren Burger, 1969-1986*. University of South Carolina Press, 2000.

The Oyez Project—Warren E. Burger, http://oyez.northwestern.edu/justices/justices.cgi?justice_id=97

Schwarz, Herman, ed. *The Burger Years: Rights and Wrongs in the Supreme Court, 1969-1986*. Penguin Books, 1988.

Warren E. Burger in *The Supreme Court of the United States: Its Beginnings and Its Justices 1790-1991*, pp. 54-55. U.S. Commission on the Bicentennial of the United States Constitution, 1992.

BURTON, HAROLD H.

Berry, Mary Frances. *Stability, Security, and Continuity: Mr. Justice Burton and Decision-Making in the Supreme Court, 1945-1958*. Greenwood Press, 1978.

Legal Information Institute: Biographies of the Justicies—Harold H. Burton http://www2.law.cornell.edu/cgi-bin/foliocgi.exe/justices/query=*/doc/{t178}

The Oyez Project—Harold Burton, http://oyez.northwestern.edu/justices/justices.cgi?justice_id=84

Harold H. Burton in *The Supreme Court of the United States: Its Beginnings and Its Justices 1790-1991*, pp. 202-203. U.S. Commission on the Bicentennial of the United States Constitution, 1992.

BUTLER, PIERCE

Brown, Francis Joseph. *The Social and Economic Philosophy of Pierce Butler*. Catholic University of America, 1945.

Danelski, David J. *A Supreme Court Justice is Appointed*. Greenwood Press, 1980 [first published 1964].

Legal Information Institute: Biographies of the Justicies—Pierce Butler, http://www2.law.cornell.edu/cgi-bin/foliocgi.exe/justices/query=*/doc/{t154}

The Oyez Project—Pierce Butler, http://oyez.northwestern.edu/justices/justices.cgi?justice_id=71

Pierce Butler in *The Supreme Court of the United States: Its Beginnings and Its Justices 1790-1991*, pp. 178-179. U.S. Commission on the Bicentennial of the United States Constitution, 1992.

BYRNES, JAMES F.

Legal Information Institute: Biographies of the Justicies—James F. Byrnes, http://www2.law.cornell.edu/cgi-bin/foliocgi.exe/justices/query=*/doc/{t172}

The Oyez Project—James F. Byrnes, http://oyez.northwestern.edu/justices/justices.cgi?justice_id=81

Robertson, David. *Sly and Able: A Political Biography of James F. Byrnes*. W.W. Norton, 1994.

James F. Byrnes in *The Supreme Court of the United States: Its Beginnings and Its Justices 1790-1991*, pp. 196-197. U.S. Commission on the Bicentennial of the United States Constitution, 1992.

Ward, Patricia Dawson. *The Threat of Peace: James F. Byrnes and the Council of Foreign Ministers, 1945-1946*. Kent State University Press, 1976.

CAMPBELL, JOHN A.

Connor, Henry G. *John Archibald Campbell, Associate Justice of the United States Supreme Court, 1853-1861.* Da Capo Press, 1971 [first published 1920].

Legal Information Institute: Biographies of the Justicies—John A. Campbell, http://www2.law.cornell.edu/cgi-bin/foliocgi.exe/justices/query=*/doc/{t90}

The Oyez Project—John A. Campbell, http://oyez.northwestern.edu/justices/justices.cgi?justice_id=33

Saunders, Robert, Jr. *John Archibald Campbell, Southern Moderate, 1811-1889.* University of Alabama Press, 1997.

John A. Campbell in *The Supreme Court of the United States: Its Beginnings and Its Justices 1790-1991*, pp. 114-115. U.S. Commission on the Bicentennial of the United States Constitution, 1992.

CARDOZO, BENJAMIN NATHAN

Kaufman, Andrew L. *Cardozo.* Harvard University Press, 1998.

Legal Information Institute: Biographies of the Justicies—Benjamin Nathan Cardozo, http://www2.law.cornell.edu/cgi-bin/foliocgi.exe/justices/query=*/doc/{t160}

Levy, Beryl Harold. *Cardozo and Frontiers of Legal Thinking, with Selected Opinions.* Press of Case Western Reserve University, 1969.

The Oyez Project—Benjamin N. Cardozo, http://oyez.northwestern.edu/justices/justices.cgi?justice_id=75

Pollard, Joseph P. *Mr. Justice Cardozo: A Liberal Mind in Action.* W. S. Hein, 1995.

Posner, Richard A. *Cardozo: A Study in Reputation.* University of Chicago Press, 1990.

Benjamin Nathan Cardozo in *The Supreme Court of the United States: Its Beginnings and Its Justices 1790-1991*, pp. 184-185. U.S. Commission on the Bicentennial of the United States Constitution, 1992.

CATRON, JOHN

Chandler, Walter. *The Centenary of Associate Justice John Catron of the United States Supreme Court: Address of Walter Chandler at the Fifty-Sixth Annual Session of the Bar Association of Tennessee at Memphis, Friday, June 11, 1937, with bibliographical notes.*

The Centenary of Associate Justice John Catron of the United States Supreme Court: Address of Walter Chandler at the Fifty-Sixth Annual Session of the Bar Association of Tennessee at Memphis, Friday, June 11, 1937, with bibliographical notes. S. C. Toof & Co., 1937.

Legal Information Institute: Biographies of the Justicies—John Catron, http://www2.law.cornell.edu/cgi-bin/foliocgi.exe/justices/query=*/doc/{t76}

The Oyez Project—John Catron, http://oyez.northwestern.edu/justices/justices.cgi?justice_id=26

John Catron in *The Supreme Court of the United States: Its Beginnings and Its Justices 1790-1991*, pp. 100-101. U.S. Commission on the Bicentennial of the United States Constitution, 1992.

CHASE, SALMON PORTLAND

Blue, Frederick J. *Salmon P. Chase: A Life in Politics*. Kent State University Press, 1987.

Chase, Salmon Portland. *Diary and Correspondence of Salmon P. Chase*. Da Capo Press, 1971 [first published 1899].

Legal Information Institute: Biographies of the Justicies—Salmon Portland Chase, http://www2.law.cornell.edu/cgi-bin/foliocgi.exe/justices/query=*/doc/{t13}

Niven, John. *Salmon P. Chase: A Biography*. Oxford University Press, 1995.

The Oyez Project—Salmon P. Chase, http://oyez.northwestern.edu/justices/justices.cgi?justice_id=39

Salmon Portland Chase in *The Supreme Court of the United States: Its Beginnings and Its Justices 1790-1991*, pp. 36-37. U.S. Commission on the Bicentennial of the United States Constitution, 1992.

CHASE, SAMUEL

Chase, Samuel. *Report of the trial of the Hon. Samuel Chase, one of the associate justices of the Supreme court of the United States, before the High court of impeachment, composed of the Senate of the United States, for charges exhibited against him by the House of representatives, in the name of themselves, and of all the people of the Unites States, for high crimes & misdemeanors, supposed to have been by him committed; with the necessary documents and official papers, from his impeachment to final acquittal. Taken in short hand, by Charles Evans, and the arguments of counsel revised by them from his manuscript.* Augmented edition. Printed for Samuel Butler and George Keatinge, 1805.

Elsmere, Jane Schaffer. *Justice Samuel Chase*. Janevar Publishing Co., 1980.

Haw, James, et. al. *Stormy Patriot: The Life of Samuel Chase*. Maryland Historical Society, 1980.

Legal Information Institute: Biographies of the Justicies—Samuel Chase, http://www2.law.cornell.edu/cgi-bin/foliocgi.exe/justices/query=*/doc/{t48}

The Oyez Project—Samuel Chase, http://oyez.northwestern.edu/justices/justices.cgi?justice_id=9

Samuel Chase in *The Supreme Court of the United States: Its Beginnings and Its Justices 1790-1991*, pp. 72-73. U.S. Commission on the Bicentennial of the United States Constitution, 1992.

CLARK, TOM C.

Larrimer, Don. *Biobibliography of Justice Tom C. Clark*. University of Texas at Austin, 1985.

Legal Information Institute: Biographies of the Justicies—Tom C. Clark, http://www2.law.cornell.edu/cgi-bin/foliocgi.exe/justices/query=*/doc/{t180}

The Oyez Project—Tom C. Clark, http://oyez.northwestern.edu/justices/justices.cgi?justice_id=86

Tom C. Clark in *The Supreme Court of the United States: Its Beginnings and Its Justices 1790-1991*, pp. 204-205. U.S. Commission on the Bicentennial of the United States Constitution, 1992.

Young, Evan A. *Lone Star Justice: A Biography of Justice Tom C. Clark*. Hendrick-Long Publishing, 1998 [young adult].

CLARKE, JOHN H.

Legal Information Institute: Biographies of the Justicies—John H. Clarke, http://www2.law.cornell.edu/cgi-bin/foliocgi.exe/justices/query=*/doc/{t150}

The Oyez Project—John H. Clarke, http://oyez.northwestern.edu/justices/justices.cgi?justice_id=68

John H. Clarke in *The Supreme Court of the United States: Its Beginnings and Its Justices 1790-1991*, pp. 174-175. U.S. Commission on the Bicentennial of the United States Constitution, 1992.

Warner, Hoyt Landon. *The Life of Mr. Justice Clarke; A Testament to the Power of Liberal Dissent in America*. Western Reserve University Press, 1959.

CLIFFORD, NATHAN

Clifford, Philip Greely. *Nathan Clifford, Democrat*. G.P. Putnam's Sons, 1922.

Legal Information Institute: Biographies of the Justicies—Nathan Clifford, http://www2.law.cornell.edu/cgi-bin/foliocgi.exe/justices/query=*/doc/{t92}

The Oyez Project—Nathan Clifford, http://oyez.northwestern.edu/justices/justices.cgi?justice_id=34

Nathan Clifford in *The Supreme Court of the United States: Its Beginnings and Its Justices 1790-1991*, pp. 116-117. U.S. Commission on the Bicentennial of the United States Constitution, 1992.

CURTIS, BENJAMIN R.

Curtis, Benjamin Robbins, Jr., ed. *A Memoir of Benjamin Robbins Curtis; With Some of his Professional and Miscellaneous Writings*. Da Capo Press, 1970 [first published 1879].

Legal Information Institute: Biographies of the Justicies—Benjamin R. Curtis, http://www2.law.cornell.edu/cgi-bin/foliocgi.exe/justices/query=*/doc/{t88}

The Oyez Project—Benjamin R. Curtis, http://oyez.northwestern.edu/justices/justices.cgi?justice_id=32

Curtis R. Benjamin in *The Supreme Court of the United States: Its Beginnings and Its Justices 1790-1991*, pp. 112-113. U.S. Commission on the Bicentennial of the United States Constitution, 1992.

CUSHING, WILLIAM

Legal Information Institute: Biographies of the Justicies—William Cushing, http://www2.law.cornell.edu/cgi-bin/foliocgi.exe/justices/query=*/doc/{t38}

The Oyez Project—William Cushing, http://oyez.northwestern.edu/justices/justices.cgi?justice_id=3

Rugg, Arthur Prentice. *William Cushing*. Yale Law Journal Co., Inc., 1920.

William Cushing in *The Supreme Court of the United States: Its Beginnings and Its Justices 1790-1991*, pp. 62-63. U.S. Commission on the Bicentennial of the United States Constitution, 1992.

DANIEL, PETER V.

Frank, John Paul. *Justice Daniel Dissenting: A Biography of Peter V. Daniel, 1784-1860*. Harvard University Press, 1964.

Legal Information Institute: Biographies of the Justicies—Peter V. Daniel, http://www2.law.cornell.edu/cgi-bin/foliocgi.exe/justices/query=*/doc/{t80}

The Oyez Project—Peter V. Daniel, http://oyez.northwestern.edu/justices/justices.cgi?justice_id=28

Peter V. Daniel in *The Supreme Court of the United States: Its Beginnings and Its Justices 1790-1991*, pp. 104-105. U.S. Commission on the Bicentennial of the United States Constitution, 1992.

DAVIS, DAVID

King, Willard L. *Lincoln's Manager, David Davis*. Harvard University Press, 1960.

Legal Information Institute: Biographies of the Justicies—David Davis, http://www2.law.cornell.edu/cgi-bin/foliocgi.exe/justices/query=*/doc/{t98}

The Oyez Project—David Davis, http://oyez.northwestern.edu/justices/justices.cgi?justice_id=37

Pratt, Harry Edward. *David Davis, 1815-1886*. Journal Printing Co., 1931

David Davis in *The Supreme Court of the United States: Its Beginnings and Its Justices 1790-1991*, pp. 122-123. U.S. Commission on the Bicentennial of the United States Constitution, 1992.

DAY, WILLIAM R.

Legal Information Institute: Biographies of the Justicies—William R. Day, http://www2.law.cornell.edu/cgi-bin/foliocgi.exe/justices/query=*/doc/{t134}

McLean, Joseph E. *William Rufus Day: Supreme Court Justice from Ohio*. John Hopkins Press, 1947.

The Oyez Project—William R. Day, http://oyez.northwestern.edu/justices/justices.cgi?justice_id=59

William R. Day in *The Supreme Court of the United States: Its Beginnings and Its Justices 1790-1991*, pp. 158-159. U.S. Commission on the Bicentennial of the United States Constitution, 1992.

DOUGLAS, WILLIAM O.

Douglas, William O. *West of the Indies*. Doubleday, 1958.

Legal Information Institute: Biographies of the Justicies—William O. Douglas, http://www2.law.cornell.edu/cgi-bin/foliocgi.exe/justices/query=*/doc/{t168}

O'Fallon, James, ed. *Nature's Justice: Writings of William O. Douglas.* Oregon State University Press, 2000.

The Oyez Project—William O. Douglas, http://oyez.northwestern.edu/justices/ justices.cgi?justice_id=79

Simon, James F. *Independent Journey: The Life of William O. Douglas.* Penguin Books, 1981.

William O. Douglas in *The Supreme Court of the United States: Its Beginnings and Its Justices 1790-1991,* pp. 192-193. U.S. Commission on the Bicentennial of the United States Constitution, 1992.

Wasby, Steven L., Ed. *"He Shall Not Pass This Way Again": The Legacy of Justice William O. Douglass.* University of Pittsburgh Press, 1990.

DUVALL, GABRIEL

Legal Information Institute: Biographies of the Justicies—Gabriel Duvall, http://www2.law.cornell.edu/cgi-bin/foliocgi.exe/justices/query=*/doc/{t60}

The Oyez Proejct—Gabriel Duvall, http://oyez.northwestern.edu/justices/justices.cgi?justice_id=17

Gabriel Duvall in *The Supreme Court of the United States: Its Beginnings and Its Justices 1790-1991,* pp. 84-85. U.S. Commission on the Bicentennial of the United States Constitution, 1992.

ELLSWORTH, OLIVER

Casto, William R. *Oliver Ellsworth and the Creation of the Federal Republic.* Second Circuit Committee on History and Commemorative Events, 1997.

Casto, William R. *The Supreme Court in the Early Republic: The Chief Justiceships of John Jay and Oliver Ellsworth.* University of South Carolina Press, 1995.

Legal Information Institute: Biographies of the Justicies—Olliver Ellsworth, http://www2.law.cornell.edu/cgi-bin/foliocgi.exe/justices/query=*/doc/{t7}

Lettieri, Ronald John. *Connecticut's Young Man of the Revolution, Oliver Ellsworth.* American Revolution Bicentennial Commission of Connecticut, 1978.

The Oyez Project—Oliver Ellsworth, http://oyez.northwestern.edu/justices/justices.cgi?justice_id=10

Oliver Ellsworth in *The Supreme Court of the United States: Its Beginnings and Its Justices 1790-1991,* pp. 30-31. U.S. Commission on the Bicentennial of the United States Constitution, 1992.

FIELD, STEPHEN J

Field, Stephen J., and George C. Gorham. *Personal Reminiscences of Early Days in California: With Other Sketches / by Stephen J. Field. To Which is Added the Story of the Attempted Assassination of Justice Field by a Former Associate on the Supreme Bench of California / by George C Gorham.* Lawbook Exchange, 2001.

Kens, Paul. *Justice Stephen Field: Shaping Liberty from the Gold Rush to the Gilded Age.* University Press of Kansas, 1997.

Legal Information Institute: Biographies of the Justicies—Stephen J. Field, http://www2.law.cornell.edu/cgi-bin/foliocgi.exe/justices/query=*/doc/{t100}

The Oyez Project—Stephen J. Field, http://oyez.northwestern.edu/justices/justices.cgi?justice_id=38

Some Account of the Work of Stephen J. Field as a Legislator, State Judge, and Judge of the Supreme Court of the United States. Reprint of 1881 ed. F. B. Rothman, 1986.

Stephen J. Field in *The Supreme Court of the United States: Its Beginnings and Its Justices 1790-1991*, pp. 124-125. U.S. Commission on the Bicentennial of the United States Constitution, 1992.

Swisher, Carl Brent. *Stephen J. Field, Craftsman of the Law.* University of Chicago Press, 1969.

FORTAS, ABE

Legal Information Institute: Biographies of the Justicies—Abe Fortas, http://www2.law.cornell.edu/cgi-bin/foliocgi.exe/justices/query=*/doc/{t196}]

Kalman, Laura. *Abe Fortas: A Biography.* Yale University Press, 1995

Murphy, Bruce Allen. *Fortas: The Rise and Ruin of a Supreme Court Justice.* William Morrow & Company, 1988. .

The Oyez Project—Abe Fortas, http://oyez.northwestern.edu/justices/justices.cgi?justice_id=95

Abe Fortas in *The Supreme Court of the United States: Its Beginnings and Its Justices 1790-1991*, pp. 220-221. U.S. Commission on the Bicentennial of the United States Constitution, 1992.

FRANKFURTER, FELIX

Hockett, Jeffrey D. *New Deal Justice: The Constitutional Jurisprudence of Hugo L. Black, Felix Frankfurter, and Robert H. Jackson.* Rowman & Littlefield Publishers, 1996.

Legal Information Institute: Biographies of the Justicies—Felix Frankfurter, http://www2.law.cornell.edu/cgi-bin/foliocgi.exe/justices/query=*/doc/{t166}

Murphy, Bruce Allen. *The Brandeis/Frankfurter Connection: The Secret Political Activities of Two Supreme Court Justices.* Oxford University Press, 1982.

The Oyez Project—Felix Frankfurter, http://oyez.northwestern.edu/justices/justices.cgi?justice_id=78

Silverstein, Mark. *Constitutional Faiths: Felix Frankfurter, Hugo Black, and the Process of Judicial Decision Making.* Cornell University Press, 1984.

Stevens, Richard G. *Frankfurter and Due Process.* University Press of America, 1982.

Felix Frankfurter in *The Supreme Court of the United States: Its Beginnings and Its Justices 1790-1991*, pp. 190-191. U.S. Commission on the Bicentennial of the United States Constitution, 1992.

FULLER, MELVILLE W.

Ely, James W. *The Chief Justiceship of Melville W. Fuller, 1888-1910.* University of South Carolina Press, 1995.

King, Willard L. *Melville Weston Fuller, Chief Justice of the United States, 1888-1910.* University of Chigago Press, 1967.

Legal Information Institute: Biographies of the Justicies—Mellville Weston Fuller, http://www2.law.cornell.edu/cgi-bin/foliocgi.exe/justices/query=*/doc/{t17}

The Oyez Project—Melville W. Fuller, http://oyez.northwestern.edu/justices/justices.cgi?justice_id=50

Melville Weston Fuller in *The Supreme Court of the United States: Its Beginnings and Its Justices 1790-1991*, pp. 40-41. U.S. Commission on the Bicentennial of the United States Constitution, 1992.

GINSBURG, RUTH BADER

Ayer, Eleanor H. *Ruth Bader Ginsburg: Fire and Steel on the Supreme Court.* Dillon Press, 1994.

Bayer, Linda N. *Ruth Bader Ginsberg.* Chelsea House Publishers, 2000.

Legal Information Institute: Biographies of the Justices—Ruth Bader Ginsberg, http://www2.law.cornell.edu/cgi-bin/foliocgi.exe/justices/query=*/doc/{t216}

The Oyez Project—Ruth Bader Ginsburg, http://oyez.northwestern.edu/justices/justices.cgi?justice_id=107

Supreme Court Historical Society—Ruth Bader Ginsburg, http://www.supremecourthistory.org/myweb/justice/ginsburg.htm

GOLDBERG, ARTHUR J.

Goldberg, Dorothy Kurgans. *A Private View of a Public Life.* Charterhouse, 1975.

Legal Information Institute: Biographies of the Justicies—Arthur J. Goldberg, http://www2.law.cornell.edu/cgi-bin/foliocgi.exe/justices/query=*/doc/{t194}

The Oyez Project—Arthur J. Goldberg, http://oyez.northwestern.edu/justices/justices.cgi?justice_id=94

Stebenne, David. *Arthur J. Goldberg: New Deal Liberal.*

Arthur J. Goldberg in *The Supreme Court of the United States: Its Beginnings and Its Justices 1790-1991*, pp. 218-219. U.S. Commission on the Bicentennial of the United States Constitution, 1992.

GRAY, HORACE

Legal Information Institute: Biographies of the Justicies—Horace Gray, http://www2.law.cornell.edu/cgi-bin/foliocgi.exe/justices/query=*/doc/{t114}

The Oyez Project—Horace Gray, http://oyez.northwestern.edu/justices/justices.cgi?justice_id=47

Sons of the Puritans: A Group of Brief Biographies. American Unitarian Association, 1908.

Horace Gray in *The Supreme Court of the United States: Its Beginnings and Its Justices 1790-1991*, pp. 138-139. U.S. Commission on the Bicentennial of the United States Constitution, 1992.

United States Supreme Court. *In Memoriam. Horace Gray.* U.S. Government Printing Office, 1903.

GRIER, ROBERT C.

Legal Information Institute: Biographies of the Justicies—Robert C. Grier, http://www2.law.cornell.edu/cgi-bin/foliocgi.exe/justices/query=*/doc/{t86}

The Oyez Project—Robert C. Grier, http://oyez.northwestern.edu/justices/justices.cgi?justice_id=31

Robert C. Grier in *The Supreme Court of the United States: Its Beginnings and Its Justices 1790-1991*, pp. 110-111. U.S. Commission on the Bicentennial of the United States Constitution, 1992.

HARLAN, JOHN MARSHALL

Legal Information Institute: Biographies of the Justicies—John Marshall Harlan, http://www2.law.cornell.edu/cgi-bin/foliocgi.exe/justices/query=*/doc/{t108}

Beth, Loren P. *John Marshall Harlan: The Last Whig Justice.* University Press of Kentucky, 1992.

The Oyez Project—John M. Harlan, http://oyez.northwestern.edu/justices/justices.cgi?justice_id=44

Przybyszewski, Linda. *The Republic According to John Marshall Harlan.* University of North Carolina Press, 1999.

John Marshall Harlan in *The Supreme Court of the United States: Its Beginnings and Its Justices 1790-1991*, pp. 132-133. U.S. Commission on the Bicentennial of the United States Constitution, 1992.

Yarbrough, Tinsley E. *Judicial Enigma: The First Justice Harlan.* Oxford University Press, 1995.

HARLAN, JOHN MARSHALL II

Legal Information Institute: Biographies of the Justicies—John Marshall Harlan II, http://www2.law.cornell.edu/cgi-bin/foliocgi.exe/justices/query=*/doc/{t184}

The Oyez Project—John M. Harlan, http://oyez.northwestern.edu/justices/justices.cgi?justice_id=89

John Marshall Harlan (II) in *The Supreme Court of the United States: Its Beginnings and Its Justices 1790-1991*, pp. 208-209. U.S. Commission on the Bicentennial of the United States Constitution, 1992.

Yarbrough, Tinsley E. *John Marshall Harlan: Great Dissenter of the Warren Court.* Oxford University Press, 1992.

HOLMES, OLIVER WENDELL., JR.

Burton, David Henry. *Political Ideas of Justice Holmes.* Fairleigh Dickinson University Press, 1992.

Frankfurter, Felix. *Mr. Justice Holmes And The Supreme Court.* Harvard University Press, 1938.

Legal Information Institute: Biographies of the Justicies—Oliver Wendell Holmes, Jr. http://www2.law.cornell.edu/cgi-bin/foliocgi.exe/justices/query=*/doc/{t132}

Monagan, John S. *The Grand Panjandrum: Mellow Years of Justice Holmes.* University Press of America, 1988.

The Oyez Project, Oliver W. Holmes, Jr., http://oyez.northwestern.edu/justices/justices.cgi?justice_id=58

Pohlman, H. L. *Justice Oliver Wendell Holmes: Free Speech and the Living Constitution.* New York University Press, 1991.

Oliver Wendell Holmes, Jr. in *The Supreme Court of the United States: Its Beginnings and Its Justices 1790-1991*, pp. 156-157. U.S. Commission on the Bicentennial of the United States Constitution, 1992.

White, G. Edward. *Justice Oliver Wendell Holmes: Law and the Inner Self.* Oxford University Press, 1993.

HUGHES, CHARLES EVANS

Glad, Betty. *Charles Evans Hughes and the Illusions of Innocence; A Study in American Diplomacy.* University of Illinois Press, 1966.

Hendel, Samuel. *Charles Evans Hughes and the Supreme Court.* Russell & Russell, 1968.

Legal Information Institute: Biographies of the Justicies—Charles Evans Hughes, http://www2.law.cornell.edu/cgi-bin/foliocgi.exe/justices/query=*/doc/{t23}

The Oyez Project—Charles E. Hughes, http://oyez.northwestern.edu/justices/justices.cgi?justice_id=62

Charles Evans Hughes in *The Supreme Court of the United States: Its Beginnings and Its Justices 1790-1991*, pp. 46-47. U.S. Commission on the Bicentennial of the United States Constitution, 1992.

HUNT, WARD

Legal Information Institute: Biographies of the Justicies—Ward Hunt, http://www2.law.cornell.edu/cgi-bin/foliocgi.exe/justices/query=*/doc/{t106}

The Oyez Project—Ward Hunt, http://oyez.northwestern.edu/justices/justices.cgi?justice_id=42

Ward Hunt in in *The Supreme Court of the United States: Its Beginnings and Its Justices 1790-1991*, pp. 130-131. U.S. Commission on the Bicentennial of the United States Constitution, 1992.

IREDELL, JAMES

Legal Information Institute: Biographies of the Justicies—James Iredell, http://www2.law.cornell.edu/cgi-bin/foliocgi.exe/justices/query=*/doc/{t42}

McRee, Griffith John. *Life and Correspondence of James Iredell, One of the Associate Justices of the Supreme Court of the United States.* Peter Smith, 1857.

The Oyez Project—James Iredell, http://oyez.northwestern.edu/justices/justices.cgi?justice_id=6

James Iredell in *The Supreme Court of the United States: Its Beginnings and Its Justices 1790-1991*, pp. 66-67. U.S. Commission on the Bicentennial of the United States Constitution, 1992.

Whichard, Willis P. *Justice James Iredell.* Carolina Academic Press, 2000.

JACKSON, HOWELL E.

Legal Information Institute: Biographies of the Justicies—Howell E. Jackson, http://www2.law.cornell.edu/cgi-bin/foliocgi.exe/justices/query=*/doc/{t126}

The Oyez Project—Howell E. Jackson, http://oyez.northwestern.edu/justices/justices.cgi?justice_id=54

Howell E. Jackson in *The Supreme Court of the United States: Its Beginnings and Its Justices 1790-1991*, pp. 150-151. U.S. Commission on the Bicentennial of the United States Constitution, 1992.

United States Supreme Court. *In Memoriam.* U.S. Government Printing Office, 1895.

JACKSON, ROBERT H.

Desmond, Charles S., et. al. *Mr. Justice Jackson: Four Lectures in His Honor.* Columbia University Press, 1969.

Gerhart, Eugene C. *Supreme Court Justice Jackson, Lawyer's Judge.* Q Corporation, 1961.

Hockett, Jeffrey D. *New Deal Justice: The Constitutional Jurisprudence of Hugo L. Black, Felix Frankfurter, and Robert H. Jackson.* Rowman & Littlefield Publishers, 1996.

Legal Information Institute: Biographies of the Justicies—Robert H. Jackson, http://www2.law.cornell.edu/cgi-bin/foliocgi.exe/justices/query=*/doc/{t174}

The Oyez Project—Robert H. Jackson, http://oyez.northwestern.edu/justices/justices.cgi?justice_id=82

Robert H. Jackson in *The Supreme Court of the United States: Its Beginnings and Its Justices 1790-1991*, pp. 198-199. U.S. Commission on the Bicentennial of the United States Constitution, 1992.

JAY, JOHN

Casto, William R. *The Supreme Court in the Early Republic: The Chief Justiceships of John Jay and Oliver Ellsworth.* University of South Carolina Press, 1995.

Legal Information Institute: Biographies of the Justicies—John Jay, http://www2.law.cornell.edu/cgi-bin/foliocgi.exe/justices/query=*/doc/{t1}

Morris, Richard Brandon. *Witnesses at the Creation: Hamilton, Madison, Jay, and the Constitution.* Holt, Rinehart, and Winston, 1985.

The Oyez Project—John Jay, http://oyez.northwestern.edu/justices/justices.cgi?justice_id=1

Pellew, George. *John Jay.* Chelsea House, 1997.

John Jay in *The Supreme Court of the United States: Its Beginnings and Its Justices 1790-1991*, pp. 26-27. U.S. Commission on the Bicentennial of the United States Constitution, 1992.

JOHNSON, THOMAS

Delaplaine, Edward S. *The Life of Thomas Johnson, Member of the Continental Congress, First Governor of the State of Maryland, and Associate Justice of the United States Supreme Court.* F. H. Hitchcock, 1927.

Legal Information Institute: Biographies of the Justicies—Thomas Johnson, http://www2.law.cornell.edu/cgi-bin/foliocgi.exe/justices/query=*/doc/{t44}

The Oyez Project—Thomas Johnson, http://oyez.northwestern.edu/justices/justices.cgi?justice_id=7

Thomas Johnson in *The Supreme Court of the United States: Its Beginnings and Its Justices 1790-1991*, pp. 68-69. U.S. Commission on the Bicentennial of the United States Constitution, 1992.

JOHNSON, WILLLIAM

Legal Information Institute: Biographies of the Justicies—William Johnson, http://www2.law.cornell.edu/cgi-bin/foliocgi.exe/justices/query=*/doc/{t54}

The Oyez Project—William Johnson, http://oyez.northwestern.edu/justices/justices.cgi?justice_id=14

William Johnson in in *The Supreme Court of the United States: Its Beginnings and Its Justices 1790-1991*, pp. 78-79. U.S. Commission on the Bicentennial of the United States Constitution, 1992.

KENNEDY, ANTHONY M.

Italia, Bob. *Anthony Kennedy.* Abdo & Daughters, 1992 [juvenile/young adult].

"Kennedy, Anthony McLeod." *Current Biography*, July 1988.

Legal Information Institute: Biographies of the Justicies—Anthony M. Kennedy, http://www2.law.cornell.edu/cgi-bin/foliocgi.exe/justices/query=*/doc/{t210}

The Oyez Project—Anthony M. Kennedy, http://oyez.northwestern.edu/justices/justices.cgi?justice_id=104

Rosen, Jeffrey. "The Agonizer: Everything About Justice Kennedy's Performance on the Supreme Court Has Been Unexpected, Particularly the Way He Has Become its Decisive Voice." *New Yorker*, Nov. 11, 1996.

Supreme Court Historical Society—Anthony M. Kennedy, http://www.supremecourthistory.org/myweb/justice/kennedy.htm

Anthony M. Kennedy in *The Supreme Court of the United States: Its Beginnings and Its Justices 1790-1991*, pp. 234-235. U.S. Commission on the Bicentennial of the United States Constitution, 1992.

LAMAR, JOSEPH RUCKER

Lamar, Clarinda Pendleton. *The Life of Joseph Rucker Lamar, 1857-1916.* Putnam, 1926.

Legal Information Institute: Biographies of the Justicies—Joseph Rucker Lamar, http://www2.law.cornell.edu/cgi-bin/foliocgi.exe/justices/query=*/doc/{t142}

The Oyez Project—Joseph R. Lamar, http://oyez.northwestern.edu/justices/justices.cgi?justice_id=64

Joseph Rucker Lamar in *The Supreme Court of the United States: Its Beginnings and Its Justices 1790-1991*, pp. 166-167. U.S. Commission on the Bicentennial of the United States Constitution, 1992.

LAMAR, LUCIUS Q. C.

Cate, Wirt Armistead. *Lucius Q. C. Lamar: Secession and Reunion.* Russell & Russell, 1969.

Legal Information Institute: Biographies of the Justicies—Lucius Q. C. Lamar, http://www2.law.cornell.edu/cgi-bin/foliocgi.exe/justices/query=*/doc/{t118}

Mayes, Edward. *Lucius Q. C. Lamar: His Life, Ttimes, and Speeches, 1825-1893.* AMS Press, 1974 [first published 1896].

Murphy, James B. *L. Q. C. Lamar: Pragmatic Patriot.* Louisiana State University Press, 1973.

The Oyez Project—Lucius Q. C. Lamar, http://oyez.northwestern.edu/justices/justices.cgi?justice_id=49

Lucius Q. C. Lamar in *The Supreme Court of the United States: Its Beginnings and Its Justices 1790-1991*, pp. 142-143. U.S. Commission on the Bicentennial of the United States Constitution, 1992.

LIVINGSTON, HENRY BROCKHOLST

Legal Information Institute: Biographies of the Justicies—Henry Brockholst Livingston, http://www2.law.cornell.edu/cgi-bin/foliocgi.exe/justices/query=*/doc/{t56}

The Oyez Project—Brockholst Livingston, http://oyez.northwestern.edu/justices/justices.cgi?justice_id=15

H. Brockholst Livingston in *The Supreme Court of the United States: Its Beginnings and Its Justices 1790-1991*, pp. 80-81. U.S. Commission on the Bicentennial of the United States Constitution, 1992.

Troup, Robert, 1757-1832. *A Letter to the Honourable Brockholst Livingston, Esq., One of the Justices of the Supreme Court of the United States.* Packard & Van Benthuysen, 1822.

LURTON, HORACE H.

Court of Appeals from the Sixth Circuit. *In Memory of Horace Hamilton Lurton.* 1914.

Legal Information Institute: Biographies of the Justices—Horace H. Lurton, http://www2.law.cornell.edu/cgi-bin/foliocgi.exe/justices/query=*/doc/{t138}

The Oyez Project—Horace H. Lurton, http://oyez.northwestern.edu/justices /justices.cgi?justice_id=61

Horace H. Lurton in *The Supreme Court of the United States: Its Beginnings and Its Justices 1790-1991*, pp. 162-163. U.S. Commission on the Bicentennial of the United States Constitution, 1992.

MARSHALL, JOHN

Beveridge, Albert Jeremiah. *The Life of John Marshall.* Chelsea House, 1980 [first published in four volumes, 1929].

Hobson, Charles F. *The Great Chief Justice: John Marshall and the Rule of Law.* University Press of Kansas, 2000.

Legal Information Institute: Biographies of the Justices—John Marshall, http://www2.law.cornell.edu/cgi-bin/foliocgi.exe/justices/query=*/doc/{t9}

The Oyez Project—John Marshall, http://oyez.northwestern.edu/justices/justices.cgi?justice_id=13

Robarge, David. *A Chief Justice's Progress: John Marshall from Revolutionary Virginia to the Supreme Court.* Greenwood Publishing Group, 2000.

John Marshall in *The Supreme Court of the United States: Its Beginnings and Its Justices 1790-1991*, pp. 32-33. U.S. Commission on the Bicentennial of the United States Constitution, 1992.

MARSHALL, THURGOOD

Bland, Randall W. *Private Pressure on Public Law: The Legal Career of Justice Thurgood Marshall: 1934-1991.* University Press of America, 1993.

Goldman, Roger L. *Thurgood Marshall: Justice for All.* Carroll & Graf, 1992.

Legal Information Institute: Biographies of the Justices—Thurgood Marshall, http://www2.law.cornell.edu/cgi-bin/foliocgi.exe/justices/query=*/doc/{t198}

The Oyez Project—Thurgood Marshall, http://oyez.northwestern.edu/justices/ justices.cgi?justice_id=96

Thurgood Marshall in *The Supreme Court of the United States: Its Beginnings and Its Justices 1790-1991*, pp. 222-223. U.S. Commission on the Bicentennial of the United States Constitution, 1992.

Thurgood Marshall, Associate Justice of the Supreme Court: Memorial Tributes in the Congress of the United States. U.S. Government Printing Office, 1994.

Williams, Juan. *Thurgood Marshall: American Revolutionary.* Times Books, 1998.

MATTHEWS, STANLEY

Legal Information Institute: Biographies of the Justicies—Stanley Matthews, http://www2.law.cornell.edu/cgi-bin/foliocgi.exe/justices/query=*/doc/{t112}

The Oyez Project—Stanley Matthews, http://oyez.northwestern.edu/justices/justices.cgi?justice_id=46

Stanley Matthews in *The Supreme Court of the United States: Its Beginnings and Its Justices 1790-1991*, pp. 136-137. U.S. Commission on the Bicentennial of the United States Constitution, 1992.

United States Supreme Court Bar. *Proceedings of the Bench and Bar of the Supreme Court of the United States in Memoriam Stanley Matthews*. U.S. Government Printing Office, 1889.

MCKENNA, JOHSEPH

Legal Information Institute: Biographies of the Justicies—Joseph McKenna, http://www2.law.cornell.edu/cgi-bin/foliocgi.exe/justices/query=*/doc/{t130}

McDevitt, Brother Matthew. *Joseph McKenna: Associate Justice of the United States*. Da Capo Press, 1976 [first published 1946].

The Oyez Project—Joseph McKenna, http://oyez.northwestern.edu/justices/justices.cgi?justice_id=57

Joseph McKenna in *The Supreme Court of the United States: Its Beginnings and Its Justices 1790-1991*, pp. 154-155. U.S. Commission on the Bicentennial of the United States Constitution, 1992.

MCKINLEY, JOHN

Legal Information Institute: Biographies of the Justicies—John McKinley, http://www2.law.cornell.edu/cgi-bin/foliocgi.exe/justices/query=*/doc/{t78}

The Oyez Project—John McKinley, http://oyez.northwestern.edu/justices/justices.cgi?justice_id=27

John McKinley in *The Supreme Court of the United States: Its Beginnings and Its Justices 1790-1991*, pp. 102-103. U.S. Commission on the Bicentennial of the United States Constitution, 1992.

MCLEAN, JOHN

Legal Information Institute: Biographies of the Justices—John McLean, http://www2.law.cornell.edu/cgi-bin/foliocgi.exe/justices/query=*/doc/{t68}

The Oyez Project—John McLean, http://oyez.northwestern.edu/justices/justices.cgi?justice_id=21

John McLean in *The Supreme Court of the United States: Its Beginnings and Its Justices 1790-1991*, pp. 92-93. U.S. Commission on the Bicentennial of the United States Constitution, 1992.

Weisenburger, Francis Phelps. *The Life of John McLean: A Politician on the United States Supreme Court*. Da Capo Press, 1971 [first published 1937].

MCREYNOLDS, JAMES CLARK

Bond, James Edward. *I Dissent: The Legacy of Chief Justice James Clark McReynolds.* George Mason University Press, 1992.

Legal Information Institute: Biographies of the Justicies—James Clark McReynolds, http://www2.law.cornell.edu/cgi-bin/foliocgi.exe/justices/query=*/doc/{t146}

The Oyez Project—James C. McReynolds, http://oyez.northwestern.edu/justices /justices.cgi?justice_id=66

James Clark McReynolds in *The Supreme Court of the United States: Its Beginnings and Its Justices 1790-1991*, pp. 170-171. U.S. Commission on the Bicentennial of the United States Constitution, 1992.

MILLER, SAMUEL F.

Fairman, Charles. *Mr. Justice Miller and the Supreme Court, 1862-1890.* Russell & Russell, 1966.

Gregory, Charles Noble. *Samuel Freeman Miller.* State Historical Society of Iowa, 1907.

Legal Information Institute: Biographies of the Justicies—Samuel F. Miller, http://www2.law.cornell.edu/cgi-bin/foliocgi.exe/justices/query=*/doc/{t96}

The Oyez Project—Samuel F. Miller, http://oyez.northwestern.edu/justices/justices.cgi?justice_id=36

Samuel F. Miller in *The Supreme Court of the United States: Its Beginnings and Its Justices 1790-1991*, pp. 120-121. U.S. Commission on the Bicentennial of the United States Constitution, 1992.

MINTON, SHERMAN

Gugin, Linda C., and James E. St. Clair, contributor. *Sherman Minton: New Deal Senator, Cold War Justice.* Indiana Historical Society, 1997.

Legal Information Institute: Biographies of the Justicies—Sherman Minton, http://www2.law.cornell.edu/cgi-bin/foliocgi.exe/justices/query=*/doc/{t182}

The Oyez Project—Sherman Minton, http://oyez.northwestern.edu/justices/justices.cgi?justice_id=87

Radcliffe, William Franklin. *Sherman Minton: Indiana's Supreme Court Justice.* Guild Press of Indiana, 1996.

Sherman Minton in *The Supreme Court of the United States: Its Beginnings and Its Justices 1790-1991*, pp. 206-207. U.S. Commission on the Bicentennial of the United States Constitution, 1992.

MOODY, WILLIAM H.

Legal Information Institute: Biographies of the Justicies—William H. Moody, http://www2.law.cornell.edu/cgi-bin/foliocgi.exe/justices/query=*/doc/{t136}

The Oyez Project—William H. Moody, http://oyez.northwestern.edu/justices/ justices.cgi?justice_id=60

William H. Moody in *The Supreme Court of the United States: Its Beginnings and Its Justices 1790-1991*, pp. 160-161. U.S. Commission on the Bicentennial of the United States Constitution, 1992.

MOORE, ALFRED

Legal Information Institute: Biographies of the Justicies—Alfred Moore, http://www2.law.cornell.edu/cgi-bin/foliocgi.exe/justices/query=*/doc/{t52}

The Oyez Project—Alfred Moore, http://oyez.northwestern.edu/justices/justices.cgi?justice_id=12

Alfred Moore in *The Supreme Court of the United States: Its Beginnings and Its Justices 1790-1991*, pp. 76-77. U.S. Commission on the Bicentennial of the United States Constitution, 1992.

MURPHY, FRANK W.

Legal Information Institute: Biographies of the Justicies—Frank W. Murphy, http://www2.law.cornell.edu/cgi-bin/foliocgi.exe/justices/query=*/doc/{t170}

The Oyez Project—Frank Murphy, http://oyez.northwestern.edu/justices/justices.cgi?justice_id=80

Frank W. Murphy in *The Supreme Court of the United States: Its Beginnings and Its Justices 1790-1991*, pp. 194-195. U.S. Commission on the Bicentennial of the United States Constitution, 1992.

NELSON, SAMUEL

Legal Information Institute: Biographies of the Justicies—Samuel Nelson, http://www2.law.cornell.edu/cgi-bin/foliocgi.exe/justices/query=*/doc/{t82}

The Oyez Project—Samuel Nelson, http://oyez.northwestern.edu/justices/justices.cgi?justice_id=29

Samuel Nelson in *The Supreme Court of the United States: Its Beginnings and Its Justices 1790-1991*, pp. 106-107. U.S. Commission on the Bicentennial of the United States Constitution, 1992.

O'CONNOR, SANDRA DAY

Legal Information Institute: Biographies of the Justicies—Sandra Day O'Connor, http://www2.law.cornell.edu/cgi-bin/foliocgi.exe/justices/query=*/doc/{t206}

Maveety, Nancy. *Justice Sandra Day O'Connor: Strategist on the Supreme Court.* Rowman & Littlefield, 1996.

McElroy, Lisa Tucker, and Courtney O'Connor. *Meet My Grandmother: She's a Supreme Court Justice.* Millbook Press, 2000 [juvenile].

The Oyez Project—Sandra Day O'Connor, http://oyez.northwestern.edu/justices/justices.cgi?justice_id=102

Supreme Court Historical Society—Sandra Day O'Connor, http://www.supremecourthistory.org/myweb/justice/o'connor.htm

Sandra Day O'Connor in *The Supreme Court of the United States: Its Beginnings and Its Justices 1790-1991*, pp. 230-231. U.S. Commission on the Bicentennial of the United States Constitution, 1992.

Williams, Jean Kinney. *Sandra Day O'Connor: Lawyer and Supreme Court Justice*. Ferguson Publishing, 2001.

PATERSON, WILLIAM

Legal Information Institute: Biographies of the Justicies—William Paterson, http://www2.law.cornell.edu/cgi-bin/foliocgi.exe/justices/query=*/doc/{t46}

O'Connor, John E. *William Paterson, Lawyer and Statesman, 1745-1806*. Rutgers University Press, 1979.

The Oyez Project—William Paterson, http://oyez.northwestern.edu/justices/justices.cgi?justice_id=8

William Paterson in *The Supreme Court of the United States: Its Beginnings and Its Justices 1790-1991*, pp. 70-71. U.S. Commission on the Bicentennial of the United States Constitution, 1992.

Wood, Gertrude Sceecy. *William Paterson of New Jersey, 1745-1806*. Fair Lawn Press, Inc., 1933.

PECKHAM, RUFUS W.

Legal Information Institute: Biographies of the Justicies—Rufus W. Peckham, http://www2.law.cornell.edu/cgi-bin/foliocgi.exe/justices/query=*/doc/{t128}

The Oyez Project—Rufus Peckham, http://oyez.northwestern.edu/justices/justices.cgi?justice_id=56

Rufus W. Peckham in *The Supreme Court of the United States: Its Beginnings and Its Justices 1790-1991*, pp. 152-153. U.S. Commission on the Bicentennial of the United States Constitution, 1992.

United States Supreme Court. *Proceedings of the Bar and Officers of the Supreme Court of the United States in Memory of Rufus Wheeler Peckham, December 18, 1909*. U. S. Government Printing Office, 1910.

PITNEY, MAHLON

Legal Information Institute: Biographies of the Justicies—Mahlon Pitney, http://www2.law.cornell.edu/cgi-bin/foliocgi.exe/justices/query=*/doc/{t144}

The Oyez Project—Mahlon Pitney, http://oyez.northwestern.edu/justices/justices.cgi?justice_id=65

Mahlon Pitney in *The Supreme Court of the United States: Its Beginnings and Its Justices 1790-1991*, pp. 168-169. U.S. Commission on the Bicentennial of the United States Constitution, 1992.

POWELL, LEWIS F., JR.

Jeffries, John Calvin. *Justice Lewis F. Powell, Jr*. Fordham University Press, 2001.

Legal Information Institute: Biographies of the Justicies—Lewis F. Powell, http://www2.law.cornell.edu/cgi-bin/foliocgi.exe/justices/query=*/doc/{t202}

The Oyez Project—Lewis F. Powell, Jr., http://oyez.northwestern.edu/justices/justices.cgi?justice_id=99

Lewis F. Powell, Jr. in *The Supreme Court of the United States: Its Beginnings and Its Justices 1790-1991*, pp. 226-227. U.S. Commission on the Bicentennial of the United States Constitution, 1992.

REED, STANLEY F.

Fassett, John D. *New Deal Justice: The Life of Stanley Reed of Kentucky*. Vantage Press, 1994.

Legal Information Institute: Biographies of the Justicies—Stanley F. Reed, http://www2.law.cornell.edu/cgi-bin/foliocgi.exe/justices/query=*/doc/{t164}

The Oyez Project—Stanley Reed, http://oyez.northwestern.edu/justices/justices.cgi?justice_id=77

Stanley F. Reed in *The Supreme Court of the United States: Its Beginnings and Its Justices 1790-1991*, pp. 188-189. U.S. Commission on the Bicentennial of the United States Constitution, 1992.

United States Supreme Court. *In Memoriam, Honorable Stanley Forman Reed: Proceedings of the Bar and Officers of the Supreme Court of the United States: Proceedings Before the Supreme Court of the United States, Washington, D.C., December 15, 1980.* U.S. Government Printing Office, 1980.

REHNQUIST, WILLIAM H.

Gottlieb, Stephen E. *Morality Imposed: The Rehnquist Court and Liberty in America.* New York University Press, 2000.

Legal Information Institute: Biographies of the Justicies—William H. Rehnquist, http://www2.law.cornell.edu/cgi-bin/foliocgi.exe/justices/query=*/doc/{t33}

The Oyez Project—William H. Renhquist, http://oyez.northwestern.edu/justices/justices.cgi?justice_id=100

Rehnquist, William H. "The Future of the Federal Courts (Speech by William H. Renquist, Chief Justice of the Supreme Court)." *Vital Speeches*, May 1, 1996.

Supreme Court Historical Society—William H. Rehnquist, http://www.supremecourthistory.org/myweb/justice/rehnquist.htm

William H. Rehnquist in *The Supreme Court of the United States: Its Beginnings and Its Justices 1790-1991*, pp. 56-57. U.S. Commission on the Bicentennial of the United States Constitution, 1992.

Tucker, D. F. B. *The Rehnquist Court and Civil Rights.* Darthmouth, 1995.

ROBERTS, OWEN J.

Legal Information Institute: Biographies of the Justicies—Owen J. Roberts, http://www2.law.cornell.edu/cgi-bin/foliocgi.exe/justices/query=*/doc/{t158}

Leonard, Charles A. *A Search for a Judicial Philosophy: Mr. Justice Roberts and the Constitutional Revolution of 1937.* Kennikat Press, 1971.

The Oyez Project—Owen J. Roberts,
http://oyez.northwestern.edu/justices/justices.cgi?justice_id=74

Owen J. Roberts in *The Supreme Court of the United States: Its Beginnings and Its Justices 1790-1991*, pp. 182-183. U.S. Commission on the Bicentennial of the United States Constitution, 1992.

RUTLEDGE, JOHN

Barry, Richard. *Mr. Rutledge of South Carolina*. Ayer, 1993 [reprint of 1942 edition].

Haw, James. *John & Edward Rutledge of South Carolina*. University of Georgia Press, 1997.

Legal Information Institute: Biographies of the Justicies—John Rutledge,
http://www2.law.cornell.edu/cgi-bin/foliocgi.exe/justices/query=*/doc/{t5}

The Oyez Project—John Rutledge,
http://oyez.northwestern.edu/justices/justices.cgi?justice_id=2

John Rutledge in *The Supreme Court of the United States: Its Beginnings and Its Justices 1790-1991*, pp. 28-29. U.S. Commission on the Bicentennial of the United States Constitution, 1992.

RUTLEDGE, WILEY B.

Legal Information Institute: Biographies of the Justicies—Wiley B. Rutledge,
http://www2.law.cornell.edu/cgi-bin/foliocgi.exe/justices/query=*/doc/{t176}

The Oyez Project—Wiley B. Rutledge, http://oyez.northwestern.edu/justices/justices.cgi?justice_id=83

Wiley B. Rutledge in *The Supreme Court of the United States: Its Beginnings and Its Justices 1790-1991*, pp. 200-201. U.S. Commission on the Bicentennial of the United States Constitution, 1992.

SANFORD, EDWARD T.

Legal Information Institute: Biographies of the Justicies—Edward T. Sanford,
http://www2.law.cornell.edu/cgi-bin/foliocgi.exe/justices/query=*/doc/{t156}

The Oyez Project—Edward T. Sanford, http://oyez.northwestern.edu/justices/justices.cgi?justice_id=72

Edward T. Sanford in *The Supreme Court of the United States: Its Beginnings and Its Justices 1790-1991*, pp. 180-181. U.S. Commission on the Bicentennial of the United States Constitution, 1992.

United States Supreme Court. *Proceedings of the Bar and Officers of the Supreme Court of the United States in Memory of Edward Terry Sanford, December 13, 1930*. U.S. Government Printing Office, 1931.

SCALIA, ANTONIN

Brisbin, Richard A. *Justice Antonin Scalia and the Conservative Revival*. Johns Hopkins University Press, 1998.

Legal Information Institute: Biographies of the Justicies—Antonin Scalia,
http://www2.law.cornell.edu/cgi-bin/foliocgi.exe/justices/query=*/doc/{t208}

The Oyez Project—Antonin Scalia,
http://oyez.northwestern.edu/justices/justices.cgi?justice_id=103

Schultz, David A., and Christopher E. Smith. *The Jurisprudential Vision of Justice Antonin Scalia*. Rowman & Littlefield, 1996.

Smith, Christopher E. *Justice Antonin Scalia and the Supreme Court's Conservative Moment*. Praeger Publishers, 1993.

Supreme Court Historical Society—Antonin Scalia,
http://www.supremecourthistory.org/myweb/justice/scalia.htm

Antonin Scalia in *The Supreme Court of the United States: Its Beginnings and Its Justices 1790-1991*, pp. 232-233. U.S. Commission on the Bicentennial of the United States Constitution, 1992.

SHIRAS, GEORGE, JR.

Legal Information Institute: Biographies of the Justicies—George Shiras, Jr.,
http://www2.law.cornell.edu/cgi-bin/foliocgi.exe/justices/query=*/doc/{t124}

The Oyez Project—George Shiras, Jr., http://oyez.northwestern.edu/justices/justices.cgi?justice_id=53

Shiras, George, III. *Justice George Shiras, Jr., of Pittsburgh, Associate Justice of the United States Supreme Court, 1892-1903: A Chronicle of his Family, Life, and Times*. University of Pittsburgh Press, 1953.

George Shiras, Jr. in *The Supreme Court of the United States: Its Beginnings and Its Justices 1790-1991*, pp. 148-149. U.S. Commission on the Bicentennial of the United States Constitution, 1992.

SOUTER, DAVID H.

Garrow, David J. "Justice Souter Emerges." *New York Times Magazine*, Sept. 25, 1994.

Italia, Bob. *David Souter*. Abdo & Daughters, 1992 [juvenile/young adult].

Legal Information Institute: Biographies of the Justicies—David H. Souter,
http://www2.law.cornell.edu/cgi-bin/foliocgi.exe/justices/query=*/doc/{t212}

The Oyez Project—David H. Souter,
http://oyez.northwestern.edu/justices/justices.cgi?justice_id=105

Supreme Court Historical Society—David H. Souter,
http://www.supremecourthistory.org/myweb/justice/souter.htm

David H. Souter in *The Supreme Court of the United States: Its Beginnings and Its Justices 1790-1991*, pp. 236-237. U.S. Commission on the Bicentennial of the United States Constitution, 1992.

STEVENS, JOHN PAUL

Legal Information Institute: Biographies of the Justicies—John Paul Stevens,
http://www2.law.cornell.edu/cgi-bin/foliocgi.exe/justices/query=*/doc/{t204}

The Oyez Project—John Paul Stevens, http://oyez.northwestern.edu/justices/
justices.cgi?justice_id=101

Pike, David F. " Standout justice; oldest member of U.S. Supreme Court remains
'maverick.'" *Los Angeles Daily Journal*, April 14, 1997.

Sickles, Robert J. *John Paul Stevens and the Constitution: The Search for Balance*.
Pennsylvania State University Press, 1988.

Supreme Court Historical Society—John Paul Stevens, http://www
.supremecourthistory.org/myweb/justice/stevens.htm

John Paul Stevens in *The Supreme Court of the United States: Its Beginnings and Its
Justices 1790-1991*, pp. 228-229. U.S. Commission on the Bicentennial of the
United States Constitution, 1992.

STEWART, POTTER

Legal Information Institute: Biographies of the Justicies—Potter Stewart,
http://www2.law.cornell.edu/cgi-bin/foliocgi.exe/justices/query=*/doc/{t190}

The Oyez Project—Potter Stewart,
http://oyez.northwestern.edu/justices/justices.cgi?justice_id=92

Potter Stewart in *The Supreme Court of the United States: Its Beginnings and Its Justices
1790-1991*, pp. 214. U.S. Commission on the Bicentennial of the United States
Constitution, 1992.

STONE, HARLAN FISKE

Konefsky, Samuel Joseph. *Chief Justice Stone and the Supreme Court*. Hafner Publishing Co., 1971 [first published 1946].

Legal Information Institute: Biographies of the Justicies—Harlan Fiske Stone,
http://www2.law.cornell.edu/cgi-bin/foliocgi.exe/justices/query=*/doc/{t25}

Mason, Alpheus Thomas. *Harlan Fiske Stone: Pillar of the Law*. Archon Books, 1968
[first published 1956].

The Oyez Project—Harlan Fiske Stone, http://oyez.northwestern.edu/justices/
justices.cgi?justice_id=73

Renstrom, Peter G. *The Stone Court: Justices, Rulings, and Legacy*. ABC-CLIO, 2001.

Harlan Fiske Stone in *The Supreme Court of the United States: Its Beginnings and Its
Justices 1790-1991*, pp. 48-49. U.S. Commission on the Bicentennial of the United
States Constitution, 1992.

Urofsky, Melvin I. *Division and Discord: the Supreme Court under Stone and Vinson,
1941-1953*. University of South Carolina Press, 1997.

STORY, JOSEPH

Dunne, Gerald T. *Justice Joseph Story and the Rise of the Supreme Court*. Simon &
Schuster, 1970.

Legal Information Institute: Biographies of the Justicies—Joseph Story,
http://www2.law.cornell.edu/cgi-bin/foliocgi.exe/justices/query=*/doc/{t62}

McClellan, James. *Joseph story and the American Constitution: A Study in Political and Legal Thought with Selected Writings*. University of Oklahoma Press, 1990 [first published 1971].

Newmyer, R. Kent. *Supreme Court Justice Joseph Story: Statesman of the Old Republic*. University of North Carolina Press, 1985.

The Oyez Project—Joseph Story, http://oyez.northwestern.edu/justices/justices.cgi?justice_id=18

Story, William W. *Life and letters of Joseph Story, associate justice of the Supreme Court of the United States, and Dane professor of law at Harvard University*. Lawbook Exchange, 2000 [first published 1851].

Joseph Story in *The Supreme Court of the United States: Its Beginnings and Its Justices 1790-1991*, pp. 86-87. U.S. Commission on the Bicentennial of the United States Constitution, 1992.

STRONG, WILLIAM

Hoar, George Frisbee. *The Charge Against President Grant and Attorney General Hoar of Packing the Supreme Court of the United States*. Press of C. Hamilton, 1896.

Legal Information Institute: Biographies of the Justicies—William Strong, http://www2.law.cornell.edu/cgi-bin/foliocgi.exe/justices/query=*/doc/{t102}

The Oyez Project—William Strong, http://oyez.northwestern.edu/justices/justices.cgi?justice_id=40

William Strong in *The Supreme Court of the United States: Its Beginnings and Its Justices 1790-1991*, pp. 126-127. U.S. Commission on the Bicentennial of the United States Constitution, 1992.

SUTHERLAND, GEORGE

Arkes, Hadley. *The Return of George Sutherland: Restoring a Jurisprudence of Natural Rights*. Princeton University Press, 1994.

Legal Information Institute: Biographies of the Justicies—George Sutherland, http://www2.law.cornell.edu/cgi-bin/foliocgi.exe/justices/query=*/doc/{t152}

The Oyez Project—George Sutherland, http://oyez.northwestern.edu/justices/justices.cgi?justice_id=70

Paschal, Joel Francis. *Mr. Justice Sutherland, a Man against the State*. Greenwood Press, 1969 [first published 1951].

George Sutherland in *The Supreme Court of the United States: Its Beginnings and Its Justices 1790-1991*, pp. 176-177. U.S. Commission on the Bicentennial of the United States Constitution, 1992.

SWAYNE, NOAH H.

Legal Information Institute: Biographies of the Justicies—Noah H. Swayne, http://www2.law.cornell.edu/cgi-bin/foliocgi.exe/justices/query=*/doc/{t94}

The Oyez Project—Noah Swayne, http://oyez.northwestern.edu/justices/justices.cgi?justice_id=35

Noah H. Swayne in *The Supreme Court of the United States: Its Beginnings and Its Justices 1790-1991*, pp. 118-119. U.S. Commission on the Bicentennial of the United States Constitution, 1992.

TAFT, WILLIAM HOWARD

Legal Information Institute: Biographies of the Justices—William Howard Taft, http://www2.law.cornell.edu/cgi-bin/foliocgi.exe/justices/query=*/doc/{t21}

The Oyez Project—William Howard Taft, http://oyez.northwestern.edu/justices /justices.cgi?justice_id=69

William Howard Taft in *The Supreme Court of the United States: Its Beginnings and Its Justices 1790-1991*, pp. 44-45. U.S. Commission on the Bicentennial of the United States Constitution, 1992.

United States Supreme Court. *Proceedings of the bar and officers of the Supreme court of the United States in memory of William Howard Taft, December 13, 1930*. U.S. Government Printing Office, 1931.

TANEY, ROGER BROOKE

Legal Information Institute: Biographies of the Justices—Roger Brooke Taney, http://www2.law.cornell.edu/cgi-bin/foliocgi.exe/justices/query=*/doc/{t11}

Newmyer, R. Kent. *The Supreme Court Under Marshall and Taney*. Harlan Davidson, 1986 [first published 1968].

The Oyez Project—Roger B. Taney, http://oyez.northwestern.edu/justices/justices.cgi?justice_id=24

Schumacher, Alvin J. *Thunder on Capitol Hill: The Life of Chief Justice Roger B. Taney*. Bruce Publishing Co., 1964.

Roger Brooke Taney in *The Supreme Court of the United States: Its Beginnings and Its Justices 1790-1991*, pp. 34-35. U.S. Commission on the Bicentennial of the United States Constitution, 1992.

Swisher, Carl Brent. *The Taney Period, 1836-64*. Macmillan, 1974.

THOMAS, CLARENCE

Gerber, Scott Douglas. *First Principles: The Jurisprudence of Clarence Thomas*. New York University Press, 1999.

Legal Information Institute: Biographies of the Justices—Clarence Thomas, http://www2.law.cornell.edu/cgi-bin/foliocgi.exe/justices/query=*/doc/{t214}

Macht, Norman, and Christopher E. Henry. *Clarence Thomas: Supreme Court Justice*. Chelsea House Publishing, 1995 [young adult].

Morrison, Toni, ed., and Nellie Y. McKay and Michael Thelwell, contributors. *Race-ing Justice, En-Gendering Power: Essays on Anita Hill, Clarence Thomas, and the Construction of Social Reality*. Pantheon Books, 1992.

The Oyez Project—Clarence Thomas, http://oyez.northwestern.edu/justices/ justices.cgi?justice_id=106

Phelps, Timothy M. *Capitol games: Clarence Thomas, Anita Hill, and the Story of a Supreme Court Nomination.* Hyperion, 1992.

Smith, Christopher E. *The Real Clarence Thomas: Confirmation Veracity Meets Performance Reality.* P. Lang, 2000.

Supreme Court Historical Society—Clarence Thomas, http://www.supremecourthistory.org/myweb/justice/thomas.htm

Clarence Thomas in *The Supreme Court of the United States: Its Beginnings and Its Justices 1790-1991*, pp. 238-239. U.S. Commission on the Bicentennial of the United States Constitution, 1992.

THOMPSON, SMITH

Legal Information Institute: Biographies of the Justices—Smith Thompson, http://www2.law.cornell.edu/cgi-bin/foliocgi.exe/justices/query=*/doc/{t64}

The Oyez Project—Smith Thompson, http://oyez.northwestern.edu/justices/justices.cgi?justice_id=19

Roper, Donald Malcom. *Mr. Justice Thompson and the Constitution.* Garland, 1987.

Smith Thompson in *The Supreme Court of the United States: Its Beginnings and Its Justices 1790-1991*, pp. 88-89. U.S. Commission on the Bicentennial of the United States Constitution, 1992.

TODD, THOMAS

Legal Information Institute: Biographies of the Justicies—Thomas Todd, http://www2.law.cornell.edu/cgi-bin/foliocgi.exe/justices/query=*/doc/{t58}

The Oyez Project—Todd Thomas, http://oyez.northwestern.edu/justices/justices.cgi?justice_id=16

Thomas Todd in *The Supreme Court of the United States: Its Beginnings and Its Justices 1790-1991*, pp. 82-83. U.S. Commission on the Bicentennial of the United States Constitution, 1992.

TRIMBLE, ROBERT

Legal Information Institute: Biographies of the Justices—Robert Trimble, http://www2.law.cornell.edu/cgi-bin/foliocgi.exe/justices/query=*/doc/{t66}

The Oyez Project—Robert Trimble, http://oyez.northwestern.edu/justices/justices.cgi?justice_id=20

Robert Trimble in *The Supreme Court of the United States: Its Beginnings and Its Justices 1790-1991*, pp. 90-91. U.S. Commission on the Bicentennial of the United States Constitution, 1992.

VAN DEVANTER, WILLIS

Legal Information Institute: Biographies of the Justicies—Willis Van Devanter, http://www2.law.cornell.edu/cgi-bin/foliocgi.exe/justices/query=*/doc/{t140}

The Oyez Project—Willis Van Devanter, http://oyez.northwestern.edu/justices/justices.cgi?justice_id=63

Willis Van Devanter in *The Supreme Court of the United States: Its Beginnings and Its Justices 1790-1991*, pp. 164-165. U.S. Commission on the Bicentennial of the United States Constitution, 1992.

VINSON, FRED M.

Legal Information Institute: Biographies of the Justicies—Fred M. Vinson, http://www2.law.cornell.edu/cgi-bin/foliocgi.exe/justices/query=*/doc/{t27}

Fred M. Vinson in *The Supreme Court of the United States: Its Beginnings and Its Justices 1790-1991*, pp. 50-51. U.S. Commission on the Bicentennial of the United States Constitution, 1992.

The Oyez Project—Fred M. Vinson, http://oyez.northwestern.edu/justices/justices.cgi?justice_id=85

Palmer, Jan. *The Vinson Court Era: the Supreme Court's Conference Votes—Data and Analysis*. AMS Press, 1990.

Urofsky, Melvin I. *Division and Discord: the Supreme Court under Stone and Vinson, 1941-1953*. University of South Carolina Press, 1997.

WAITE, MORRISON R.

Legal Information Institute: Biographies of the Justicies—Morrison R. Waite, http://www2.law.cornell.edu/cgi-bin/foliocgi.exe/justices/query=*/doc/{t15}

Magrath, C. Peter. *Morrison R. Waite: The Triumph of Character*. Macmillan, 1964.

The Oyez Project—Morrison R. Waite, http://oyez.northwestern.edu/justices/justices.cgi?justice_id=43

Morrison R. Waite in *The Supreme Court of the United States: Its Beginnings and Its Justices 1790-1991*, pp. 38-39. U.S. Commission on the Bicentennial of the United States Constitution, 1992.

Trimble, Bruce R. *Chief Justice Waite, Defender of the Public Interest*. Russell & Russell, 1970 [first published 1938].

WARREN, EARL

Cray, Ed. *Chief Justice: A Biography of Earl Warren*. Simon & Schuster, 1997.

Herda, D. J. *Earl Warren: Chief Justice for Social Change*. Enslow Publishers, 1995 [young adult].

Horwitz, Morton J. *The Warren Court and the Pursuit of Justice*. Hill & Wang, 1999.

Legal Information Institute: Biographies of the Justicies—Earl Warren, http://www2.law.cornell.edu/cgi-bin/foliocgi.exe/justices/query=*/doc/{t29}

The Oyez Project—Earl Warren, http://oyez.northwestern.edu/justices/justices.cgi?justice_id=88

Earl Warren in *The Supreme Court of the United States: Its Beginnings and Its Justices 1790-1991*, pp. 52-53. U.S. Commission on the Bicentennial of the United States Constitution, 1992.

WASHINGTON, BUSHROD

Legal Information Institute: Biographies of the Justices—Bushrod Washington, http://www2.law.cornell.edu/cgi-bin/foliocgi.exe/justices/query=*/doc/{t50}

The Oyez Project—Bushrod Washington, http://oyez.northwestern.edu/justices/justices.cgi?justice_id=11

Bushrod Washington in *The Supreme Court of the United States: Its Beginnings and Its Justices 1790-1991*, pp. 74-75. U.S. Commission on the Bicentennial of the United States Constitution, 1992.

Washington, Lawrence. *Address of Lawrence Washington in Presenting on May 3, 1910, at Montrose, Va., the Portrait of Judge Bushrod Washington*. F.B. Toothtaker, 1912.

WAYNE, JAMES M.

Lawrence, Alexander A. *James Moore Wayne, Southern Unionist*. Greenwood Press, 1970 [first published 1943].

Legal Information Institute: Biographies of the Justices—James M. Wayne, http://www2.law.cornell.edu/cgi-bin/foliocgi.exe/justices/query=*/doc/{t72}

The Oyez Project—James M. Wayne, http://oyez.northwestern.edu/justices/justices.cgi?justice_id=23

James M. Wayne in *The Supreme Court of the United States: Its Beginnings and Its Justices 1790-1991*, pp. 96-97. U.S. Commission on the Bicentennial of the United States Constitution, 1992.

WHITE, BYRON R.

Hutchinson, Dennis J. *The Man Who Once Was Whizzer White: A Portrait of Justice Byron R. White*. Free Press, 1998.

Legal Information Institute: Biographies of the Justices—Byron R. White, http://www2.law.cornell.edu/cgi-bin/foliocgi.exe/justices/query=*/doc/{t192}

The Oyez Project—Byron R. White, http://oyez.northwestern.edu/justices/justices.cgi?justice_id=93

Byron R. White in *The Supreme Court of the United States: Its Beginnings and Its Justices 1790-1991*, pp. 216-217. Commission on the Bicentennial of the United States Constitution, 1992.

WHITE, EDWARD DOUGLASS

Highsaw, Robert Baker. *Edward Douglass White, Defender of the Conservative Faith*. Louisiana State University Press, 1981.

Legal Information Institute: Biographies of the Justices—Edward Douglass White, http://www2.law.cornell.edu/cgi-bin/foliocgi.exe/justices/query=*/doc/{t19}

The Oyez Project—Edward D. White, http://oyez.northwestern.edu/justices/justices.cgi?justice_id=55

Pratt, Walter F. *The Supreme Court under Edward Douglass White, 1910-1921*. University of South Carolina Press, 1999.

Edward Douglass White in *The Supreme Court of the United States: Its Beginnings and Its Justices 1790-1991*, pp. 42-43. U.S. Commission on the Bicentennial of the United States Constitution, 1992.

WHITTAKER, CHARLES E.

Legal Information Institute: Biographies of the Justicies—Charles E. Whittaker, http://www2.law.cornell.edu/cgi-bin/foliocgi.exe/justices/query=*/doc/{t188}

The Oyez Project—Charles E. Whittaker, http://oyez.northwestern.edu/justices/justices.cgi?justice_id=91

Charles E. Whittaker in *The Supreme Court of the United States: Its Beginnings and Its Justices 1790-1991*, pp. 212-213. U.S. Commission on the Bicentennial of the United States Constitution, 1992.

United States Supreme Court. *In Memoriam, Honorable Charles Evans Whittaker: Proceedings of the Bar and Officers of the Supreme Court of the United States: Proceedings of the Supreme Court of the United States, Washington, D.C., February 19, 1975*. U.S. Government Printing Office, 1975.

WILSON, JAMES

Delahanty, Mary T. *The Integralist Philosophy of James Wilson*. Pageant Press, 1969.

Legal Information Institute: Biographies of the Justicies—James Wilson, http://www2.law.cornell.edu/cgi-bin/foliocgi.exe/justices/query=*/doc/{t36}

The Oyez Project—James Wilson, http://oyez.northwestern.edu/justices/justices.cgi?justice_id=4

Seed, Geoffrey. *James Wilson*. KTO Press, 1978.

Smith, Page. *James Wilson, Founding Father, 1742-1798*. Greenwood Press, 1973 [first published 1956].

James Wilson in in *The Supreme Court of the United States: Its Beginnings and Its Justices 1790-1991*, pp. 60-61. U.S. Commission on the Bicentennial of the United States Constitution, 1992.

WOODBURY, LEVI

Cole, Donald B. *Jacksonian Democracy in New Hampshire, 1800-1851*. Harvard University Press, 1970.

Legal Information Institute: Biographies of the Justicies—Levi Woodbury, http://www2.law.cornell.edu/cgi-bin/foliocgi.exe/justices/query=*/doc/{t84}

The Oyez Project—Levi Woodbury, http://oyez.northwestern.edu/justices/justices.cgi?justice_id=30

Levi Woodbory in in *The Supreme Court of the United States: Its Beginnings and Its Justices 1790-1991*, pp. 108-109. U.S. Commission on the Bicentennial of the United States Constitution, 1992.

Woodbury, Charles Levi. *Memoir of Hon. Levi Woodbury, Ll.D*. David Clapp & Son, 1894.

WOODS, WILLIAM B.

Legal Information Institute: Biographies of the Justicies—William B. Woods, http://www2.law.cornell.edu/cgi-bin/foliocgi.exe/justices/query=*/doc/{t110}

The Oyez Project—William B. Woods, http://oyez.northwestern.edu/justices/justices.cgi?justice_id=45

William B. Woods in *The Supreme Court of the United States: Its Beginnings and Its Justices 1790-1991*, pp. 134-135. U.S. Commission on the Bicentennial of the United States Constitution, 1992.

United States Supreme Court Bar. *Proceedings of the Bench and Bar of the Supreme Court of the United States in Memoriam William B. Woods*. U.S. Government Printing Office, 1887.

Glossary

abrogate Abolish.

act A bill passed through the various legislative steps necessary, and signed into law by the executive.

actuarial tables Statistical calculations based on life expectancy yielding insurance annuities and premiums.

admiralty law Laws and statutes which govern maritime questions and disputes.

affirmative action Government policy which encourages institutions of various kinds to focus on hiring minorities such as women, African Americans, Hispanics, etc.

alcade The chief judicial officer in a Spanish town.

alma mater A school, college, or university from which one has graduated.

amend To change, revise, or alter a worded document, such as a piece of legislation or a constitution.

amicus curiae Latin for "Friend of the court; a legal brief filed by a party not directly involved in a legal dispute on behalf of the plaintiff or defendant.

anarchistic Favoring total disarray within the political and social make-up of a nation or state.

annexed A piece of land which is incorporated through a treaty or agreement to a sovereign nation.

anti–trust Term used for legislation designed to prevent businesses from establishing unfair advantages and circumventing the free market to their benefit.

appeal Request filed to ask a superior court to review a case decided by a lesser court; in nations such as the United States, the appeals process stops at the Supreme Court.

apprentice A young individual who learns a craft or skill under the supervision of a professional in that person's place of business or trade.

aristocracy Governing body made up of wealthy individuals of inherited nobility.

augmented Made greater.

bar examination An written test given to individuals seeking to become certified by the state in which they wish to practice law.

barrister A litigation specialist who limits his or her legal practice to the court room.

belligerents Individuals involved in waging war or conflict.

bench A judge in court session.

board of regents A group of elected members governing a public university or college.

burgeoning Growing in prosperity and opportunity.

buttress Support.

Cabinet Group of advisers of the head of the executive branch, appointed by the executive and confirmed to serve by the legislative body of the federal government.

canon law Rule of the Christian Church, which has little or no legal significance today.

capital punishment Also known as the death penalty, the punishment of death given by the state.

carpetbagger Derogatory political term applied to individuals who are seen as running for elected office in an area with which they have little or no association.

case law The sum of published legal decisions of the courts which contribute to the resolution of modern legal disputes.

certiorari A grant by the Supreme Court meaning it has decided to hear a case based on the legal merits; follows a writ of certiorari, filed by the party who wishes to have a case heard before the Court.

chattel Moveable items of property which are not attached to a building or land.

citation A court order directing a particular action or summons to appear before a court.

civil libertarians Individuals concerned with upholding the rights they see the Constitution providing to all citizens.

commander in chief An individual who holds the supreme command and final authority in an armed force.

common law Judge–made law; law which exists based on legal precedents built up over hundreds of years, and examined by judges when ruling in cases.

comptroller A public official who audits government accounts.

concurrence A concurring opinion written by one or more of the justices which agrees with the majority opinion, but may differ with the reasoning in reaching that decision.

confession A statement made by a person charged with a crime that he or she committed that crime.

contemporaries Individuals in the same relative age class and/or profession.

constitution The basic law or laws under which a nation or state is governed and the organization of the government and authorities.

conviction The formal decision of a criminal trial proclaiming the accused guilty of a crime.

court martial A military court established to try and punish members of the military.

convenant A written document in which parties agree to do a certain thing, not do a certain thing, or agree to a certain act.

counsel An attorney engaged in a trial; an attorney hired for the purposes of legal advice to a corporate or public entity.

crime An act prohibited by law.

Croix de Guerre A French military medal for distinguished and gallant service in war.

cum laude To graduate from a higher educational institution with distinction.

de facto Latin term referring to a circumstance which is not necessarily legal but exists in fact.

de jure Latin term meaning complete adherence to the law.

despot A tyrannical leader exercising an abuse of power.

dicta; dictum Latin term describing an observation by a judge in an opinion which does not concern itself with the case at hand.

diplomat An individual representing the nation and skilled in negotiation and mediation in foreign affairs on behalf of that nation.

dispensation Exemption.

dissent To disagree; a written opinion by a judge or group of judges who disagree with the majority finding of a case.

docket An official court record book containing the cases before a court.

doctrine An established principle or rule of law reinforced by its continued use in legal cases.

due process Term of United States law promising each citizen the full rights and privileges of the law without interference from the government or any other body.

dueling An armed conflict between two principles with witnesses, the primary purpose being the settling of a dispute.

eludicate To give clarity to an issue or word.

emanation The action of an object or thing coming out of another source.

emancipation Term used to describe the release of a person who is under the legal control of another.

eminence A high degree of importance.

enactment A law or statute.

exculpate Something which excuses a wrong action.

exigencies Situations which demand urgent action or a sudden change of previous plans.

ex parte Latin term meaning one party; when there is only one party to a case who has been notified and represented.

ex post facto Latin term for the after the fact; a law is ex post facto if it attempts to govern events which have already taken place.

expunge To delete all references to something in court records.

fledgling A newly formed group or effort attempting to become established.

flogging The beating of a criminal with a stick or rod.

foray Journey.

fraud Deceitful conduct by intending to manipulate someone to give something of value by lying, or concealing facts.

gavel A wooden mallet used by judges to open and close court proceedings, as well as to maintain order during those proceedings.

general counsel Traditionally, the senior attorney in a corporation.

gentry The ruling class of wealthy landowners or proprietors.

gout A disease characterized by painful inflammation of joints and large amounts of uric acid in the blood.

grand jury An American court proceeding in which 16-23 citizens are assembled to listen to criminal complaints brought by a prosecutor, and decide if a trial is warranted.

habeus corpus A legal writ requiring a law enforcement body bringing a party who is being charged with a crime or offense to the court in person.

hack Derisive term used to describe a politician or political appointee as entirely beholden to the party he or she represents.

harangue A loud, controversial speech in a public forum.

hauteur Arrogance.

hearsay evidence Evidence based on the knowledge of a witness on a matter told to him or her by someone else.

House of Burgesses A legislative body giving representation to residents of certain colonies in the years prior to the American Revolution.

Huguenot A member of a Swiss political movement of the sixteenth and seventeenth centuries.

imperialism A practice or policy of a nation to extend its power and domination by acquiring territories or conquering other nations for political and economic superiority.

immunity An exception in which an individual has exemption from the normal laws of a nation or state.

indictment The formal accusation brought by a grand jury.

injunction A court order prohibiting a party from executing a particular action.

insurrection An act of resistance or rebellion against an established civil authority or government.

internment Removal of Japanese-Americans from their homes by the United States government to camps during World War II.

interpolation Insertion of a word or words into a text which did not previously exist in that text.

interrogation A formal period of questioning under systematic rules.

invalidism A chronic state of suffering from disability or disease.

itinerant An individual who travels to complete the duties of his occupation.

J.D. Abbreviation for juris doctor, the formal title conferred on law school graduates in the United States.

judicial review A process by where a court of law is asked to review the decision of an administrative entity or other tribunal decision.

jurisdiction A court's authority to rule in a particular dispute.

jurisprudence The science of the law.

kangaroo court A court making decisions without regard to proper authority or procedures.

law The rules of conduct approved by the government which are in force and must be obeyed by those within the territory of that government.

law review A journal published by a law school containing scholarly articles by prominent figures in academia, usually edited by high-ranking students of that law school.

legislation Written and approved laws.

libertarian Political outlook advocating an extremely limited influence of government on the individual citizen.

litigation A dispute between two or more parties before a court of law.

litmus test Term used in reference to Supreme Court appointees' views on particularly controversial issues.

malaria A disease in humans caused by the bite of certain mosquitoes and characterized by periodic attacks of chills and fever.

maritime Relating to issues of navigation or commerce on the seas.

mediate To attempt to bring agreement or accord between two opposing parties.

merchant marines Personnel of a privately or publicly owned commercial ship.

meticulous Careful and precise.

Miranda warning Warning given by arresting law enforcement officers notifying suspects of their lawful rights, as advised by the Supreme Court in *Miranda v. Arizona*.

misdemeanor A crime less serious than a felony for which the penalty is not as harsh.

mistrial A trial which does not come to completion due to a technicality or other error.

mitigating circumstances Facts which may give grounds for a defendant to have acted in a certain manner, while not releasing the defendant from the wrong.

monopoly Ownership or control of an entity or product by one person or group, excluding all others.

moot A side issue which does not have to be resolved.

mustermaster A military position in which an individual is charged with assembling his or her particular regiment for inspection.

nation A group or race of people who share history, culture, and traditions.

oath A religious or solemn affimation of faith or promise.

obstructing justice Act with the express purpose of impeding the administration of justice.

offense A crime.

onus Latin for "the burden."

order A formal declaration of instruction from a member of the judiciary; a court decision given without reasons.

ordinance An executive decision of a government not reviewed or subjected to review by a legislative body.

pardon A government action excusing an individual from responsibility for a crime for which he or she has been convicted; in the United States the power of pardon rests with the President.

patronage A system in politics wherein an elected official dispenses available jobs and posts to supporters and friends.

paucity Lacking.

penumbra A surrounding or adjoining region wherein something exists in a smaller degree.

perjury An intentional lie told under oath or in a sworn legal document.

perspicacious Of sharply keen mental vision.

petitioner Individual or group bringing suit in a court case.

Phi Beta Kappa Organization of individuals winning high scholastic distinction in undergraduate education in the United States.

philanthropic Charitable.

plaintiff The person or party who brings a case to court; the one who sues.

pleading The formal recitation of facts and arguments which support a party's case.

polemic The art of political or adversarial conversation.

precedent A case which established a legal principle or principles, to be referred to by future judges applying the law in similar cases.

prescient Having the attributes to correctly anticipate events.

presidential elector An individual elected to serve in the Electoral College, which is constitutionally mandated to select the president and vice president of the United States.

pro bono Latin term meaning "public good"; the execution of legal services in exchange for no financial compensation.

pro forma Latin meaning to keep within practice.

probate judge A judge who determines the validity of a deceased person's estate.

probity Adherance to high ideals and principles.

proclivities Tendencies or leanings.

protectorate A nation under the military protection and governmental control of another.

provisional government Government installed in conquered territory immediately after an armed conflict by the victor to restore law and order.

puckish Impish, whimsical.

punctilious Careful and precise in matters of conventional style or wisdom.

Puritan A member of a group of Protestants in England and New England during the sixteenth and seventeenth centuries opposed to the dominance of the Church of England.

Purple Heart A military decoration awarded by the United States to any member of the armed forces wounded or killed in action.

Raceketeering Participating in a fraudulent operation the primary purpose of which is to obtain money, usually by intimidation and threat.

Remand Court order which refers a case back to the lower court from which it came, usually with instructions to proceed in a different manner.

repeal To invalidate a law or legislative act previously passed by a legislative body.

respondent The person or party who responds to a claim against them; more commonly known as a defendant.

retainer A fee paid by a client to an attorney for services in the present and future.

schisms Divisions between people, groups, or two points of land.

search warrant A court order permitting law enforcement officers or agencies to search a private property for evidence of the commission of a crime; the order is granted following a sworn statement describing the exact area to be searched and the property being sought.

secede To remove oneself from a united group or governmental body.

sedition Incitement of resistance or the actual action of insurrection of an established authority.

segregationist Supporter of the policy of legal separation of the races in public accommodations such as schools, restaurants, hotels, and other places.

semiprofessional An athlete paid to play a sport for an organized team.

slavery Situation in which a person has complete and total control of another, including life and liberty.

solicitor An attorney who restricts his or legal practice to the court room; see *Barrister*.

Speaker of the House of Representatives An individual elected by the majority of the members of the U.S. House of Representatives to serve as the leader of the entire House; third in line of succession to the presidency.

squatters Individuals who settle on property without title or payment of rent.

stacks A compact storage space for books usually found in college libraries.

state A term of international law signifying a group of people who are recognized as an independent country.

statutes The written laws of a legislature of a state, also known as legislation.

subpoena Latin for a written document ordering an individual or party to appear before a court subject to penalty.

subversive Description of acts contrary to the benefit of one's native nation; acting in behalf of a nation's enemies.

surfeit Overabundance.

tarriff A duty or tax added by a government to imported or exported goods.

testimony The verbal answers of a witness during a trial.

treason The overt act or attempt to overthrow the government of a state to which an individual owes allegiance.

treaty A formal written agreement signed by governmental officials of two states which may or may not be law–binding.

tribunal A forum or court of justice.

valedictorian The student achieving the best grades in a graduating class.

venue Location of a judicial proceeding.

verdict The decision of a jury.

Whig A political party which preceded and was replaced by the Republican Party in American politics.

witness A person who delivers testimony during a legal proceeding verbally or in writing.

writ of mandamus A judicial action taken by a superior court commanding the performance of a specific duty.

Zionist An individual who was part of the Zionist movment which advocated the formation of a Jewish state in Palestine; a supporter of modern Israel.

Index